Medical Masterclass third edition

Editor-in-Chief

Dr John D Firth DM FRCP
Consultant Physician and Nephrologist
Addenbrooke's Hospital
Cambridge
UK

Endocrinology

Editor

Professor Mark Gurnell MA(MEd) PhD FRCP
Clinical SubDean and Honorary Consultant Physician
University of Cambridge School of Clinical Medicine and
Addenbrooke's Hospital
Cambridge
UK

Third edition

Disclaimer

List of contributors

Dr Benjamin Challis PhD MRCP(UK)
Honorary Consultant in Endocrinology and Diabetes
Addenbrooke's Hospital
Cambridge
UK

Professor Mark Gurnell MA(MEd) PhD FRCP
Clinical SubDean and Honorary Consultant Physician
University of Cambridge School of Clinical Medicine and Addenbrooke's Hospital
Cambridge
UK

Dr Sanjeev Sharma MD FRCP-Endo/Diab FHEA
Consultant in Endocrinology and Diabetes
Ipswich Hospital
East Suffolk and North Essex NHS Foundation Trust
Ipswich
UK

Professor Jeremy W Tomlinson PhD FRCP
Professor of Metabolic Endocrinology
Consultant Endocrinologist
Oxford Centre for Diabetes, Endocrinology and Metabolism
University of Oxford
Churchill Hospital
Oxford
UK

Dr Alison M Wren PhD MRCP(UK)
Consultant Physician and Honorary Senior Lecturer
Chelsea and Westminster Hospital and Imperial College London
London
UK

Acknowledgements

The third edition of Medical Masterclass has been produced by a team. The names of those who have written and edited are clearly indicated, and along with all these contributors I gratefully acknowledge the contributions of those who wrote and edited the first and second editions. This third edition is based on their foundations, and some of their material has been retained. But my acknowledgements must not stop there, because the Medical Masterclass would not have been published without the efforts of many other people. Naming names is risky, but I must name Claire Daley, who has worked as editor of the third edition with a wonderful combination of quietness and efficiency, and with an attention to detail that has made me feel triumphant if I have ever spotted a misplaced comma in a proof.

Dr John Firth DM FRCP
Medical Masterclass Editor-in-Chief

Cover image courtesy of: Lea Paterson / Science Photo Library

Published by:
Royal College of Physicians of London
11 St Andrews Place
Regent's Park
London NW1 4LE
United Kingdom

Typeset by Manila Typesetting Company, Makati City, Philippines

Printed by The Lavenham Press Limited, Suffolk

First edition published 2001
Reprinted 2004
Second edition published 2008
Updated and reprinted 2010
Third edition published 2018

ISBN: 978-1-86016-664-8 (this book)
eISBN: 978-1-86016-665-5 (this book)
ISBN: 978-1-86016-670-9 (set)
eISBN: 978-1-86016-671-6 (set)

Royal College of Physicians of London
11 St Andrews Place
Regent's Park
London NW1 4LE
United Kingdom
Tel: +44 (0)20 3075 1379
Email: medical.masterclass@rcplondon.ac.uk
Web: www.rcplondon.ac.uk/medicalmasterclass

Contents

Preface

This third edition of Medical Masterclass is produced and published by the Royal College of Physicians of London. It comprises 12 books and an online question bank. Its aim is to interest and help doctors in their first few years of training, to enable them to improve their medical knowledge and skills, and to pass postgraduate medical examinations, most particularly the MRCP(UK): Part 1, Part 2 and PACES (the practical assessment of clinical examination skills that is the final part of the exam).

The 12 textbooks are divided as follows: two cover the scientific background to medicine; one is devoted to general clinical skills, including medicine for older people, palliative care and specific guidance on exam technique for PACES; one deals with acute medicine; and the other eight cover the range of medical specialties.

The medical specialties are dealt with in eight sections:

- Case histories – you are presented with letters of referral that are commonly received in each specialty and led through the ways in which the patients' histories should be explored, and what investigations and/or treatments should follow, as in Station 2 of PACES.
- Physical examination scenarios – these emphasise solid and reliable clinical method, logical analysis of physical signs and sensible clinical reasoning ('having found this, what would you want to do next?'), as in Stations 1 and 3 of PACES.
- Communication and ethical scenarios – you are presented with difficult issues that can arise in each specialty. What should you actually say in response to the 'frequently asked (but nonetheless tricky) questions', as required in Station 4 of PACES?
- Brief clinical consultations – how should you take a focused history and perform a focused examination of a patient who has a medical problem when there isn't much time? This section explains how to do this while working as a medical registrar on take, or in Station 5 of PACES.
- Acute presentations – what are your priorities if you are the doctor seeing a patient in the emergency department or the medical admissions unit? The material in this section is relevant to all parts of the MRCP(UK) exam.
- Diseases and treatments – concise structured notes that are of particular relevance to the Part 1 and Part 2 exams.
- Investigations and practical procedures – short and concise notes.
- Self-assessment questions – in the form used in the Part 1 and Part 2 exams.

The online question bank, which is continually updated, enables you to take mock Part 1 and Part 2 exams, or to be selective in the questions that you tackle (if you want to do 10 questions on cardiology, or any other specialty, then you can do so). You can see how your scores compare with those of others who have attempted the same questions, which helps you to know where to focus your learning.

I hope that you enjoy using the Medical Masterclass to learn more about medicine. I know that medicine is tough at the moment, with hospital services under unprecedented pressure and the medical registrar bearing more than their fair share of the burden. But careers are a long game, and being a physician is a wonderful occupation. It is sometimes intellectually and/or emotionally very challenging, but with these challenges come great rewards, and few things give more substantial satisfaction than being a doctor who provides good care for a patient. The Medical Masterclass should help you do to that, as well as to pass the MRCP(UK) exam along the way.

Dr John Firth DM FRCP
Medical Masterclass Editor-in-Chief

Key features

We have created a range of icon boxes that sit among the text of the various Medical Masterclass books. They are there to help you identify key information and to make learning easier and more enjoyable. Here is a brief explanation:

This icon is used to highlight points of particular importance.

Key point

A patient with a normal physical examination, a normal ECG and a normal echocardiogram is at very low risk of significant arrhythmia.

This icon is used to indicate common or important drug interactions, pitfalls of practical procedures, or when to take symptoms or signs particularly seriously.

Hazard

Acute lymphoblastic leukaemia may present in an identical manner to infectious mononucleosis.

Case examples / case histories are used to demonstrate why and how an understanding of the scientific background to medicine helps in the practice of clinical medicine.

Case history

A man with a renal transplant is immunosuppressed with ciclosporin, azathioprine and prednisolone. He develops recurrent gout and is started on allopurinol.

Endocrinology

Authors

Dr B Challis, Professor M Gurnell, Dr S Sharma, Professor JW Tomlinson and Dr A Wren

Editor

Professor M Gurnell

Editor-in-Chief

Dr JD Firth

The endocrinology section of the second edition of Medical Masterclass was written by Dr MZ Qureshi, Dr RK Semple, Dr JW Tomlinson, Dr AM Wren and Dr M Gurnell (editor). This third edition of Medical Masterclass contains entirely new material, but many sections from the second edition have been retained and updated, and we gratefully acknowledge the contribution of these authors.

Endocrinology: Section 1

1 PACES stations and acute scenarios

1.1 History taking

1.1.1 Hypercalcaemia

Letter of referral to the endocrinology outpatient clinic

Dear Doctor,

Re: Mrs Sally-Anne Cooke, aged 54 years

This 54-year-old teacher presented with loin pain to the acute surgical take and was found on computerised tomography (CT) to have several left-sided renal calculi. These have been managed conservatively, but further investigation has revealed a serum calcium of 2.8 mmol/L (normal range 2.20–2.60) and an endocrinology opinion has been recommended. I would be grateful for your advice regarding further investigation and management.

Yours sincerely,

Introduction

Most urinary tract calculi contain calcium and most patients (~65%) have idiopathic hypercalciuria, but some 5% have underlying hypercalcaemia, as in this case, which ideally should be confirmed on an uncuffed venous sample. Although the differential diagnosis of hypercalcaemia is broad (Table 1), the presence of a renal stone usually implies that it is long-standing and therefore unlikely to be secondary to malignancy. The most likely diagnosis here is primary hyperparathyroidism.

History of the presenting problem

With increasingly frequent use of biochemical testing hypercalcaemia is often found incidentally, or as a result of directed screening such as in this case. This means that frank symptomatology is uncommon, but symptoms of hypercalcaemia should be specifically sought. These usually occur when the serum calcium exceeds 3 mmol/L and comprise:

> thirst and polyuria
> constipation
> anorexia and general malaise
> depression and anxiety.

More severe hypercalcaemia can lead to vomiting, severe dehydration, confusion and even coma.

Other relevant history

Careful enquiry should be directed towards possible causes and complications of hypercalcaemia. Bear in mind the conditions listed in Table 1 as you proceed.

Functional enquiry

A full systematic functional enquiry is needed. Respiratory symptoms might suggest sarcoidosis as the cause of hypercalcaemia. Gastrointestinal symptoms might be a consequence of hypercalcaemia, but could be causal if leading to excessive consumption of milk or alkali. Any features suggesting malignancy should be explored, especially in patients presenting acutely.

Drug history

> ask specifically about lithium – the mechanism of action remains unclear but may involve altered calcium sensing by the parathyroids and enhanced effects of parathyroid hormone (PTH)
> thiazide diuretics – reduce urinary calcium excretion and potentiate the effects of PTH
> vitamin D intake (either oral or topical, for example for psoriasis)
> milk, alkali, antacids.

Hazard

Don't forget to ask about over-the-counter medications

A detailed drug history, including use of over-the-counter treatments for indigestion ('white medicine') or of vitamin D-containing preparations, is essential in the patient with hypercalcaemia.

Family history

A family history of hypercalcaemia or a personal history of pituitary or pancreatic islet cell tumours may suggest the presence of multiple endocrine neoplasia type 1 (MEN-1) (see Sections 2.5.7 and 2.7.1). Familial hypocalciuric hypercalcaemia (FHH) should also be considered in familial cases of hypercalcaemia.

Complications of hypercalcaemia

These include peptic ulceration and acute pancreatitis. Is there a history of bone pain or pathological fracture? If not due to malignancy, these may be caused by long-standing hyperparathyroidism. Ask directly about urinary stones, which were the presenting feature of this case.

Table 1 Causes of hypercalcaemia[1]

Frequency	Type of disorder	Example
Common	Primary hyperparathyroidism	—
	Malignancy	Carcinoma with skeletal metastases, eg breast, lung
		Carcinoma without skeletal metastases, ie humoral hypercalcaemia of malignancy
		Haematological disorders, eg myeloma
Less common	Vitamin D toxicity	Consumption of medicines/compounds containing vitamin D
	Vitamin D 'sensitivity'	Granulomatous disorders, eg sarcoidosis
	Excess calcium intake	Milk-alkali syndrome
	Reduced calcium excretion	Thiazide diuretics, lithium
		Familial hypocalciuric hypercalcaemia[2]
	Endocrine/metabolic	Thyrotoxicosis
		Adrenal failure
		Phaeochromocytoma
	Other	Acute kidney injury
		Long-term immobility
		Tertiary hyperparathyroidism

1 Note that artefactual hypercalcaemia is common and can be due to venous stasis at phlebotomy, hyperalbuminaemia or hypergammaglobulinaemia.
2 Familial hypocalciuric hypercalcaemia (FHH) is a benign condition caused by inactivating mutations in the calcium-sensing receptor (*CASR*) gene, leading to impaired negative feedback with raised parathyroid hormone (PTH) and compensatory hypercalcaemia and hypocalciuria.

Plan for investigation and management

First explain to the patient that under normal circumstances you would perform a full physical examination looking for signs associated with the conditions described in Table 1.

Investigation

Routine haematological and biochemical tests (full blood count, inflammatory markers (erythrocyte sedimentation rate (ESR), C-reactive protein (CRP)), electrolytes, renal/liver/bone function tests), together with measurement of vitamin D and PTH should be considered in all patients presenting with hypercalcaemia, looking for the following clues:

- anaemia – may indicate malignancy, including myeloma
- ESR, CRP – raised in malignancy, especially multiple myeloma
- impaired renal function – usually a consequence of hypercalcaemia, but remember that advanced long-standing chronic renal failure can cause tertiary hyperparathyroidism
- phosphate – low in hyperparathyroidism, raised in multiple myeloma (particularly when accompanied by renal failure)
- alkaline phosphatase (bone isoenzyme) – reflecting osteoclast activation
- abnormal liver function tests – consider malignancy
- PTH – suppressed in virtually all causes of hypercalcaemia except hyperparathyroidism.

Hazard

Normal may not be normal!

A serum/plasma PTH within the 'normal range' is inappropriate in the context of hypercalcaemia and suggests that the patient has hyperparathyroidism.

Key point

Distinction between hypercalcaemia with suppressed versus non-suppressed PTH helps guide further management, eg the finding of hypercalcaemia with a clearly detectable PTH indicates a parathyroid origin and further investigation for occult malignancy is not indicated.

Key point

Vitamin D status should be determined at diagnosis as vitamin D insufficiency/deficiency may be associated with a raised PTH, in which case consideration should be given to careful replacement which may lead to resolution of hypercalcaemia and normalise PTH. However, caution is required as vitamin D therapy in those with underlying primary hyperparathyroidism predisposes to marked hypercalcaemia, hence it is important to obtain specialist endocrine advice before implementing this strategy.

Other tests will be driven by clinical suspicion and the results of these initial investigations:

- chest radiograph / CT – look for primary or secondary malignancy, or hilar lymphadenopathy suggestive of sarcoidosis
- abdominal imaging (ultrasound and/or CT) – look for urinary tract calcification (already established in this case)
- serum electrophoresis, urinary testing for Bence Jones proteinuria and a skeletal survey – if multiple myeloma is suspected
- isotope bone scan for bony metastases
- vitamin D levels – may be helpful if intoxication is suspected, but require careful interpretation given their wide seasonal variation
- plasma or urinary metanephrines, thyroid function tests and Synacthen test
- 24-hour urinary calcium excretion – low in FHH (see Section 2.5.7).

Hazard

To avoid unnecessary and ineffective surgery

FHH must be excluded in any patient presenting with hypercalcaemia and a raised PTH in order to avoid unnecessary parathyroid exploration. Diagnosis depends on demonstrating a low urinary calcium:creatinine clearance ratio and can be confirmed by screening for mutations in the calcium-sensing receptor (*CASR*) gene.

In this case primary hyperparathyroidism is the most likely diagnosis, and after normal or high PTH is confirmed in the presence of hypercalcaemia, investigation should be directed towards assessing complications (eg nephrocalcinosis/nephrolithiasis and reduced bone mineral density), and, depending on local practice, identification of the overactive gland(s) (see Section 2.5.7).

Management

Hypercalcaemia associated with complications

Specific treatment will depend on the underlying disorder. In this case, given the history of nephrolithiasis and assuming the diagnosis of primary hyperparathyroidism, definitive treatment should be offered. For a solitary parathyroid adenoma the preferred option is surgical excision. The only controversy is whether preoperative imaging should be performed, for example with ^{99m}technetium (^{99m}Tc)-sestamibi scanning, neck ultrasound and/or 4D-CT; currently this depends on local practice/expertise (see Section 2.5.7). Postoperatively transient hypocalcaemia may occur, which should be treated with intravenous (IV) 10% calcium gluconate in the acute setting, or with a combination of oral vitamin D and calcium supplements in milder cases.

Asymptomatic hypercalcaemia

With a diagnosis of primary hyperparathyroidism, a calcium level that is only mildly elevated (eg 2.8 mmol/L as in this case), in the absence of symptoms of polyuria and polydipsia or confusion, and with no evidence of urinary tract calcification, it is debatable whether any immediate specific treatment is required based on the biochemistry alone, other than ensuring adequate hydration. It would be appropriate to give the patient advice to drink around 3 L of fluid daily.

For details of the approach to the investigation and management of renal calculi see the *Nephrology* book of Medical Masterclass.

Further discussion

Surgery for asymptomatic primary hyperparathyroidism

In recent years practice has changed, and it is now more common to offer early parathyroidectomy, especially as expertise in minimally invasive day-case surgery grows, rather than waiting for hypercalcaemia to become more marked or complications to develop. In the absence of symptoms or clinically overt complications, guidelines have been developed for whom should be offered surgery based on evidence of hypercalciuria and bone mineral density loss (see Section 2.5.7).

Familial cases of hypercalcaemia/hyperparathyroidism

If associated with suspected or confirmed MEN-1, then it is important to counsel the patient that hyperplasia of all four glands generally requires total parathyroidectomy (see Section 2.7.1). FHH is typically associated with a family history of mild hypercalcaemia: as indicated above, screening with a urine calcium:creatinine ratio is mandatory if inappropriate parathyroidectomy is to be avoided.

1.1.2 Polyuria

Letter of referral to the endocrinology outpatient clinic

Dear Doctor,

Re: Mrs Jane Parry, aged 63 years

Thank you for seeing this hotel receptionist who has recently been troubled by passing excessive amounts of urine. She says that she is very thirsty and drinking 'gallons of water' every day. Her migraine also seems to have returned of late, although she thinks that the headaches are somewhat different to previously.

Her past medical history includes surgery and radiotherapy 4 years ago for left-sided breast cancer. She is on tamoxifen and co-codamol.

On examination, she appeared somewhat anxious, but there was nothing else of note except for a slightly high blood pressure of 148/93 mmHg.

She has a normal fasting glucose level, and her electrolytes and creatinine are also normal. I am not sure as to the cause of her polyuria and would appreciate your advice regarding further investigations and management.

Yours sincerely,

Table 2 Causes of polyuria

Problem	Example
Osmotic diuresis	DM (glucose)
	CRF (urea)[1]
	Intravenous infusions (saline, mannitol)
	Diuretics
Abnormal renal tubular water handling	Hypothalamic/pituitary (cranial) DI
	Nephrogenic DI
Excessive fluid intake	Primary polydipsia (dipsogenic DI) – due to habitual excessive drinking or psychogenic polydipsia
	Iatrogenic

1 Polyuria is most likely in CRF associated with damage to the renal medulla, which prevents the elaboration of concentrated urine.
CRF, chronic renal failure; DI, diabetes insipidus; DM, diabetes mellitus.

Introduction

Polyuria is defined as the passage of an abnormally large volume of urine and must be distinguished from frequency of micturition. It is usually taken to indicate the passage of at least 3 L in 24 hours, a useful surrogate marker being nocturia on two or more occasions each night. If polyuria is confirmed, there are a large number of possible causes (Table 2), and the history, clinical examination and initial investigations should be used to direct more detailed study. In essence, diabetes mellitus (DM), chronic renal failure (CRF) and use of diuretics should be excluded before distinguishing between hypothalamic/pituitary (often referred to as simply as hypothalamic) or nephrogenic diabetes insipidus (DI) and primary polydipsia (dipsogenic DI) with water intoxication.

History of the presenting problem

Hazard

Does the patient really have polyuria?

The first requirement is to be sure that polyuria really is present – investigation for a problem that the patient does not have is futile. If there is any doubt, a 24-hour urine collection should be performed before embarking on other tests. The patient does not have polyuria if all the urine fits in one of the standard containers, although he or she may have frequency associated with it.

Polyuria or frequency of micturition?

'Tell me about a typical day – for instance, how was it yesterday, starting with when you woke up in the morning?' Enquire about the frequency of visits to the toilet and roughly how much urine is passed on each occasion – small, medium or large amounts? How often do you wake up to pass urine during a typical night? If the patient can sleep undisturbed for 8 hours, then it is unlikely that they have primary polyuria. Does it hurt or burn when passing urine? Is there any accompanying discomfort in the abdomen/loin/groin areas? All of these might point to a chronic urinary tract infection leading to urinary frequency.

Daily fluid intake

In all cases take a careful history of drinking behaviour. Exactly what did the patient have to drink yesterday, and why did they drink it? It is not at all uncommon for someone referred with polyuria to have drunk several cups of tea and/or coffee, one to two cans of fizzy drink and 0.5 L of water before lunch, the reason being recognised by them as 'habit' rather than thirst, but often also driven by a belief that it is good to 'keep the kidneys flushed'. However, even in cases where it seems immediately apparent that excessive fluid intake out of habit is the reason for polyuria, it is appropriate to look for evidence on history, examination and simple testing of the other conditions listed in Table 2, since it can be difficult to know which came first – the polydipsia or the polyuria; the chicken or the egg?

Thirst

Is the patient drinking because of a genuine thirst rather than because of a dry mouth such as that encountered with a head cold and compensatory mouth breathing? Patients with primary polyuria drink water/fluids to quench their thirst rather than as a matter of habit or routine. Does he/she have to get up and drink water (rather than just to pass urine) during the night, which suggests that the problem is not psychogenic.

Common causes of polyuria

Ask directly about DM (already excluded in this case), CRF and use of diuretics.

Hypothalamic or nephrogenic diabetes insipidus

Table 22 lists many of the causes of DI. Questions should be directed at screening for these disorders, eg when considering pituitary dysfunction, a history of head injury, surgery or radiotherapy should be sought, together with evidence of anterior pituitary failure (lassitude, weight gain, cold intolerance, constipation, diminished libido).

Primary polydipsia (dipsogenic DI)

Compulsive water intoxication (rather than simple habitual non-psychiatric excessive drinking) is likely to be concealed and details may need to be sought from a relative, partner or carer (in routine practice, although not possible in PACES).

Other relevant history

Headaches

Although the patient has a history of migraine, the letter from the general practitioner (GP) says that the current headaches are probably different from those that she experienced in the past, which may suggest alternative pathology. Which part of the head? Are they constant or intermittent? Is there any visual disturbance? Are there any other features such as nausea, vomiting, aura or flashing lights? Patients with pituitary/peripituitary pathology may have frontal headaches ('behind the eyes'), bitemporal hemianopia and/or visual disturbance due to involvement of the third, fourth or sixth cranial nerves.

Past history of breast cancer

Lung and breast cancers may metastasise to the pituitary and cause central DI. Are there any features that might suggest local or metastatic recurrence?

Psychiatric and drug history

Key point

When taking a history from a patient with polyuria, ask directly if they have any psychiatric history or if they have taken lithium in the past. They may not volunteer this information unless asked directly.

Lithium, a cause of nephrogenic DI, is often used in the treatment of bipolar affective disorders and depression.

Plan for investigation and management

Key point

Investigation of polyuria

- Confirm that polyuria is present before embarking on tests (if necessary with 24-hour urine collection).
- Exclude osmotic diuresis (high glucose).
- Exclude CRF (high creatinine and urea).
- Consider hypothalamic or nephrogenic DI.
- Consider primary polydipsia (dipsogenic DI).

Investigation

Explain to the patient that under normal circumstances you would examine her, and then proceed as follows.

Routine tests

These should include a full blood count (anaemia), electrolytes and renal function (dehydration, hypokalaemia, CRF), blood glucose (DM), liver and bone biochemistry (specifically calcium, phosphate and alkaline phosphatase). Urinalysis for glycosuria (DM or renal disease), haematuria and proteinuria. Chest radiograph – look for evidence of granulomatous disease (eg sarcoidosis, tuberculosis) or possible metastases (particularly relevant in this case).

Further tests

These include plasma and urine osmolalities and the water deprivation test.

Having excluded an osmotic basis for polyuria, the diagnosis now rests between hypothalamic or nephrogenic DI and primary polydipsia. Begin with 'spot tests' of plasma and urine osmolality:

- Plasma osmolality – this is usually lower than 290 mosmol/kg (normal range 278–300) in polydipsia, reflecting volume overload, and greater than normal in hypothalamic or nephrogenic DI, reflecting volume depletion.
- Urine osmolality – test on the first voided sample of the day (especially if the patient has not drunk excessively overnight) as this may prevent the need for a more detailed investigation: a value greater than 750 mosmol/kg excludes DI.

However, often these initial 'spot results' are inconclusive, and it is necessary to proceed to either a water deprivation test or hypertonic saline infusion with measurement of plasma antidiuretic hormone (ADH) (vasopressin) (see Sections 2.1.7 and 3.3.2).

If hypothalamic/pituitary DI is confirmed, the pituitary and hypothalamus should be imaged by magnetic resonance imaging (MRI) and dynamic tests of pituitary function should be considered (see Sections 2.1.8 and 3.1). Patients with nephrogenic DI require more detailed tests of renal tubular function.

Management

Excessive drinking

The patient who has simply got into the habit of drinking excessively should be reassured after simple screening that there is nothing seriously wrong and that their urinary volume, and any attendant embarrassment caused by the need for frequent micturition, will be eased if they can gradually wean down the amount of fluid that they drink.

Hypothalamic/pituitary DI

Symptomatic relief may be provided with the synthetic vasopressin analogue desmopressin. This can be administered orally, or via a nasal spray (see Section 2.1.7). Any associated anterior pituitary failure should also be corrected with appropriate hormone replacement (see Section 2.1.8). If imaging reveals a structural abnormality then specific treatment may be required, eg radiotherapy or chemotherapy for a patient with known metastatic breast carcinoma.

Nephrogenic DI

Wherever possible, correct the underlying cause (eg electrolyte disturbances). In cases where a reversible cause cannot be identified, thiazide diuretics (eg hydrochlorothiazide) in combination with mild sodium restriction are often effective. Amiloride may be of benefit, especially in lithium-induced DI.

Primary polydipsia (dipsogenic DI)

Polyuria in this setting can be controlled by limiting fluid intake, but this is easier said than done. Patients may have a known psychiatric disorder, and formal psychiatric input should be considered. However, the reason for trying to restrain drinking and polyuria in this condition needs to be considered. Unless of massive degree, it is likely that the only complication of primary polydipsia is the inconvenience of urinary frequency, and reassurance to the patient, relatives and carers that there is no 'serious pathology' may be the limit of useful medical contribution.

Further discussion

Pituitary metastases from lung, breast and other malignancies are well recognised, and occasionally DI may be the presenting manifestation. There may be accompanying symptoms and signs due to local mass effect, including optic chiasmal compression or cranial nerve palsies. MRI/CT does not always distinguish between metastases and other pituitary lesions (Fig 1), but it is worth noting that pituitary adenomas themselves rarely present with DI. Accordingly, in a patient with hypothalamic DI and a pituitary fossa lesion it is important to consider other possible diagnoses, eg intrasellar craniopharyngioma, metastasis, infiltration. If there are no other obvious pointers to the diagnosis, then pituitary exploration and biopsy may be necessary.

1.1.3 Faints, sweats and palpitations

Letter of referral to the endocrinology outpatient clinic

Dear Doctor,

Re: Miss Anne Davies, aged 46 years

Thank you for seeing this woman who has had recurrent episodes of light-headedness associated with sweating and palpitations. These are occurring with increasing frequency and are affecting her ability to perform her job as a company director. She has a toddler at home and is finding the life–work balance a challenge.

She has no significant past medical history and the only family history of note is that her mother suffers from type 2 diabetes mellitus. I am grateful for your assessment as to the likely cause of these episodes.

Yours sincerely,

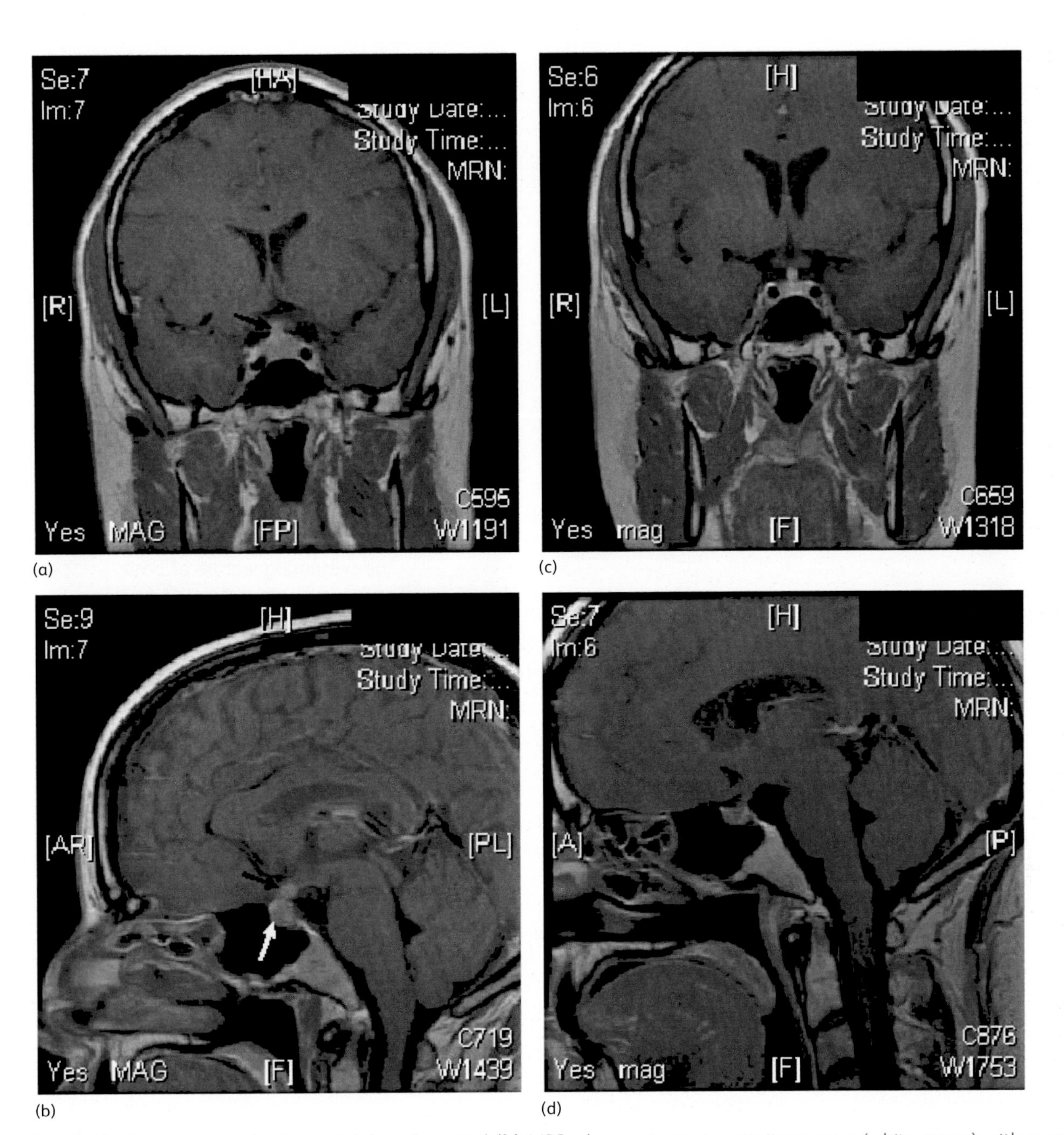

Fig 1 Pituitary metastasis. Coronal **(a)** and sagittal **(b)** MRIs demonstrating a pituitary mass (white arrow) with suprasellar extension (black arrow) in a 36-year-old woman with known metastatic breast carcinoma. Following radiotherapy (**c** and **d**) there has been a marked improvement in appearances.

Introduction

> **Hazard**
>
> This presentation could be simply due to stress – but it would be most unwise not to explore the history carefully in routine clinical practice or in PACES.

A fundamental issue here is to determine whether there is a true organic basis for the presentation. In most cases such as this the diagnosis can be made after taking a thorough history, and clinical examination often adds little. Although the symptoms described may have no clear physical basis and simply represent a response to difficult social circumstances, a diagnosis of a non-organic disorder is a diagnosis of exclusion. In addition, 'light-headedness' means different things to different people: individuals with this symptom find their way into various clinics (neurology, cardiology, endocrinology, etc) and a wide range of diagnoses need to be considered. The combination of light-headedness with sweating and palpitations is more specific in that it suggests enhanced autonomic sympathetic activity (Table 3).

Table 3 Conditions presenting with light-headedness, sweating and palpitations	
Psychological/psychiatric	Anxiety state
'Toxic'	Excess use of stimulants, eg caffeine
	Alcohol withdrawal
	Drug withdrawal
Cardiovascular	Primary arrhythmia
	Vasovagal
	Postural hypotension
Endocrine/metabolic	Menopausal vasomotor instability
	Hypoglycaemia
	Thyrotoxicosis
	Phaeochromocytoma

History of the presenting problem

It is important to ask the woman to explain as precisely as possible the nature of the episodes of light-headedness, sweating and palpitations, and – in routine practice, although not possible in PACES – to obtain a report from a witness if available, since by the very nature of the problem the patient may not be able to give a lucid account. Ask both the patient and any witness about the following:

- When and how often do the episodes occur?
- What is she typically doing at the time?
- Are there any obvious precipitants?
- Are the onset and recovery sudden or gradual?
- What happens during an attack and how long does it last?
- Can she tap out how her heart beats at the time?
- Are some episodes worse than others?

While answers to these questions may give a firm clue to one of the diagnoses listed in Table 3, it is also possible that the account given may broaden the differential diagnosis still further, and the full range of causes of presyncope, syncope or vertigo may need to be considered (see the *Cardiology* book of Medical Masterclass).

Other relevant history

In addition to sweating and palpitations, are there any other autonomic symptoms, eg dry mouth, tremor, altered bowel habit? Consider the possibilities listed in Table 3 when talking with the patient.

Anxiety/depression

Does the patient experience pins and needles in the hands and feet, suggesting possible hyperventilation? Ask in detail about social circumstances, both at home and work, which seem likely to be relevant in this case from the information initially available. Does the woman have a long history of presenting with medically unexplained symptoms (see the *Psychiatry* book of Medical Masterclass)?

Alcohol/drugs

How much alcohol does the patient drink? Does she take any drugs, prescribed or non-prescribed? These questions must be approached with tact and care (see the *Clinical skills for PACES* and *Gastroenterology and hepatology* books of Medical Masterclass). Is she 'addicted to coffee'?

Cardiac arrhythmias

Both tachyarrhythmias and bradyarrhythmias can be associated with light-headedness as a consequence of impaired cardiac output, and may be noted by the patient as 'palpitations'. Ask about shortness of breath, chest pain and any previous cardiac history (see the *Cardiology* book of Medical Masterclass).

Endocrine/metabolic disorders

Autonomic symptoms can be the presenting feature of both common (eg thyrotoxicosis) and uncommon (eg phaeochromocytoma) endocrine and metabolic conditions. Ask carefully about symptoms that would suggest thyrotoxicosis, eg weight loss, tremor, dislike of hot weather. Neuroglycopenia is a possible cause of 'light-headedness' and hypoglycaemia must be considered in this woman (Table 4): if there is weight gain consider insulinoma.

Social circumstances

While most of the history is directed at determining the accurate diagnosis, attention should also be paid to the impact that these symptoms are having on the patient's life, regardless of underlying aetiology, eg the ability to perform her job and to look after her child.

Plan for investigation and management

In a case such as this your initial assessment is very important in gauging whether the symptoms have a psychological rather than physical origin – but beware of jumping to prejudiced conclusions. Always perform a full physical examination and relevant investigations unless the history is clear cut.

Table 4 Causes of hypoglycaemia

Category	Examples
Diabetes treatment related	Inadequate carbohydrate intake, excessive exercise, pregnancy, inadvertent insulin/sulfonylurea overdose
Alcohol or drug induced	Salicylates, quinine, pentamidine
Tumour related	Insulinoma,[1] non-islet cell tumour hypoglycaemia
Endocrine disorders	Hypopituitarism, Addison's disease, congenital adrenal hyperplasia
Hepatic dysfunction	Liver failure, inborn errors of metabolism, eg hereditary fructose intolerance
Reactive[2] (postprandial)	Idiopathic, postgastrectomy ('dumping syndrome')
Factitious	Sulfonylurea or insulin administration

1 A history of fasting or exertion-related hypoglycaemia in an otherwise healthy adult should prompt consideration of insulinoma.
2 Hypoglycaemia occurring within 5 hours of ingestion of food: in most cases the diagnosis is one of exclusion, with hypoglycaemia documented during the presence of symptoms.

Key point

Light-headedness, sweating and palpitations

In any patient with episodic symptoms it is invaluable if they can be assessed during an attack – priorities (after ensuring airway, breathing and circulation) are to observe the general appearance, check the pulse, measure the blood pressure (BP), obtain an electrocardiogram (ECG) rhythm strip, and test for hypoglycaemia with a finger-prick blood glucose monitor.

Investigation

Check full blood count (macrocytosis of chronic liver disease), electrolytes and renal function (low sodium and high potassium in Addison's disease), liver function (hepatic failure, metastases), fasting glucose, thyroid function tests (TFTs). Check chest radiograph (cardiac disease, metastases) and ECG (arrhythmia).

Further tests should be as dictated by clinical suspicion:

- cardiac disease – consider echocardiography and 24-hour tape (see the *Cardiology* book of Medical Masterclass)
- thyrotoxicosis (see Section 2.3.2)
- phaeochromocytoma (see Section 2.2.4)
- Addison's disease (see Section 2.2.6)
- hypoglycaemia (see below).

Hypoglycaemia

If hypoglycaemia is shown to be the cause of symptoms, then in most instances the aetiology (Table 4) can be readily identified without recourse to further studies, eg diabetes related, liver disease, but occasionally additional investigations are indicated.

Insulinoma

Key point

Diagnosis of the cause of hypoglycaemia

If hypoglycaemia is found on a finger-prick blood glucose sample, immediately take a blood sample for laboratory estimation of plasma glucose and a sample for storage for analysis of insulin, C-peptide and toxicological studies as appropriate.

A supervised 72-hour fast with regular measurements of glucose and insulin profiles (every 6 hours, and at any time when the patient is symptomatic) will unmask hypoglycaemia in most cases. Biochemical confirmation of hypoglycaemia (laboratory blood glucose <2.2 mmol/L) should be accompanied by demonstration of inappropriate hyperinsulinaemia and elevated C-peptide levels.

The tumour may be visible on ultrasound (especially endoscopic ultrasound), CT (Fig 2), MRI, octreotide scintigraphy or positron emission tomography (PET), or angiography (Fig 3), but some cases are sufficiently small to evade detection. Accordingly, some centres advocate localisation at surgery by palpation under direct vision. Intraoperative ultrasound may aid detection of tumours that are too small to feel.

Factitious hypoglycaemia

Exogenous insulin administration causes hypoglycaemia with hyperinsulinaemia, but C-peptide levels are low because endogenous insulin secretion is suppressed. By contrast, the surreptitious use of sulfonylureas (which enhance endogenous insulin secretion) gives rise to a biochemical profile similar to that seen with insulinoma: diagnosis is made by assay of plasma or urinary sulfonylurea levels.

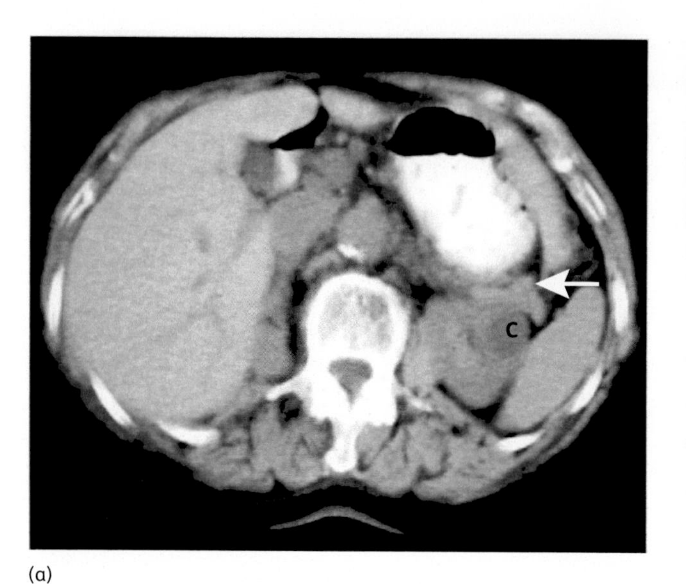

(a)

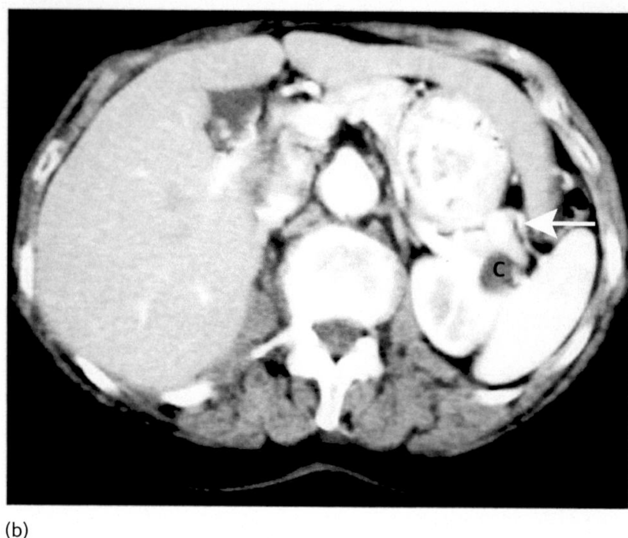

(b)

Fig 2 Insulinoma. CTs **(a)** before and **(b)** after contrast demonstrating an insulinoma (arrow) projecting anteriorly from the tail of the pancreas, in close proximity to an incidental left renal cyst – 'C'.

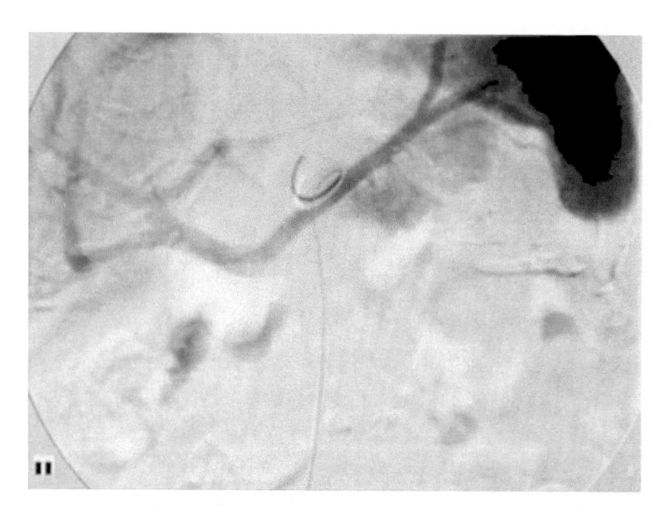

Fig 3 Insulinoma tumour 'blush'. Digital subtraction angiogram of the splenic artery revealing the typical tumour 'blush' of an insulinoma within the tail of the pancreas.

Hazard

Beware factitious hypoglycaemia

Factitious hypoglycaemia should be considered in those allied to the medical profession or, as perhaps in this case, where there is ease of access to insulin / oral hypoglycaemic agents (especially sulfonylureas).

Management

Insulinoma

Surgical excision is the treatment of choice. Regular snacking or the use of corn starch will minimise the number of hypoglycaemic episodes prior to surgery. Diazoxide or somatostatin analogues which inhibit insulin secretion may be useful adjuncts in more refractory cases, or in those considered unfit for operation (although some patients may experience a worsening of hypoglycaemia with somatostatin analogue therapy due to inhibition of counter-regulatory hormones).

Reactive hypoglycaemia

Postgastrectomy patients should be advised to eat little and often, avoiding rapidly absorbed carbohydrate. 'Idiopathic' (ie 'unexplained, but no sinister cause found') hypoglycaemia may respond to dietary manipulation with avoidance of refined carbohydrate and reassurance that there is no serious underlying disorder.

Factitious hypoglycaemia

Treatment is difficult: confrontation often leads to denial despite convincing evidence. An underlying psychiatric condition is frequently present and appropriate referral is advisable, although often declined by the patient.

Further discussion

Multiple endocrine neoplasia type 1

Many cases of insulinoma are due to solitary benign tumours arising within the pancreas, but a small number have malignant potential and a few are seen in the context of the multiple endocrine neoplasia type 1 (MEN-1) syndrome (see Section 2.7.1). The latter should always be borne in mind, and genetic counselling/screening considered if there is a personal or close family history of hyperparathyroidism (ask about neck surgery, renal stones), pituitary adenomas or other neuroendocrine tumours (eg gastrinoma).

1.1.4 Gynaecomastia

Letter of referral to the endocrinology outpatient clinic

Dear Doctor,

Re: Mr Lee Hopwood, aged 29 years

I would be grateful for your further assessment of this young teacher who has had 18 months of progressive enlargement of both breasts, which are also intermittently uncomfortable. He is a keen sportsman and is increasingly embarrassed socially by his appearance. He is well in other respects, not having attended the practice for some 4 years. I would be most grateful for your advice on the cause and treatment of this problem.

Yours sincerely,

Introduction

Gynaecomastia is the presence of palpable breast tissue in a male. Clinically apparent gynaecomastia is found at about 1% of autopsies, while corresponding histological changes have been reported in up to about 40%, suggesting that in many cases it may be a normal variant.

Gynaecomastia results from an increase in the net effective oestrogen: androgen ratio acting on the breast, either as a consequence of a decrease in androgen production/action, or an increase in oestrogen formation (including conversion of circulating androgens to oestrogens by aromatisation). Physiological gynaecomastia may be seen in the newborn, at puberty and in older people: other causes are listed in Table 5, but many cases are idiopathic.

The principal problems associated with gynaecomastia are cosmetic and psychological. In young men, gynaecomastia may lead to bullying and social isolation. It is not associated with an excess risk of breast carcinoma, except in Klinefelter's syndrome.

History of the presenting problem

When did the gynaecomastia start?

The age of the patient presenting with gynaecomastia is of great importance – this man lies between puberty and old age, both times at which 'physiological' breast enlargement may be seen.

The duration and tempo of the enlargement should be noted, and the timing of pubertal milestones documented. Check whether the problem is unilateral or bilateral.

Table 5 Causes of gynaecomastia

Cause	Example/condition
Physiological	Neonatal
	Puberty
	Older people
Idiopathic	—
Drugs that inhibit androgen synthesis or action[1]	Antiandrogens (eg cyproterone acetate, flutamide) or GnRH analogues (used in the treatment of prostate cancer)
	Digoxin
	Spironolactone
	Ketoconazole
	Metronidazole
	Cimetidine
	'Recreational' use or abuse of anabolic steroids
Primary or secondary testosterone deficiency	Klinefelter's syndrome (XXY), Kallmann's syndrome
	Testicular failure secondary to mumps orchitis, trauma or orchidectomy
	Hyperprolactinaemia
	Renal failure
Increased oestrogen production (or increased aromatisation)	Testicular, adrenal or bronchogenic tumours producing hCG, oestrogens or androgens
	Chronic liver disease
	Starvation
	Obesity
	Thyrotoxicosis

1 Note that many other drugs have been implicated (some with no clear mechanism of action).
GnRH, gonadotrophin-releasing hormone; hCG, human chorionic gonadotrophin.

Has he noticed any other features?
Ask about tenderness, discharge and discrete lumps: lactation suggests hyperprolactinaemia.

What impact has this had psychologically?
It is very important to establish the reason for presentation and to document the degree of psychological distress caused by the problem.

Other relevant history

Has the patient gained a lot of weight over the course of the appearance of the breast enlargement? If so, this may be the reason.

Drug history
A careful drug history is essential, focusing on the drugs implicated in Table 5. In this case specific questioning about anabolic steroid use would be appropriate in view of the patient's involvement in sport: this is something that the patient might not volunteer in routine clinical practice, or in PACES, unless prompted to do so.

Testicular function
Evidence of testicular function should be garnered through questions about libido, shaving frequency, morning erections and the onset of puberty. Whether the patient has been aware of any testicular lumps is also important.

Pituitary function
This presentation may be associated with a pituitary macroadenoma (and associated hypogonadism), hence ask about fertility: has he had any children? Does he have a partner, and if so, are they trying to have children? Also ask about any visual symptoms or headaches.

Other systemic diseases
Known liver disease, or risk factors for chronic liver disease should be sought, as should symptoms of thyroid disease.

Plan for investigation and management

Explain to the patient that you would normally conduct a full physical examination.

Investigation
Some experts argue that gynaecomastia is so common that it should only be investigated when breast enlargement is symptomatic, progressive, has no simple explanation or is accompanied by abnormal findings on examination. In these circumstances laboratory assessment should include:

- renal, liver and thyroid function tests
- luteinising hormone (LH), follicle-stimulating hormone (FSH) and testosterone (with or without dehydroepiandrosterone sulphate (DHEAS) as a marker of adrenal androgen production)
- oestradiol (E_2)
- human chorionic gonadotrophin (hCG) (with or without alpha-fetoprotein (AFP))
- prolactin – if there are other clinical features of hyperprolactinaemia
- karyotype analysis – especially if gynaecomastia is accompanied by tall stature and small testes suggestive of Klinefelter's syndrome.

If E_2 or hCG is elevated or testicular examination is abnormal, then a testicular ultrasound is indicated.

Management
Where identified, the underlying cause should be treated, including withdrawal, where possible, of any drug that is implicated.

In idiopathic gynaecomastia, patients may simply need reassurance that there is no sinister underlying cause. Testosterone therapy is only effective in those cases associated with hypogonadism. Tamoxifen may be of benefit in some patients, although this is an unlicensed use of the drug. For gynaecomastia associated with obesity there is a theoretical place for aromatase inhibitors such as letrozole, but again this is not a licensed indication. Cosmetic surgery (either liposuction or reduction mammoplasty) is the only effective definitive treatment.

Key point

After taking a history, examining a patient and conducting appropriate investigations, do not underestimate the importance of reassuring a patient that nothing terrible has been found.

In practice it would be appropriate to arrange relevant blood tests and to review the patient again in clinic in 4–8 weeks to discuss any evidence for an underlying problem, and to explore his desire for therapy.

Further discussion

Most males with gynaecomastia find the condition distressing and a cause of social embarrassment, eg when partaking in sporting activities, as in this case. It can cause significant psychological morbidity, leading to teasing and social isolation in young men in particular. It is very important to address these concerns and to reassure the patient that you are arranging appropriate tests to exclude specific treatable conditions, although in many cases no underlying cause can be identified. Many men will appreciate reassurance that they are not 'becoming less masculine and more feminine', and it is also important to emphasise that even if no aetiological factor comes to light, then there are still a number of treatment options that can be considered.

There is little evidence to suggest that gynaecomastia is associated with an excess risk of breast carcinoma, except in Klinefelter's syndrome.

1.1.5 Hirsutism

Letter of referral to the endocrinology outpatient clinic

Dear Doctor,

Re: Miss Carly Denton, aged 33 years

Thank you for seeing this hairdresser with long-standing irregular menses who presented with gradually worsening hirsutism and weight gain. Both the beautician doing her electrolysis and a fellow 'Weight Watcher' have suggested that 'there might be something wrong with (her) glands' and hence she is keen to seek 'expert' medical advice. I would be grateful for your views on diagnosis and treatment.

Yours sincerely,

Introduction

Knowledge of the normal biology of hair growth is central to the understanding of hirsutism, a common disorder in endocrine clinics. Although most cases represent predominantly a cosmetic problem, occasionally hirsutism is a sign of serious underlying pathology (see Table 42).

Key point
Hair

- Hair can be classified as either vellus (soft, non-pigmented) or terminal (coarse, pigmented) – before puberty most of the body is covered by vellus hair, notable exceptions being the scalp and eyebrows.
- At puberty, under the influence of androgens, vellus hairs are transformed into terminal hairs. In females this process is limited mainly to the pubic and axillary regions.
- The development in a female of terminal hairs in a male distribution (face, chest, back, lower abdomen and inner thighs) is referred to as hirsutism.
- Enhanced conversion of testosterone to dihydrotestosterone (active metabolite) through increased 5alpha-reductase activity in skin is believed to account for most cases of idiopathic hirsutism.
- Hirsutism should be distinguished from hypertrichosis, which is a generalised increase in vellus hair.

History of the presenting problem

Time course of hirsutism

How long have the symptoms been present? Polycystic ovary syndrome (PCOS) typically presents with gradual onset of hirsutism and weight gain on a background of long-standing oligomenorrhoea, usually dating back to puberty.

Extent and previous treatment of hirsutism

Is the hirsutism restricted to certain body areas (eg chin, upper lip) or is it more extensive? Remember that the clinical picture may be modified by hair removal or make-up. Ask what measures the patient has used to control the hair growth (eg depilatory creams, waxing, plucking, shaving, electrolysis) and how frequently this is done. This will give an indication of the severity of the problem.

Other relevant history

Weight gain

A recent history of weight gain, as in this patient, is common and exacerbates the clinical features by promoting insulin resistance and suppressing sex hormone-binding globulin (SHBG) levels, thereby increasing circulating free androgens.

Virilisation

Increasing muscularity, deepening of the voice and/or clitoromegaly should prompt specific consideration of an androgen-secreting adrenal or ovarian tumour.

Disturbances of menstruation or concerns about fertility

A detailed menstrual history is critical, including current or previous hormonal contraceptive use. It is important to know whether the patient is currently concerned about fertility, as this may influence the course of treatment you recommend.

Key point
Oral contraceptive pill

Remember that many women on the combined oral contraceptive pill regard their withdrawal bleeds as 'normal periods' and will truthfully say that they are regular, but perhaps forget to mention that they are taking the pill.

Underlying disorders

Ask about symptoms of endocrine conditions, in particular Cushing's syndrome and hypothyroidism, and use of any prescribed or non-prescribed medications that may be associated with hirsutism (Table 42).

Family history

Remember there are significant variations in the extent and distribution of body hair in normal women from different ethnic backgrounds. Ask about whether female relatives have had similar problems. PCOS is associated with insulin resistance, hence a family history of metabolic syndrome or type 2 diabetes should be sought.

Plan for investigation and management

Investigation

Opinions differ as to the extent to which women with hirsutism should be investigated. A suggested practical approach based on clinical findings is shown in Table 43. The features described in this case are suggestive of PCOS.

Key point

Investigation of hirsutism

> If suspected clinically, Cushing's syndrome and hypothyroidism require specific exclusion (see Sections 2.1.1 and 2.3.1).

> Dehydroepiandrosterone sulphate (DHEAS), a pure adrenal androgen, is useful in differentiating adrenal from ovarian sources of hyperandrogenism (see Section 2.2.3).

> If fertility is an issue, check mid-luteal (day 21 in a 28-day cycle) progesterone to determine whether cycles are ovulatory.

Management

Specific treatment will clearly depend on the underlying diagnosis:

> Cushing's syndrome (see Section 2.1.1)

> adrenal virilising tumour (see Section 2.2.3)

> ovarian virilising tumour (see Section 2.2.3 and the *Oncology* book of Medical Masterclass)

> congenital adrenal hyperplasia (CAH) (see Section 2.2.5)

> hypothyroidism (see Section 2.3.1).

Polycystic ovary syndrome

In the patient with PCOS, the following aspects are important:

> Communication – having excluded sinister underlying pathology, the patient should be reassured that, although there is a slight imbalance between the male and female hormones in her body, all women have some circulating male sex hormones and she is not being 'masculinised' in any way. Patients with relationship problems or eating disorders may benefit from liaison counselling or psychotherapy.

> Weight loss – weight loss ameliorates all of the symptoms of PCOS. Frequently, however, the patient has struggled to lose weight for many years, and may be unimpressed if – despite a hormonal imbalance being detected – there is nothing on offer other than a referral to the dietitian.

> Hirsutism – patients are usually experts on all forms of hair removal, having invested both time and money on a variety of cosmetic measures. Specific pharmacological options are discussed in Section 2.4.6.

> Oligomenorrhoea/infertility – normalisation of the cycle can be achieved with a combined oral contraceptive pill, but ensure that you recommend a non-androgenic variety. Always enquire whether fertility is currently an issue, or likely to be so in the future – clomifene and/or metformin (see Sections 2.4.5 and 2.4.8) are likely to be more effective than the combined oral contraceptive pill in this setting!

> Other cardiovascular risk factors – patients with the metabolic form of PCOS may be obese and have impaired glucose tolerance: other cardiovascular risk factors (eg hypertension, smoking, lipid profile) should be reviewed and treated as necessary (see Section 1.1.15).

> Review – the patient described has experienced a gradual onset of hirsutism with several features suggestive of PCOS and no worrying features to indicate malignancy. Having established that initial blood tests (luteinising hormone (LH), follicle-stimulating hormone (FSH), testosterone, DHEAS, SHBG, 17alpha-hydroxyprogesterone) fit with the clinical diagnosis and agreed a management plan (in the first instance probably diet and exercise with or without Dianette (co-cyprindiol)) it would be reasonable to arrange a follow-up appointment at 6 months. Significant effects are not seen before this time due to the long duration of the hair-growth cycle, with maximal effects not seen until 9–12 months.

Hazard

Treatment of hirsutism

Whatever treatment is given, patients are often disappointed that 6–12 months may pass before any benefit is seen. It is important to emphasise this before initiating therapy.

Further discussion

Tailoring treatment for different needs

The patient has been referred with hirsutism, but she is 33 and her main concern may really be sub-fertility in view of her irregular periods. If this is the case she will likely need clomifene (and/or metformin), with consideration of referral for specialist fertility treatment earlier rather than later as age restrictions apply for interventions such as *in vitro* fertilisation (IVF) on the National Health Service (NHS). Patients' needs continually evolve and fertility should be discussed at each review.

Prognosis of PCOS

While the patient's main concern may be cosmetic appearances, it should be borne in mind that this condition is associated with insulin resistance, type 2 diabetes and features of the metabolic syndrome. Cardiovascular risk factors should be sought and addressed, but this will require good communication with the patient as she may be unhappy coming away from clinic with several prescriptions, none of which helps her hirsutism.

1.1.6 Post-pill amenorrhoea

Letter of referral to the endocrinology outpatient clinic

Dear Doctor,

Re: Mrs Tasmin Jayasena, aged 28 years

This woman presented after 2 years of failing to conceive. Her previous menstrual history is unremarkable, with menarche at 13 years of age and a regular cycle prior to going onto the oral contraceptive pill (OCP) aged 18. However, she has had no menstrual bleeds since coming off the pill 15 months ago and she remains keen to start a family. I would be grateful for your opinion as to whether this is simple 'post-pill amenorrhoea', or whether further investigation is indicated at this stage.

Yours sincerely,

Introduction

The presentation is one of secondary amenorrhoea with infertility. 'Post-pill amenorrhoea' is not a diagnosis in itself: 6 months after stopping an oral contraceptive preparation the risk of secondary amenorrhoea is no higher than in the general population, meaning that in amenorrhoea prolonged beyond this time, some other pathology must be implicated. True secondary amenorrhoea may be related to failure at any level of the hypothalamic–pituitary–gonadal axis, whether functional (eg in the context of very low body mass index (BMI)) or due to direct neoplastic or inflammatory involvement of relevant organs, as detailed in Table 6.

History of the presenting problem

The history should begin by confirming that the patient had a normal menarche and regular menses prior to OCP use, and establish whether there is any possibility of pregnancy (even allowing for the duration of amenorrhoea, pregnancy must be excluded in all cases).

Other relevant history

The rest of the history should be devoted to teasing out clues to the underlying problem, bearing in mind the conditions listed in Table 6.

Exercise/dieting/stress

Excessive exercise, weight loss or psychological stress can suppress the activity of the gonadotrophin-releasing hormone (GnRH) pulse generator. Patients may be evasive in their answers to questions concerning these issues. Similarly, severe illnesses with significant weight loss may also lead to hypothalamic amenorrhoea.

Pituitary disease

Secondary amenorrhoea can reflect direct damage to the gonadotrophs (eg pituitary adenoma, infarction) or hyperprolactinaemia (which disrupts GnRH neuronal activity). Enquire about galactorrhoea and other symptoms of pituitary disease, focusing both on symptoms of hormone hypersecretion, and direct effects of a pituitary tumour such as visual disturbance, and new onset migraine (Section 2.1). If there is a history of previous pregnancy, then evidence of major haemorrhage or severe hypotension peripartum should be sought, and any general history of head trauma may also be relevant: the gonadal axis is particularly vulnerable to damage in both of these situations.

Table 6 Causes of secondary amenorrhoea

Cause	Example/condition
Physiological	Pregnancy
	Lactation
	Postmenopausal
Pathological	PCOS (although more typically the patient reports oligomenorrhoea)
	Hypothalamic–pituitary dysfunction (including excessive weight loss or exercise, stress, pituitary tumours/infiltration, hyperprolactinaemia)
	Premature ovarian failure
	Congenital adrenal hyperplasia
	Adrenal/ovarian neoplasms

PCOS, polycystic ovary syndrome.

Premature ovarian failure

This is most commonly autoimmune in origin and characterised by hypergonadotrophic hypogonadism. Ask about menopausal symptoms (eg hot flushes, dyspareunia), check for a family history of early menopause, also for any personal or family history of autoimmune disease.

Adrenal or ovarian tumours

Enquire about hirsutism and virilising features (see Sections 2.2.3 and 2.4.6). Given the regular menses prior to OCP use, both PCOS and congenital adrenal hyperplasia (CAH) are less likely.

Exogenous sex steroids

It should be confirmed that the patient is not taking any exogenous preparations containing sex steroids.

Plan for investigation and management

In practice, it should be explained that the lack of periods is not due to an after-effect of the OCP alone, and that the problem may lie at one of various different levels of the hormonal system which controls the ovaries.

Investigation

Pregnancy test

Key point

Exclude pregnancy!

However unlikely it may seem, it is imperative to exclude pregnancy before embarking on further investigations for amenorrhoea. Explain this to the patient and obtain her consent to testing.

Routine blood tests

Full blood count, electrolytes, renal/liver/bone biochemistry and thyroid function will often have been checked before referral.

Specific endocrine assessment

Check:

- LH, FSH and oestradiol (E_2) – to distinguish hypogonadotrophic and hypergonadotrophic hypogonadism
- prolactin – elevated in prolactinoma or with stalk disconnection
- testosterone and DHEAS – to exclude an androgen-secreting ovarian or adrenal tumour.

Further investigations will be guided by the clinical features and initial biochemical screen:

- hyperprolactinaemia and hypopituitarism (see Sections 2.1.3 and 2.1.8)
- PCOS (see Section 2.4.5)
- premature ovarian failure (see Section 2.4.3).

Management

Management will clearly depend on the diagnosis:

- Pregnancy – it is rare but not unheard of for pregnancy to present to an endocrine clinic. The chances are that you will not be the only surprised person in the room!
- Excessive exercise / weight loss / stress – explain the physiological basis for the amenorrhoea and encourage moderation. Psychological/psychiatric input may be required.

For management of hyperprolactinaemia and hypopituitarism, PCOS and premature ovarian failure see sections indicated above.

Further discussion

Advice for a patient with a pituitary tumour

Patients with microprolactinomas who are not trying to conceive need to be aware of the importance of complying with treatment to prevent osteoporosis: many women are quite happy not having periods when they know there is 'nothing to worry about'. If they find the side effects of bromocriptine upsetting, oestrogen replacement therapy is a good alternative.

Key point

Important advice for patients

Patients with pituitary problems need to understand a little anatomy and physiology, otherwise their disease, its monitoring and treatment can seem very mysterious. They will often have their own ideas about 'brain tumours': it is important to find out what these are and if necessary provide reassurance that their type of tumour will not spread elsewhere in the body, and will not need treatment that results in baldness, etc. Patient information leaflets produced by the Pituitary Foundation (www.pituitary.org.uk/) are a useful aid.

1.1.7 A short girl with no periods

Letter of referral to the endocrinology outpatient clinic

Dear Doctor,

Re: Miss Joanna Otai, aged 15 years

Thank you for seeing this schoolgirl who has not yet started her menstrual periods. She is more concerned about her height and says that she is 'the shortest person' in her class. Her growth chart, maintained until the age of 9 years, shows that she has always been quite short. Her current height is 135 cm. She is otherwise healthy but it is quite obvious that she has not yet developed any secondary sexual characteristics.

There is no family history of note and a recent set of blood tests, including full blood count, electrolytes and renal function and blood glucose were all within normal limits.

I suspect that she has some hormonal cause for her delayed growth and puberty and would appreciate your evaluation and advice on further management.

Yours sincerely,

Introduction

'Delayed growth and puberty' are often linked presentations (see Sections 2.4.1, 2.4.3 and 2.4.4). In general, investigations should be initiated if there are no secondary sexual characteristics by $13^1/_2$ years in girls and $14^1/_2$ years in boys, and/or if the child's height falls below the third centile and is inappropriate for the height of the parents. There are many causes (Table 7), but remember that up to 3% of children exhibit constitutional pubertal delay.

Table 7 Causes of delayed growth and puberty[1]

Frequency	Condition
Common	'Constitutional delay'
	Chronic/severe illness
Rarer causes of short stature	Chromosomal abnormalities
	Single-gene defects
	Dysmorphic syndromes
	Endocrine disorders
Rarer causes of delayed puberty	Hypogonadotrophic hypogonadism
	Hypergonadotrophic hypogonadism
	Androgen excess

1 For further details see Table 38.

History of the presenting problem

Birth and growth history

Enquire about birth weight and problems during pregnancy / at delivery: low birth weight is associated with short stature.

Are data showing the time course of growth failure available, eg child health records which include growth charts? In this case the GP's letter suggests that she has always been of short stature, but obtaining the actual charts allows you to determine whether there was a period of arrested growth from which she has never recovered the 'lost ground', or whether her growth velocity has been constant but low (Fig 4). Has she experienced any dramatic changes in body weight?

Childhood/chronic illness

Does she have a history of other chronic illness, eg asthma, cystic fibrosis, Crohn's disease, chronic renal impairment, childhood cancer treated with chemotherapy and/or radiotherapy? Any of these can lead to short stature and/or delayed puberty.

Other relevant history

Past medical history

If Turner's syndrome is considered a possibility, ask about associated features: history of structural cardiac or renal disease; history of recurrent middle-ear infections or of hearing impairment; symptoms/signs to suggest hypothyroidism.

Family history

Enquire about a family history of short stature or delayed puberty. Ascertain the height of each of her parents.

Social history

Once you have gained the confidence/ trust of the patient (and her parents) ask about eating habits – both nutritional deficiency and disorders such as anorexia nervosa may be associated with short stature and/or delayed puberty. Ask about her social circumstances – emotional stress can have adverse effects on growth.

Plan for investigation and management

Explain to the patient that under normal circumstances you would examine her and then proceed as follows.

Investigation

Recommended blood tests, imaging and further investigations are discussed in more detail in Sections 2.4.1, 2.4.3 and 2.4.4, but in brief may include the following.

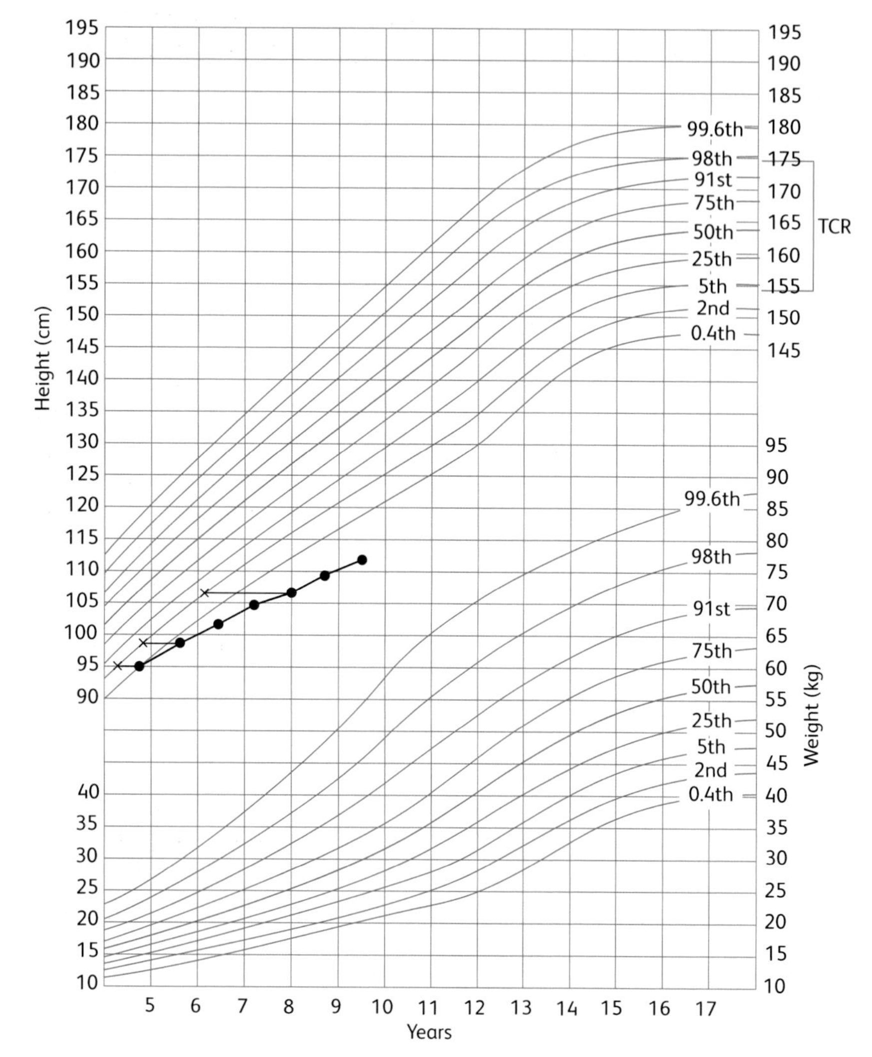

Fig 4 Growth chart from a young girl with Turner's syndrome. The dots denote measurements plotted according to chronological age, while the crosses refer to bone age. TCR, target centile range.

Exclusion of chronic diseases

There are a number of chronic diseases that can be easily diagnosed and are worth screening for on a fairly universal basis:

> full blood count (anaemia)

> electrolytes and renal function tests (chronic renal impairment)

> glucose (diabetes mellitus)

> C-reactive protein (CRP) and/or erythrocyte sedimentation rate (ESR) (systemic disorders)

> thyroid function tests (TFTs) (free thyroxine (FT4) and thyroid-stimulating hormone (TSH))

> anti-tissue transglutaminase antibodies and immunoglobulin A (IgA) (coeliac disease)

> plasma bicarbonate and urinalysis (renal tubular acidosis).

Specific investigations

These will be determined by your clinical impression and initial screening tests, but may include:

> Bone age (typically plain radiograph of the wrist) – can be compared with chronological age and may aid in the diagnosis of pubertal delay as well as in predicting future growth potential.

> Karyotype analysis – all girls with delayed puberty and growth should have a karyotype analysis as Turner's syndrome is not always clinically apparent.

> Paired luteinising hormone (LH), follicle-stimulating hormone (FSH) and oestrogen levels – will help to differentiate between hypergonadotrophic hypogonadism (primary gonadal failure as in Turner's syndrome) and hypogonadotrophic hypogonadism (secondary gonadal failure or constitutional delay).

Depending on the results of these investigations, more complex tests of pituitary function (eg a GnRH test – see Section 3.1.4; assessment of growth hormone (GH) status – see Section 2.1.8) may be indicated, together with structural studies, eg MRI of the pituitary fossa, visual field assessment and pelvic ultrasound.

Management

Where identified, specific underlying disorders should be treated appropriately, eg juvenile hypothyroidism should be corrected with thyroxine replacement therapy. The management of Turner's syndrome is complex and requires a multidisciplinary approach as outlined in Section 2.4.4.

Further discussion

Children of parents with short stature

Children of parents with short stature and/or constitutional delayed puberty are at increased risk of being affected themselves. Determination of gonadotrophin (LH and FSH) and sex steroid (oestrogen or testosterone) levels together with assessment of bone age may help to establish the diagnosis. Low gonadotrophins and a relatively delayed bone age are more likely to be associated with normal (but delayed) pubertal development, while low gonadotrophins and a more advanced bone age are suggestive of underlying pathology, and require further investigation.

Turner's syndrome

Key point

All girls with delayed puberty and short stature should have their karyotype checked

Turner's syndrome occurs in one in 2,000 to one in 2,500 live-born females and is not always clinically apparent. If the karyotype in peripheral blood-derived lymphocytes is normal, but the clinical index of suspicion for Turner's syndrome remains high, then consider checking karyotype in a second tissue, eg skin fibroblasts, just in case the patient exhibits mosaicism.

1.1.8 Young man who has 'not developed'

Letter of referral to the endocrinology outpatient clinic

Dear Doctor,

Re: Mr Gregory Clear, aged 18 years

Thank you for seeing this 18-year-old student who does not appear to have gone through puberty as yet. He originally presented to me with an upper respiratory tract infection, and at the time I noted a lack of facial and axillary hair. Subsequent examination revealed a general absence of secondary sexual characteristics, and his testosterone level has come back as very low. I would be grateful for your advice on diagnosis and management.

Yours sincerely,

Introduction

The importance of the history in this case is first to confirm that the subject is indeed prepubertal, suggesting failure of onset of puberty rather than pubertal arrest (although there is overlap between these conditions, they should be considered as distinct clinical entities) and, secondly, to try to identify the underlying cause. Table 8 outlines the major groups of disorders associated with male hypogonadism, a term that denotes deficiency of both testosterone secretion (from Leydig cells) and sperm production (by the seminiferous tubules).

History of the presenting problem

Androgen status

Ask about frequency of shaving and beard growth; axillary and pubic hair development; deepening of the voice; and libido and erectile function (and where appropriate fertility).

Hypogonadotrophic hypogonadism

Enquire about problems with sense of smell (hyposmia or anosmia in Kallmann's syndrome), features suggesting other pituitary hormone deficiencies (Section 2.1.8), headaches / visual problems (hypothalamic/pituitary space-occupying lesion) and galactorrhoea (hyperprolactinaemia).

Hypergonadotrophic hypogonadism

Ask about testicular surgery/trauma or bouts of orchitis in the past, and gynaecomastia (Klinefelter's syndrome).

Other relevant history

Enquire about his previous medical history, in particular chronic illnesses during childhood and the teenage years. A family history of delayed puberty may be relevant in Kallmann's syndrome and in simple constitutional delayed puberty. Potential fertility may also need to be considered, although it would be appropriate to reserve this discussion for a later visit when the results of initial investigations are available.

Plan for investigation and management

Explain to the patient that under normal circumstances you would examine him to confirm his GP's findings. The objectives of investigation are first to confirm the presence of hypogonadism and then to determine the aetiology.

Table 8 Causes of male hypogonadism

Cause	Example/condition
Primary hypogonadism (ie testicular dysfunction)	Idiopathic
	Post chemotherapy, surgery, trauma or viral orchitis
	Klinefelter's syndrome (see Section 2.4.2)
	Systemic disorders, eg renal failure, haemochromatosis, myotonic dystrophy
Secondary hypogonadism (ie hypothalamic/pituitary in origin)	Constitutional delayed puberty
	Hyperprolactinaemia
	Hypothalamic/pituitary tumour/infiltration/surgery/radiotherapy
	Isolated hypogonadotrophic hypogonadism, including Kallmann's syndrome (see Section 2.4.2)

Investigation

Routine blood tests

Unless the clinical features suggest a specific underlying disorder, some simple screening tests should be performed including: full blood count (anaemia), electrolytes and renal function tests (chronic renal impairment), fasting glucose, thyroid function, prolactin, liver biochemistry and serum transferrin saturation/iron studies (iron overload).

Gonadotrophins (LH, FSH) and testosterone

The finding of a low testosterone level (ideally measured at 9am and with correction for a low sex hormone-binding globulin (SHBG) level) on more than one occasion confirms hypogonadism. Measurement of LH and FSH allows distinction between hypogonadotrophic (secondary) and hypergonadotrophic (primary) hypogonadism, although remember that the former may simply indicate constitutional delay.

Specific investigations

These will be guided by your clinical impression and preliminary screening tests, and are discussed in more detail in Section 2.4.2, but may include:

> karyotype analysis – to exclude Klinefelter's syndrome

> assessment of pituitary function / MRI pituitary fossa – in cases of secondary hypogonadism/hyperprolactinaemia (see Sections 2.1.3 and 2.1.8)

> genetic screening – if haemochromatosis is suspected (see Section 2.5.3), although this would be an unusual presentation for primary as opposed to secondary iron overload

> ultrasound of the testes – in cases of cryptorchidism

> semen analysis

> human chorionic gonadotrophin (hCG) stimulation – to help differentiate primary and secondary gonadal failure

> bone densitometry (dual-energy X-ray absorptiometry (DXA)) – to help identify those at significant risk of fracture.

Management

The general principles governing management of the hypogonadal male are discussed in more detail in Sections 2.1.8, 2.4.2 and 2.4.8, but include patient and sympathetic explanation, treatment of any underlying disorder, correction/replacement of hormone deficiency and referral for specialist fertility advice if appropriate.

Further discussion

Testosterone replacement

Testosterone replacement can be efficiently delivered using gel (care needed to avoid transfer to partner or children; use may also be limited by local skin reaction), intramuscular depot injection (3–4 weekly or 3 monthly depending on preparation) or (less commonly) implant. Oral preparations are not recommended as it is rarely possible to achieve therapeutic blood levels with this mode of delivery. Monitoring of testosterone replacement should include measurement of serum testosterone levels, liver chemistry and full blood count (haemoglobin and haematocrit) and, where appropriate, prostate surveillance (digital rectal examination and prostate-specific antigen (PSA)).

1.1.9 Depression and diabetes

Letter of referral to the endocrinology outpatient clinic

Dear Doctor,

Re: Mrs Cynthia Scott, aged 72 years

This normally active widow was brought to our surgery by her daughters who are concerned about her mental state: they fear she is depressed. Her past medical history is unremarkable, although she is overweight and routine urinalysis has revealed glycosuria. Could she have an underlying endocrine cause for her problems?

Yours sincerely,

Introduction

Depression is very common. There may be several contributing factors, eg social isolation, neglect, bereavement, poverty and chronic health problems: all are major risk factors that should be sought in the history. Remember, however, that depression can be a manifestation of many physical illnesses, particularly in older people (Table 9).

History of the presenting problem

Is this depression?

What features have led the daughters to conclude that their mother is depressed? Has she directly complained of 'feeling down' or has she exhibited unusual thoughts/behaviour? Has she suffered any recent 'life events', eg bereavement, physical ill-health? How long have the symptoms been present for?

Table 9 Physical illnesses with depression as a common presenting feature

Type of problem	Example	
'Obvious'	Any condition causing severe physical debility	Malignancy
		'Systemic illness', eg advanced cardiac/ respiratory failure or chronic renal failure (dialysis)
		Parkinson's disease
	Any condition causing chronic pain	'Arthritis/rheumatism'
		Refractory headache
		Postherpetic neuralgia
'More subtle'	Endocrine	Hypothyroidism
		Hyperparathyroidism
		Cushing's syndrome
		Pseudo-Cushing's syndrome
	Neurological	Dementia

Primary depressive disorder

Enquire about physical and psychological features of depressive illness (see the *Psychiatry* book of Medical Masterclass). Also check if there is a personal or family history of psychiatric disease.

Depression secondary to underlying physical illness

Several physical disorders can present with or masquerade as depression, and accordingly a full medical history and systems enquiry is required to look for evidence of any of the conditions listed in Table 9. This will clearly involve exploration of matters related to diabetes given that she has been found to have glycosuria. Has this been documented previously? Have there been symptoms of thirst and polyuria (see Section 2.6)? Has she recently gained or lost weight?

Also think about the following as you take the history:

- Cushing's syndrome / pseudo-Cushing's syndrome – type 2 diabetes is common in obese older people, but when associated with mood change, should prompt consideration of Cushing's syndrome. Enquire about symptoms of glucocorticoid excess, eg easy bruising, difficulty climbing stairs (see Section 2.1.1). Check for an obvious cause (eg exogenous corticosteroid usage) and enquire about alcohol consumption. Remember depression and excessive alcohol intake can result in pseudo-Cushing's syndrome (see Section 2.1.1). Care and tact will be required to elicit this history (see the *Clinical skills for PACES* book of Medical Masterclass).
- Hypothyroidism – mood change and weight gain are recognised features of hypothyroidism (see Section 2.3.1).
- Hypercalcaemia – remember 'bones, stones, abdominal groans and psychic moans' (see Section 2.5.8).
- Dementia, eg Alzheimer's disease, multi-infarct dementia – may be mistaken for a depressive illness in the early stages (see the *Medicine for older people* book of Medical Masterclass).
- Parkinson's disease – remember other physical features may go undiagnosed for some considerable period of time (see the *Neurology* book of Medical Masterclass).

Other relevant history

Enquire about home circumstances and social support.

Plan for investigation and management

Initial tests

- full blood count and ESR (normochromic normocytic anaemia of systemic disease)
- electrolytes and renal function (renal impairment; hypokalaemia – Cushing's syndrome)
- liver chemistry and calcium (hypercalcaemia, metastases)
- fasting glucose ± glycated haemoglobin A_{1c} (HbA_{1c}) (diabetes mellitus (DM))
- thyroid function tests (hypothyroidism)
- consider performing a full dementia screen (see the *Medicine for older people* book of Medical Masterclass)
- chest radiograph to look for evidence of bronchial neoplasia / lymphadenopathy
- ECG.

Specific investigations and management

These will be directed by the suspicions raised on history, examination and initial testing:

- DM (see Section 2.6)
- Cushing's syndrome (see Section 2.1.1)
- hypothyroidism (see Section 2.3.1)
- hypercalcaemia (see Section 2.5.8)
- Parkinson's disease (see the *Neurology* book of Medical Masterclass)
- dementia (see the *Medicine for older people* book of Medical Masterclass).

Further discussion

Coping with the diagnosis of diabetes

Many patients who are diagnosed with diabetes fear that this will inevitably mean insulin injections. While this might ultimately be the case, it is important to emphasise that there are other ways to treat the condition, including diet, exercise and tablets, and that the diabetes may even regress with successful treatment of an underlying disorder such as Cushing's syndrome.

It is also important to consider whether the patient and/or her family would be capable of monitoring blood glucose levels and administering/supervising treatment, or whether a district nurse may need to visit each day.

1.1.10 Acromegaly

Letter of referral to the endocrinology outpatient clinic

Dear Doctor,

Re, Mr Stephen Lee, aged 37 years

This accountant recently underwent bilateral carpal tunnel decompression. During the preoperative assessment it was noted that he had acromegalic features, and a random growth hormone (GH) level was found to be high. An endocrine referral was recommended on the discharge summary, and I would be grateful for your assistance.

Yours sincerely,

Introduction

Clearly a clinical suspicion of acromegaly in a patient awaiting carpal tunnel decompression must be taken seriously. However, the diagnosis has not been confirmed by a single 'high' growth hormone (GH) measurement. Normal GH secretion is highly pulsatile, with spikes of secretion several times a day, hence random GH levels do not reliably discriminate between normal subjects and those with acromegaly unless markedly elevated.

History of the presenting problem

Symptoms of a GH-secreting pituitary adenoma are most usefully considered in terms of those that are attributable to direct local effects of tumour expansion, those that result from exposure to supraphysiological GH levels, and those that are due to associated hypopituitarism. Ask about the following symptoms.

Symptoms due to local tumour expansion

- headaches, double vision and visual field loss.

Symptoms due to growth hormone excess

- changes in ring, shoe or hat size
- alteration/coarsening of features, or dental problems
- snoring, nocturnal apnoea, daytime somnolence (there is a high prevalence of obstructive sleep apnoea due to soft tissue overgrowth in the upper airway)
- excessive sweating
- arthritis and arthralgia
- symptoms of cardiac failure
- symptoms of diabetes mellitus (DM) such as polyuria, polydipsia, tiredness and lethargy (GH antagonises the action of insulin). A rare difficulty in the clinical diagnosis of acromegaly is that patients with syndromes of severe insulin resistance may develop a strikingly acromegalic appearance (pseudoacromegaly) without GH excess. This is believed to be due to cross-reaction of extremely high insulin levels with the insulin-like growth factor (IGF)-1 receptor, and perhaps also upregulation of the receptor. A clinical clue to this condition is the presence of severe acanthosis nigricans, or diabetes requiring very large doses of insulin to control (>300 units/day)
- hypertension – has his BP ever been measured? Hypertension is a major factor contributing to the excess morbidity and mortality seen in untreated acromegaly.

Symptoms due to associated hypopituitarism

Enquire about reduced libido and difficulties achieving/maintaining an erection (hypogonadism), tiredness and dizziness (adrenocorticotropic hormone (ACTH) deficiency), weight gain and lethargy (hypothyroidism), and galactorrhoea (hyperprolactinaemia). Also see Section 2.1.8.

Other relevant history

Long-standing GH excess is associated with an increased risk of colonic polyps and carcinomas, hence ask about alterations in bowel habit. Also remember that acromegaly can arise in the setting of multiple endocrine neoplasia type 1 (MEN-1) (see Section 2.7.1). Check for a history of hypercalcaemia and ask about relatives with similar problems.

Plan for investigation and management

These are covered in detail in Sections 2.1.2 and 3.2.4. In brief, after you have completed a thorough physical examination of the patient, consider the following.

Investigation

Hazard

Random GH levels do not reliably distinguish between normal subjects and those with acromegaly.

Growth hormone (GH) excess

- Oral glucose tolerance test (OGTT) – this remains the 'gold standard' investigation for confirming/excluding acromegaly, with the benefit also of establishing whether or not it has been complicated by the development of diabetes.
- IGF-1 – levels are typically elevated above the age-related normal range and can be used to monitor the effectiveness of treatment.

Local tumour expansion

- MRI of the pituitary fossa – distinguishes macroadenomas from microadenomas and gives vital information about the proximity of the tumour to key anatomical structures such as the optic chiasm and cavernous sinuses. It is also important postoperatively to guide the choice of adjunctive treatment in cases where transsphenoidal surgery is not curative.
- Formal visual field testing – should establish the presence and extent of any temporal field defect.

Associated hypopituitarism

Luteinising hormone (LH), follicle-stimulating hormone (FSH), testosterone, thyroid-stimulating hormone (TSH), free thyroxine (FT4), prolactin and an assessment of adrenal reserve, eg short Synacthen test or insulin tolerance test.

It is very unusual for diabetes insipidus to be a presenting feature of a pituitary adenoma, and polyuria in this case would be more likely to be due to previously undiagnosed DM. However, if there is any doubt, then check electrolytes and paired serum/plasma and urine osmolalities and ask the patient to record their fluid intake and output for a 24-hour period.

Complications of acromegaly

Further investigation will be determined by clinical findings and planned therapy, but formal polysomnography will pick up obstructive sleep apnoea in many patients with acromegaly and is of relevance to perioperative anaesthesia and airway management. Any clinical suspicion of colonic tumours should lead to formal examination of the large bowel endoscopically or radiologically. Do not forget to screen for other cardiovascular risk factors, eg dyslipidaemia.

Management

This is discussed in detail in Section 2.1.2. In brief, transsphenoidal surgery remains the mainstay of treatment for most patients with acromegaly, although there is increasing use of medical treatments – both somatostatin analogues such as octreotide in sustained release form (which suppress GH secretion from the adenoma directly) and pegvisomant, a GH receptor antagonist. In addition, radiotherapy remains an effective means of controlling tumour growth and lowering GH levels, although the latter may take several months/years to achieve.

Further discussion

Key point

Acromegaly

A picture is worth a thousand words. Ask the patient to bring along old photographs that may allow you to determine the approximate date of onset of the condition.

1.1.11 Relentless weight gain

Letter of referral to the endocrinology outpatient clinic

Dear Doctor,

Re: Miss Kathy Macdonald, aged 24 years

Thank you for seeing this 24-year-old single mother who came to see me because she has gained 12 kg in weight over the last 7 or 8 months. Although she has always had a tendency to be slightly overweight, since the birth of her daughter her weight has increased at an alarming rate, despite the fact (she tells me) that she is hardly eating anything.

Currently, she weighs 94 kg, which gives her a body mass index (BMI) of 35 kg/m^2 (normal range 18–25). She has stretch marks over her lower abdomen. Her blood pressure is 145/85 mmHg. I have checked her electrolytes, full blood count and fasting glucose and they are all within normal limits.

I would be most grateful if you could see her to exclude a serious underlying medical cause for her weight gain.

Yours sincerely,

Introduction

Weight gain of such magnitude and velocity always warrants thorough assessment and evaluation to exclude possible secondary causes (Table 10).

History of the presenting problem

Time course of weight gain

Was there an event/trigger that started it off? She may have lost her job, contracted an illness, stopped smoking, suffered a personal/family stress or had a

Table 10 Causes of weight gain / obesity

Cause	Example/condition
Lifestyle	Habitual/social overeating (quantity or quality, eg energy-dense foods)
	Excessive alcohol consumption
	Lack of exercise (voluntary or inability)
Psychological/psychiatric	Anxiety/depression
	Eating disorders, eg binge/comfort eating
Physiological	Pregnancy, post-pregnancy
	Ageing
Genetic predisposition	Simple forms of obesity – likely to reflect interaction between the individual's genetic predisposition and his/her environment
	Severe monogenic obesity, eg congenital leptin deficiency
	Other syndromic disorders, eg Prader–Willi, Laurence–Moon–Biedl
Other	Endocrine disorders, eg hypothyroidism, PCOS, Cushing's syndrome, insulinoma
	Hypothalamic dysfunction, eg tumour, infiltration, surgery
	Fluid retention, eg cardiac failure, nephrotic syndrome, cirrhosis
	Iatrogenic, eg glucocorticoids, lithium, antidepressants

PCOS, polycystic ovary syndrome.

baby (as in this case). Was she overweight as a child or teenager? Has she been prone to fluctuations in weight?

Eating habits

Ask her to describe what she would eat during a typical day – both quantity and quality are important. Has there been any change in recent weeks/months? Ask (sensitively) about comfort/binge eating. Enquire about alcohol intake (current and past).

Exercise

Ask about formal exercise, eg gym, running, swimming, also about exercise at home or at work – does she have an active or sedentary job, or is she stuck indoors all the time with the baby?

Features to suggest an underlying psychological/psychiatric disorder

Check for clues to the presence of an underlying anxiety/depressive disorder, eg early morning waking (also see the *Psychiatry* book of Medical Masterclass).

Underlying physical disorder

Consider asking about features of:

- hypothyroidism (see Section 2.3.1)
- PCOS (see Section 2.4.5)
- Cushing's syndrome (see Section 2.1.1)
- hypothalamic–pituitary dysfunction (see Section 2.1.8)
- insulinoma (see Section 1.1.3)
- cardiac impairment / nephrotic syndrome / cirrhosis.

Associated features

Ask about menstrual disturbance, eg oligomenorrhoea/amenorrhoea, also features of androgen excess, eg hirsutism/androgenic alopecia, which are a consequence of associated insulin resistance.

Other relevant history

Drug history

A full drug history should be taken (Table 11).

Family history

Ask about other family members who are overweight (especially if childhood/early onset), thyroid disease, PCOS and type 2 diabetes.

Social history

Once you have gained the confidence/trust of the patient, enquire about social circumstances and employment/financial stresses.

Plan for investigation and management

Explain to the patient that under normal circumstances you would examine her and then proceed as follows.

Investigation

Simple blood tests

Check electrolytes, renal function tests (renal impairment), liver function tests (hepatic steatosis, cirrhosis), fasting glucose ± HbA_{1c} (diabetes mellitus), fasting lipid profile (metabolic dyslipidaemia) and thyroid function (hypothyroidism).

Specific investigations

Depending on clinical suspicion and the results of preliminary investigations it may be appropriate to look for evidence of one or more of the following conditions:

- PCOS (see Section 2.4.5)
- Cushing's syndrome (see Section 2.1.1)
- hypopituitarism (see Section 2.1.8)
- insulinoma (see Section 1.1.3).

Management

Where identified, specific underlying disorders should be treated appropriately (see relevant subsections in Section 2: Diseases and treatments).

Dietary assessment/advice

Most patients who are overweight/obese will benefit from referral for formal dietary assessment – especially those who claim that they are only eating lettuce and cucumber! Key issues to address include:

- composition of current diet and total calorie intake – patients are often genuinely surprised at how many calories they are consuming each day (a food diary can be helpful)
- food substitution, ie replacing current high-calorie energy-dense foodstuffs with healthier alternatives
- limitation of total calorie intake
- restriction of alcohol consumption.

Specific dietary advice will also be required if the patient is discovered to be diabetic or hypercholesterolaemic.

Exercise/lifestyle

Encourage regular exercise, eg brisk walking, swimming or cycling for 30–40 minutes four to five times per week. Adjustments to work routines (eg taking the stairs rather than the lift) can also help.

Key point

Losing weight is not easy to do!

Most patients with simple dietary / lifestyle-related obesity require significant support in their quest to lose weight – encouragement and supervision can be provided through support groups (eg Weightwatchers®), the GP practice or specialist hospital clinics.

Assessment of cardiovascular risk

Other cardiovascular risk factors (eg hypertension, smoking, dyslipidaemia) should be reviewed and treated as necessary (see Section 1.1.15).

Medical therapy

See further discussion below.

Surgery

This is reserved for morbidly obese patients who are attending a specialist clinic and who have failed to lose weight or maintain weight loss despite intensive intervention and medical therapy. Two main types of surgery are available: 'restrictive', which limits the size of stomach, and 'malabsorptive', which shortens the length of the gut by creating a bypass.

Further discussion

Drug treatments for obesity

Various agents are now licensed for use in subjects who are obese (BMI >30 kg/m^2) or overweight (BMI >27 kg/m^2 with a major obesity-related comorbidity, eg diabetes mellitus, hypertension) (Table 11).

1.1.12 Weight loss

Letter of referral to the general medical outpatient clinic

Dear Doctor,

Re: Mrs Mandy Chang, aged 22 years

I would be grateful if you could see this healthcare assistant in your clinic. She has been previously fit and well and on no regular medications, but over the past 4 months she has lost more than 10 kg in weight and feels tired most of the time. There is not a lot to find on examination.

I have arranged for her to have some blood tests, the results of which should be available for when you see her in clinic. Thank you for advising on further investigation and management.

Yours sincerely,

Table 11 Drugs used to treat obesity

Drug	Action	Comments
Orlistat	Gastric and pancreatic lipase inhibitor which reduces the absorption of dietary fat by ~30%	To prevent possible malabsorption of fat-soluble vitamins, co-prescription of a daily multivitamin is advised by some clinicians
		May potentiate the effect of warfarin
		Main adverse effect is faecal urgency/soiling, especially if non-compliant with dietary restriction of fat intake
Liraglutide	Glucagon-like peptide-1 analogue	In animal studies, high-dose liraglutide usage has been linked with an increased risk of MTC; treatment should therefore be avoided in those with a personal or family history of MTC or MEN type 2
		Other recognised adverse effects include pancreatitis, biliary disease and hypoglycaemia in patients with type 2 diabetes who are taking other medications such as sulfonylureas

MEN, multiple endocrine neoplasia; MTC, medullary thyroid carcinoma.

Introduction

Weight loss is a non-specific symptom and may be the presenting manifestation of a large number of disorders (Table 12). However, the relatively short duration of symptoms in a previously fit young person makes some diagnoses, eg thyrotoxicosis, diabetes mellitus (DM), more likely than others.

History of the presenting problem

Allow the patient to explain what her major concerns are, then adopt a systematic approach with direct questions to screen for potential diagnoses for which relevant information has not been forthcoming.

General symptoms

Ask about other non-specific symptoms such as fever, night sweats and lymphadenopathy. Lymphoma is not uncommon in this age group and weight loss is one of the classical B symptoms.

Appetite and calorie intake

Key point

Some patients lose weight intentionally!

Before embarking on a chase for causes of weight loss it is always important to find out if the patient is trying to lose weight.

What is her attitude to eating and to her loss of weight? Appetite may be increased in hypermetabolic states, reduced in true anorexia of chronic disorders, and is usually normal in anorexia nervosa where the problem is food refusal. Has she ever made herself vomit?

Abdominal symptoms

Ask about dysphagia, vomiting/regurgitation, abdominal pain or distension, and bowel habit (frequency, consistency, blood, mucus, difficulty flushing).

It may be that a clear lead will emerge to suggest malignancy, malabsorption or anorexia nervosa, in which case these possibilities should be pursued as indicated in the *Gastroenterology and hepatology* and *Psychiatry* books of Medical Masterclass. Is it possible that other conditions listed in Table 12 are present? In this young woman consider the following.

Table 12 Causes of weight loss

Type of disorder	Example
Hypermetabolic states	Thyrotoxicosis
	DM
	Acute sepsis/trauma
Anorexia of chronic disorders	Infections, eg gastrointestinal, HIV
	Systemic inflammatory disorders
	Malignancy, including lymphoma
	Addison's disease
Reduced calorie intake	Anorexia nervosa or other eating disorder
	Upper gastrointestinal tract pathology, eg oesophageal stricture
	Neurological disorders, eg motor neurone disease
Malabsorption	Coeliac disease
Increased physical activity	Competitive athlete

DM, diabetes mellitus; HIV, human immunodeficiency virus.

Thyrotoxicosis

Ask specifically about:

- heat intolerance – does the patient need fewer/thinner clothes/bedclothes than those around her?
- palpitations, breathlessness
- tiredness (mentioned by the patient), weakness, difficulty with sleeping
- mood – has she been 'irritable of late'? Patients with thyrotoxicosis often report feeling unusually anxious/irritable / bad tempered
- bowel habit – particularly increased frequency
- menses – especially oligomenorrhoea/amenorrhoea
- goitre – has there been any swelling or tenderness in the neck? Check for difficulty with swallowing/breathing
- eye symptoms, eg prominence, dryness/itching, double vision
- recent pregnancy – consider postpartum thyroiditis.

Diabetes mellitus

Elicit further symptoms, eg polyuria, polydipsia.

Other relevant history

Past medical history

Is there any history of previous surgery (especially abdominal) or chronic illness, or of any autoimmune disease.

Drug history

Check that she is not taking any non-prescription medications or herbal remedies that contain iodine or thyroid extract. Keep in mind the possibility of surreptitious use of thyroxine, laxatives, diuretics, etc.

Family/social history

Autoimmune thyroid disease may be associated with other organ-specific autoimmune conditions, hence enquire about a personal or family history of thyroid disorders, DM, Addison's disease, pernicious anaemia, premature ovarian failure (POF) and vitiligo (see Section 2.7.2).

Ask about recent travel abroad. If you suspect anorexia nervosa, concentrate on taking a careful social history. Ask about alcohol consumption and smoking – the latter can exacerbate dysthyroid eye disease.

Plan for investigation and management

Explain to the patient that under normal circumstances you would examine her, and then proceed as follows.

Investigation

This should begin with 'screening tests' that are indicated in all cases of weight loss where the cause is not obvious.

Routine tests

- full blood count and C-reactive protein (CRP) / erythrocyte sedimentation rate (ESR) (anaemia, infection, inflammation)
- electrolytes and renal function (Addison's disease, anorexia nervosa, chronic renal impairment)
- fasting glucose
- liver chemistry and calcium (intrinsic liver disease, malignancy)
- haematinics (ferritin, folate, vitamin B_{12})
- thyroid-stimulating hormone (TSH)
- anti-tissue transglutaminase antibodies and IgA (coeliac disease)
- chest radiograph (lymphadenopathy, malignancy).

Further investigations should be directed by the findings on history, examination and screening tests. If these suggest gastrointestinal disease, see the *Gastroenterology and hepatology* book of Medical Masterclass, or if an eating disorder, see the *Psychiatry* book.

Thyroid disease

If you suspect thyroid disease, check:

- free thyroxine (FT4) with or without free triiodothyronine (FT3)
- TSH
- thyroid autoantibody titres (see Section 2.3).

Radioisotope scans are not routinely performed in most centres but may help to differentiate between the various causes of hyperthyroidism when the clinical picture is not clear, eg in the absence of dysthyroid eye disease and with a negative autoantibody screen (see Section 2.3.2).

The presence of a retrosternal goitre and associated tracheal compression/deviation may be evident on plain radiography (Fig 5a) and can be confirmed if necessary by ultrasound (Fig 5b) and/or flow–volume loop analysis.

Other specific investigations

Consider Addison's disease (see Section 2.2.6), lymphoma (see the *Haematology* book of Medical Masterclass) and human immunodeficiency virus (HIV); the latter diagnosis will need to be considered if no other explanation for weight loss emerges but needs to be approached carefully (see the *Clinical skills for PACES* and *Infectious diseases* books of Medical Masterclass).

Management

Thyrotoxicosis

The various available treatment options are discussed in detail in Section 2.3.2. Reassure the patient that she has a treatable condition that is not malignant. It is important to point out, however, that she might not feel 'completely back to normal' for some time, while fine adjustments are made to the medication. It may be useful to explain the concept of an autoimmune disease. For a woman of childbearing age, as in this case, it is important to find out whether she could be pregnant or is planning a pregnancy in the near future, as this limits your treatment options (see Section 2.3.2).

Other specific disorders

Where identified, other specific underlying disorders should be treated appropriately (see relevant subsections in Section 2: Diseases and treatments).

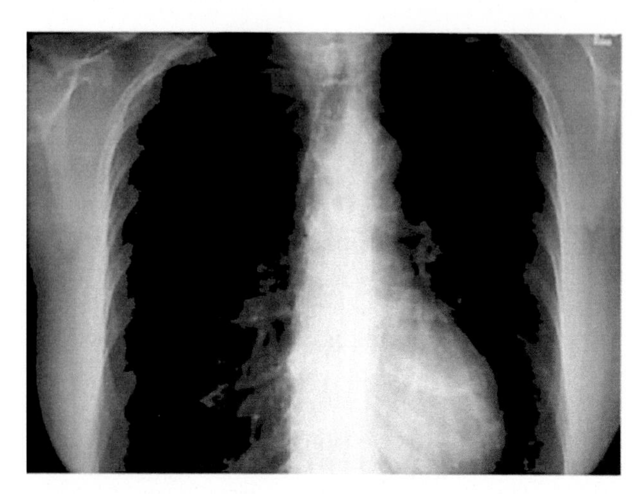

(a)

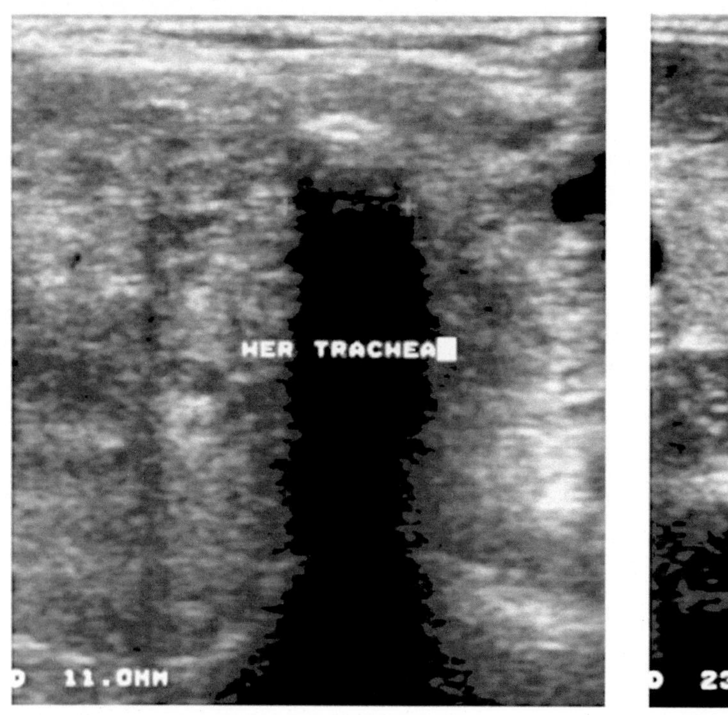

(b)

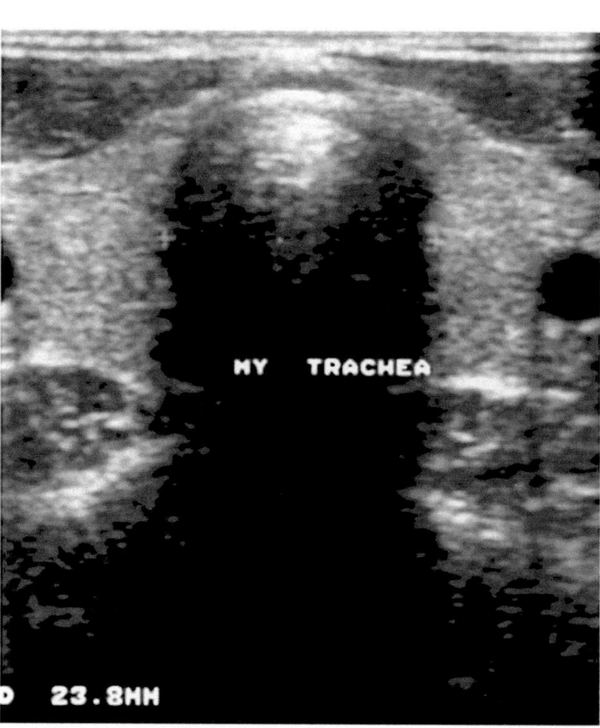

(c)

Fig 5 Retrosternal goitre with tracheal compression. **(a)** Chest radiograph and **(b)** thyroid ultrasound showing tracheal narrowing by a large retrosternal goitre. **(c)** Normal tracheal dimensions for comparison.

Further discussion

Graves' disease

Features that would point to Graves' disease as the likely cause of this woman's thyrotoxicosis include:

- age – toxic multinodular goitre is unusual in young females, although other causes of thyrotoxicosis (eg solitary adenoma, thyroiditis) must be considered
- family history of thyroid or other autoimmune disease
- dysthyroid eye signs – exophthalmos, ophthalmoplegia, periorbital oedema, chemosis
- pretibial myxoedema
- thyroid acropachy (looks like clubbing)
- diffuse symmetrical goitre – clinically and on radioisotope scanning
- positive anti-TSH receptor antibodies.

1.1.13 Tiredness and lethargy

Letter of referral to the general medical outpatient clinic

Dear Doctor,

Re: Mr Charles George, aged 54 years

Thank you for seeing this 54-year-old businessman who is no longer able to meet the demands of his job. He has become excessively tired over the past 6 months and complains of extreme lethargy. The only past medical history of note is that of palpitations, which are now well controlled on amiodarone.

It may be that he is simply trying to work too hard, but I would be grateful for your opinion as to whether there could be a medical explanation for his symptoms.

Yours sincerely,

Table 13 Disorders presenting with tiredness and lethargy

Type of condition	Common or important example
'Normal variant'	Hard work
	Childcare
Psychological/psychiatric disorder	Anxiety
	Depression
	Alcohol dependence
	Chronic fatigue syndrome
Chronic/systemic illness, usually obvious in this context	Malignancy
	Heart failure
	Respiratory failure
Systemic illness, not always obvious	Anaemia
	Thyroid deficiency (or occasionally excess)
	Diabetes mellitus
	Primary hyperparathyroidism
	Addison's disease
	Hypopituitarism

Introduction

Tiredness and lethargy are non-specific symptoms, which most of us experience from time to time – just think of the average junior doctor! A key part of the history is to try to determine whether tiredness and lethargy are features of an underlying medical disorder rather than everyday life. The differential diagnosis is broad, including those conditions listed in Table 13.

History of the presenting problem

Tiredness and lethargy

Exactly what does the patient mean by 'tiredness and lethargy'? When did the symptoms first appear? Have they been continuous or intermittent? Do they stop him doing anything that he would like to do? What activities has he had to cut out?

If the problem is that he falls asleep every night at 7pm, then this is certainly unusual; if he is unable to sustain working from 7am until midnight for five or six nights a week for very long, then few are able to do this and they (or their boss!) expect too much of themselves.

Hazard

Exclude medical causes before making psychiatric diagnoses

With any presentation that could have a 'physical' or a 'psychological/psychiatric' basis, always consider 'physical' conditions carefully before making a 'psychological/psychiatric' diagnosis.

Specific diagnoses

Consider the diagnoses listed in Table 13 as you take the history:

- Anaemia – is there any history of indigestion or peptic ulcer disease? Carefully pursue any suggestion of altered bowel habit (see the *Gastroenterology and hepatology* book of Medical Masterclass). Consider other causes of anaemia (see the *Haematology* book of Medical Masterclass).
- Thyroid disease – both hypothyroidism and hyperthyroidism (see Sections 2.3.1 and 2.3.2) can present in this manner. This is likely to be of particular importance in this case since the patient is on amiodarone, which can be associated with both conditions (Fig 6). Although unlikely, consider the possibility that his original palpitations

The antiarrhythmic agent amiodarone has a high organic iodine content (approximately 1/3 by weight) and bears structural similarities to both T4 and T3:

Thyroxine (T4)

Triiodothyronine (T3)

Amiodarone

Standard maintenance doses of amiodarone (100–200 mg/day) result in a massive expansion of the iodide pool and can influence thyroid physiology in various ways:

1 Abnormalities of thyroid function in clinically euthyroid individuals:

- ↑T4 and rT3, ↓T3 — through inhibition of the type 1 deiodinase
- ↑TSH during early stages of treatment (? an effect on the pituitary type 2 deiodinase)

In the absence of overt symptoms of thyroid disease, specific treatment is usually not required, but thyroid function tests should be monitored periodically.

2 Amiodarone-induced thyrotoxicosis occurs in some patients and can arise through several mechanisms including:

- stimulation of excess hormone synthesis in response to an iodine load (more common in iodine deficient regions and may represent unmasking of occult thyroid disease, the so-called Jod–Basedow effect)
- destruction of thyroid follicles with subsequent release of thyroid hormones (essentially an inflammatory thyroiditis). Treatment can be difficult since it is often not possible to stop amiodarone. Medical therapy including antithyroid drugs and glucocorticoids may be necessary, with surgery reserved for difficult cases.

3 Amiodarone-induced hypothyroidism is more common in iodine-replete areas and in those with detectable thyroid autoantibodies. Again various mechanisms have been invoked, including the Wolff–Chaikoff effect in which high intra-thyroidal iodide concentrations inhibit thyroid hormone biosynthesis. Treatment is generally easier than for thyrotoxicosis since amiodarone can be continued if necessary, and T4 replacement therapy given.

Accordingly, it is wise to check thyroid function tests (FT4, FT3 and TSH) prior to commencing amiodarone and to periodically life, abnormalities of thyroid function may persist for several months after discontinuation of therapy.

Fig 6 Amiodarone and thyroid function.

were a manifestation of thyroid hormone excess, now followed by thyroid hormone deficiency (a feature of thyroiditis – Section 2.3.2).

Key point

Amiodarone often causes abnormalities of thyroid function, and predisposes to both hypothyroidism and hyperthyroidism.

> Diabetes mellitus – excessive tiredness and lethargy are well-recognised presenting features of diabetes. Elicit further symptoms including polyuria, polydipsia and weight loss (see Section 2.6).

> Adrenal insufficiency – tiredness and lethargy may be the only presenting symptoms of hypoadrenalism (see Section 2.2.6).

> Primary hyperparathyroidism – tiredness and constipation are common manifestations of chronic hypercalcaemia (see Section 2.5.7). Has the patient had urinary stones?

> Hypopituitarism – tiredness and lethargy are extremely common findings in subjects with hypopituitarism, frequently reflecting combined hormonal deficits (see Section 2.1.8).

> Anxiety and depression – ask about the physical manifestations of depressive illness such as early morning wakening and poor appetite; also regarding the psychological/social factors that may be causative, eg stress at the office/home.

> Chronic fatigue syndrome – this is a difficult diagnosis that remains one of exclusion. Ask about poor concentration and memory, irritability, altered sleep and muscle aches.

Other relevant history

This should include details of chronic/systemic illness, any autoimmune illnesses in the patient or their family, other medication (eg beta-blockers) and alcohol consumption.

Plan for investigation and management

First explain to the patient that normally you would perform a full physical examination looking for signs associated with the conditions listed in Table 13.

Investigation

The presenting symptoms here are vague, hence initial investigations may need to cover a broad range of conditions.

Screening tests

Check full blood count (anaemia), electrolytes and renal function (chronic renal impairment, Addison's disease), liver chemistry and calcium (chronic liver disease, metastases, hypercalcaemia), fasting glucose and thyroid function tests (TFTs). Check chest radiograph (malignancy). Measurement of inflammatory markers including erythrocyte sedimentation rate (ESR) and C-reactive protein (CRP) would also be appropriate.

Specific investigations

Further investigations should be directed by the findings on history, examination and screening tests. In some cases, psychiatric assessment may be needed if depression or anxiety are felt to be key features.

Management

Where identified, specific underlying disorders should be treated appropriately (see relevant subsections in Section 2: Diseases and treatments).

Further discussion

What if no cause for tiredness is found?

If all of the initial investigations are negative and there are no other specific clinical pointers, then there is little to be gained by 'blind investigation', eg whole body imaging. In many cases an underlying medical cause for symptoms of tiredness and lethargy cannot be found, and lifestyle really is to blame. In these circumstances (which often form the basis of a communication skills scenario in Station 4 of PACES) it is important to explain the results of investigations that have been performed and to explain why you are not planning to arrange any further tests at this stage. While some patients might be reassured that there is nothing physical amiss, others will be unhappy that no cause for their symptoms has been identified, especially if they sense that an underlying psychological cause is being inferred. Make sure that the patient knows that you have taken their symptoms seriously, but at the same time explain why continued 'blind investigation' is not justified, nor in the patient's interest (inappropriate radiation exposure, the possibility of identifying an 'incidentaloma' which does not account for the presenting symptoms, etc).

1.1.14 Flushing and diarrhoea

Letter of referral to the endocrinology outpatient clinic

Dear Doctor,

Re: Mr James Hill-Wheatley, aged 50 years

This man has been unable to enjoy the recent festivities over Christmas because any over-indulgence with alcohol resulted in severe facial flushing. He has also been troubled by watery diarrhoea. We would both be grateful for your advice regarding further investigations and management.

Yours sincerely,

Introduction

Although it is important to bear in mind the possibility that the symptoms of flushing and diarrhoea are unrelated, taken together they suggest a number of specific diagnoses (Table 14).

Table 14 Conditions associated with flushing and diarrhoea

Condition	Comment
Anxiety attacks	Common
Thyrotoxicosis	–
Carcinoid syndrome	–
Diabetic autonomic neuropathy	Gustatory sweating and diarrhoea
Side effect of medication	–
Systemic mastocytosis	Very rare

Note that true 'flushing' episodes are not typical of phaeochromocytoma, although the pallor and profuse sweating that accompany catecholamine release may be perceived/interpreted as such by patients or their doctors.

History of the presenting problem

Flushing episodes

Can you describe a typical episode? How often do 'attacks' happen, and how long do they last? Which areas of the body are affected (eg whole body, face, hands)? Are there any precipitating factors (eg alcohol, tea/coffee, exercise, 'stressful' circumstances)? Do you experience any other symptoms at the time of an 'attack' (eg palpitations, sweating)? What tablets/medications are you taking? For example, calcium channel antagonists and the sulfonylurea chlorpropamide are recognised causes of facial flushing.

Bowel symptoms

First find out what the patient considers to be his normal bowel habit, then enquire: could you explain what you mean by 'diarrhoea' (eg increased frequency of stool or loose motions)? Has there been any blood or mucus with the stool? Are there any precipitating factors (eg specific foods, alcohol, 'stressful' circumstances)? Have you travelled abroad recently?

Also check for other systemic symptoms (eg weight loss, malaise, abdominal pain).

Other relevant history

Bearing in mind the possible diagnoses in Table 14, ask about the following if the information is not forthcoming spontaneously:

- Anxiety attacks – these would almost certainly be the commonest cause of this presentation. Are there other features to support this diagnosis? Has he experienced pins and needles affecting the hands and feet, 'atypical' chest pain or a history of medically unexplained symptoms?
- Thyrotoxicosis – enquire about weight loss, heat intolerance, tremor, proximal myopathy, etc (see Section 2.3.2).
- Diabetes mellitus (DM) – gustatory sweating and altered bowel habit are

recognised features of diabetic autonomic neuropathy, but this is a feature of long-established diabetes and not a presentation of this condition (see Section 2.6).

- Carcinoid syndrome – most carcinoid tumours arise from enterochromaffin cells of the intestine. Generally, they are slow-growing tumours and many remain asymptomatic until metastases develop. Carcinoid syndrome only occurs in the presence of hepatic metastases or (rarely) a pulmonary primary releasing 5-hydroxytryptamine (5-HT) directly into the systemic circulation (thereby circumventing first-pass metabolism in the liver). It commonly leads to flushing (which may be spontaneous or precipitated by food, alcohol or stress) and recurrent watery diarrhoea. Other less common characteristics include abdominal pain, wheeze, right-sided heart disease and pellagra (dermatitis, diarrhoea and dementia due to niacin deficiency).
- Phaeochromocytoma – ask about related symptoms, eg anxiety, palpitations, hypertension (see Section 2.2.4).

Plan for investigation and management

Investigation

Initial tests

Check full blood count, electrolytes and renal function, liver chemistry, calcium, fasting glucose ± HbA_{1c}, thyroid function tests, inflammatory markers (ESR and/or CRP).

Specific investigations

These should be guided by the patient's presentation: for thyrotoxicosis see Section 2.3.2; for DM see Section 2.6; for phaeochromocytoma see Section 2.2.4. For carcinoid syndrome look for biochemical and structural evidence with the following investigations:

- 24-hour urinary 5-hydroxyindoleacetic acid (5-HIAA) excretion – 5-HIAA is a metabolite of 5-HT; a 24-hour collection is a sensitive (~75%) and specific (approaching 100%) test for carcinoid syndrome.

Hazard

False positive 24-hour 5-HIAA results

Some foods (avocados, bananas, plums, walnuts, pineapples, tomatoes, aubergines, cough medicine) can cause false positives in measurement of 24-hour urinary 5-HIAA and need to be avoided during the collection period.

- Fasting plasma gut hormones including chromogranins, a marker of neuroendocrine tumours.
- Ultrasound/CT – once the diagnosis has been confirmed biochemically, the liver should be imaged with ultrasound or CT. If the liver is clear, perform a chest CT to look for a pulmonary primary.
- Functional nuclear medicine imaging – an octreoscan using radiolabelled octreotide can visualise about 85% of tumours (Fig 7). Uptake indicates that the tumour may respond to treatment with somatostatin analogues. New radionuclides based on gallium (Ga)-68 have higher sensitivity and improved spatial resolution for detection of neuroendocrine tumours.

Key point

The carcinoid primary

Note that there is usually little to be gained in undertaking a protracted search for a primary carcinoid tumour unless it is causing symptoms in its own right, eg intestinal obstruction.

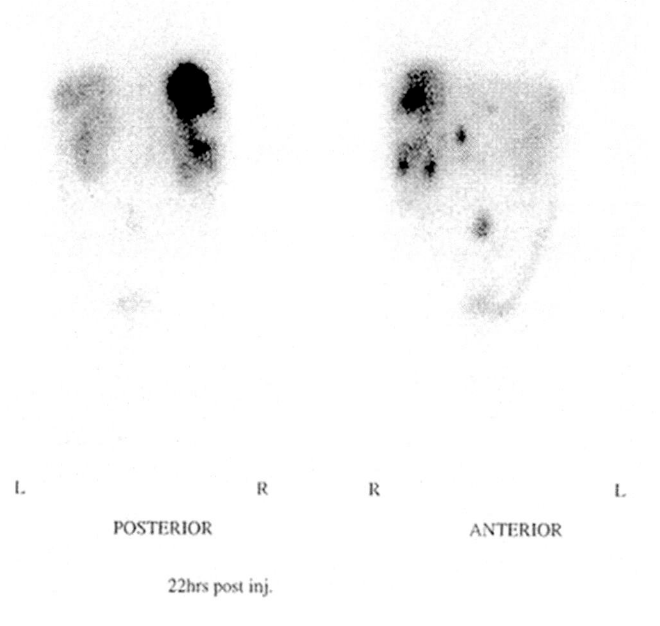

Fig 7 Octreoscan. Radiolabelled octreotide scan demonstrating focal uptake centrally within the abdomen (primary tumour) and multiple areas of hepatic uptake (metastases) in a 67-year-old man with carcinoid syndrome.

Management

This will clearly be dependent on the particular diagnosis. For anxiety/panic attacks the patient may respond to reassurance that there is no sinister diagnosis, but consider referral for specialist psychological/psychiatric input if symptoms are persistent and intrusive (see the *Psychiatry* book of Medical Masterclass). For thyrotoxicosis see Section 2.3.2; for DM see Section 2.6; for phaeochromocytoma see Section 2.2.4.

Carcinoid syndrome

The condition is rare, few doctors have much experience of it, and therefore carcinoid syndrome is optimally managed in a specialist centre. The patient's management will involve a multidisciplinary team, which may comprise an endocrinologist, interventional radiologist, gastroenterologist, pathologist, oncologist, surgeon, dietician, specialist endocrine laboratory and endocrine specialist nurse. This has obvious benefits in terms of receiving 'state of the art' treatment, but it may also have several inconveniences (eg lengthy travel, admission to hospital far from home) and these issues will need to be considered and discussed.

It is important to explain to the patient the nature of his condition. Carcinoid tumours can fall anywhere along a spectrum from indolent to highly malignant. This degree of uncertainty is difficult for both patients and doctors to deal with, but one can be cautiously optimistic as survival for 10–15 years is not uncommon. It remains unclear as to whether any of the following treatment options significantly affect life expectancy.

Lifestyle and simple remedies

Patients may be able to identify precipitating factors that they can avoid, such as alcohol, spicy food or strenuous exercise. Symptomatic treatment of diarrhoea with loperamide is worthwhile. Nicotinic acid supplements should be recommended. Antihistamines with antiserotoninergic activity (eg cyproheptadine) may be useful. Asthma (if present) can be treated with inhaled beta-agonists.

Surgery

Symptomatic primaries and occasionally single hepatic metastases (depending on their size and position) may be amenable to resection.

Somatostatin analogues

Octreotide and the longer-acting somatostatin analogues frequently relieve symptoms of flushing and diarrhoea, with more recent evidence suggesting they possess anti-proliferative properties that may inhibit tumour growth. Somatostatin analogues are administered by injection and side effects may include steatorrhoea (which can be treated with CREON), nausea/vomiting (often transient) and gallstones. Intravenous octreotide is useful in the event of a carcinoid crisis (see below).

Selective embolisation via the hepatic artery

The premise for hepatic artery embolisation is that tumours receive most of their blood supply from the hepatic artery, while hepatocytes are also able to derive blood from the portal venous circulation. Selective embolisation should be undertaken in specialist centres only. The patient is likely to experience fever, pain and nausea. Treatment carries a risk of massive hepatic necrosis and may precipitate a carcinoid crisis (hypotension, tachycardia and bronchoconstriction). The risk of carcinoid crisis can be minimised with careful hydration, oral cyproheptadine and intravenous octreotide infusion.

Peptide receptor radionuclide therapy

Peptide receptor radionuclide therapy (PRRT), using ^{111}In-, ^{177}Lu- or ^{90}Yt-labelled somatostatin analogues, is used for treatment of metastatic neuroendocrine tumours expressing somatostatin receptors.

Chemotherapy

Chemotherapy (eg 5-fluorouracil; interferon-alpha) has a limited role in the treatment of patients with carcinoid syndrome as the benefits are often outweighed by the side effects. Local transcatheter arterial 'chemoembolisation' (TACE) therapy may be tried, when an emulsion of the chemotherapeutic agent (Adriamycin or streptozotocin) is injected into the hepatic artery branches, followed by embolisation using gelatin sponge particles or microspheres. It is difficult to assess how much benefit accrues from the chemotherapy and how much from the embolisation as outcomes thus far appear similar to conventional embolisation.

Response to treatment

Response to treatment can be assessed clinically, radiologically and by monitoring levels of 24-hour urinary 5-HIAA and fasting gut hormones.

1.1.15 Avoiding another coronary

Letter of referral to the general medicine outpatient clinic

Dear Doctor,

Re: Mr John Smith, aged 55 years

This man suffered a heart attack 6 months ago. He has not had any angina since the event, and the cardiologists are not planning any further intervention at this stage as his post-infarct exercise test was reassuring. Not surprisingly, however, Mr Smith is worried about the possibility that he might have another event, and is keen to seek further advice as to what can be done to help prevent this. He stopped smoking at the time of his admission, but is struggling to follow a healthy diet and lifestyle.

Currently, he is overweight (BMI = 34 kg/m^2 (normal range 18–25)) and hypertensive (BP 160/96 mmHg). There are no signs of heart failure. His most recent lipid profile has shown a total cholesterol of 4.5 mmol/L, high-density lipoprotein cholesterol (HDL-C) 0.8 mmol/L, low-density lipoprotein cholesterol (LDL-C) 3.0 mmol/L and triglycerides of 2.5 mmol/L. He is taking aspirin, simvastatin, atenolol and ramipril.

I would be grateful for your advice as to how we can further help him to reduce his risk of another cardiovascular event.

Yours sincerely,

Introduction

The aim is to identify all modifiable risk factors and then decide how best to address them in discussion with the patient.

History of the presenting problem

In the history you will explore symptoms suggestive of vascular disease and enquire about chest pain, evidence of cardiac failure and symptoms suggestive of cerebrovascular or peripheral vascular disease. Following these lines of enquiry, your attention should then focus on risk factors.

Diet

What, and how much, does he eat during a typical day? Does he eat a lot of saturated fats? Does he take dietary/vitamin supplements (eg antioxidant vitamins, folic acid, omega-3 unsaturated fatty acids (fish oil))?

Ask about his average weekly alcohol intake – is it within recommended 'safe' limits?

Exercise

Does he take regular exercise? If yes, how much and how often? Aside from formal exercise, what does his typical working day involve?

Smoking

It is important to confirm that he has completely given up smoking, and that he is not still having the occasional cigarette.

Hypertension

Is his hypertension long-standing? Was he overweight at the time of diagnosis? Have secondary causes been excluded? Is there a family history of hypertension?

Diabetes / impaired glucose tolerance

Has he ever been tested for diabetes mellitus (DM)? Is there a family history of DM?

Dyslipidaemia

This man has had his lipid profile checked and he takes a statin, but if this information was not available has he had his cholesterol level checked? Does he take cholesterol-lowering medications? Is there a family history of dyslipidaemia?

Overweight/obesity

How long has he been overweight/obese? Ask about symptoms that might indicate a secondary cause for his obesity including hypothyroidism (see Section 2.3.1) or Cushing's syndrome (see Section 2.1.1).

Other relevant history

Medication

Take a thorough drug history that includes current doses.

Family history

In addition to checking for a family history of hypertension, diabetes and dyslipidaemia, ask about premature coronary, cerebrovascular or peripheral vascular disease in close relatives.

Plan for investigation and management

Explain to the patient that under normal circumstances you would undertake a physical examination focusing on the cardiovascular system and specific metabolic parameters (eg waist circumference – see below), and then proceed as follows.

Investigation

Routine tests

These include a full blood count (anaemia or polycythaemia), electrolytes and renal function (renovascular disease and other secondary causes of hypertension), fasting blood glucose, liver biochemistry (hepatic steatosis), lipid profile and thyroid function tests (hypothyroidism). Perform urinalysis, checking specifically for glycosuria and proteinuria.

Organise a chest radiograph, looking for cardiomegaly, left ventricular failure and/or smoking-related lung disease, also an ECG, checking for evidence of his previous infarct, ongoing ischaemic changes, left ventricular hypertrophy (Fig 8).

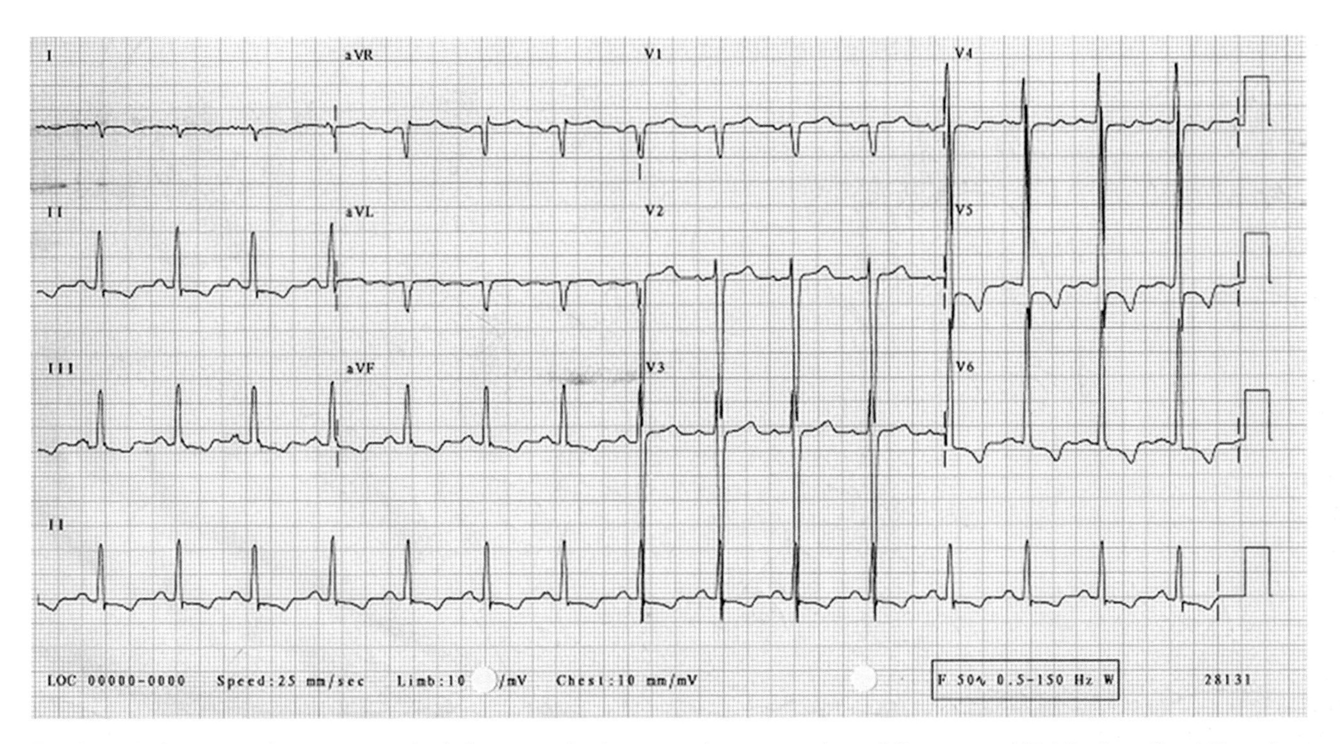

Fig 8 ECG showing voltage criteria for left ventricular hypertrophy – note the tall R-waves in V5–V6, deep S in V2 and inverted T-waves in II, III, aVF, V5–V6.

Further investigations

These will be guided by the history, findings on physical examination and results of initial screening investigations, but may include:

- Oral glucose tolerance test (OGTT) – if impaired glucose tolerance is suspected (see Section 3.1.7).
- Echocardiogram – if there is evidence of left ventricular hypertrophy or cardiac failure.
- Renal ultrasound – if renovascular or intrinsic renal disease is suspected.
- Screening tests for Cushing's syndrome (see Section 2.1.1) and other secondary causes of hypertension (see Section 1.1.16), but these are much less likely to be appropriate.

Management

What can this man do to help himself, and what can be done for him?

Diet

Refer to a dietician to ensure that the diet is low in saturated fat (red meat, dairy products, egg yolks, fried food), low in refined carbohydrates, reduced in calories (to promote weight loss) and high in antioxidant vitamins, folic acid, omega-3 fatty acids (fresh fruit and green vegetables and oily fish).

Exercise

Advise moderate exercise for at least 30–40 minutes three to four times per week. If he has not taken exercise for several years, then he should begin gradually.

Smoking

Absolute cessation is required.

BP control

Target ≤140/90 mmHg. Consider increasing the dose of his angiotensin-converting enzyme (ACE) inhibitor or introducing another agent (note: although beta-blockers are still important in the secondary prevention of ischaemic heart disease, they are no longer preferred as front-line agents in the management of hypertension).

Diabetes

See Section 2.6; if the patient has impaired fasting glycaemia (IFG) or impaired glucose tolerance (IGT), then dietary modification and exercise are the mainstay of treatment. Initiation of glucose-lowering agents may also be required (see Section 2.6).

Lipid lowering

Aim to achieve total cholesterol <4 mmol/L, LDL-C <2 mmol/L, HDL-C >1 mmol/L and triglycerides <2.0 mmol/L (see Section 2.5.1). In the first instance it would be appropriate to consider adjusting his statin dose in conjunction with dietary review.

Weight reduction

This is usually best achieved through a combination of dietary modification and increased exercise.

Antiplatelet therapy

Either with aspirin (as in this case) or clopidogrel.

Alcohol

Intake should be kept within 'safe' limits.

Further discussion

Metabolic syndrome / syndrome X

Central obesity is recognised to be a major risk factor for cardiovascular disease. This is reflected in recommendations published by the International Diabetes Federation (IDF) for the diagnosis of the metabolic syndrome (see below), in which central obesity is the only absolute requirement. Indeed, determining BMI alone is no longer considered to be acceptable in the assessment of cardiovascular risk, eg a middle-aged male patient with a BMI of 27 kg/m^2, but obvious visceral adiposity, is at greater risk of occlusive coronary disease than a younger female with a BMI of 33 kg/m^2 whose fat is predominantly distributed in the gluteal region.

Key point

IDF criteria for diagnosis of the metabolic syndrome (2006)

Central obesity (this is the only core requirement) defined as waist circumference ≥ ethnicity-specific cut-offs (eg ≥94 cm for Europid men and ≥80 cm for Europid women) plus two or more of the following:

- hyperglycaemia – fasting plasma glucose ≥5.6 mmol/L or previously diagnosed type 2 DM
- hypertriglyceridaemia – triglycerides (TG) >1.7 mmol/L or treated for this lipid abnormality
- reduced HDL-C – <1.03 mmol/L (men) or <1.29 mmol/L (women) or treated for this lipid abnormality
- hypertension – BP ≥130/85 mmHg or treated for hypertension.

1.1.16 High blood pressure and low serum potassium

Letter of referral to the endocrinology outpatient clinic

Dear Doctor,

Re: Mr Jack Lewis, aged 40 years

Thank you for seeing this 40-year-old man in whom I have recently diagnosed hypertension (BP 160/105 mmHg). He had originally presented to me with generalised weakness and tiredness. Blood tests have shown that he is not anaemic, but his serum potassium is 2.4 mmol/L (normal range 3.5–4.9). I am concerned that he may have primary hyperaldosteronism (Conn's syndrome) and would be grateful for your opinion.

Yours sincerely,

Introduction

The history in this case should be directed towards establishing the cause of hypertension and seeking evidence of target organ damage. Although essential hypertension can strike at any age, a concern in any young patient presenting with high BP is to exclude a secondary cause (Table 15). The tiredness and weakness, although non-specific, are probably related to hypokalaemia in this case and would favour some of the secondary causes, including primary hyperaldosteronism as suggested by the GP.

History of the presenting problem

The history should begin by encouraging the patient to describe their symptoms of tiredness and weakness, also details of how his hypertension was discovered, and whether he has ever had his BP measured previously, before moving on to cover causes and consequences of both hypertension and hypokalaemia.

Table 15 Causes of secondary hypertension

Type of condition	Example
Renal	Chronic kidney disease,[1] eg glomerulonephritis, chronic pyelonephritis, polycystic kidney disease
	Renovascular disease,[1] eg atheromatous renal artery stenosis
Endocrine	Primary hyperaldosteronism (Conn's syndrome)[1]
	Phaeochromocytoma[1]
	Cushing's syndrome
	Primary hyperparathyroidism
	Acromegaly
	DM / insulin resistance (metabolic syndrome / syndrome X)
Drugs	Corticosteroids, oral contraceptive pill
Others	Coarctation of aorta[1]
	Pregnancy-associated hypertension[1] Mendelian causes,[1] eg glucocorticoid-remediable aldosteronism, the syndrome of apparent mineralocorticoid excess, Liddle's syndrome and Gordon's syndrome

1 Conditions in which hypertension is always or often a prominent feature.
DM, diabetes mellitus.

Causes of hypertension

Ask about the following if the details are not forthcoming:

- Is there a family history of high BP? Does he know if his parents, brothers or sisters are on antihypertensive drugs? If they are, 'essential' hypertension becomes an even more likely diagnosis (although a rare familial form of hypertension would be an outside possibility).
- Is there any history of renal disease? Has he had medicals for work or insurance where his urine has been checked in the past? A report of a 'just a bit of protein and/or blood' may indicate that he has long-standing renal disease and hypertension secondary to this.
- Could there be a phaeochromocytoma? Most patients with phaeochromocytoma will have some symptoms suggestive of catecholamine excess, the commonest being headache, sweating, palpitations and episodes of pallor (see Section 2.2.4). This is a very uncommon condition, but if you are not alert to the diagnosis you are unlikely to make it.
- Are there any features to suggest Cushing's syndrome (see Section 2.1.1) or acromegaly (see Section 2.1.2)? These are very unlikely, but again you will never make these diagnoses unless you consider them.

Consequences of hypertension

Enquire about any symptoms related to target organ damage:

- cardiac – chest pain / myocardial infarction, dyspnoea, peripheral oedema
- cerebrovascular accidents / transient ischaemic attacks
- retinopathy (Fig 9).

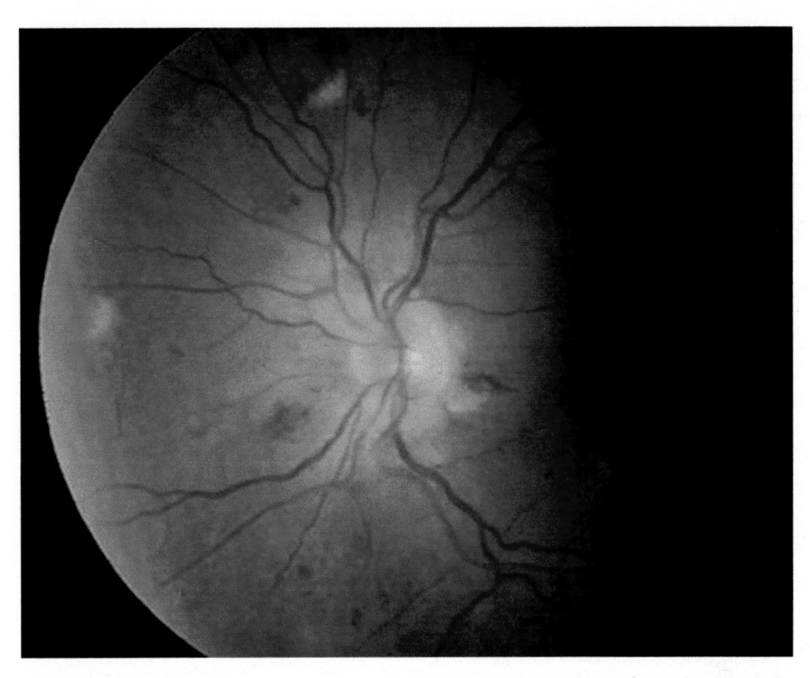

Fig 9 Hypertensive retinopathy. Advanced retinal changes (cotton-wool exudates, flame and blot haemorrhages, blurring of the optic disc margins) identified in a 50-year-old man with hypertensive cardiomyopathy.

Causes of hypokalaemia

Given that hypertension is common, it is possible that hypokalaemia in this case is not associated with it and other causes must be considered (Table 16). Ask about the following:

- diarrhoea or vomiting
- diuretics – has he been prescribed these for his hypertension?
- consumption of laxatives or liquorice
- proximal myopathy or other symptoms of steroid excess – hypokalaemia is most prominent in the setting of ectopic adrenocorticotropic hormone (ACTH) secretion, but can occur in any form of Cushing's syndrome when circulating cortisol levels are sufficiently high that they 'spill over' to act on the mineralocorticoid receptor. Ectopic ACTH secretion is extremely unlikely to be the diagnosis if there is a long prodromal phase: the usual cause is malignancy and the pace of deterioration rapid (see Section 2.1.1)
- family history of 'a potassium problem'.

Key point

Making the diagnosis of primary hyperaldosteronism

There are no clinical features beyond hypertension and symptoms related to hypokalaemia that might support the diagnosis of primary hyperaldosteronism: a high index of suspicion is therefore needed to make the diagnosis.

Consequences of hypokalaemia

Enquire about other symptoms that might be due to hypokalaemia, eg thirst, polyuria (nephrogenic diabetes insipidus), paraesthesia (hypokalaemic alkalosis).

Other relevant history

In any patient with hypertension it is clearly important to enquire about other cardiovascular risk factors – smoking, cholesterol, diabetes mellitus (DM) and family history.

Table 16 Causes of hypokalaemia

Total body potassium	Mechanism	Common or important example
Normal	Shift of potassium into cells	Beta-adrenergic stimulation
		Periodic paralysis
Reduced	Renal potassium wasting	Alkalosis, eg due to vomiting[1]
		Diuretics (thiazides, loop)[1]
		Primary hyperaldosteronism
		Cushing's syndrome
		Liquorice excess
		Genetic: Gitelman's, Bartter's syndromes
		Various renal tubular disorders
	Gastrointestinal potassium loss	Any cause of diarrhoea[1]
		Intestinal fistulae
		Colonic villous adenoma

1 The commonest causes of hypokalaemia, which must always be excluded before more exotic diagnoses are considered.

Plan for investigation and management

Investigation

Hypertension

In any patient presenting with hypertension it would be appropriate to check the following:

- dipstick urinalysis – if this shows proteinuria or haematuria send specimen for microscopy (casts)
- full blood count – anaemia of chronic disease, eg renal failure
- electrolytes and renal function – to confirm hypokalaemia and look for renal failure
- random glucose, with subsequent fasting sample if abnormal – impaired glucose tolerance / DM is associated with acromegaly and Cushing's syndrome
- ECG/echocardiography – looking for changes of left ventricular hypertrophy seen with long-standing hypertension (Fig 8)
- chest radiograph – to look for evidence of cardiomegaly, pulmonary oedema or rib notching (coarctation).

Hypokalaemia

In most cases the cause of hypokalaemia is obvious – in outpatient practice the patient is taking a diuretic and in inpatient practice they are (or have been) vomiting. In such cases investigation is not required, but if the cause is not apparent then the following should be considered:

- electrolytes and renal function – to confirm hypokalaemia
- plasma bicarbonate and chloride – to check for metabolic alkalosis, usually a consequence of hyperaldosteronism (primary or secondary). A low plasma chloride would most commonly be explained by vomiting, which may be concealed
- urinary chloride – the diagnosis is hypokalaemia due to vomiting if the urinary chloride is very low
- urinary assay for diuretics and laxatives (in some cases).

Key point

Always consider concealed vomiting in any case of unexplained hypokalaemia – the finding of a very low urinary chloride is often the crucial diagnostic test.

Specific investigations

These will be guided by the clinical findings and results of routine testing.

- renal or renovascular disease:
  - urinary albumin:creatinine ratio (ACR) or protein:creatinine ratio (PCR) to quantitate proteinuria
  - ultrasound to determine renal size and look for parenchymal abnormalities
  - renal artery imaging if renal artery stenosis (RAS) suspected (angiography – various techniques)
  - renal biopsy if renal parenchymal disease is likely
- primary hyperaldosteronism, Cushing's syndrome, acromegaly, phaeochromocytoma, primary hyperparathyroidism (see relevant subsections in Section 2: Diseases and treatments).

Management

Treatment is directed where possible at the underlying cause, with correction of hypertension and attention to target organ damage. Specific aspects of management relating to endocrine hypertension are outlined in the relevant sections of this book.

1.1.17 Tiredness, weight loss and amenorrhoea

Letter of referral to endocrinology outpatient clinic

Dear Doctor,

Re: Mrs Mary Pearce, aged 42 years

Thank you for seeing this 42-year-old woman who has a 6-month history of tiredness and lethargy. Although 'routine bloods' were initially unremarkable, subsequent repeat thyroid function tests (TFTs) have shown a slightly elevated thyroid-stimulating hormone (TSH) with a low normal free thyroxine (FT4). She has also lost a 'significant amount' of weight and her periods have stopped. More recently she has been troubled by nausea and vomiting. I wonder if this could be related to hypothyroidism, but am concerned that there might be another diagnosis?

Yours sincerely,

Introduction

Hazard

If the clinical picture does not fit, do not jump to a diagnosis because a test shows an abnormality.

Although tiredness and lethargy are commonly reported symptoms of hypothyroidism, the relatively mild derangements of thyroid biochemistry reported here seem unlikely to account fully for the clinical picture. In particular, weight loss and oligomenorrhoea/amenorrhoea are more in keeping with thyroid hormone excess than deficiency. It is therefore important to keep an open mind during the clinical assessment. Failure to do so, with treatment given simply on the basis of the biochemical abnormality, could lead to dire consequences.

History of the presenting problem

When did the woman last feel completely well? In retrospect, many patients can identify symptoms or signs in the past, which they ignored at the time or failed to associate with their current problem.

Tiredness and lethargy

Tiredness and lethargy are non-specific symptoms seen in the context of many different physical and psychological illnesses as well as in normal individuals, especially when overworked. See Section 1.1.13 and Table 13 for details of the approach to this problem. The most important issue to decide at the beginning is whether or not the tiredness and lethargy really amount to much more than might be expected given the woman's lifestyle. Does it affect her daily routine, eg is she still able to work/take exercise? Has the tiredness become progressively worse with time? Does she find it necessary to sleep during the day?

In this case a key point to note is the presence of other symptoms: weight loss, nausea and vomiting cannot simply be ascribed to 'overdoing it'.

Weight loss, nausea and vomiting

Important points are:

- How much weight has she lost and over what time period?
- Has this been associated with deliberate dieting or, alternatively, a loss of appetite?
- Confirm the timing of the onset of nausea and vomiting in relation to the weight loss.
- As a younger woman, did she have trouble with anorexia nervosa or bulimia? Has she ever made herself vomit?

Could a primarily gastrointestinal disease explain all of this woman's problems? Weight loss might be a reflection of reduced calorie intake, malabsorption or an underlying neoplastic process, while the development of anaemia could explain the tiredness and lethargy. Ask about appetite/dietary intake, abdominal pain/discomfort, altered bowel habit, eg frequency/constipation, blood, mucus. Further discussion of the clinical approach to weight loss with gastrointestinal symptoms can be found in the *Gastroenterology and hepatology* book of Medical Masterclass.

Oligomenorrhoea/amenorrhoea

Key point

Significant weight loss can cause menstrual irregularities.

Take a careful menstrual history. Ask about age at menarche and regularity of cycle thereafter, pregnancies and oral contraceptive use, previous episodes of oligomenorrhoea/amenorrhoea or menorrhagia, date of her last period and whether it was 'lighter or heavier' than usual.

Further discussion on the clinical approach to amenorrhoea can be found in Sections 1.1.6 and 1.1.7.

Other features

This woman does not have symptoms confined to one organ system: how can this all be put together? Consider the following possibilities as you continue the history:

- Malignancy and systemic disorders – weight loss and lethargy are common presenting features of malignancy (including lymphoma) and other systemic conditions (eg hepatitis, HIV-related disease). Ask about night sweats, lymphadenopathy and where appropriate assess risk factors (including sexual partners, intravenous drug use and previous blood transfusions; see the *Clinical skills for PACES* book of Medical Masterclass).

- Depression/psychological illness – check for other physical manifestations of depression, including early morning wakening. Ask about mood and social circumstances.
- Thyroid disease – this has been suggested on the basis of the blood tests taken by the GP. Check if there are any other symptoms to suggest thyroid dysfunction (Section 2.3).
- Addison's disease – remember that many of the symptoms of Addison's disease are non-specific, often leading to considerable delay in its diagnosis. Tiredness, weakness, anorexia, weight loss and gastrointestinal disturbances are commonly reported, and menstrual disturbance can be a feature. Has the patient noticed a desire to eat salt? Salt craving is not uncommon in Addison's disease.
- Pituitary disease – hypogonadotrophic hypogonadism and secondary adrenal insufficiency may complicate primary pituitary disease (eg non-functioning adenomas). Ask about headaches and visual disturbance (suggesting a local mass effect); galactorrhoea (hyperprolactinaemia – prolactinoma or stalk disconnection). Bear in mind, however, that the elevated TSH would be against coexistent central hypothyroidism.
- DM – enquire about polyuria and polydipsia; prominent osmotic symptoms might be expected given the duration of illness and degree of systemic upset. Did the initial set of 'routine bloods' include a fasting glucose measurement?

Other relevant history

Is there is a personal or family history of organ-specific autoimmune disease, eg pernicious anaemia, vitiligo, thyroid disease (see Section 2.7.2)? Ask about smoking and alcohol consumption.

Plan for investigation and management

First, explain to the patient that under normal circumstances you would perform a full physical examination to look for signs associated with the conditions outlined above.

Investigation

The differential diagnosis here is very broad and it would be appropriate to begin with some 'routine' tests, although the history may direct you to more specific investigations.

Routine tests

Full blood count (anaemia, haematological disorders), electrolytes and renal function (chronic renal impairment, Addison's disease), liver chemistry (malignancy, intrinsic liver disease), fasting glucose (DM), thyroid function tests, ESR and CRP (systemic disorders), chest radiograph (cardiac disease, intrinsic lung disease, lymphoma, metastases) (Fig 10). With a history of amenorrhoea, pregnancy must always be excluded: gonadotrophins (luteinising hormone (LH) and follicle-stimulating hormone (FSH)), oestradiol and prolactin should also be measured. Dipstick urinalysis (renal disease).

Specific tests

These will depend on the history, physical findings and the results of routine tests described above, but may range from blood cultures and echocardiography if endocarditis is suspected, to testing for Addison's disease or pituitary disease (see relevant subsections in Section 2: Diseases and treatments) to psychiatric assessment (if depression/psychological illness are thought likely).

Management

As always, management is directed at the underlying cause.

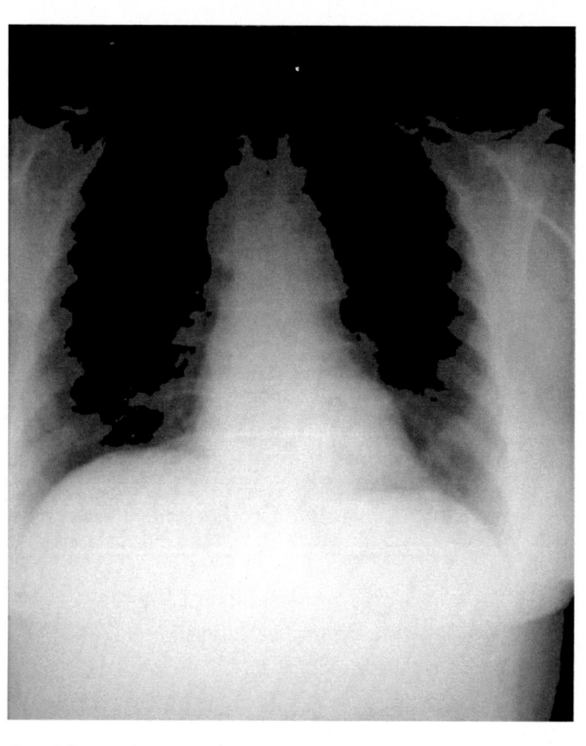

Fig 10 Mediastinal lymphadenopathy. Chest radiograph demonstrating paratracheal lymphadenopathy in a patient with lymphoma.

Hazard

Treat adrenal insufficiency before hypothyroidism

In both primary and secondary adrenal insufficiency glucocorticoid replacement must be initiated before coexisting hypothyroidism is treated to avoid the risk of precipitating a hypoadrenal crisis.

Addison's disease

The rules and regulations governing glucocorticoid and mineralocorticoid replacement in both the emergency and routine settings are discussed in detail in Section 2.2.6. Note, as in this case, that minor abnormalities of thyroid function may revert to normal with satisfactory steroid replacement.

Hypopituitarism: In addition to treating the underlying cause, appropriate hormone-replacement therapy (HRT) should be instituted (see Section 2.1.8).

Key point

Mineralocorticoid replacement is not necessary for patients with secondary adrenocortical insufficiency.

Further discussion

Key point

Patient education

It is extremely important that patients with adrenal insufficiency are educated such that they can assume responsibility for a life-maintaining therapy that requires adjustment at times of stress and which may cause significant side effects, particularly weight gain.

1.2 Communication skills and ethics

1.2.1 Explaining an uncertain outcome

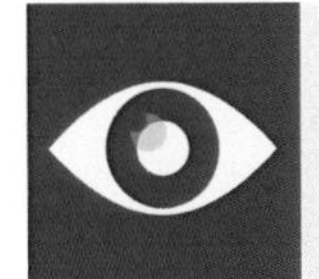

Scenario

Role: you are a junior doctor on the admitting medical team.

Scenario: Mrs Olivia Benson, a 72-year-old woman, previously well apart from mild hypertension, has been admitted to the emergency department after she was found unconscious by a neighbour. On admission her Glasgow Coma Scale (GCS) score was 8/15. A CT of her head has shown no abnormality, but her serum sodium is 112 mmol/L (normal range 137–144). This is almost certainly caused by the thiazide diuretic that she takes for her high BP (although other possible causes have not been excluded), and is the only obvious cause for her coma.

The management plan is to give her a controlled infusion of hypertonic saline, with frequent monitoring of the serum sodium concentration until this is corrected into the mildly hyponatraemic range.

Her son arrives and is very worried about his mother's condition. The staff nurse asks you to explain the situation to him.

Your task: to explain the management plan and the uncertainty of the prognosis to Mrs Benson's son.

Key issues to explore

Although the son will understandably be concerned for the health of his mother, are there any specific worries or questions that he would like you to address? Is there a hidden agenda or worry? For example, is he concerned that she has been confused or depressed and may have accidentally or deliberately taken an overdose of tablets that has contributed to her condition?

Is he the next of kin, and are there other close relatives or friends who would be appropriate to speak to?

Key points to establish

Outline the basis and prognosis of his mother's condition by explaining the following in simple language:

> Cause of the problem – a 'low level of salt (or sodium) in the blood', which can have many causes; and that the low salt level can itself cause loss of consciousness, but that you are also excluding other causes of coma.

> Treatment – that the low salt level can be corrected with a drip and by restricting water intake.

> Outlook – uncertain. The very low level of sodium can cause irreversible brain damage or death; and the longer-term outlook depends on the underlying cause of the condition.

Appropriate responses to likely questions

Son: *so she is going to get better then doctor?*

Doctor: I'm not hiding anything when I say that I don't know. We have only just started treatment and I'm afraid that I cannot give a guarantee that she will get better. We're trying to rule out other causes, but we think the reason for her being unconscious is the very low level of salt in her blood and we're trying to correct this. However, this has to be done slowly and carefully: doing it too rapidly can itself cause or worsen damage to the brain.

Son: *is she going to die, or end up like a vegetable?*

Doctor: I'm afraid that I don't know. As you can see, she is unconscious now, which means that her brain has been badly affected by the problem. It is possible for people to make a complete recovery from this situation, but that isn't certain. She could die, or could be left with some permanent brain damage. I'm afraid that we just can't tell at the moment.

Son: *so why is the salt in her blood so low?*

Doctor: again we're not 100% sure. The most likely reason for it is a reaction to a tablet that she was taking for her high blood pressure, but there are other causes that we need to check for.

Son: *could it be cancer then?*

Doctor: as I've said before, we're not absolutely sure what's causing the problem. The most likely thing is a reaction to one of her tablets, so I think that cancer is unlikely, but at the moment I can't rule it out and it is one of the things we need to consider. Is there something that makes you suspect that your mother may have cancer?

Son: *why was she put on a tablet that can cause this sort of problem?*

Doctor: the tablet that she was on is one of the drugs that is most widely used to treat high blood pressure, and it normally doesn't cause any serious side effects at all. However, rarely it can cause the salt in the blood to drop very low, and that's what we think is most likely to have happened in your mother's case.

1.2.2 The possibility of cancer

Scenario

Role: you are the admitting doctor working on an acute medical ward.

Scenario: Mrs Harriet Claremont, a 64-year-old woman, has presented with severe but non-specific lethargy and fatigue, and is found to have a serum calcium of 3.2 mmol/L (normal range 2.20–2.60). The initial history and examination fail to provide a clear diagnosis for this. There are no features to suggest malignancy, but the possibility cannot be excluded.

The patient's daughter visits the ward wanting to discuss the possible causes of her mother's condition with you, and Mrs Claremont gives you permission to talk with her. She is particularly worried because of the recent demise of her aunt (the patient's sister) from lung cancer.

Your task: to explain what is meant by hypercalcaemia, and to discuss likely investigation and possible diagnoses.

Key issues to explore

What does the daughter already know, and what are her main concerns? Ask her to tell you about these before embarking on explanations.

Key points to establish

Explain the following in simple terms:

> the diagnosis and possible causes of hypercalcaemia

> that the underlying diagnosis is not certain and that it will not be possible to give a reliable prognosis until it is, but there is a range of possibilities from the benign to the malignant.

Appropriate responses to likely questions

Daughter: *what is the abnormality in the blood tests?*

Doctor: there is an abnormally high level of calcium in the blood, which can cause the tiredness and fatigue that your mother is suffering from.

Daughter: *what's causing the high calcium?*

Doctor: I don't know at the moment, but there are many possible causes that we need to check for. One of the most common is overactivity of the glands which normally control the blood calcium level – called parathyroid glands – and this is usually caused by a small benign tumour that can be removed with a simple operation. But there are some more worrying possible causes, including some types of cancer.

Daughter: *cancer is the most likely thing, isn't it?*

Doctor: no, I'm not sure that it is. As I've said, it's certainly a possibility that we need to look for, but I'm not hiding anything when I say that we don't know what the cause of the problem is at the moment. It could turn out to be a cancer, but it could turn out to be something much more straightforward.

Daughter: *if it is cancer, you won't tell her, will you?*

Doctor: I won't force any information on her that she doesn't want to know, but I won't keep things from her if she does want to talk about them.

Daughter: *but she won't cope at all if you tell her. Her sister has just died from lung cancer and she couldn't cope with that.*

Doctor: I hear what you say and I understand it. As I've said, I won't force anything on her that she doesn't want to hear, but I will ask her if she's got any questions about things, and if she has I will answer them as simply, honestly and kindly as I can. But if she doesn't ask, then I certainly won't force information on her.

1.2.3 No medical cause for hirsutism

Scenario

Role: you are a junior doctor working in the endocrine outpatient clinic.

Scenario: Miss Irene Harris has come back to the clinic to discuss the results of investigations for hirsutism. She is 21 years old and has been troubled by mild to moderate hirsutism since menarche. She bleaches or shaves her upper lip weekly, and waxes her abdomen and thighs monthly.
She has regular periods. Her blood tests, including luteinising hormone, follicle-stimulating hormone and testosterone, are all normal. The opinion of the endocrinology consultant is that she has idiopathic hirsutism.

Your task: to explain to the patient that she has idiopathic hirsutism, and that treatment options include cosmetic hair removal and Dianette (an oral contraceptive pill, with limited efficacy for hirsutism, that typically reduces hair growth by one-third).

Key issues to explore

What is the patient's main worry?
Is she concerned that she has a serious underlying disorder, in which case the diagnosis will be a relief, or does she simply want you to give her a tablet to make things better for her forthcoming summer holiday, in which case she is likely to be disappointed.

Does she have other concerns? For example, is she worried about fertility? This is unlikely to be a problem in view of her regular periods and normal blood tests.

Key points to establish

Explain the following in simple terms:

- Reassure her that there is no sinister underlying pathology – the diagnosis of idiopathic hirsutism is good news, and no further investigations are needed. But at the same time remember to be sensitive and ensure that you do not sound as if you are dismissing any concerns that she might have as no longer being important.
- Explain the basis for her condition – she may find it helpful to learn that some of the hair follicles on her body are simply a little more sensitive to the normal levels of circulating androgens (which all women have), leading to a coarsening of these hairs. This is a very common problem, and indeed can be viewed as one end of the normal spectrum for hair distribution in women. Emphasise that she is not becoming 'masculinised' in any way. If appropriate, mention that there are significant racial differences in hair biology and that hirsutism can run in families – she may know relatives who have had similar problems.
- Address the patient's expectations – while it is important not to minimise symptoms that are troubling a patient, it may be appropriate to discuss the difference between the ideal woman portrayed by the media and the biological norm (in terms of body fat and hair distribution).

Appropriate responses to likely questions

Patient: *people will think I'm turning into a man.*

Doctor: although many women express this concern, I can reassure you that it's not the case at all. You have normal periods and you're not going to turn into a man, but your body is more sensitive to the normal levels of male hormones that you and all other women have, and this shows itself in the way that the hair grows.

Patient: *is this going to get worse?*

Doctor: no, that's unlikely. This condition most often causes a reasonably stable level of unwanted excess hair throughout life, although weight gain can make the situation worse. It can also become more pronounced at the menopause with the change in balance between male and female sex hormones.

Patient: *you said earlier on that this problem can run in families, so why isn't my sister affected?*

Doctor: it is true that the condition tends to run in families, but different individuals are affected to varying degrees, and some not at all – just as some people with the same parents are taller or shorter, or have different hair or eye colour.

Patient: *why can't you give me a tablet to cure this illness?*

Doctor: if I could give you something that would take away the problem and didn't have any side effects then I would, but there isn't anything capable of doing this. It is important to appreciate that this is not an illness, but rather one end of the range of body hair growth that is normal for women. No drugs are without side effects, and although we can give you a tablet that is likely to reduce the hair growth by about a third, you would still almost certainly continue to need local hair removal treatments. The most commonly used tablet has a contraceptive action (eg Dianette), so is not suitable if you want to get pregnant and has risks associated with other oral contraceptives, including an increased risk of developing blood clots in the veins.

1.2.4 A short girl with no periods

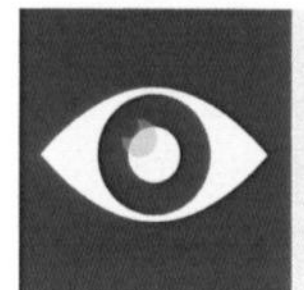

Scenario

Role: you are a junior doctor working in the endocrine outpatient clinic.

Scenario: Miss Alison Jackson, aged 17 years, presented to her GP with short stature and primary amenorrhoea. Your initial clinical assessment has revealed numerous features (webbed neck and cubitus valgus) that are suggestive of an underlying diagnosis of Turner's syndrome. The GP had already mentioned this as a possibility, and the patient has read up about the condition on the Internet.

Your task: to explain the meaning of 'karyotype analysis' and to ensure that the patient has an appropriate understanding of Turner's syndrome.

Key issues to explore

What does the patient already know, and what are her main concerns? Has she heard or read about 'karyotyping' or 'chromosome analysis'? What has she learnt about Turner's syndrome from discussions with her GP and her reading on the Internet? Explore these matters before embarking on explanations.

Key points to establish

In simple terms:

> Explain why you (and the GP) believe that the patient might have Turner's syndrome – recap the salient features from the history and examination (and any relevant available investigations).

> Emphasise the importance of confirming the diagnosis through biochemical testing and karyotype (chromosome) analysis.

> Explain how studying the chromosome pattern helps to establish the diagnosis.

> Briefly mention the associated features of the condition, but try to avoid an overdetailed discussion at this stage when confirmation of the diagnosis is still awaited. It is important to point out that not all patients manifest all features of the condition.

Appropriate responses to likely questions

Patient: *why do you want to check my chromosomes?*

Doctor: because I think it's likely that you have a condition called Turner's syndrome, and checking your chromosomes is the best way of making this diagnosis.

Patient: *chromosomes – what are chromosomes?*

Doctor: the chromosomes contain the genetic information that governs how all of the cells and tissues in the body develop. In Turner's syndrome there is a distinctive alteration in the chromosome arrangement – one of the chromosomes called the X chromosome is missing in some or all of the cells of the body – and this can be detected in most patients by looking at the chromosome pattern in a small number of cells taken from a simple blood sample. This test is called chromosome analysis or karyotyping/karyotype analysis.

Patient: *do I have to have the test done?*

Doctor: no, you don't have to have any test done that you don't want, but I think it would be a good idea to do it. You went to your doctor because you were worried that you hadn't grown as much as your friends and that your periods hadn't started. If we can find out why this is, then we should be able to help; but if we don't do any tests and don't find out what's causing the problem, then I'm afraid that we're not going to be able do anything about it.

Patient: *if you find that I have Turner's syndrome, does it mean that I'm not a proper woman?*

Doctor: no, it doesn't mean that at all. The absence of one of the X chromosomes, and the impact that this has on some of the tissues of the body such as the ovaries, is the reason why you haven't grown as tall as your friends and have not yet developed fully. But with the correct hormone replacement treatment we will be able to help you grow and develop.

Patient: *would the treatment make me absolutely normal?*

Doctor: you might not finish up quite as tall as other girls of your age, but remember that there's a lot of variation anyway, as I'm sure you're aware from looking at your friends – some are shorter and some are taller. Many women with Turner's syndrome have similar thoughts/questions about their femininity. You may find the Turner's Society, a patient support group, helpful: I can give you their details if you'd like them and haven't got them. Women with Turner's syndrome should have no doubt about their femininity: physically, behaviourally or sexually.

Patient: *do I have lots wrong with my body? On the Internet I read about possible heart, thyroid and kidney problems with Turner's syndrome.*

Doctor: I think we need to do the chromosome analysis before we say that we're sure that you have Turner's syndrome, so at this stage I don't think we should get into very detailed discussion about other conditions that may be associated with it. But if the diagnosis is confirmed then we will need to talk things through thoroughly, but it's important to say now that not all patients with Turner's syndrome are affected by complications.

1.2.5 Simple obesity, not a problem with 'the glands'

Scenario

Role: you are a junior doctor working in the endocrine outpatient clinic.

Scenario: Miss Manju Patel, aged 26 years, was referred by her GP because of concern that there may be an endocrine cause for her obesity (weight 90 kg; body mass index (BMI) 38 kg/m^2 (normal range 18–25)). Her periods are regular. She is mildly hirsute and has faint striae over her lower abdomen. Examination is otherwise unremarkable.

Investigations have excluded polycystic ovary syndrome (PCOS), hypothyroidism and Cushing's syndrome, and the diagnosis is one of 'simple obesity'. Both of her parents are also obese.

Miss Patel remains convinced that 'her glands are to blame' and states that she 'wants something done about it'.

Your task: to explain to the patient that no underlying endocrine cause for her obesity has been identified and to provide advice on weight loss management.

Key issues to explore

In this common scenario, as in others, it is important to allow the patient time to explain her view of things before launching in with explanations. Why does she continue to believe that her 'glands' are at fault, and which 'glands' does she believe are not working properly? What is she hoping/expecting the doctor to offer her in terms of treatment?

Key points to establish

In simple terms:

- Explain that there are many different reasons as to why somebody might become overweight or obese (Table 10), but that in most cases it is due to an imbalance between energy intake and expenditure. An individual's genetic make-up can affect their predisposition to weight gain, but environmental and behavioural factors are equally important in determining whether or not this occurs.
- Emphasise that endocrine causes of weight gain/obesity (eg polycystic ovary syndrome (PCOS), hypothyroidism and Cushing's syndrome) have been looked for and excluded.
- Explain that further medical tests are not required and that attention must now focus on helping her to lose weight through dietary and lifestyle modifications, supplemented with pharmacological/surgical interventions where necessary/appropriate.

Appropriate responses to likely questions

Patient: *how can you be sure that I don't have a problem with my glands? Have you checked all of them?*

Doctor: no, we haven't checked all of your glands, but we have checked the ones that can be relevant to problems with body weight. In particular we've done tests on the thyroid, the ovaries and the adrenal glands, and we've not found any evidence to indicate a specific problem with any of these. Are there any other glands that you are worried about specifically?

Patient: *does this mean that you think that I am fat just because I eat too much, because that can't be the case as I hardly eat anything?*

Doctor: how heavy a person is depends on the balance of how much energy they take in – how much they eat and drink – and how much energy they burn – how much exercise they do. But people are variable: we all know some people who can eat what they like and stay thin; and we know other people who put on a lot of weight without eating an enormous amount, just more than their body can burn off. I know that life's unfair, and you may not be eating more than some thin people do, but you are eating more than your body can burn off.

Patient: *so are you telling me that I just have to go on a diet and join a gym?*

Doctor: those are easy things to say and they might do some good, but as I'm sure you know it's often not as straightforward as that. I'd like to offer some help if you'd like to have some: I would like to refer you to a dietician who will be able to provide you with information on the calorie content of different foods and how to achieve a healthy, balanced diet that will help you to lose weight; and I think that it would also be very important for you to undertake regular exercise. This could begin with taking a brisk walk each day or swimming, and doesn't mean that you have to join a gym. But if you would like to take up regular supervised exercise, then many gyms can help out with this. It is also important to alter your day-to-day routine, for example use the stairs rather than taking the lift, walk or cycle to work rather than using the car – all these things can help.

Patient: *what if I still do not lose weight despite doing everything that you are saying. Would you check my glands again?*

Doctor: I am confident that if you do manage to alter your diet and lifestyle to achieve a situation where you are expending more calories than you are taking in, then you will lose weight. If this is proving difficult to achieve, then we could consider prescribing one or other treatments to try to help with this, but I don't think we will need to reinvestigate your 'glands' unless there are some new symptoms or changes to indicate that we should do so. The glands aren't the problem, and I don't think it's going to be helpful to keep focusing on them.

Patient: *why can't you give me a tablet now or just send me for an operation?*

Doctor: there are three reasons for not racing into tablets or operations straight away. First, adjusting your diet and exercise are the most appropriate and logical first steps to tackle weight gain in this situation because they directly address the underlying cause of the problem. Secondly, tablets or surgery rarely work in isolation, and lifestyle adaptation is an important component if these are to succeed. Thirdly, tablets and surgery can both have side effects and complications, so we should start with the simple things: diet and exercise.

1.2.6 I don't want to take the tablets

Scenario

Role: you are a junior doctor working in the endocrine outpatient clinic.

Scenario: Mrs Isabel Burns, a 35-year-old woman recently diagnosed with primary adrenal insufficiency (Addison's disease), has raised several concerns over her lifelong requirement for steroid treatment. She is particularly worried about weight gain.

Your task: to explain the rationale behind physiological glucocorticoid replacement and the necessity of taking it.

Key issues to explore

Patient education is extremely important for those with adrenal insufficiency: this woman will have to assume responsibility for a life-maintaining therapy that requires adjustment at times of stress. But before embarking on a worthy lecture, encourage her to express her concerns. Why is she worried about taking steroids? Has she ever taken them in the past, or known anyone else who has? And did they have problems?

Key points to establish

Explain the following in straightforward terms:

> Physiological versus pharmacological steroid treatment – it is important for the patient to realise that steroid treatment in this setting is to replace what is normally produced by the body and not to administer a pharmacological dose, as would be required for treating inflammatory conditions such as rheumatoid arthritis or asthma. A physiological dose is most unlikely to have side effects.

> The importance of compliance – she requires lifelong steroid replacement therapy. Failure to take an appropriate dose leaves her vulnerable to adrenal crises, which are potentially life-threatening. It is also important to carry a steroid card or bracelet so that in the event of being unable to communicate (eg if involved in a car accident) appropriate medical treatment can be given without delay.

Appropriate responses to likely questions

Patient: *why do I need steroids anyway?*

Doctor: steroids are essential for life: everyone's body produces steroids, and the most important one is cortisol. The condition that you have destroys the glands that make this. Cortisol is important for controlling many systems in the body, including those that regulate blood pressure and the response to stress. Without cortisol your body cannot respond properly to stress: your blood pressure can fall, you may suddenly become very unwell and in rare cases the problem can be fatal. So steroids are important, they're not something that you or I could just decide to do without.

Patient: *some of my friends have been on steroids and have put on a huge amount of weight, will this happen to me?*

Doctor: no, it won't. They were almost certainly being given steroids as a drug to treat an illness: asthma, arthritis (do you know what it was?). The aim of treating you with steroid is quite different. Everyone's body normally makes some steroid, but in you this doesn't happen because the adrenal glands are damaged. So what we're aiming to do is to give you back only the amount of steroid that your body would produce naturally: we're not intending to give you any extra, so you shouldn't suffer excess weight gain as a result of this steroid treatment.

Patient: *I don't like the idea of wearing a MedicAlert bracelet: I don't want to advertise that I've got a problem. I don't have to wear one, do I?*

Doctor: I can understand what you're saying. The issue is that, if you were to become unwell, you might not be able to tell a doctor looking after you about the fact that you had Addison's disease and needed steroids. So you need to carry something on you at all times that would give the doctor this information. Some people carry a steroid card in their purse or handbag, some people wear a MedicAlert bracelet or necklace – but it's important that you carry something.

Patient: *I'm confused about this business of increasing the dose when I'm ill – what's all that about?*

Doctor: when someone gets ill their body naturally makes more steroid, but yours can't do that, so the simple rule is that you take double the normal dose if you feel unwell and go back to the normal dose as soon as you feel better. There are no side effects from a few days of double dose steroid, so if in doubt just increase the dose. If you're back to normal the following day, then cut back the dose to normal.

1.3 Brief clinical consultations

1.3.1 Hypertension and a lump in the neck

Instruction

Mr Harry Linton, a 26-year-old man, has refractory hypertension and has recently noticed a firm lump on the right side of his neck. What is the likely diagnosis, and how should he be managed?

Introduction

This is likely a case of secondary hypertension (Table 15) and you should approach the patient with these differential diagnoses in mind. The finding of a neck mass may be relevant and should alert you to possible inherited tumour syndromes.

Beginning the encounter

Doctor: hello, my name is Dr A, I understand the problems are that you have been found to have high blood pressure and more recently, a neck lump: is that right?

Patient: *yes.*

Doctor: before we get onto the details of these, can you tell me if you have any major medical problems? Any problems with bruising, diabetes mellitus, renal stones or blood calcium levels? Any previous surgery?

Patient: [gives list (with doctor politely but firmly discouraging lengthy detail).]

Doctor: and are you on any tablets or medications?

Patient: [gives details (and will probably have been asked to produce a written list).]

These introductory questions will provide useful clinical context and may immediately give a clue to the likely diagnosis, eg in a young person with a history of manifestations of hypercalcaemia or previous neck surgery a diagnosis of multiple endocrine neoplasia type 2a (MEN-2) may be suspected. Alternatively, the presence of easy bruising or newly diagnosed diabetes may suggest cortisol excess due to Cushing's syndrome.

Focused history

Doctor: going back to the high blood pressure, just some general questions. Have you noticed any associated symptoms, for example palpitations, chest discomfort, sweating or headache? [And if the patient has had any such symptoms] Do you have them all the time, or do they come and go?

Most patients who present with high blood pressure will be asymptomatic. The presence of episodic symptoms should raise suspicion of increased sympathetic activity.

If the patient has had episodic symptoms, specific questions that may be helpful in this case are:

- How long have these episodes been going on for?
- How long do these episodes last?
- Are there any precipitating factors?
- Are there any other associated symptoms?
- Is there a family history of hypertension?
- Do you smoke, consume alcohol or take recreational drugs?
- Do you have any current relationship, work or financial problems?

Doctor: now please tell me, when did you first notice the neck lump?

Ask some general questions:

- Is the lump increasing in size?
- Is the lump hard or soft; tender or non-tender?
- Is there a history of previous neck lumps?
- Has there been a recent history of sore throat or viral illness?
- Is there a past history of head and neck cancer?
- Is there any significant family history of head, neck or intra-abdominal tumours?

Focused examination

Look quickly for evidence of any conditions associated with secondary hypertension, including acromegaly and Cushing's syndrome.

Cardiovascular – check the following:

- pulse – rate and rhythm
- blood pressure – lying and standing (ask the examiner: they will almost certainly give you the readings)
- signs of heart failure – look for evidence of congestive cardiac failure which may result from a dilated catecholamine cardiomyopathy
- heart sounds – mitral regurgitation is common in patients with impaired, dilated left ventricles.

Thyroid examination (if appropriate) – check the following:

- neck and thyroid examination – note size, mobility, texture and tenderness of the lump
- palpate cervical lymph nodes.

Abdominal examination – check the following:

- palpate for abdominal masses, specifically renal masses
- palpate for hepatomegaly.

Other relevant examination (if appropriate):

> fundoscopy (tell the examiner that you would like to do this: they will almost certainly decline this offer, but they will note that you have made it).

Questions from the patient

[Assuming that the patient has symptoms suggesting catecholamine excess, and you think that the lump in the neck may be a paraganglionoma:]

Patient: *why do I have high blood pressure?*

Doctor: high blood pressure in young adults is unusual and in some cases can be caused by too much of a particular hormone. There are several different hormones that can cause high blood pressure, and in most cases the hormone is produced from a tumour.

Patient: *is my neck lump related?*

Doctor: I'm not sure, but yes, I think it might be. I think you might have a tumour called a paraganglioma – that's a tumour of a nerve – that could be overproducing catecholamines, which are hormones similar to adrenaline.

Patient: *what will you do next?*

Doctor: the first thing we need to do is to find out whether or not you do have a tumour of this sort. In the first instance I will arrange for you to have blood tests to measure the levels of catecholamine metabolites (metanephrine, normetanephrine and methoxytyramine) in your blood. I will then request a CT of your whole body to look at the lump in your neck, and see if there are any other lumps anywhere else.

Questions from the examiner

Examiner: *if a functional paraganglioma is the confirmed diagnosis in this patient, how will you prepare the patient, preoperatively, for surgery?*

Doctor: surgery in this context carries potential risks including hypertensive and hypotensive crises, cardiac arrhythmias, myocardial infarction and stroke, due to tumoral release of catecholamines during anaesthetic induction and tumour manipulation. Preoperatively, alpha-adrenoceptor blockade is the mainstay of management in order to minimise perioperative haemodynamic instability. Beta-adrenoceptor antagonists are contraindicated in the absence of effective alpha1-receptor blockade due to the risk of a potentially fatal hypertensive crisis secondary to unopposed alpha-adrenoceptor stimulation. Beta-blockers should be considered in the management of tachycardia or tachyarrhythmias induced by adrenaline-secreting phaeochromocytomas. Close monitoring of fluid balance is also critical in these patients, and some may require IV fluids prior to surgery.

Examiner: *which genetic conditions predispose individuals to the development of phaeochromocytoma and/or paraganglioma (PPGL)?*

Doctor: multiple endocrine neoplasia (MEN)-2a (MEN-2), MEN-2b (MEN-3), von Hippel–Lindau syndrome, neurofibromatosis type 1 all predispose to phaeochromocytoma. Germline mutations in components of mitochondrial succinate dehydrogenase (for example SDHA, SDHB, SDHC, SDHD) predispose to familial paraganglioma and phaeochromocytoma syndromes.

Further discussion

The reported incidence of phaeochromocytoma/paraganglioma in normotensive asymptomatic subjects is increasing due to increased use of high-resolution imaging and surveillance strategies in subjects known to have a predisposing gene mutation. Up to 25% of all phaeochromocytomas may be discovered incidentally during imaging undertaken for unrelated reasons, and about 5% of adrenal incidentalomas are phaeochromocytomas.

Hazard

Biopsy or surgical removal of a neck lump may be required to confirm the diagnosis, but do not undertake a fine-needle aspirate (FNA) of something that may be highly vascular (aneurysm or paraganglioma) until the lesion has been radiologically and biochemically characterised.

1.3.2 Tiredness and lethargy

Instruction

Mrs Tracey Lumb, a 31-year-old woman, has been complaining of progressive tiredness and lethargy over the past 3 months. She is now 4 months postpartum having had a complicated delivery. What is the likely diagnosis, and how should she be managed?

Introduction

Tiredness and lethargy are common complaints and the list of differential diagnoses is broad. The challenge lies in identifying those cases with a clear organic basis. A temporal relationship with pregnancy is relevant and may signify an underlying endocrine aetiology.

Beginning the encounter

Doctor: hello, my name is Dr A, I understand that the problems are that you have been struggling with tiredness and lethargy. Is that right?

Patient: *yes.*

Doctor: before we get onto the details of these, can you tell me if you have any major medical problems? Any problems with bleeding (including heavy periods), dizziness, visual disturbance or headache?

Patient: [gives list (with doctor politely but firmly discouraging lengthy detail).]

Doctor: and are you on any tablets or medications?

Patient: [gives details (and will probably have been asked to produce a written list).]

These introductory questions will provide useful clinical context and may immediately give a clue to the likely diagnosis; for example, a history of autoimmunity, low blood pressure and postural dizziness may signify primary adrenal insufficiency. Pituitary failure following pregnancy may be due to severe blood loss during delivery resulting in pituitary infarction, or Sheehan's syndrome. Alternatively, the presence of heavy menstrual bleeding may suggest anaemia secondary to a gynaecological pathology, such as uterine fibroids.

Focused history

Doctor: going back to the tiredness, just some general questions. When did the tiredness first appear? Is it there all the time, or does it come and go? Have you noticed any other symptoms, for example changes in body weight or bowel habit, intolerance of cold or dry skin? Have you had a recent sore throat? Have you had any neck swelling, and [if so] was this tender?

Doctor: relating to the pregnancy, I know that the delivery was complicated. Were you very unwell? Did you have to have a blood transfusion? Did you try to breast feed, and [if so] did you have any difficulty doing this?

These questions will help to establish whether the patient's symptoms are due to:

- thyroiditis (Hashimoto's or postpartum) – tiredness, constipation, weight gain, goitre, cold intolerance
- hypoadrenalism – tiredness, weight loss, dizziness (primary adrenal insufficiency), salt craving (primary adrenal insufficiency)
- hypopituitarism – failure of lactation (prolactin deficiency), tiredness (hypoadrenalism, hypothyroidism, growth hormone deficiency).

Focused examination

Observe the patient's general appearance. What is her BMI? What is her thyroid status?

Cardiovascular – check the following:

- pulse – rate and rhythm
- blood pressure – lying and standing (ask the examiner: they will almost certainly give you the readings).

Thyroid examination – check the following:

- palpate for a goitre.

Other relevant examinations (if appropriate):

- neurology – visual fields (bitemporal quadrantanopia/hemianopia, indicating a pituitary lesion), reflexes (slowly relaxing, indicating hypothyroidism)
- dermatology – generalised pigmentation of the skin, palmar creases, scars, buccal mucosa (indicating hypoadrenalism).

Questions from the patient

[Assuming that the patient has features suggesting postpartum hypopituitarism:]

Patient: *why do I feel so tired and lethargic?*

Doctor: there are a number of possible causes, including problems with endocrine glands such as the thyroid, adrenal or pituitary glands. It may be that you are not making adequate amounts of hormones, and this may be causing your symptoms.

Patient: *what will you do next?*

Doctor: in the first instance I would like to request blood tests including those that measure the levels of specific hormones. Some of these tests can be done today, and – depending on the results of these, we may need to do some more later. We may also need to do some special scans, including an MRI of the pituitary gland.

Patient: *could my symptoms be related to my pregnancy?*

Doctor: yes, that is possible. Some endocrine conditions, that's problems with the glands, can develop in the context of pregnancy. For example, hypothyroidism – having an underactive thyroid – is more common following pregnancy, and pituitary failure – that's failure of a special gland in the brain – can occur if there is severe blood loss during delivery.

Questions from the examiner

Examiner: *if hypopituitarism is confirmed, what hormone would you replace first?*

Doctor: if pituitary (or adrenal) insufficiency is suspected, cortisol should be replaced first, with treatment started even before the diagnosis is biochemically confirmed. Replacing thyroxine first may precipitate an adrenal crisis.

Key point

Hormone replacement in pituitary insufficiency – give cortisol first; replacing thyroxine first may precipitate an adrenal crisis.

Examiner: *why do patients with primary adrenal insufficiency often have low blood pressure, whereas patients with secondary (central) adrenal insufficiency may not?*

Doctor: in secondary adrenal insufficiency aldosterone production by the adrenal gland is preserved.

Further discussion

Following replacement with cortisol, then thyroxine, additional pituitary hormones may be replaced. In women, oestrogen and progesterone should be replaced (men require testosterone replacement therapy). In adults, a requirement to meet specific biochemical and clinical criteria is mandated before growth hormone replacement can be considered.

1.3.3 Weight loss and gritty eyes

Instruction

Mrs Wilma Eagle, a 43-year-old woman, has been complaining of progressive weight loss and gritty eyes. What is the likely diagnosis, and how should she be managed?

Introduction

There are several causes of thyrotoxicosis (Table 17), with a limited number of diagnostic possibilities that unify progressive weight loss and gritty eyes. The challenge lies in recognising this association, making the correct diagnosis, and initiating the correct management plan by involving the appropriate clinical experts as soon as possible.

Beginning the encounter

Doctor: hello, my name is Dr A, I understand that you have been losing weight and having a problem with gritty eyes. Is that right?

Patient: *yes.*

Doctor: before we get onto the details of these, can you tell me if you have any major medical problems or history of autoimmune disorders? Any problems with your vision, chest pain, shortness of breath, ankle swelling? Have you noticed any change in your appetite?

Patient: [gives list (with doctor politely but firmly discouraging lengthy detail).]

Doctor: and are you on any tablets or medications? Specifically, have you ever taken a drug called amiodarone?

Patient: [gives details (and will probably have been asked to produce a written list).]

These introductory questions will provide useful clinical context and may immediately identify any 'red flags' that require immediate medical or surgical intervention. For example, severe Graves' ophthalmopathy may require urgent referral to ophthalmology. Use of specific medications, such as amiodarone, may cause thyrotoxicosis and should be identified to ensure the correct investigations are performed and management is initiated.

Weight loss in the context of reduced appetite may signify a sinister pathological process, such as malignancy or chronic illness. Alternatively, marked weight loss in association with increased appetite may signify an underlying metabolic disturbance.

Focused history

Doctor: going back to the weight loss, just some general questions. How much weight have you lost and over what period of time? Have you noticed any other symptoms, for example palpitations, chest pain, tremor, irregular periods, diarrhoea or sweating? Have you noticed any changes to your skin? Have you had any difficulty getting up out of a chair? Any changes in your mood? Have you had a sore throat recently? Has your neck been swollen and/or tender?

Doctor: with regards to your gritty eyes, have you noticed any double vision? Are your eyes sore? Have they changed in appearance? Do you smoke?

These questions will help to establish the severity of the patient symptoms and the correct diagnosis.

Focused examination

Observe the patient's general appearance.

Thyroid status – check the following:

- hands – onycholysis, acropachy, palmer erythema, tremor
- eyes – lid lag and retraction, proptosis, exophthalmos, chemosis, periorbital oedema, ophthalmoplegia, fundoscopy (tell the examiner that you would like to do this: they will almost certainly decline this offer, but they will note that you have made it)
- skin – pretibial myxoedema.

Table 17 Causes of thyrotoxicosis

Cause	Condition
Primary	Grave's disease Toxic multinodular goitre Toxic adenoma Postpartum thyroiditis Drug induced (ie amiodarone) Viral thyroiditis Struma ovarii
Secondary	TSH-secreting pituitary adenomas[1] Thyroid hormone resistance (usually euthyroid)

1 A pituitary tumour that secretes TSH is sometimes referred to as a TSHoma.
TSH, thyroid-stimulating hormone.

Neck examination – check the following:

- thyroid – examine for a goitre and a bruit.

Cardiovascular – check the following:

- pulse – rate and rhythm
- blood pressure (ask the examiner: they will almost certainly give you the reading)
- signs of heart failure.

Questions from the patient

[Assuming that the patient has features suggesting hyperthyroidism due to Graves' disease:]

Patient: *why have I lost weight and got such sore eyes?*

Doctor: the most likely cause is an overactive thyroid gland which is producing too much thyroid hormone. Although there are several causes for an overactive thyroid, I think the most likely cause is Graves' disease. Although overactivity of the thyroid gland is the main problem for most patients, the condition can also affect the eyes.

Patient: *how will you work out what's going on with the thyroid gland?*

Doctor: in the first instance I will request blood tests to confirm that your thyroid is overactive and the diagnosis is Graves' disease. If the gland is overactive but the blood tests don't confirm Graves' disease, then we will probably need to do some imaging studies – special X-rays – including a thyroid uptake scan to investigate for other possible causes of an overactive thyroid.

Patient: *what about my eyes?*

Doctor: I plan to refer you to my ophthalmology colleagues for detailed assessment of your eyes. In this regard [if the patient has said that she smokes], I would advise you to stop smoking because smoking may cause your eye disease to deteriorate.

Questions from the examiner

Examiner: *if Graves' disease is confirmed how will you initially manage this patient?*

Doctor: I will treat her with antithyroid drugs such as carbimazole or propylthiouracil. I could treat by titrating the dose of antithyroid drug to maintain the thyroid hormones in the normal range, or using a 'block and replace' regimen (ie give a large dose of antithyroid drug to fully block thyroid hormone production and replace with an adequate dose of thyroxine therapy). If necessary, beta-blockers could be given to alleviate symptoms associated with thyrotoxicosis in the short term.

Examiner: *will you counsel your patient on any specific side effects associated with antithyroid drugs?*

Doctor: agranulocytosis is the most serious complication of antithyroid drugs. I would advise the patient to immediately report to their doctor if they develop a temperature, sore throat or mouth ulcers. A more common minor side effect is a rash which often responds to antihistamine treatment. A small number of patients develop abnormalities of liver function.

Hazard

Agranulocytosis is the most serious complication of antithyroid drugs.

Further discussion

Key point

Thyroid eye disease – in any patient with suspected Graves' ophthalmopathy it is important to formally assess visual acuity, examine the fundi and to check for loss of colour vision. If there is any concern or if the patient has evidence of ophthalmoplegia or complains of pain, then urgent referral to an ophthalmologist is required.

1.3.4 Depression and diabetes

Instruction

Mr Daniel Davis, a 28-year-old man, has recently been diagnosed with diabetes. His body weight has noticeably increased over the past 4 months and he has a low mood. What is the likely diagnosis, and how should he be investigated?

Introduction

Due to the increasing prevalence of obesity, new onset diabetes in a young adult is not uncommon. However, it is important to differentiate type 2 diabetes from secondary causes of diabetes that may have an underlying endocrine aetiology.

Beginning the encounter

Doctor: hello, my name is Dr A, I understand that you have been recently diagnosed with diabetes, that your body weight has increased, and that your mood has been low. Is this correct?

Patient: *yes.*

Doctor: before we get onto the details of these, can you tell me if you have any major medical problems such as hypertension, asthma, inflammatory diseases or recurrent infections? Do you have a family history of any hormone problems or diabetes?

Patient: [gives list (with doctor politely but firmly discouraging lengthy detail).]

Doctor: and are you on any tablets or medications? Specifically, do you take steroid tablets or steroid inhalers?

Patient: [gives details (and will probably have been asked to produce a written list).]

These introductory questions will provide useful clinical context and may immediately give a clue to the likely diagnosis. For example, a patient with poorly controlled asthma or rheumatoid arthritis may develop Cushing's syndrome secondary to exogenous glucocorticoid therapy.

Focused history

Doctor: going back to the diabetes and increased body weight, just some general questions. Have you noticed any other symptoms, for example easy bruising, muscle weakness, poor libido, stretch marks on your abdomen, fatness of your face or your abdomen, or acne? Has anyone mentioned that your appearance has changed? Do you have difficulty standing from a seated position?

Doctor: do you suffer from headaches? Have you noticed any changes in your vision? Tell me about your mood.

These questions will help to establish whether the patient's diabetes is secondary to glucocorticoid excess and will also check for features of a pituitary tumour (although most cases of Cushing's disease are caused by pituitary microadenomas).

Focused examination

Observe the patient's general appearance and thyroid status. Does the face appear moon-like and plethoric? Is there truncal obesity or prominent supraclavicular and interscapular (buffalo hump) fat pads?

Thyroid – check the following:

> goitre, dry skin.

Dermatology – check the following:

> acne
> thin skin with easy bruising
> purple abdominal striae.

Neuromuscular – check the following:

> muscle wasting
> proximal myopathy.

Cardiovascular – check the following:

> blood pressure (ask the examiner: they will almost certainly give you the reading).

Abdomen – check the following:

> palpate for abdominal masses and hepatomegaly (adrenal carcinoma – not likely in PACES).

Musculoskeletal – check the following:

> examine the spine for evidence of osteoporosis (vertebral collapse), kyphoscoliosis.

Questions from the patient

[Assuming that the patient has features suggesting Cushing's syndrome:]

Patient: *what is the cause of my diabetes?*

Doctor: the most likely cause is Cushing's syndrome, which is caused by excessive production of a steroid called cortisol.

Patient: *what causes Cushing's syndrome?*

Doctor: there are several possible causes of it, including tumours of the pituitary gland, which is a special gland in the brain, or of the adrenal glands, and very rarely it can be caused by other things.

Patient: *tumours – does that mean I've got cancer?*

Doctor: most of the tumours that cause Cushing's syndrome are benign, which means that they don't spread, but – although I think this is unlikely to be the problem in your case – some can be cancerous. We need to do some tests to find out exactly what's going on.

Patient: *what will you do next?*

Doctor: in the first instance, we need to confirm the diagnosis with a series of tests including measurement of cortisol levels in blood, saliva and urine. If these confirm that you are producing excessive amounts of cortisol, then we will need more blood and radiological (X-ray) tests to establish the cause.

Questions from the examiner

Examiner: *if an ACTH-dependent cause is suspected, which investigations will you request?*

Doctor: further biochemical testing (for example a high-dose dexamethasone suppression test and/or a corticotropin-releasing hormone (CRH) test) may help to distinguish Cushing's disease from ectopic ACTH production. However, bilateral inferior petrosal sinus sampling and an MRI of the pituitary are the preferred investigations for confirming or excluding a pituitary source. If ectopic ACTH production is suspected, cross-sectional imaging (CT/MRI) of the neck, chest and abdomen will be required to localise an ectopic source of ACTH production. Scintigraphy (octreotide) or PET-CT may also help localise an occult ectopic tumour.

Examiner: *how would you manage a patient with Cushing's disease?*

Doctor: initial treatment will aim to reduce circulating cortisol levels using drugs that block adrenal steroidogenesis, such as metyrapone or ketoconazole. I will then refer the patient to the neurosurgeons for transsphenoidal adenomectomy or hemi-hypophysectomy. In patients unsuitable for surgery, or in whom surgical resection is incomplete, radiotherapy may be required.

Further discussion

Key point

Cushing's syndrome and pseudo-Cushing's syndrome

Signs that most reliably differentiate Cushing's syndrome from pseudo-Cushing's syndrome are proximal myopathy, easy bruising and thinness and fragility of the skin. Centripetal obesity, buffalo hump and hirsutism are also classical clinical features but relatively poor discriminators.

1.3.5 Headache and sweating

Instruction

Mr Harry Sullivan, a 37-year-old man, has been troubled with headache and sweating for the past few months. He has also recently been diagnosed with carpal tunnel syndrome. What is the likely diagnosis and how should he be investigated?

Introduction

Headache and sweating are common symptoms that may be related to an underlying endocrine aetiology or result from independent pathologies. Possible endocrine causes include hypogonadism, phaeochromocytoma, growth hormone excess or carcinoid syndrome. It is important to ascertain additional external clues that may point towards a diagnosis. Similarly, it is critical to exclude sinister causes of headache.

Beginning the encounter

Doctor: hello, my name is Dr A. I understand that you have been suffering with headaches and sweating. Is this correct?

Patient: *yes.*

Doctor: before we get onto the details of these, can you tell me if you have any major medical problems such as hypertension, diabetes, bowel cancer, gallstones, arthritis or obstructive sleep apnoea? Do you have a family history of hormone problems?

Patient: [gives list (with doctor politely but firmly discouraging lengthy detail).]

Doctor: and are you on any tablets or medications?

Patient: [gives details (and will probably have been asked to produce a written list).]

These introductory questions will provide useful clinical context and may immediately give a clue to the likely cause of the headache or other unifying diagnosis.

Focused history

Doctor: going back to the headaches, I would like to ask some specific questions. How long do they last? Are they constant or episodic? How frequent are they? Where are the headaches? Are they worse on waking? Do they wake you from your sleep? Do you get any warning that a headache is going to come on (aura)? Nausea and/or vomiting? Do bright lights make your eyes sore? Have you noticed any changes to your vision? Is there anything that makes the headaches worse or better?

Key point

Headaches worse on wakening may indicate raised intracranial pressure. It is always important to explore the history of a patient presenting with new onset headache for features suggestive of migraine.

Doctor: going back to the sweating, is it continuous or does it come and go? Is there any association with flushing? Have you had any gastrointestinal symptoms, such as diarrhoea or abdominal cramps? Is there any association with palpitations or chest discomfort? Have you identified anything that makes the sweating worse, for example specific foods? Have you noticed any changes to your libido? Do you get regular erections?

These questions will help to establish whether the patient's sweating may have an underlying endocrine aetiology that requires further investigation. Both headaches and sweating are common symptoms in acromegaly and hence this specific diagnosis should be explored.

> Have you noticed a change in your shoe or ring size?

> Have you or others noticed a change in your appearance?

> Do you snore, or has anyone mentioned that you stop breathing when you sleep?

> Is your skin greasy? Do you suffer with acne?

> Do you have painful joints?

> Have you noticed a change in bowel habit or blood in the stool?

Focused examination

Observe the patient's general appearance and look for features of acromegaly including greasy skin (seborrhoea), prominent supraorbital ridges, prognathism, interdental separation and macroglossia.

Hands – check the following:

> large (spade-like), sweaty

> carpal tunnel syndrome (a feature in this case).

Neurology – check the following:

> eyes – visual fields (bitemporal quadrantanopia/hemianopia), visual acuity, ophthalmoplegia (reflecting lateral extension of a pituitary tumour).

Cardiovascular – check the following:

> blood pressure (ask the examiner: they will almost certainly give you the reading)

> features of heart failure, cardiomegaly.

Dermatology – check the following:

> skin tags (axillae)

> acanthosis nigricans.

Abdomen – check the following:

> palpate for abdominal masses and hepatomegaly

> gynaecomastia.

Questions from the patient

[Assuming that the patient has features suggesting acromegaly:]

Patient: *what is the cause of my headaches and sweating?*

Doctor: the most likely cause is a condition called acromegaly, which is due to excessive production of growth hormone from a benign pituitary tumour.

Patient: *are you saying that I've got cancer?*

Doctor: no, I'm not. Cancer is something that spreads in the body. The cause here is almost certainly a benign growth in the pituitary gland, which is a special gland in the brain.

Patient: *how will you find out if I have got acromegaly?*

Doctor: if someone has acromegaly, then they have too much growth hormone in their blood. The first thing will be to do a test that involves you drinking a sugary drink and then having several blood samples taken over the following 2 hours. This should make the growth hormone fall to a very low level, but in acromegaly this doesn't happen and the level of the growth hormone remains high. We will also do blood tests to check the levels of other pituitary hormones, arrange for a special scan – an MRI – of the pituitary gland to find the pituitary tumour, and arrange to have a check of your vision because sometimes this can be affected by things in the pituitary.

Key point

Diagnosis of acromegaly is made when a glucose tolerance test demonstrates failure of normal suppression of growth hormone.

Questions from the examiner

Examiner: *if acromegaly is confirmed, what therapeutic options are available?*

Doctor: medical therapy with somatostatin analogues, dopamine agonists (ie bromocriptine) or growth hormone receptor antagonists (ie pegvisomant) can be used in patients unfit for surgery or to minimise disease activity prior to surgery. Transsphenoidal adenomectomy is first-line treatment for acromegaly. Radiotherapy may be given if there is residual tumour postoperatively or if a patient is unfit for surgery.

Examiner: *what are the complications of acromegaly?*

Doctor: complications include hypertension, cardiac failure, secondary diabetes, osteoarthritis, obstructive sleep apnoea, carpal tunnel syndrome, hypopituitarism, spinal stenosis, colon cancer, visual field defects and cholecystitis.

Further discussion

It is useful to appreciate the difference between evidence of active growth hormone hypersecretion (such as headaches, poorly controlled diabetes, seborrhoea, progressive enlargement of hands and feet, sweating) and evidence of past, inactive disease (presence of morphological features).

Aggressive treatment of other risk factors is essential, including for hypertension, diabetes, dyslipidaemia and sleep apnoea. Most centres also offer screening colonoscopy because the risk of colon cancer in acromegalic subjects is twice that of the general population. Those with a family history of colon cancer are likely to be at particular risk.

1.3.6 Amenorrhoea and low blood pressure

Instruction

Mrs Amanda Barton, a 27-year-old woman, has a 7-month history of secondary amenorrhoea. Her GP has noted that she has low blood pressure (100/65 mmHg). What is the likely diagnosis and how should she be investigated?

Introduction

Secondary amenorrhoea may be a consequence of ovarian, pituitary or hypothalamic dysfunction, but the combination with low blood pressure immediately raises the possibility of two scenarios: (1) a pituitary or hypothalamic disorder with malfunction of the hypothalamic–pituitary–adrenal and hypothalamic–pituitary–gonadal axes; or (2) Addison's disease with associated autoimmune ovarian failure. The initial approach to the case should concentrate on these two possibilities.

Beginning the encounter

Doctor: hello, my name is Dr A. I understand that you have stopped having regular menstrual periods and have been found to have a low blood pressure. Is this correct?

Patient: *yes.*

Doctor: before we get onto the details of these, can you tell me if you have any other medical problems such as visual problems, diabetes or so-called autoimmune diseases? Do you have a family history of autoimmunity or hormone problems? Have you ever broken or fractured a bone?

Patient: [gives list (with doctor politely but firmly discouraging lengthy detail).]

Doctor: are you taking any tablets or medications? Have you ever taken the oral contraceptive pill or other hormone-based therapies?

Patient: [gives details (and will probably have been asked to produce a written list).]

Focused history

Doctor: going back to missed menstrual periods, I would like to ask some specific questions:

> Is it possible you could be pregnant? Have you had a recent pregnancy test? (It is always important to exclude pregnancy as a cause for amenorrhoea!)

> When did you last have a menstrual period?

> At what age did you first have a period? Were they regular or irregular thereafter?

> Have you lost or gained significant body weight?

> How much exercise do you take?

> Have you experienced breast tenderness or milky nipple discharge? (features of prolactin excess)

> Have you experienced any flushing?

Hazard

Don't forget to exclude pregnancy as a cause of secondary amenorrhoea!

These questions will provide useful clinical context and may immediately give a clue to the likely cause of the amenorrhoea or other unifying diagnosis. If there is a history of significant weight loss or an unusual (excessive) exercise pattern, it may be necessary to consider the possibility of an underlying primary eating disorder.

Doctor: going back to the low blood pressure, do you know how long this has been for? Do you feel dizzy when you stand up? Is there any association with fatigue or weight loss? Are you often thirsty? Do you crave salty foods?

These questions will help to establish whether the patient's symptoms may be due to primary adrenal insufficiency or hypothalamic–pituitary dysfunction. Additional questions that may help to further distinguish between these possibilities may include:

> Do you have vitiligo?

> Have you or others noticed changes in your skin, such as increased pigmentation?

> Do you often feel cold?

> Have you noticed a change in bowel habit?

> Have you experienced any hair loss?

> Do you struggle climbing stairs or getting up from a chair?

Focused examination

Observe the patient's general appearance and look for features of Addison's disease including general pallor, palmar/buccal/scar pigmentation or vitiligo.

Does the patient appear to be of normal, high or low body mass index? If the latter, then consider possible causes of weight loss (eg anorexia nervosa, malabsorption, etc).

While acromegaly could present with secondary amenorrhoea, low blood pressure is not a common finding. Similarly, in Cushing's syndrome the patient is likely to be hypertensive due to cortisol excess.

Specific examination should focus on the likely affected glands, with respect to both anatomical abnormalities caused by mass lesions and hypofunction of the relevant hormonal axes.

Evidence of a pituitary mass lesion

Check for:

> bitemporal hemianopia or quadrantanopia

> eye movement abnormalities

> reduced visual acuity / red extinction / optic disc pallor / relative afferent pupillary defect.

Key point

Make sure that you have a smooth and well-practised technique to examine for bitemporal hemianopia or quadrantanopia – it is very likely that you will need to do so in PACES.

Evidence of dysfunction of hypothalamic–pituitary-target organ axes

Hyperfunction – examine for features of:

> acromegaly

> Cushing's syndrome

> hyperprolactinaemia.

Hypofunction – examine for features of:

> hypothalamic–pituitary–adrenal dysfunction – scanty axillary hair; postural hypotension, but without excess pigmentation (ACTH levels are not increased)
> hypothalamic–pituitary–thyroid dysfunction – slow relaxing reflexes, bradycardia, slow mentation, hypothermia
> hypothalamic–pituitary–gonadal dysfunction – loss of secondary sexual hair/diminished secondary sexual characteristics
> hypothalamic–posterior pituitary dysfunction – evidence of dehydration, but this is not likely to be present in any patient who is well and able to drink freely, such as when assisting in PACES, but may become a significant problem in any situation where they are not able to access or absorb water (eg intercurrent illness/vomiting). May be masked by concomitant glucocorticoid deficiency.

Questions from the patient

[Assuming that the patient probably has an endocrine cause, but that the precise diagnosis is not clear:]

Patient: *what is causing my abnormal menstrual periods and low blood pressure?*

Doctor: the most likely causes are either a problem with your pituitary gland, which is a small gland in the brain, or a combination of problems affecting your adrenal glands and ovaries.

Patient: *how will you find out what the diagnosis is?*

Doctor: in the first instance I think we should check some specific hormone tests (short Synacthen test, renin/aldosterone, full pituitary hormone profile, oestrogen) to identify the source of the problem and the possible cause (adrenal and ovarian autoantibodies). If these tests indicate that a pituitary problem seems likely, then the next step will be to have a special scan – an MRI – of the pituitary gland to see what the problem is.

Patient: *what sort of pituitary problem might it be?*

Doctor: we don't know yet, but if there is a problem in the pituitary, then the most likely cause is a benign tumour.

Questions from the examiner

Examiner: *how would you manage this patient if the underlying diagnosis is Addison's disease?*

Doctor: I would start the patient on replacement glucocorticoids (ie hydrocortisone) and mineralocorticoid (ie fludrocortisone).

Examiner: *what else would be important in the management of a patient with Addison's disease?*

Doctor: I would want to educate them regarding 'steroid sick day rules', recommend that they wear a MedicAlert bracelet and carry a steroid card, and consider providing them with intramuscular glucocorticoids for use in emergencies.

Key point

Steroid deficiency can kill – all patients with Addison's disease must be educated about steroid sick day rules and advised to wear a MedicAlert bracelet and carry a steroid card.

Further discussion

Visual field defects in pituitary disease

The classical visual field abnormality in a patient with a pituitary macroadenoma causing optic chiasmal compression is bitemporal hemianopia. However, it is important to remember that pressure on the optic chiasm from below initially results in a superior quadrantanopia (either unilateral or bilateral), before progressing to a complete bitemporal field defect. By contrast, a mass arising in the suprasellar region and primarily compressing the chiasm from above (ie a craniopharyngioma) is likely in the early stages to be associated with an inferior quadrantanopia.

1.3.7 Young man who has 'not developed'

Instruction

Mr Nigel Duncan, an 18-year-old student, presented to his GP with an upper respiratory tract infection and was noted to lack facial and axillary hair, as well as a general absence of secondary sexual characteristics. Initial investigations found his testosterone level to be very low.

What is the likely diagnosis and how should he be investigated?

Introduction

The importance of the history in this case is first to establish whether the patient is prepubertal, suggesting failure of onset of puberty rather than pubertal arrest (although there is overlap between these conditions, they should be considered as distinct clinical entities) and, secondly, to try to identify the underlying cause. Table 8 outlines the main groups of disorders associated with male hypogonadism, a term that denotes deficiency of both testosterone secretion (from Leydig cells) and sperm production (by the seminiferous tubules).

Beginning the encounter

Doctor: hello, my name is Dr A. I understand that you have been found to have low testosterone levels. Is this correct?

Patient: *yes.*

Doctor: before we get onto the details of this, can you tell me if you have any other medical problems such as chronic illnesses during childhood, visual problems, poor sense of smell (anosmia), previous cranial radiotherapy or testicular infections, trauma or surgery? Do you have a family history of hormone problems or other diseases?

Patient: [gives list (with doctor politely but firmly discouraging lengthy detail).]

Doctor: are you taking any tablets or medications? Specifically, have you ever taken prescribed or non-prescribed testosterone preparations, or other types of steroids (anabolic or glucocorticoids), or opioid-based painkillers? Do you take any recreational drugs? How much alcohol do you drink?

Patient: [gives details.]

Focused history

Doctor: going back to the low testosterone measurement, I would like to ask some specific questions.

> How often do you shave, and are you able to grow a beard?
> Do you have axillary and pubic hair?
> Has your voice become lower with age?
> Do you have regular morning erections?
> Is your libido normal?
> Do you have any children?
> Do you find it difficult to build muscle?
> Have you lost or gained significant body weight recently?
> How much do you exercise?
> Have you developed any breast tissue?
> Have you experienced breast tenderness or milky nipple discharge?

These questions will provide useful clinical context and may immediately establish whether this is a case or delayed puberty or pubertal arrest.

Doctor: I would now like to ask you some additional specific questions.

> Have you noticed any change in your vision?
> Do you suffer from headaches?
> Do you often feel tired and lethargic?
> Do you experience flushing?

These questions will help to establish whether the patient's symptoms may be related to pituitary or testicular dysfunction.

Focused examination

General

Observe for evidence of long-standing hypogonadism including an absence of facial/body hair, and fine wrinkles around the corners of the eyes and mouth. Observe body habitus and muscularity. Is there evidence of chronic liver disease?

Endocrine

Check for:

> an impaired sense of smell (Kallmann's syndrome)
> eunuchoid habitus (ie span greater than height, and heel to pubis distance greater than pubis to crown), which is common in those in whom hypogonadism precedes puberty, eg Klinefelter's syndrome
> gynaecomastia – indicates a decrease in the androgen:oestrogen ratio.

Assess pubertal development

The Tanner staging system allows for an objective assessment of sexual maturity. In recognition of the differing actions of adrenal androgens and gonadal steroids, it distinguishes between genital and pubic hair development in boys, and breast and pubic hair development in girls. In routine clinical practice assessment is performed by comparing the patient's development with that described on Tanner scale charts or images. It is most unlikely that these will be available in PACES, or that you would be expected to perform such intimate examination, but you should explain what you would do (with a chaperone present) in routine clinical practice to the examiner.

In routine clinical practice the presence of bilateral descended testes should be confirmed by palpation and testicular volume assessed with an orchidometer – in PACES offer to do this, but anticipate that the examiner will not wish you to proceed.

Assess pituitary status

Check for features suggestive of a pituitary tumour, eg bitemporal quadrantanopia/hemianopia, Cushing's syndrome, galactorrhoea, hypopituitarism.

Questions from the patient

[Assuming that there is no obvious reason for the patient to have a low serum testosterone:]

Patient: *why do I have a low testosterone?*

Doctor: I'm not sure. A low testosterone measurement may be due to problems with the pituitary gland (hypogonadotrophic hypogonadism) or testes (hypergonadotrophic hypogonadism).

Patient: *how will you work out what the cause is?*

Doctor: in the first instance I will arrange for blood tests, including measurement of some specific hormones to confirm the low testosterone measurement and identify the source of the problem (paired measurements of testosterone and gonadotrophins). In some instances (eg Klinefelter's syndrome) a genetic test (karyotype analysis) may be required.

Key point

Measurement of serum gonadotrophins (eg luteinising hormone (LH) and follicle-stimulating hormone (FSH)) will distinguish primary hypogonadism (high LH/FSH) from secondary hypogonadism (low LH/FSH).

Patient: *will I need any tests other than these blood tests?*

Doctor: depending on results of the initial blood tests, I may recommend additional blood tests to further assess the function of the pituitary gland, which is a small gland in the brain that is very important for producing hormones. I may also want to do a special scan – an MRI – to look at the pituitary gland. Sometimes a benign tumour of the pituitary can be the cause of the problem. Sometimes a low testosterone level is associated with reduced bone density and increased fracture risk, so I will also request a special type of X-ray known as a bone density scan.

Questions from the examiner

Examiner: *if this patient has confirmed hypogonadism how will you manage him medically?*

Doctor: this patient is likely to be a candidate for testosterone replacement therapy. Testosterone replacement is most commonly delivered using gel (popular, although care needed to avoid transfer to partner or children), or intramuscular depot injection (3–4 weekly or 3 monthly depending on preparation), and occasionally by implant. Oral preparations are not recommended as it is rarely possible to achieve therapeutic blood levels with this mode of delivery. It is also important to consider future fertility and in some patients initial, or subsequent, gonadotrophin therapy (eg with human chorionic gonadotrophin (hCG) and recombinant FSH) may be required (this should be supervised by a fertility clinic).

Examiner: *if this patient is started on testosterone replacement therapy how will you monitor him?*

Doctor: monitoring of testosterone replacement should include measurement of serum testosterone levels (most commonly trough, but sometimes post-dose with transdermal therapy), liver chemistry and full blood count (haemoglobin and haematocrit) and, where appropriate, prostate surveillance (digital rectal examination and prostate-specific antigen (PSA)).

1.4 Acute scenarios

1.4.1 Coma with hyponatraemia

Case history

A 72-year-old woman, previously well apart from mild hypertension, has been admitted comatose to the emergency department. A CT of her head has shown no abnormality, but her plasma sodium is 112 mmol/L (normal range 137–144).

Introduction

Key point

The unconscious patient

The first priority in dealing with the unconscious patient is to check and initiate management for problems with:

- airway
- breathing
- circulation.

Next consider rapidly reversible causes:

- hypoglycaemia – check finger-prick blood glucose: if <2.5 mmol/L give 50 mL of 50% IV dextrose
- opioid overdose – look for pin point pupils and slow respiratory rate: if present give 0.4 mg naloxone IV.

Next:

- Check Glasgow Coma Scale (GCS) score, noting in particular whether there are lateralising neurological signs, which suggest a focal cause (eg stroke).

For further details of the approach to the unconscious patient, see the *Acute medicine* book of Medical Masterclass.

The priority in this case is clearly to ensure safe management of the unconscious patient, as described in the key point box above. This will include consideration of the possibility that the patient's coma and their hyponatraemia are not connected, although it is likely that they are.

There are many causes of hyponatraemia (Fig 11). When considering the differential diagnosis, consider the following:

- Is the patient hypovolaemic, euvolaemic or hypervolaemic? (See Fig 11.)
- Are there clues to any of the diagnoses listed in Fig 11 or Table 18?

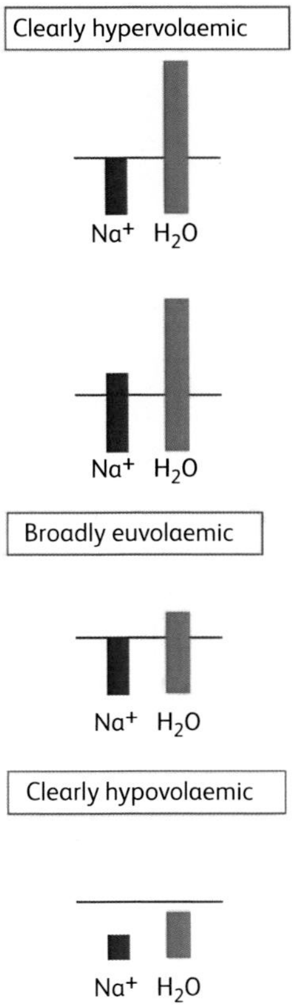

Clearly hypervolaemic

Na^+ H_2O

- Secondary hyperaldosteronism – cardiac failure, cirrhosis / liver failure, nephrotic syndrome
- Iatrogenic – inappropriate administration of 5% dextrose IV, eg postoperatively, or to a patient with acute kidney injury or chronic kidney disease

Na^+ H_2O

Broadly euvolaemic

- Diuretics (the patient may not be clearly hypovolaemic)
- Syndrome of inappropriate antidiuretic hormone secretion (SIADH)
- Glucocorticoid deficiency
- Hypothyroidism
- 'Sick cells'

Na^+ H_2O

Clearly hypovolaemic

Renal causes
- Diuretics
- Sodium-wasting renal diseases (including – rarely – cerebral salt wasting)
- Mineralocorticoid deficiency

Non-renal causes
- Excessive fluid losses – vomiting, diarrhoea, burns, sweating

Na^+ H_2O

Fig 11 Hyponatraemia and volume status.

History of the presenting problem

This woman is unconscious, hence any history will need to be obtained from others – has anyone accompanied her to the hospital? Extract as much information as you can from the GP's letter (if any) and the notes of ambulance/paramedical staff.

General circumstances

It is essential to get the following information:

> Who found her?

> What were the circumstances?

> When was she last seen before that, and did she appear to be well?

> Is there any possibility that she has taken an overdose?

> If anyone who knows anything about the woman is available, then ask for details that might give a clue as to why she is hyponatraemic and why she might be comatose (if the two are different).

Table 18 Causes of inappropriate secretion of antidiuretic hormone (ADH)

Source of ADH	Type of problem	Example
Ectopic ADH production	Malignancy	Small-cell lung cancer
Inappropriate pituitary ADH secretion	Malignancy	Lung cancer, lymphoma, prostate cancer, pancreatic cancer
	Inflammatory lung disease	Pneumonia, lung abscess
	Neurological disease	Meningitis, head injury, subdural haematoma, tumours, post surgery
	Drugs	Antidepressants (tricyclics, SSRIs), carbamazepine, chlorpropamide, phenothiazines (eg chlorpromazine), vincristine, cyclophosphamide, ecstasy
	Postoperative[1]	–
	Others	Nausea, pain, porphyria

1 Secretion of ADH is inappropriate to plasma tonicity, being driven by anaesthesia, nausea, pain and intravascular volume depletion, all of which are more powerful stimuli than plasma osmolality.
ADH, antidiuretic hormone; SSRIs, selective serotonin reuptake inhibitors.

Clues to other neurological problems

The neurological history is clearly of prime importance in someone who is comatose, since a neurological problem could cause coma in its own right, or in this case via hyponatraemia induced by the syndrome of inappropriate antidiuretic hormone secretion (SIADH). Try to ascertain whether there is a history of:

- head injury
- epileptic fits
- fluctuating consciousness – suggestive of subdural haematoma
- headaches – especially with features of raised intracranial pressure
- symptoms suggestive of meningeal irritation – neck stiffness, photophobia.

Clues to the cause of hyponatraemia

Think of the conditions listed in Fig 11 and Table 18 as you seek information about the following.

Drug history

Diuretics are a very common cause of hyponatraemia and this woman has hypertension. Is she taking a diuretic? Enquire also about drugs associated with SIADH (Table 18), exogenous steroids and nephrotoxins. Check with the patient's GP, and if possible ask a relative or friend to bring all her bottles of pills into the hospital for you to check.

Key point

Diuretics are the commonest cause of hyponatraemia.

Fluid loss and fluid intake

Has the woman had diarrhoea or vomiting? What has she been drinking, and how much? Psychogenic polydipsia is extremely unlikely in a woman of this age, most commonly being seen in young psychiatric patients when excessive intake is frequently concealed.

Features of malignancy

Has there been weight loss, unexplained fever, night sweats, pruritus? Could this woman have lung cancer complicated by SIADH? What are her current or past smoking habits? Have there been features of lung cancer (eg cough, haemoptysis, dyspnoea, pleuritic chest pain) or symptoms of pulmonary inflammation (eg purulent cough, dyspnoea)?

Other aspects

Is there a history of cardiac, renal or liver failure, or of nephrotic syndrome? Is it possible that there is an endocrine or metabolic cause of hyponatraemia? Consider the following:

- Hypothyroidism – ask about weight gain, cold intolerance, constipation (see Section 2.3.1).
- Hypopituitarism – enquire specifically about symptoms of hypocortisolism, hypothyroidism and hypogonadism (see Section 2.1.8).
- Addison's disease – unexplained hyponatraemia in a comatose patient should prompt immediate consideration of primary hypoadrenalism (see Section 2.2.6).
- Porphyria – abdominal pain, neuropathy and preceding psychiatric illness in a younger patient are important clues to the diagnosis (see Section 2.5.2).

Examination

In any comatose patient the immediate priorities are:

- check airway, breathing, circulation – insert oropharyngeal airway if tolerated
- check Glasgow Coma Scale (GCS) score.

In this case pursue the cause of hyponatraemia as follows.

Key point

Assessment of fluid volume status

Accurate assessment of fluid volume status is vital in diagnosis of the cause of hyponatraemia. Check carefully for:

- Hypovolaemia – the most reliable signs are a low jugular venous pressure (JVP) and postural hypotension.
- Hypervolaemia – look for a raised JVP, gallop rhythm, pulmonary oedema, peripheral oedema.

Look specifically for evidence of:

- infection/inflammation as a cause of SIADH – pyrexia
- malignancy/other chest pathology as a cause of SIADH – clubbing (malignancy or pyogenic lung disease), lymphadenopathy (malignancy), Horner's syndrome (Pancoast's tumour)
- features suggesting an endocrine cause of hyponatraemia – buccal/palmar/generalised pigmentation (Addison's disease), myxoedematous features (hypothyroidism), diminished body hair (hypopituitarism).

A full physical examination is required:

- Cardiac – is there evidence of heart failure?
- Respiratory – many chest pathologies can be associated with SIADH.
- Abdominal – in particular looking for signs of chronic liver disease.
- Neurological – check for neck stiffness, photophobia, papilloedema or any focal neurological deficits.

Investigation

In any comatose patient immediate investigations should exclude hypoglycaemia, opioid toxicity and significant head injury. This woman has already had a CT, which is normal, and attention is clearly focused on her hyponatraemia.

Hazard

Beware factitious hyponatraemia

Although highly unlikely in this case, factitious hyponatraemia (eg sampling from a 'drip' arm) and pseudohyponatraemia (eg in the context of gross hyperlipidaemia) should be excluded before embarking on more detailed investigations, particularly if the serum sodium is extremely low and yet the patient seems well.

Routine tests

Check full blood count (anaemia, leucocytosis, low haematocrit); creatinine, urea and electrolytes (dehydration, hypoadrenalism); glucose; liver biochemistry (intrinsic liver disease, malignancy); calcium (malignancy); phosphate (renal tubular defects); free thyroxine (FT4) and thyroid-stimulating hormone (TSH) (primary or secondary hypothyroidism); chest radiograph (lung pathology, including malignancy; aspiration).

Paired plasma (or serum) and urine osmolalities

This is a key investigation in the diagnosis of SIADH, but must be supplemented by measurement of a 'spot' urinary sodium concentration, since SIADH cannot be diagnosed in the face of a low urinary sodium concentration. The latter indicates that the kidney is conserving sodium because of 'real' or 'perceived' intravascular volume depletion, which will stimulate antidiuretic hormone (ADH) release and water retention that is appropriate for the defence of intravascular volume, although inappropriate for regulation of osmolality. With reference to Fig 11 note the following:

- Urinary sodium concentration is generally low (<10 mmol/L) in non-renal causes of hyponatraemia, eg when the kidney is responding appropriately to real (eg vomiting) or perceived (eg hyperaldosteronism of cardiac failure) intravascular volume depletion.
- Urinary sodium concentration is generally high (>30 mmol/L) in renal causes of hyponatraemia (eg diuretics, sodium-losing renal disease).
- Intermediate urinary sodium concentrations (10–30 mmol/L) are difficult to interpret but should probably be regarded as indicating non-renal causes of hyponatraemia.

Key point

Criteria for the diagnosis of SIADH

- clinically euvolaemic
- true hyponatraemia (plasma sodium <135 mmol/L)
- low serum/plasma osmolality (<275 mosmol/kg)
- inappropriately high urinary sodium concentration (>30 mmol/L)
- less than maximally dilute urine (ie urine osmolality >100 mosmol/kg)
- normal adrenal, renal and thyroid function.

Hazard

SIADH should never be diagnosed if the urinary sodium concentration is low (<20 mmol/L); 20–30 mmol/L represents a grey zone for diagnosis.

Key point

Calculation of plasma osmolality

The measured plasma osmolality can be compared with a calculated value to exclude the presence of other osmotically active substance(s) in plasma:

Calculated osmolality = $\{([Na^+] + [K^+]) \times 2\} + [urea] + [glucose]$

This is most often useful in the context of poisoning, eg ethylene glycol (antifreeze) overdose.

Other investigations

These will be determined by your clinical findings: CT head scan is normal in this case; lumbar puncture may be appropriate.

Management

In any comatose patient the immediate priorities are:

- ensure protection of the airway
- give high-flow oxygen by face mask.

Hazard

Treatment of acute adrenal insufficiency in an emergency

If there is any suggestion of acute adrenal insufficiency, treatment with hydrocortisone (100 mg IV stat) must not be delayed. A serum sample should be saved for subsequent cortisol estimation (see Section 2.2.6), and the patient established on regular hydrocortisone replacement until biochemical testing has excluded hypocortisolism.

Specific management will depend on the underlying condition, and this should be treated vigorously whenever possible.

Acute symptomatic hyponatraemia

Urgent treatment is required if there are neurological complications attributable to hyponatraemia, as in this case, but even here it is important not to undertake too rapid a correction, which has been associated with irreversible and sometimes fatal central pontine and/or extrapontine myelinolysis. Treatment is as follows.

Key point

Beware calculations!

No formula can accurately predict the patient's response to giving hypertonic saline: all assume a 'closed system' and take no account of the patient's ongoing water losses, which are not predictable.

- Treatment with 3% saline, 2 mL/kg to a maximum of 100 mL, infused over 10–20 minutes (or 150 mL of 1.8% saline): this is likely to increase the serum sodium concentration by 1–2 mmol/L.
- Repeat 3% saline bolus once or twice until encephalopathy improves: hyponatraemic encephalopathy is unlikely if there is no clinical improvement following an acute rise in serum sodium of 5–6 mmol/L.
- Stop further therapy with hypertonic saline if: (1) the patient's symptoms resolve – they are awake, alert, responding to commands, with resolution of headache and nausea; (2) there is a rise in serum sodium of 10–12 mmol/L over 24 hours and 15–20 mmol/L over 48 hours.
- Monitor the serum sodium concentration every 1–2 hours while infusing hypertonic saline and replace hypertonic saline with 0.9% saline if the serum sodium is rising more quickly than desired.

Hazard

Treatment of severe hyponatraemia

Correction of symptomatic hyponatraemia with hypertonic saline requires very close monitoring – check serum sodium every 1–2 hours.

- Stop infusion of hypertonic saline when serum sodium >125 mmol/L (possibly sooner if neurological symptoms have improved) and institute appropriate ongoing measures (eg fluid restriction in SIADH while seeking/treating the underlying cause). Remember, the aim is to return the plasma sodium to a 'safe level' and not 'back to normal' – do not allow rapid correction into the normal range.
- The European Society of Endocrinology (in conjunction with the European Society of Intensive Care Medicine and the European Renal Association-European Dialysis and Transplant association) has published guidance (2014) on the use of infusions of 3% hypertonic saline for the treatment of patients with hyponatraemia and severe symptoms. Such management must only be undertaken by those with appropriate expertise in a high-dependency setting.

Key point

Giving hypertonic saline in hyponatraemia

- Infusion of hypertonic saline is potentially dangerous and should be restricted to those cases where hyponatraemia is causing neurological sequelae such as altered conscious level or fits. In these circumstances the plasma sodium will almost always be <120 mmol/L. If not consider other causes of coma.
- Administration of hypertonic saline must only be undertaken in a high-dependency or intensive-care setting, via a pump and with regular monitoring of plasma sodium levels (1–2 hourly).
- Hypertonic saline should not be given where there is an increase in total body sodium with oedema, eg in advanced liver disease.

Further comments

Chronic asymptomatic hyponatraemia

Chronic hyponatraemia is much commoner than acute hyponatraemia and is usually well tolerated, producing no clear-cut symptoms or symptoms that are rather vague. In this situation plasma sodium should always be corrected over days rather than hours, and there is no indication whatsoever for attempting to raise the plasma sodium rapidly.

- If hypovolaemic with no major symptoms from hyponatraemia – give IV 0.9% saline replacement cautiously until volume is restored, then restrict water intake if hyponatraemia persists.

- If euvolaemic or hypervolaemic with no major symptoms from hyponatraemia – restrict water to 750 mL per day or less, giving this as ice in aliquots through the day and ensuring that swabs are available to moisten the mouth. In those cases where the underlying cause cannot be corrected (eg lung cancer) demeclocycline or vaptan therapy may be useful, inducing a form of nephrogenic diabetes insipidus (DI) and reversing the inappropriate antidiuresis.
- Deal with precipitant, eg stop diuretics; diagnose and treat cause of vomiting.

Hazard

Chronic asymptomatic hyponatraemia should never be treated with hypertonic saline.

1.4.2 Hypercalcaemic and confused

Case history

A 73-year-old woman has been admitted from home. She was confused and dehydrated, with a Glasgow Coma Scale (GCS) score of 11/15. Initial blood tests sent on arrival revealed a serum calcium of 4.0 mmol/L (normal range 2.20–2.60).

Introduction

Hypercalcaemia typically gives rise to insidious symptoms and may go undetected for a considerable period of time before presenting acutely. Patients with hypercalcaemia who become confused tend not to drink, which conspires to produce a vicious circle of worsening dehydration and hypercalcaemia. This is a medical emergency: immediate treatment is required before investigation aimed at establishing the underlying cause (Table 1).

History of the presenting problem

As described in Section 1.1.1, enquire about:

- symptoms of acute hypercalcaemia – fatigue, lethargy, constipation, polyuria and polydipsia
- symptoms suggesting chronic hypercalcaemia – renal stones, abdominal pain, bone pain/fracture
- causes of hypercalcaemia – known malignancy, or symptoms suggestive of malignancy (eg weight loss, night sweats, change in bowel habit, haemoptysis or breathlessness); drug history, with particular reference to calcium and vitamin D-containing preparations, antacids, and thiazide diuretics.

Although it seems very likely that this woman's confusion is caused by hypercalcaemia, do not neglect to consider, even if only briefly, other possible diagnoses such as sepsis.

Examination

Key point

How unwell is the woman? Is she well, ill, very ill or nearly dead? If very ill or nearly dead, get help immediately.

Check vital signs – temperature, pulse, respiratory rate, blood pressure, pulse oximetry.

Conduct a thorough physical examination, looking in particular for signs of the following related to hypercalcaemia:

- intravascular volume depletion – postural tachycardia, postural hypotension, low JVP
- dehydration – reduced skin turgor, dry axillae, dry mucous membranes
- possible malignancy, eg cachexia, anaemia, digital clubbing, lymphadenopathy, breast lumps, chest signs, abdominal/rectal masses
- chronic hypercalcaemia – there are few signs, but band keratopathy (calcium deposition at the edge of the cornea at 3 and 9 o'clock) may be seen in chronic severe cases.

With regard to other causes of confusion, note in particular:

- any evidence of sepsis
- focal neurological signs – which would raise the possibility of cerebral metastases in this context.

Investigation

Key point

The higher the serum calcium, the more likely that there is a malignant cause.

Investigate as described in Section 1.1.1, but noting that this degree of hypercalcaemia is likely to be associated with:

- Acute kidney injury – electrolytes, creatinine and urea will require close monitoring.
- A malignant cause – hyperparathyroidism is unlikely to cause a serum calcium of 4.0 mmol/L. Look very carefully at the chest radiograph; make sure that all elements of a myeloma screen are pursued (immunoglobulins, serum electrophoresis, urinary Bence Jones proteins); and have a low threshold for pursuing further investigations if the history, examination or routine screening tests raise suspicions.

A CT brain should be organised urgently to look for cerebral metastases if the patient has any focal neurological signs.

Management

The aim must be to reduce the serum calcium level while a diagnosis is made and appropriate definitive treatment initiated.

Key point

Treatment of severe hypercalcaemia

The most important measures are:

- saline diuresis
- intravenous bisphosphonate, eg pamidronate.

Immediate treatment

The first aspect of emergency management should be rehydration with intravenous saline:

- Correct intravascular volume depletion – if this is present (postural tachycardia, postural hypotension, low JVP) give 0.9% (normal) saline rapidly until replete (as judged by correction of postural tachycardia/postural hypotension and elevation of JVP to normal).
- When intravascular volume depletion is corrected – insert urinary catheter to monitor urine output and give 0.9% (normal) saline IV at a rate sufficient to maintain a urinary output of 100–150 mL/hour. Consider giving furosemide 40–80 mg IV to encourage diuresis. Examine the patient regularly for signs of fluid overload or deficit, ensure accurate fluid charts are kept and adjust fluid input accordingly.
- Monitor the calcium level, and also levels of potassium and magnesium which may fall rapidly with rehydration. Replace as necessary.

Other calcium-lowering measures

- Bisphosphonates – following initial rehydration, the drug of first choice for most patients is disodium pamidronate. A dose of 60–90 mg, depending on the magnitude of hypercalcaemia, is administered by IV infusion over 2 or more hours. Calcium levels typically fall over the next few days. The hypocalcaemic effect may persist for up to 6 weeks; further doses can be given as required.
- Calcitonin (initially 5–10 IU/kg per day – in divided doses) – a relatively weak agent, but safe and a useful alternative antiresorptive agent that is suitable for acutely lowering serum calcium levels in severe hypercalcaemia because of rapid action (4–6 hours). Its beneficial effects are short-lived, however, with most patients becoming refractory to treatment within a few days.
- Denosumab – an option for patients in whom bisphosphonates are contraindicated (eg severe renal impairment) or have failed.
- Glucocorticoids (eg prednisolone 20–40 mg per day) – limited use, except in hypercalcaemia associated with granulomatous diseases (eg sarcoidosis) and lymphoma.

1.4.3 Thyrotoxic crisis

Case history

A 38-year-old woman has been brought to the emergency department with palpitations and a high fever. She had undergone treatment for a dental abscess just 24 hours prior to admission.

On examination she was restless and tremulous, with 'staring eyes' and an obvious goitre. Vital signs included temperature 40°C, pulse 180 beats per minute and BP 95/60 mmHg.

Her friend who brought her to hospital reported that she had not been well for several months and seemed to have lost a significant amount of weight, but had refused to see her GP.

Introduction

Thyrotoxic crisis (thyroid storm) is a rare but life-threatening complication of thyrotoxicosis/hyperthyroidism that is typically seen in previously undiagnosed or inadequately treated patients.

Hazard

Even with appropriate management the mortality rate of thyrotoxic crisis (storm) approaches 20%.

History of the presenting problem

A brief history should be taken focusing on features that would support the clinical suspicion of thyrotoxicosis (see Section 2.3.2), but ensuring that an open mind is kept with regards to other potential causes of this presentation, although none apart from thyrotoxic crisis would explain all features of the presentation (eg primary cardiac disease, septicaemia following treatment of dental abscess). Enquire specifically about:

- symptoms of thyrotoxic crisis – weight loss, heat intolerance, sweating, palpitations, diarrhoea, tremor and anxiety/agitation/irritability.
- factors that can precipitate a thyrotoxic crisis – intercurrent illness (eg sepsis, surgery), radioiodine therapy, pregnancy (eg toxaemia) and drugs (eg thyroxine, amiodarone, iodine-containing radiographic contrast media).

Hazard

Thyrotoxic crisis (storm) leads to apathy, hypotension, seizures, coma and death if not treated appropriately.

Examination

The approach to the examination of the very ill patient is described in the *Acute medicine* book of Medical Masterclass, but in this case you would obviously look for features that would be consistent with a diagnosis of thyrotoxic crisis as follows.

- General – agitation, anxiety, restlessness; tremor; skin usually warm and moist. Hyperpyrexia is a feature of thyrotoxic crisis but does not necessarily indicate infection, although this should always be looked for.
- Cardiovascular compromise – sinus tachycardia is usually greater than 140/min in thyroid crisis (storm); fast atrial fibrillation or supraventricular tachycardia are common, as found in this case. Establish whether cardiac failure is present – raised JVP, gallop rhythm, pulmonary oedema and peripheral oedema.
- Neurological/psychological – altered consciousness, frank psychosis, delirium, seizures and coma can all be seen in thyrotoxic crisis.

Findings that might indicate the likely cause of the thyroid pathology are:

- signs of Graves' disease – exophthalmos, lid retraction and lid lag
- goitre (as in this case) – if present, what are its characteristics (smooth, nodular, painful) and is there an associated bruit?
- vitiligo – associated with autoimmune thyroid disease.

Investigation

Hazard

Thyrotoxic crisis is a clinical diagnosis

There are no laboratory criteria to diagnose thyrotoxic crisis – the levels of thyroid hormones are the same as in uncomplicated hyperthyroidism. Start treatment immediately if the clinical diagnosis is thyrotoxic crisis – do not delay while waiting for laboratory confirmation.

Check the following immediately:

- full blood count (anaemia, leucocytosis or leucopenia); electrolytes, creatinine and urea (dehydration, electrolyte imbalance, renal failure); glucose (hypoglycaemia or hyperglycaemia); liver and bone biochemistry (abnormalities of liver function, hypercalcaemia); thyroid function tests (free thyroxine (FT4), free triiodothyronine (FT3) and thyroid-stimulating hormone (TSH))
- ECG – to confirm rhythm and check for evidence of ischaemia
- chest radiograph – looking for evidence of pulmonary oedema or consolidation
- blood and urine cultures, urinalysis – to identify potential sites of infection
- arterial blood gases – to look for hypoxia and metabolic acidosis.

Further investigations will be determined by the findings on clinical examination and the results of initial investigations. If and when the diagnosis of thyrotoxicosis is confirmed biochemically, then attention should turn to identifying its cause (see Section 2.3.2).

Management

Hazard

Danger of cardiovascular collapse

Patients with thyrotoxic crisis (storm) are at risk of cardiovascular collapse, may require sedation to facilitate effective management, and should be managed on a high-dependency unit / intensive care unit.

Immediate and acute management

General supportive measures

Emergency resuscitation is the priority:

- check airway, breathing, circulation
- administer high-flow oxygen via reservoir bag
- establish intravenous access and take bloods as indicated above
- begin active cooling and give paracetamol – not aspirin, which may displace thyroid hormones from thyroid-binding globulin and exacerbate the situation
- commence appropriate antibiotics where there is suspicion/evidence of an infective precipitant (as is likely in this case given the recent history of a dental abscess)
- consider sedation if the patient is particularly anxious/confused – chlorpromazine is the drug of choice
- commence strict fluid balance – consider placement of a urinary catheter to help monitor output. If the patient is hypotensive, determine whether this is due to absolute or relative hypovolaemia (eg in a patient with systemic sepsis), which requires fluid resuscitation, or whether it is secondary to cardiac failure, requiring treatment with diuretics and digoxin (also see below for the role of beta-blockers in this setting).

Specific antithyroid measures

These are described in detail in Section 2.3.2 but in brief include the use of the following.

- Beta-blockers – give propranolol 1 mg IV, repeated every 20 minutes as necessary up to total of 5 mg; or give 40–80 mg per os (PO) four times daily. Be careful if the patient has cardiac failure. Esmolol, a short-acting beta-blocker, can be used as an infusion for immediate management of sympathetic overactivity.
- Propylthiouracil or carbimazole – propylthiouracil is the preferred drug as it both blocks further synthesis of thyroid hormones and inhibits

peripheral conversion of T4 to T3, but it is often not immediately available on the wards, whereas carbimazole usually is. If propylthiouracil is available, give a loading dose of 600 mg PO or by nasogastric (NG) tube, then 200 mg every 6 hours. If propylthiouracil is not available (you should not wait for 'the pharmacy to get some up to the ward tomorrow'), give carbimazole 20 mg, then 20 mg three times daily.

> Lugol's iodine (saturated solution of potassium iodide), five drops every 6 hours, or sodium iodide (0.5–1 g every 12 hours by IV infusion), beginning at least 1 hour after starting propylthiouracil/carbimazole (not before as thyroid hormone stores may be increased) to inhibit further release of thyroxine.

Hazard

Iodide must *not* be given until organification has been blocked.

> Steroids – eg hydrocortisone 100 mg IV, then 100 mg every 6 hours; or dexamethasone 2 mg PO four times daily.

Consider digitalisation if the patient is in fast atrial fibrillation, but note that higher doses of digoxin than usual may be needed due to relative resistance to the drug.

Further management

Definitive treatment for thyrotoxicosis will be required, eg surgery or radioiodine under antithyroid drug and beta-blocker cover.

1.4.4 Adrenal crisis

Case history

A 35-year-old woman was brought into the emergency department having collapsed in the supermarket. On arrival her vital signs included temperature 38°C, pulse 115 beats per minute and BP 75/50 mmHg. Oxygen saturation was 93% on air, and capillary blood glucose was 2.9 mmol/L.

She was unable to give any history, but was carrying a steroid alert card in her purse that stated a diagnosis of Addison's disease. Rapid analysis of serum electrolytes revealed Na^+ 128 mmol/L (normal range 137–144) and K^+ 5.5 mmol/L (normal range 3.5–4.9).

Introduction

Hazard

Adrenal crisis (acute adrenal insufficiency)

Failure to recognise and treat this condition promptly can lead to death. Fluid resuscitation and administration of parenteral hydrocortisone are life-saving and must be given immediately, before detailed assessment and investigation. If hypoglycaemia is present, then this should be corrected with intravenous dextrose.

History of the presenting problem

A collateral history will be required in this case: details of the 'collapse' should be sought from any source available – relatives, friends or other witnesses who were present, and from the GP's or paramedics' notes. The differential diagnosis of 'collapse' is wide, but in this case a great deal of evidence points towards the diagnosis of adrenal (Addisonian) crisis, in which case important aspects to explore include:

> Precipitants for adrenal crisis – most commonly there will be some prodromal illness, eg intercurrent infection; very rarely there may be a history of flank pain attributable to adrenal infarction.

> Drug/medication history – is there any suggestion of non-compliance with steroid replacement therapy? Has there been any recent change to medication, eg introduction of an enzyme-inducing agent (eg phenytoin, carbamazepine or rifampicin), without a corresponding increase in the regular hydrocortisone regimen?

> Symptoms of adrenal crisis – many cases develop non-specific abdominal pain in conjunction with nausea and/or vomiting, also restlessness and confusion, which in some patients can progress to stupor and coma.

Examination

In any comatose or semi-comatose subject, the immediate priorities are:

> check airway, breathing, circulation: insert oropharyngeal airway if tolerated

> check Glasgow Coma Scale (GCS) score.

See the *Acute medicine* book of Medical Masterclass for further information.

In the patient with suspected adrenal crisis take particular note of the following:

> hypotension/postural hypotension – these are expected in all cases

> infection – look for evidence of an infective precipitant

> features of Addison's disease – look for hyperpigmentation, also for vitiligo.

Investigation

In any comatose or semi-comatose patient immediate investigations should exclude hypoglycaemia, opioid toxicity and significant head injury (see the *Acute medicine* book of Medical Masterclass for further information).

Routine investigations

Key point

Investigations in adrenal crisis

Typical findings are hyponatraemia, hyperkalaemia and hypoglycaemia.

Check full blood count (anaemia, leucocytosis, low haematocrit); electrolytes, creatinine and urea (dehydration, hypoadrenalism); glucose (hypoglycaemia or hyperglycaemia); liver biochemistry (intrinsic liver disease); calcium (may be elevated); thyroid function tests (may be associated hypothyroidism). Blood and urine cultures, urinalysis and chest radiograph may identify potential sites/sources of infection. Arterial blood gases – to confirm adequate oxygenation and look for acidosis. CT of the head is indicated if there is focal neurology, or if the cause for the reduced conscious level remains unclear.

Further investigation

This will be determined by the findings on clinical examination and the results of initial investigations. In this case of a subject with known chronic adrenal insufficiency (Addison's disease) and suspected adrenal crisis, take a serum sample for later cortisol measurement before giving hydrocortisone – an inappropriately low serum cortisol in this setting is diagnostic of acute adrenal insufficiency.

Management

Key point

Shoot first – ask questions afterwards

Give steroids immediately if you suspect Addisonian crisis.

Immediate and acute management

Emergency resuscitation must be instigated as a priority:

- check airway, breathing, circulation
- administer high flow oxygen via reservoir bag
- establish intravenous access and take bloods as indicated above
- commence fluid resuscitation with 0.9% (normal) saline: infuse 1 L stat and then re-examine. If hypotension/postural hypotension persist, then repeat rapid infusion. Stop rapid infusion when hypotension abolished, JVP normal or signs of fluid overload develop (basal crackles)
- give intravenous hydrocortisone 100 mg stat, followed by 50–100 mg IV 6-hourly
- if the patient is hypoglycaemic, give intravenous dextrose (eg 10% dextrose bolus, followed by drip if necessary at a rate sufficient to keep the glucose >5 mmol/L), but do not give more than is needed and avoid using 5% dextrose because this is likely to exacerbate hyponatraemia
- consider infection – have a low threshold for starting antibiotics.

Further management

Confirm the reason for the recent collapse. Continue parenteral hydrocortisone until there has been a sustained clinical improvement, at which point a transition back to oral hydrocortisone can be undertaken. While the patient is receiving high-dose hydrocortisone there is no need for additional mineralocorticoid replacement, but fludrocortisone must be re-commenced once the dose of hydrocortisone is lowered.

Key point

Avoiding adrenal crisis

Before discharge the patient should be seen by an endocrinologist or endocrine nurse specialist to ensure that she:

- is aware of 'sick day rules', ie when and how to increase her hydrocortisone dose at times of illness and stress, and that she should seek medical attention urgently if she is unable to take her medication orally (eg due to recurrent vomiting)
- has an 'emergency pack' – whenever possible the patient and her next of kin should be provided with an emergency pack and taught how to administer intramuscular hydrocortisone at home in the event of an emergency, while stressing that this is not a substitute for seeking medical help
- is advised how to titrate her dose of hydrocortisone back down to an appropriate maintenance regimen if she is being discharged on an increased dose to cover an intercurrent illness.

Most patients with chronic adrenal insufficiency will already be under long-term endocrine follow-up: an appointment should be made to allow for early review following discharge.

1.4.5 'Off legs'

Case history

A 72-year-old woman was brought to the emergency department by ambulance after one of her carers found that she had not moved from her chair between 9.30am, when the carer left after helping her to get up in the morning, and 8pm, when the carer returned to help her go to bed.

She gave a history of widespread aches and pains and increasing immobility, with particular difficulty in getting to her feet, that had been getting worse over the last 2–3 months.

Her past medical history was unremarkable, apart from long-standing idiopathic epilepsy that was well controlled on treatment. She was not febrile or confused.

Introduction

The differential diagnosis of immobility in older people is broad. The principal clue in this history is the suggestion of proximal muscle weakness with pain. The history, examination and investigation should be directed at confirming this, while excluding other causes of weakness.

A broad differential diagnosis for proximal muscle weakness is provided in Table 19. A possible clue to the diagnosis in this case is the history of epilepsy and long-term anticonvulsant therapy, raising the possibility of osteomalacia exacerbated by hypercatabolism of vitamin D. Polymyalgia rheumatica is a common cause of aches and pains in older people, predominantly involving the muscles of the shoulder and pelvic girdle, and clearly needs to be considered, but it does not cause weakness.

History of the presenting problem

Given the wide range of causes of weakness in older people, and of proximal myopathy in particular, a full history is required, beginning with careful consideration of the symptoms themselves.

Weakness, aches and pains

The brief details given suggest that weakness might be due to proximal myopathy. The first priority is to confirm that weakness is indeed present, and that limitation of movement is not simply caused by pain. It would be misleading to probe extensively for causes of proximal myopathy if, in fact, the problem was due to lumbar back pain with nerve root irritation. Ask carefully about the following if the details do not emerge spontaneously.

- Is the problem in one or both legs? If the problem is much worse in one leg than the other, then a myopathic condition is less likely and attention should focus on 'local' disorders, eg spinal pain with nerve root irritation; undeclared hip fracture.
- How did the problem start? Onset after a fall would suggest a traumatic cause of pain, perhaps fracture of a lumbar vertebra or hip.
- Which things are most difficult to do? When is the weakness most noticeable? With proximal myopathy there is particular difficulty when rising from a chair or on climbing stairs. With rheumatic disorders, eg rheumatoid arthritis, there may be diurnal variation, with pain and stiffness worst in the morning and then improving as the patient 'warms up'.
- What is the distribution of aches and pains? Pain in the affected muscles is suggestive of an inflammatory myositis or diabetic amyotrophy. Pain in a radicular distribution suggests nerve root irritation. Generalised aches and pains are in keeping with osteomalacia, and also with the much commoner condition of polymyalgia rheumatica, but polymyalgia rheumatica does not cause weakness, although pain and stiffness in the affected muscle groups may be perceived as such. Are there any other symptoms to support this diagnosis? Ask about headaches, scalp tenderness, visual symptoms and jaw or tongue claudication.

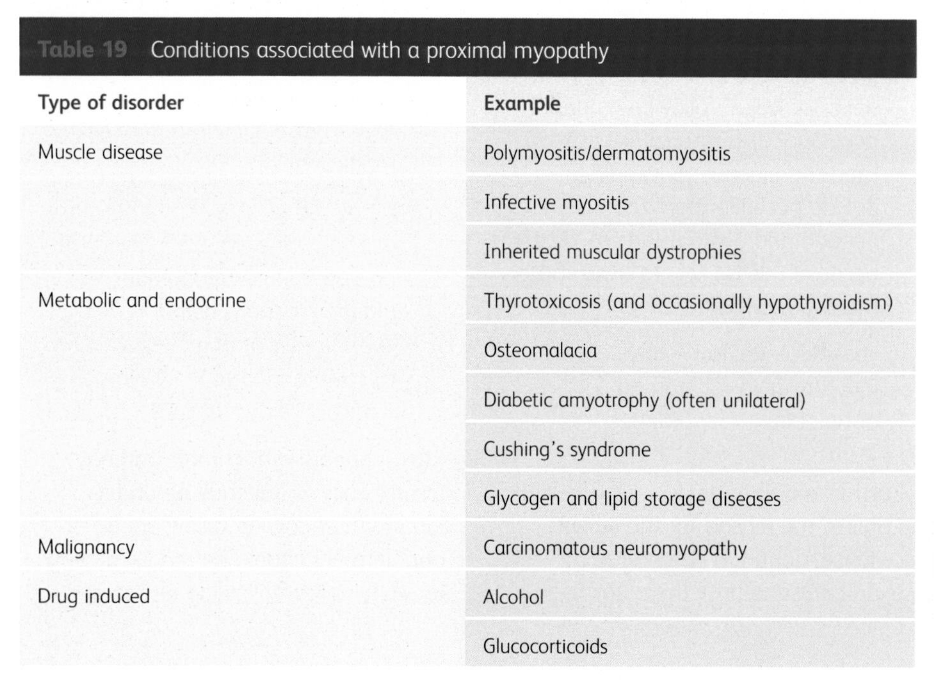

Table 19 Conditions associated with a proximal myopathy

Type of disorder	Example
Muscle disease	Polymyositis/dermatomyositis
	Infective myositis
	Inherited muscular dystrophies
Metabolic and endocrine	Thyrotoxicosis (and occasionally hypothyroidism)
	Osteomalacia
	Diabetic amyotrophy (often unilateral)
	Cushing's syndrome
	Glycogen and lipid storage diseases
Malignancy	Carcinomatous neuromyopathy
Drug induced	Alcohol
	Glucocorticoids

Key point

Polymyalgia rheumatica does not cause weakness.

Neurological symptoms

Weakness could have a primarily neurological cause. Focal symptoms, eg weakness of one leg rather than both as in this case, would imply focal pathology, eg unrecognised stroke. The presence of sensory symptoms, eg numbness and paraesthesia, would suggest neuropathy rather than myopathy.

Other symptoms

A full systems enquiry is needed, particularly bearing in mind the diagnoses listed in Table 19.

- Osteomalacia – a history of long-term anticonvulsant use (eg phenytoin, barbiturates or carbamazepine) but also of renal disease, previous gastric surgery, coeliac disease or other malabsorptive states should prompt consideration of osteomalacia. Older people and Asian populations are at particular risk, reflecting reduced skin synthesis of vitamin D together with dietary insufficiency (see Section 2.5.5).
- Polymyositis/dermatomyositis – ask about arthralgia/arthritis, especially affecting the small joints of the hand (~50% of cases), and rashes, eg the heliotrope rash of dermatomyositis.
- Diabetic amyotrophy – typically seen in older patients (especially men), who present with asymmetrical weakness and wasting of the quadriceps muscles. Ask about pain in the thigh, which often keeps the patient awake at night.
- Cushing's syndrome – many of the features of Cushing's syndrome (eg easy bruising, thin skin, weight gain) may be mistaken for part of the 'normal ageing process' (see Section 2.1.1).
- Thyroid disease – ask about the classical symptoms of thyrotoxicosis and hypothyroidism (see Sections 2.3.1 and 2.3.2), but remember that the clinical features may be modified in older people.

Other relevant history

Check for a history of asthma, arthritis or other illnesses requiring long-term corticosteroid treatment. Ask about alcohol intake: this could be a pseudo-Cushing's syndrome presentation (see Section 2.1.1).

Examination

A full physical examination will be required, with particular emphasis on the following:

- Hydration state – this woman has been immobile at home and therefore vulnerable to dehydration: check for postural tachycardia, postural hypotension, low JVP (features of intravascular volume depletion) and reduced skin turgor, dry axillae, dry mucous membranes (features of dehydration).
- General features – is there anything to support any of the diagnoses listed in Table 19?
- Legs – does she have a proximal myopathy (wasting, weakness)? Consider and look for features of stroke/other upper motor neurone lesion, spinal cord compression, radiculopathy/nerve root/peripheral nerve lesion (see the *Clinical skills for PACES* book of Medical Masterclass). Could she have fractured a hip? Look for shortening and external rotation of a leg.

> **Hazard**
>
> **Hip fractures are common and not always obvious**
>
> Always check that an older patient who is admitted 'off legs' has not broken their hip – aside from being bad medicine to miss such a diagnosis, it is embarrassing!

Investigation

Investigations will be directed by the findings on careful history and examination, but assuming a proximal myopathy has been confirmed, carry out the following.

Routine tests

Many of the causes of proximal myopathy can be screened for with simple blood tests. These include: full blood count (anaemia suggestive of chronic disease or iron deficiency); erythrocyte sedimentation rate (ESR)/ C-reactive protein (CRP) (raised in inflammatory muscle diseases or polymyalgia rheumatica); electrolytes, creatinine and urea (renal failure, severe hypokalaemia); glucose; creatine kinase (raised in inflammatory muscle disease and hypothyroidism); liver chemistry (low albumin in malabsorption, raised alkaline phosphatase in osteomalacia); calcium, phosphate (low/low normal in osteomalacia); TSH (suppressed in thyrotoxicosis and elevated in hypothyroidism).

Chest radiograph – look for evidence of malignancy.

Further tests

Other investigations will depend on clinical suspicion and the results of routine tests.

- Osteomalacia – perform the following:
  - parathyroid hormone raised (also in renal osteodystrophy)
  - 25-hydroxyvitamin D_3 typically low, although 1,25-dihydroxyvitamin D_3 may be normal
  - radiological studies (see Section 2.5.5)
  - when malabsorption is suspected as a cause – measure serum folate, vitamin B_{12} and ferritin; prothrombin time to screen for vitamin K malabsorption; and anti-tissue transglutaminase antibodies as indicators of coeliac disease.
- Cushing's syndrome – perform 24-hour urinary free cortisol estimation and/or dexamethasone suppression test (see Section 2.1.1).

Further tests including electromyography and/or muscle biopsy will be required if these investigations fail to identify a cause for the proximal myopathy.

Management

Osteomalacia

Treatment is with vitamin D supplementation (see Section 2.5.5). The most commonly used daily regimen of combined calcium and 4–800 units of vitamin D will not be sufficient, and high-dose oral therapy (eg 10,000 units ergocalciferol on alternate days) or parenteral therapy (eg 300,000 units ergocalciferol intramuscularly (IM)) may well be required. In cases of renal failure or malabsorption, the vitamin D metabolites alfacalcidol (1alpha-hydroxycholecalciferol) or calcitriol (1,25-dihydroxycholecalciferol) are usually required, often with dietary calcium supplements.

Other diagnoses

Other causes of proximal myopathy will require specific treatment: for thyroid disease see Section 2.3; for Cushing's syndrome see Section 2.1.1; for diabetes mellitus see Section 2.6; for polymyositis/dermatomyositis see the *Rheumatology and clinical immunology* book of Medical Masterclass.

Endocrinology: Section 2

2 Diseases and treatments

2.1 Hypothalamic and pituitary diseases

2.1.1 Cushing's syndrome

The clinical disorder resulting from prolonged exposure to supraphysiological levels of glucocorticoid.

Aetiology

Key point

Aetiology of Cushing's syndrome

This is most easily thought of in terms of adrenocorticotropic hormone (ACTH)-dependent and ACTH-independent causes (Table 20). The term 'Cushing's disease' refers exclusively to those cases arising as a consequence of ACTH-secreting corticotroph adenomas of the pituitary gland, as described in 1932 by Harvey Cushing, an American neurosurgeon.

Table 20 Aetiology of Cushing's syndrome

Type	Example
ACTH-dependent	Pituitary adenoma (Cushing's disease)
	Ectopic ACTH secretion
	Ectopic CRH secretion (very rare)
ACTH-independent	Exogenous glucocorticoid administration
	Adrenal adenoma
	Adrenal carcinoma
	AIMAH
	PPNAD (sporadic or associated with Carney complex)

ACTH, adrenocorticotropic hormone; AIMAH, ACTH-independent bilateral macronodular adrenal hyperplasia; CRH, corticotropin-releasing hormone; PPNAD, primary pigmented nodular adrenal disease.

Clinical presentation

The clinical features of Cushing's syndrome have often been present for some time before the diagnosis is made. Patients may have been treated for individual components of the condition, eg obesity, hypertension or diabetes before the 'penny drops' and the diagnosis is considered. Women may present with oligomenorrhoea and infertility, while children can exhibit isolated growth failure.

Physical signs

Patients often exhibit many, if not all, of the classical signs (Fig 12) of Cushing's syndrome, including:

- moon-like facies and plethora
- central (truncal) obesity ('orange on match-sticks')
- prominent supraclavicular fat pads and 'buffalo hump' (interscapular)
- acne, thin skin with easy bruising and purple striae (abdomen, thighs)
- hypertension
- muscle wasting and proximal myopathy
- hirsutism (due to excess adrenal androgen production in ACTH-dependent disease or adrenal carcinoma)
- kyphoscoliosis due to osteoporosis
- psychiatric features, eg emotional lability, depression, psychosis.

Key point

Patients with ectopic ACTH may not look typically Cushingoid

In patients with ectopic ACTH secretion the clinical picture is often modified, with wasting, cachexia and pigmentation more prominent, the latter reflecting very high circulating levels of ACTH.

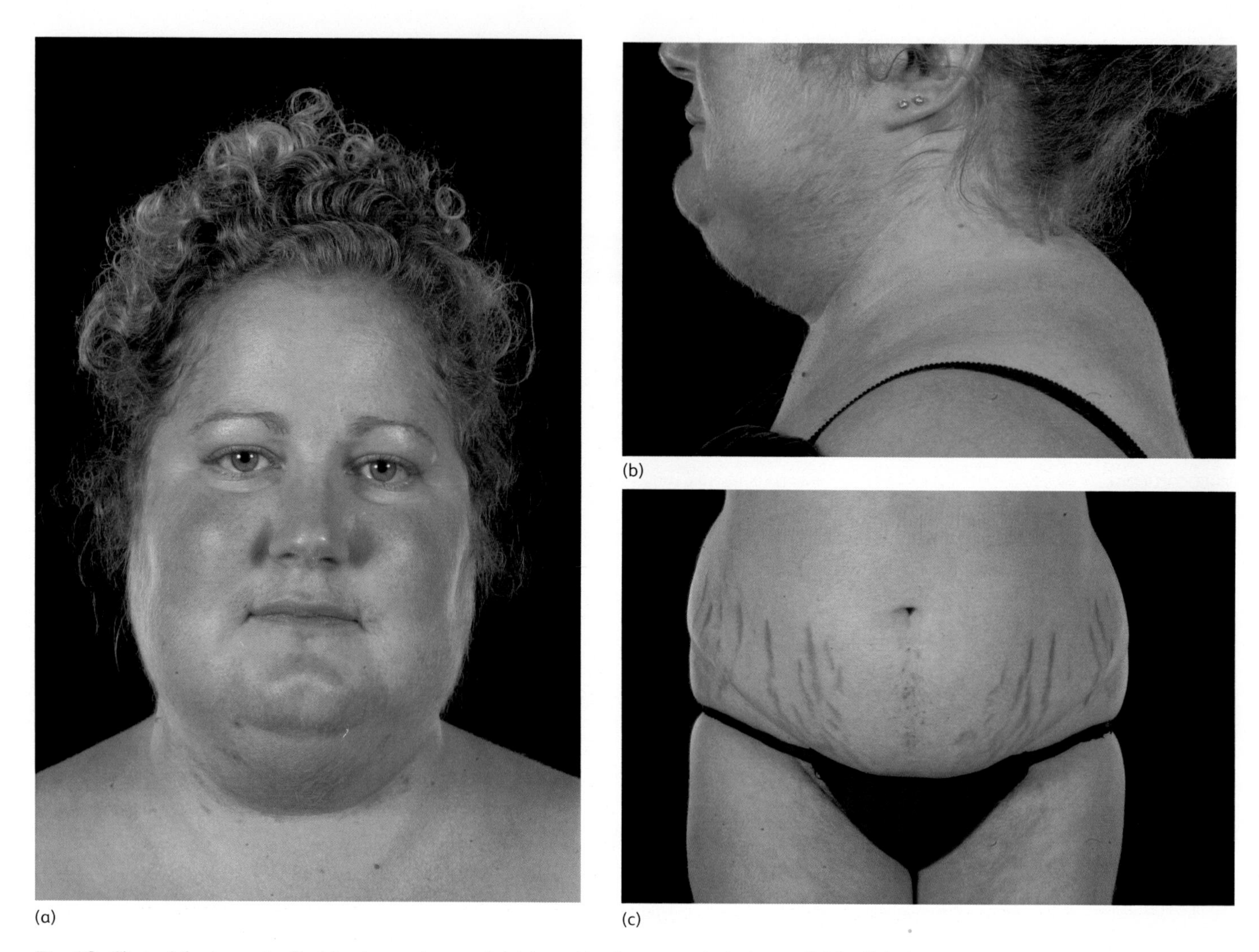

Fig 12 Clinical features in Cushing's syndrome. **(a)** Moon-like facies and plethora, **(b)** buffalo hump and hirsutism, and **(c)** purple striae.

Investigation

This should be approached in two stages:

- confirmation of the diagnosis
- definition of the aetiology.

Confirming the diagnosis

Most centres use one or more of the following for screening purposes, with confirmation / further investigation of positive results. Clinical index of suspicion is important when deciding whether a single 'rule out' test is sufficient, or whether to proceed to additional investigations (which is generally recommended in cases where there is a moderate or higher suspicion of hypercortisolism).

24-hour urinary free cortisol estimation

Ideally at least three collections of urinary free cortisol (UFC) should be performed.

Overnight dexamethasone suppression test

See Section 3.2.1.

Low-dose dexamethasone suppression test

See Section 3.2.2.

Loss of diurnal cortisol variation

Measure cortisol at 9am and midnight – normal midnight serum/plasma cortisol, asleep, is <100 nmol/L (and in many instances actually <50 nmol/L). For subjects who are awake, a higher cut-off is used (~200 nmol/L). Alternatively, late-night salivary cortisol measurement offers an excellent reflection of the plasma free cortisol concentration and, due to the simple non-invasive collection procedure, can be conveniently performed at home.

Key point

Pseudo-Cushing's syndrome (physiologic/ non-neoplastic)

This is a disorder mimicking Cushing's syndrome, and sometimes seen in the setting of excess alcohol consumption or severe endogenous depression, in which the overnight and low-dose dexamethasone suppression tests and UFC estimation can be abnormal. However, other indices (eg mean corpuscular volume (MCV), gamma-glutamyltransferase) may suggest the underlying cause, and the cortisol response to insulin-induced hypoglycaemia (see Section 3.1.5) is preserved, contrasting with the subnormal response typically seen in Cushing's syndrome. In addition, the low-dose dexamethasone suppression test followed at its conclusion by a corticotropin-releasing hormone (CRH) test (see Section 3.1.2) has been proposed as a means of discriminating pseudo-Cushing's from Cushing's disease.

Key point

Cyclical Cushing's syndrome

This is a variant in which hypercortisolism occurs periodically. Serial UFC and/or late-night salivary cortisol collections, timed to when the patient is symptomatic, may help to establish the diagnosis. All subsequent testing must be completed when the patient is in an active phase of the disease.

Defining the aetiology

Once the diagnosis has been confirmed, tests are undertaken to establish the cause as follows.

Plasma ACTH

Distinguishes between ACTH-dependent and ACTH-independent causes.

ACTH-dependent cause

If an ACTH-dependent cause is suspected, consider the following:

- Selective venous sampling for ACTH: bilateral inferior petrosal sinus sampling with measurement of ACTH before and after CRH stimulation, provides a sensitive and specific means of discriminating Cushing's disease from the ectopic ACTH syndrome: an ACTH ratio of >2 (pre-CRH) or >3 (post-CRH) between inferior petrosal and peripheral samples is indicative of a pituitary source of ACTH. Furthermore, an intersinus gradient (between left and right or vice versa) of >1.4 aids lateralisation of an adenoma within the pituitary fossa in approximately two-thirds of cases.
- Imaging:
  - MRI pituitary – an adenoma can be identified in approximately 60–65% of patients with Cushing's disease, but MRI findings must be interpreted with care, since corticotroph adenomas may be too small to be detected, while pituitary incidentalomas (which are not clinically significant) are increasingly reported (up to 10% of normal individuals).
  - CT/MRI neck, chest and abdomen – although a good quality chest radiograph may identify a bronchial carcinoma or carcinoid tumour as the source of ectopic ACTH production, in virtually all cases detailed cross-sectional imaging is required.
  - Other – octreotide scintigraphy and positron emission tomography (PET) may help identify small tumours within the thorax or abdomen that are not visible with CT/MRI.
- Urea and electrolytes – unprovoked hypokalaemia (ie in the absence of diuretics or other confounding factors) favours an ectopic source, reflecting the tendency for ACTH (and hence cortisol) levels to be higher in this setting.
- High-dose dexamethasone suppression test – (see Section 3.2.3).
- CRH test – (see Section 3.1.2).

The latter two are now less commonly used, reflecting their relative lack of sensitivity and specificity when compared with bilateral inferior petrosal sinus sampling.

ACTH-independent cause

If an ACTH-independent cause is suspected, consider CT/MRI of the adrenal glands. Providing the patient is not receiving exogenous steroids, the main objective is to differentiate the possible adrenal causes, in particular adenoma (Fig 13) and carcinoma.

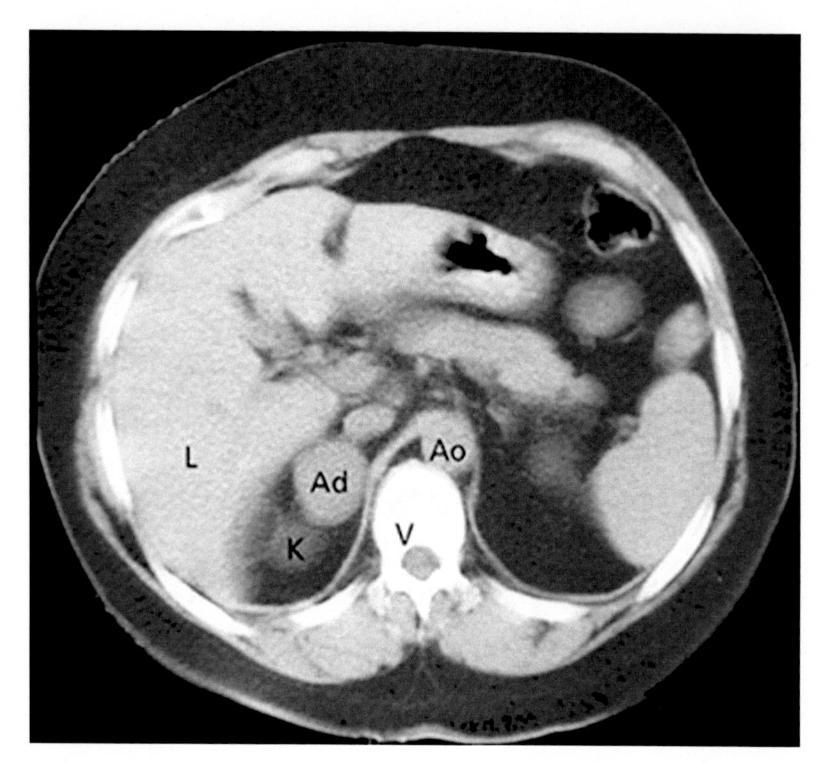

Fig 13 Adrenal adenoma. CT showing a right-sided adrenal adenoma (Ad) in a patient with Cushing's syndrome. Ao, aorta; K, kidney; L, liver; V, vertebral body.

Treatment

Initial treatment should aim to reduce circulating cortisol levels using drugs that block steroid biosynthesis, eg metyrapone or ketoconazole. Use of these agents should be restricted to clinicians with experience of dose titration and monitoring for adverse events (including rendering the patient hypoadrenal). Attention must also be paid to correcting hyperglycaemia and hypertension. Thereafter, specific treatment is directed at the source of hypercortisolism as follows:

- Pituitary adenoma – transsphenoidal adenomectomy or hemi-hypophysectomy. Radiotherapy may be required where surgical removal is incomplete or in patients judged unsuitable for surgery. The second-generation somatostatin receptor ligand pasireotide may help control hypercortisolism in some patients, but is associated with hyperglycaemia.
- Ectopic ACTH – surgical resection of tumour where possible.
- Adrenal tumour – surgical resection/debulking. For malignant tumours adjunctive medical treatment is often necessary in the form of the adrenolytic agent mitotane (1-(2-chlorophenyl)-1-(4-chlorophenyl)-2,2-dichloroethane), with or without systemic chemotherapy. Radiotherapy may also be useful in some instances.
- Exogenous corticosteroids – reduce dose or substitute steroid-sparing agents.

Key point

Bilateral adrenalectomy

This is reserved for those patients in whom the primary source cannot be localised, or when conventional treatment measures have failed. In Cushing's disease, however, this can be complicated by expansion of the corticotroph adenoma, leading to enhanced ACTH secretion, pigmentation and local problems due to tumour growth (so-called Nelson's syndrome). Pituitary irradiation may help to prevent/limit this.

Prognosis

Untreated Cushing's syndrome is often fatal, predominantly as a consequence of the complications of sustained hypercortisolism, including hypertension, cardiovascular disease, venous thromboembolism and susceptibility to infection. However, with modern surgical techniques, benign pituitary and adrenal tumours can often be removed in their entirety, thereby curing the patient.

2.1.2 Acromegaly

Acromegaly is the clinical disorder resulting from hypersecretion of growth hormone (GH).

Aetiology/pathophysiology

The majority of cases are caused by a pituitary adenoma. Of these, 70–75% are macroadenomas (>1 cm in diameter) and 25–30% are microadenomas (<1 cm in diameter). A small number of cases have been reported in which acromegaly results from ectopic growth hormone-releasing hormone (GHRH) secretion. Many of the growth-related aspects of this disorder are mediated by insulin-like growth factor (IGF)-1, which is produced by the liver in response to GH, while GH itself has direct metabolic effects, eg induction of insulin resistance (see the *Physiology* section of Medical Masterclass book 1).

Epidemiology

The incidence of acromegaly is estimated at approximately three to five cases per million people per year, with a prevalence of 40–70 per million. Patients are typically diagnosed in their early middle age, although the onset of disease, and hence symptoms, often predates the diagnosis by 5–15 years.

Clinical presentation

The diagnosis of acromegaly is often first raised by a clinician, dentist or optometrist, who encourages the patient to seek advice for changes that they had attributed to 'ageing'. Commonly reported symptoms include:

- an increase in the size of the hands and feet (often noted as changes in ring and shoe size respectively)
- coarsened facial features, altered bite and prominence of the jaw (prognathism)
- features of carpal tunnel syndrome
- snoring – reflecting sleep apnoea (which may be central or obstructive in aetiology)
- arthralgia
- sweating / greasy skin
- thirst and polyuria (reflecting impaired glucose tolerance or overt diabetes mellitus (DM))
- local symptoms due to the space-occupying effects of a pituitary tumour, eg headache and visual disturbance
- amenorrhoea, loss of libido or erectile dysfunction secondary to hypogonadotrophic hypogonadism.

Tubulovillous adenomas and colonic carcinoma, also thyroid nodules (including malignant), are recognised to be more common in patients with long-standing acromegaly.

GH excess before puberty is associated with gigantism.

Physical signs

Many of the symptoms reported by the patient correlate with specific signs on examination, including evidence of large 'spade-like' hands and feet, prognathism and coarsened facial features (see Figs 14 and 15). Hypertension is a common finding and long-standing untreated disease may lead to concentric myocardial hypertrophy and ultimately cardiac failure.

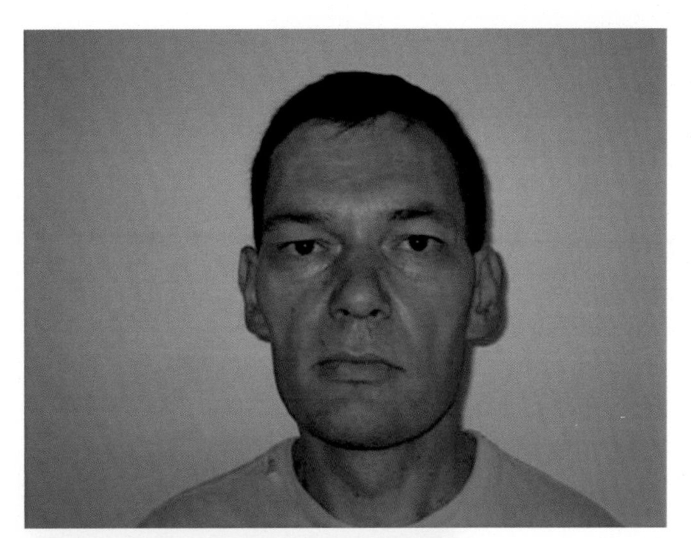

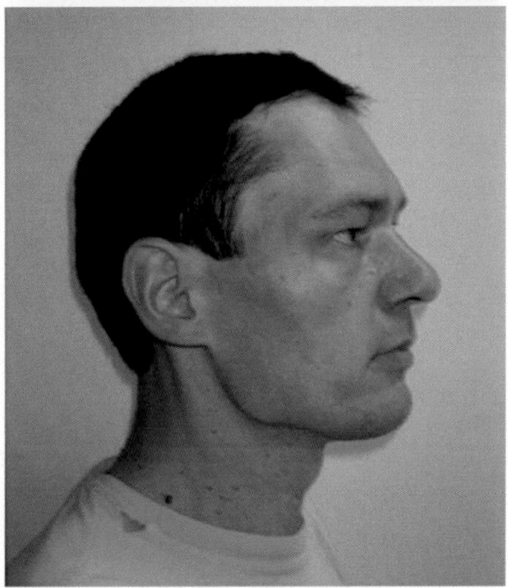

Fig 14 Acromegalic facies, showing the typical coarse facial features with prominent supraorbital ridges, prognathism and multiple skin tags.

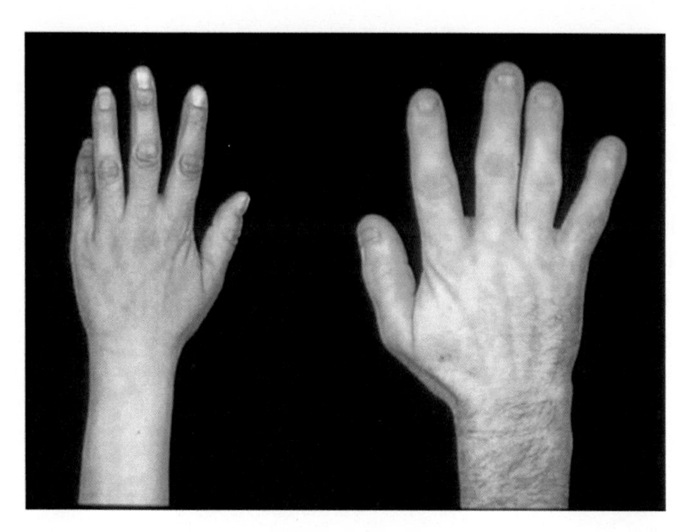

Fig 15 Acromegalic hands. Soft tissue growth leads to marked enlargement and thickening of the digits, such that the hand takes on a 'spade-like' appearance when compared with that of an unaffected subject.

Key point

Chiasmal compression

Careful examination of the visual fields is essential to check for evidence of a bitemporal quadrantanopia/hemianopia.

Investigation

Biochemical confirmation of the diagnosis is usually made using an oral glucose tolerance test (OGTT) (see Section 3.2.4) in which GH levels show a paradoxical rise or failure to suppress in response to a glucose challenge. In addition, the IGF-1 concentration is typically elevated above the age-related normal range.

Once the diagnosis has been established, imaging of the pituitary fossa should be carried out (preferably by MRI – Fig 16) and visual acuity and visual fields formally assessed (see Figs 19 and 20 in Section 2.1.4). A full appraisal of anterior pituitary function is also necessary (see Section 2.1.8). Remember that 20–25% of GH-producing tumours also co-secrete prolactin.

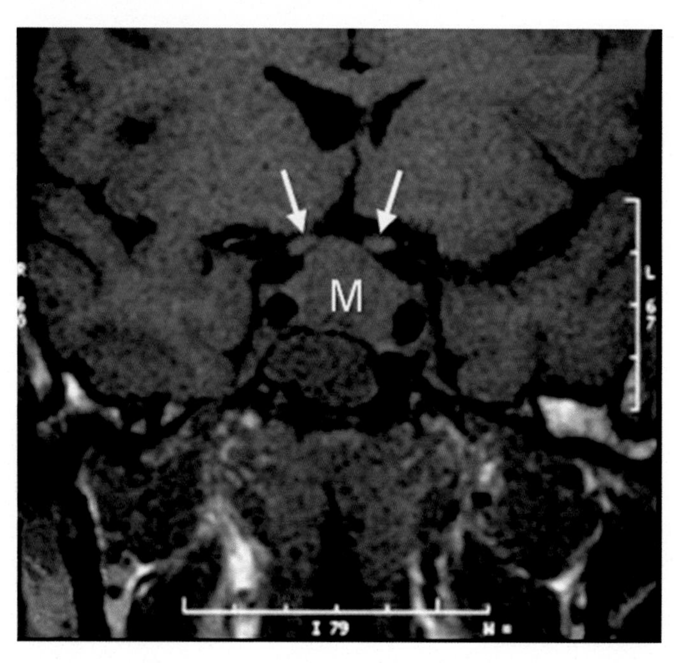

Fig 16 Pituitary macroadenoma in acromegaly. Coronal pituitary MRI demonstrating a macroadenoma (M) with suprasellar extension abutting the optic chiasm/nerves (arrows).

Treatment

Key point

Treatment goals in acromegaly

These are to effect a cure, preserve/restore remaining pituitary function, and reverse/control complications. Evidence suggests that, even if a cure can not be achieved, then providing that GH can be reduced to less than 1 μg/L and IGF-1 normalised, the life expectancy of patients with acromegaly approximates that of the general population.

Surgery

The first-line treatment for acromegaly is usually surgery. In experienced hands, transsphenoidal adenomectomy offers a surgical cure rate of approximately 80–90% for microadenomas, but drops to about 50% for macroadenomas. Recurrence rates are estimated at 2–7% over 5 years in patients originally considered to be 'cured' postoperatively.

Radiotherapy

Radiotherapy may be given if there is residual tumour postoperatively with persistent elevation of GH or if the patient is medically unfit for surgery. Note that although beneficial effects of conventional fractionated radiotherapy are usually evident within 12–24 months of treatment, it can take much longer for GH to fall to 'safe' levels (approximately 50% of patients achieve adequate suppression at 10 years). A similar proportion of patients at the same time point have hypopituitarism involving one or more trophic axes.

Stereotactic radiosurgery (in which the total treatment dose is administered in a single or small number of fractions) may be an option in some patients (eg when the residual tumour is not in close proximity to the optic chiasm) and can lead to more rapid control of GH excess.

Medical therapy

The role of medical therapy in the management of acromegaly is evolving. Traditionally it has been used as an adjunct to surgical treatment, as a 'holding exercise' in patients who have had radiotherapy, or as first-line treatment in patients who are unfit for surgery.

Somatostatin analogues (somatostatin receptor ligands)

First-generation somatostatin analogues (octreotide/lanreotide and their longer-acting preparations) improve symptoms in most patients and achieve good biochemical and tumour control, especially when used as an adjunct following incomplete surgical resection. Gastrointestinal side effects, including nausea and diarrhoea in the acute phase and an increased tendency to gallstone formation in the longer term, are relatively common.

The second-generation somatostatin receptor ligand pasireotide has recently been introduced and appears to offer greater efficacy, especially in patients whose condition is refractory to octreotide and lanreotide. However, it predisposes to hyperglycaemia, with many treated patients requiring commencement or escalation of antihyperglycaemic therapy.

Dopamine agonists

Dopamine agonists (eg bromocriptine, cabergoline) only suppress GH levels to acceptable 'safe' levels in <15% of patients, although they may be useful if the tumour co-secretes prolactin, or when combined with a somatostatin analogue.

Growth hormone receptor antagonist

Pegvisomant, a growth hormone receptor antagonist, lowers circulating IGF-1 levels in to the normal range in most patients, thereby improving many of the clinical features of acromegaly. However, it does not reduce pituitary tumour size nor lower GH secretion, and indeed during treatment GH levels can rise by up to 70% over baseline, which is probably caused by a loss of negative feedback due to the reduction in IGF-1. The drug is also expensive, and is given by daily subcutaneous (SC) injection. Currently, its use in the UK is limited to those patients who still have uncontrolled disease despite surgery, radiotherapy and somatostatin analogue therapy. However, in other countries it is increasingly being used at an earlier stage in the treatment pathway. Liver function tests must be monitored during treatment (especially in the early phase), and MRI repeated at 6 months or sooner if there are any concerns regarding tumour growth.

Other risk factors

Key point

Aggressive treatment of other risk factors is essential, including hypertension, DM, dyslipidaemia and sleep apnoea. Most centres also offer screening colonoscopy once the patient is of an appropriate age, as the risk of colon cancer in acromegalic subjects is about twice that of the general population.

A holistic approach

Other causes of morbidity should not be overlooked, with patients frequently requiring rheumatological/orthopaedic assessments, dental/maxillofacial opinions and psychological input or support to address problems of body image. They may find contact with The Pituitary Foundation (www.pituitary.org.uk/) helpful.

Follow-up

Following treatment, periodic MRIs are required, together with assessment of visual fields, the GH–IGF-1 axis, and anterior pituitary function.

Prognosis

The mortality of subjects with acromegaly has been estimated to be 1.5 to 4 times that of the general population, mainly due to an excess of cardiovascular, cerebrovascular and respiratory disease. Remember, the mortality rate approaches that of the general population if mean post-treatment GH levels are <1 μg/L and IGF-1 is normalised.

Disease associations

Acromegaly may be associated with parathyroid and pancreatic tumours as part of the multiple endocrine neoplasia type 1 (MEN-1) syndrome (see Section 2.7.1), or with cutaneous and cardiac myxomas, primary pigmented nodular adrenal disease and testicular tumours in the Carney complex.

2.1.3 Hyperprolactinaemia

Aetiology and pathophysiology

Varying degrees of hyperprolactinaemia are found in an array of physiological and pathological states (Table 21). Prolactin inhibits hypothalamic GnRH secretion and hence gonadal function.

Epidemiology

The incidence of prolactinoma has been estimated at 25–30 cases per 1 million people per year, with a prevalence of 500 per million. Microprolactinomas are diagnosed much more commonly in females (typically in the age range 20–30 years), and account for approximately one-third of all cases of secondary amenorrhoea in young women. Macroprolactinomas show no major gender difference.

Clinical presentation

- Females typically present with oligomenorrhoea/amenorrhoea and/or galactorrhoea. Some are referred with infertility. On questioning, they may report symptoms of reduced libido and vaginal dryness with dyspareunia.
- Males commonly present with larger tumours (macroadenomas) causing local pressure effects (eg headache or visual disturbance), although reduced libido/potency, subfertility and galactorrhoea may occur.

Physical signs

Always examine for visual field defects (bitemporal hemianopia) and check for galactorrhoea. Signs of other underlying disorders (eg chronic liver or renal disease) may be present.

Investigation

Prolactin

The finding of an elevated prolactin level should be confirmed on at least one separate occasion.

Key point

Prolactin level gives a clue to diagnosis

A prolactin concentration in excess of 5,000 mU/L usually indicates the presence of a prolactinoma, while values up to this level may be seen with several other conditions shown in Table 21. Pituitary stalk compression is typically associated with a serum prolactin <2,000 mU/L. Prolactin levels in excess of 10,000 mU/L are usually indicative of a macroprolactinoma.

Table 21 Causes of hyperprolactinaemia

Condition	Examples
Physiological	Pregnancy, lactation, postpartum, physical activity
Idiopathic	—
Stress	Venepuncture (up to two-fold rise)
Drugs	Dopamine antagonists, eg phenothiazines, metoclopramide
Liver/renal disease	Cirrhosis, chronic renal impairment
Hypothalamic–pituitary disorders	Microprolactinoma/macroprolactinoma, stalk disconnection syndrome (eg non-functioning tumour, infiltration)
Other endocrine disorders	Primary hypothyroidism (TRH is a trophic stimulus for prolactin release), PCOS

PCOS, polycystic ovary syndrome; TRH, thyrotropin-releasing hormone.

Routine bloods

Check renal, liver and thyroid function and carry out a pregnancy test if applicable. Follicle-stimulating hormone (FSH, luteinising hormone (LH) and oestradiol (E_2) may be useful in the differential diagnosis of oligomenorrhoea/amenorrhoea (see Section 2.4.3).

Radiological imaging

Unless there is an obvious explanation for mild hyperprolactinaemia, an MRI (or CT) scan of the pituitary fossa is indicated in virtually all cases (Fig 17). With modest hyperprolactinaemia, although a microadenoma may be identified, the principal objective of the scan is to exclude tumour/infiltration causing disconnection hyperprolactinaemia.

Visual fields / pituitary function

Formal assessment of visual fields (see Figs 19 and 20 in Section 2.1.4) and anterior pituitary function (see Section 2.1.8) may be indicated, depending on the clinical and MRI findings.

Differential diagnosis

The differential diagnosis of oligomenorrhoea/amenorrhoea is discussed in detail in Section 2.4.3.

Treatment

Hyperprolactinaemia not associated with a pituitary tumour

Treatment depends on the cause:

- Drug treatment that is causing hyperprolactinaemia is sometimes amenable to change, in liaison with the original prescriber (often a psychiatrist). Some of the newer antipsychotic agents (eg quetiapine) are much less prone to inducing hyperprolactinaemia.
- Women with unwanted postpartum galactorrhoea (and their partners) need to be advised to avoid nipple stimulation completely for a while, including 'checking to see if it is still happening'. Bromocriptine or cabergoline can be tried (see below), although some women find the benefit–side-effect profile unfavourable.
- Underlying renal or liver disease requires appropriate treatment.
- Idiopathic hyperprolactinaemia – dopaminergic agonists are often effective in restoring prolactin levels to normal in symptomatic patients.

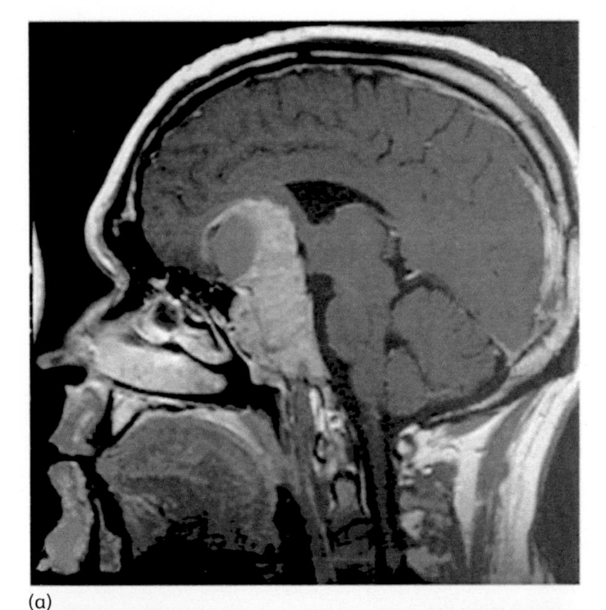

(a)

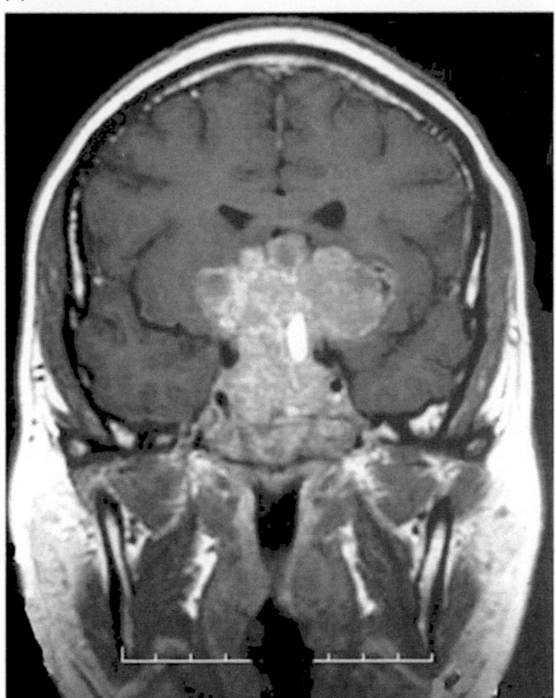

(b)

Fig 17 Macroprolactinoma. Sagittal **(a)** and coronal **(b)** MRIs demonstrating a massive macroprolactinoma. Note the heterogeneous appearance with cystic components and areas of haemorrhage (high signal).

Hyperprolactinaemia caused by a pituitary tumour

Prolactinomas are unusual among pituitary tumours in that the primary treatment for both microadenomas and macroadenomas is medical (providing there is no immediate significant threat to vision). Dopaminergic agonists (eg bromocriptine, cabergoline, quinagolide) are often highly effective in shrinking tumours, relieving symptoms and preserving/restoring anterior pituitary function.

Key point

Immediate side effects of bromocriptine

These include nausea, hypotension, nasal congestion and fatigue. These side effects can be minimised if the patient is started on a very low dose and advised to take the tablet with a snack at bedtime. Unfortunately, due to its short duration of action, bromocriptine requires bd or tds dosing. Longer-acting preparations (eg cabergoline and quinagolide) are therefore preferred in most cases, although again it is best to start with a low dose and gradually titrate up according to the serum prolactin level and tolerability. Even if the patient experiences significant side effects on starting treatment it is worth encouraging him/her to persist with therapy if possible, as tolerance usually develops over a relatively short period of time.

Key point

Long-term side effects of bromocriptine

Both bromocriptine and cabergoline have been linked with fibrotic disorders (cardiac valvular, pulmonary and retroperitoneal) when used at higher doses for a longer period of time. While these seem to be rare in patients being treated for hyperprolactinaemia, continued vigilance is advised in those likely to have significant drug exposure over time.

Hazard

Mood and behavioural changes with dopamine agonists

Hypersexuality, impulse control disorders and gambling have been linked with dopamine agonist therapy, and all patients (and where possible their relatives) should be advised to report any concerns immediately as treatment discontinuation may be necessary.

Microprolactinomas

Following normalisation of prolactin, follow-up is on an annual basis unless there is evidence of progression. Treatment may be withdrawn every 2–3 years to check for remission.

Macroprolactinoma

For those with macroprolactinomas, serial prolactin concentrations should be checked during the early stages of treatment and a repeat MRI performed (at 3–6 months) to monitor the response to medical therapy. Additional bone protection measures (eg bisphosphonate and/or calcium/vitamin D therapy) may be necessary in patients whose prolactin concentration does not come down sufficiently to permit restoration of gonadal function. Remember that exogenous oestrogens should be used with caution because of their potential trophic effect on the tumour, although many clinicians will permit oestrogen at hormone replacement therapy (HRT) doses once the tumour has shrunk in response to dopamine agonist therapy, and providing that there is no clinical, biochemical or radiological evidence to suggest tumour regrowth after commencing HRT. Surgical intervention (transsphenoidal adenomectomy) is generally preferred as second-line treatment in the UK. Radiotherapy is usually held in reserve for refractory tumours as it takes time to have an effect and often leads to hypopituitarism.

Non-functioning adenomas

Surgery is generally considered to be the treatment of choice (see Section 2.1.4). For mid-range prolactin concentrations (2,000–5,000 mU/L), when it is difficult to distinguish between a prolactinoma and a non-functioning adenoma, a trial of bromocriptine or cabergoline may be considered to see if the tumour shrinks in response to medical therapy.

> **Key point**
>
> **Serial imaging**
>
> The prolactin concentration is likely to come down with dopamine agonist therapy in patients with both prolactinomas and non-functioning adenomas, hence the size of the tumour must be monitored.

Contraception and pregnancy

> **Key point**
>
> **Risk of pregnancy**
>
> Women must be warned that they may get pregnant on starting treatment, even before they have a menstrual period.

Women who wish to defer pregnancy should use barrier contraception, although the combined oral contraceptive pill is also safe for use in women with microadenomas. Those with microprolactinomas who do not wish to conceive do not need to take bromocriptine or cabergoline but may require HRT or other agents such as a bisphosphonate to prevent osteoporosis. Again, contraceptive advice should be given. For those who elect for no treatment at all, then close surveillance of bone status with periodic dual-energy X-ray absorptiometry (DXA) scanning is mandatory if the patient is oligomenorrhoeic or amenorrhoeic.

Bromocriptine is generally considered safe in pregnancy. There are fewer published data with cabergoline, although reassuringly to date there is no evidence that it is detrimental to the pregnant woman or fetus. In contrast, some concerns have been raised regarding higher rates of miscarriage and fetal malformation in females taking quinagolide, and hence this should be avoided in pregnancy and in women trying to conceive.

In general, patients with microadenomas are usually advised to discontinue treatment once pregnancy is confirmed, as there is very little risk of clinically relevant tumour expansion during the remainder of the pregnancy. Most endocrinologists recommend clinical review during each trimester, but it is extremely rare for intervention to be required. Patients should be reassessed following cessation of breastfeeding. With macroadenomas some physicians recommend continuing bromocriptine throughout pregnancy, with avoidance of breastfeeding postpartum, in view of the small risk of clinically significant tumour expansion. Others withdraw bromocriptine but alert the patient to present immediately should they develop visual symptoms or a severe headache. Close follow-up is required in either setting.

Complications

Prolonged oligomenorrhoea/amenorrhoea is associated with an increased risk of osteopaenia and osteoporosis.

Disease associations

Prolactinomas may be associated with parathyroid and pancreatic tumours in the context of multiple endocrine neoplasia type 1 (MEN-1) syndrome (see Section 2.7.1).

2.1.4 Non-functioning pituitary tumours

Aetiology/pathophysiology

Non-functioning pituitary tumours ('chromophobe adenomas') are usually benign macroadenomas (>1 cm diameter).

Epidemiology

The incidence of clinically relevant non-functioning pituitary tumours is estimated at 10 cases per 1 million people per year.

Clinical presentation

Local pressure effects often result in a headache and visual disturbances. The patient may present with symptoms of hypopituitarism or hyperprolactinaemia due to pituitary stalk compression (fatigue, lack of well-being and hypogonadism). Alternatively, it may be an incidental finding following routine eye testing or a head scan for unrelated purposes.

Physical signs

It is important to check carefully for evidence of a bitemporal (sometimes only upper quadrantic) hemianopia. Features of hyperprolactinaemia and hypopituitarism may also be present (see Section 2.1.3).

Investigation

A full assessment should include tests of anterior pituitary function (see Section 2.1.8), an MRI of the pituitary fossa (Fig 18), and formal tests of the patient's visual fields (Figs 19 and 20) and visual acuity.

> **Key point**
>
> The serum prolactin result must be seen before surgery is considered in any patient with a suspected non-functioning tumour to exclude the possibility of a prolactinoma that would be amenable to medical therapy (see Section 2.1.3).

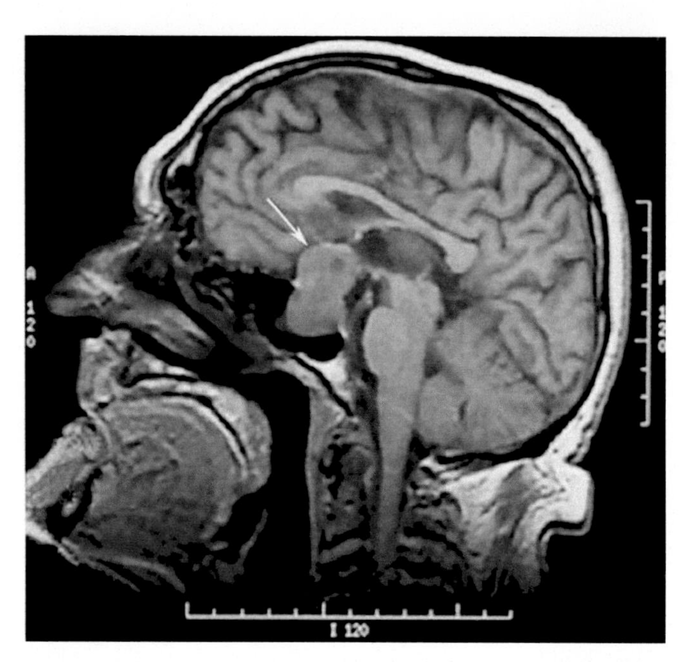

Fig 18 Non-functioning tumour. Sagittal MRI showing a large non-functioning tumour arising from the pituitary fossa with suprasellar extension (arrow) in a 45-year-old man presenting with a bitemporal visual field defect.

Key point

Visual field defects in pituitary disease

The classical visual field abnormality in a patient with a pituitary macroadenoma causing optic chiasmal compression is a bitemporal hemianopia (Fig 19). However, it is important to remember that pressure on the optic chiasm from below initially results in a superior quadrantanopia (either unilateral or bilateral) (Fig 20), before progressing to a complete bitemporal field defect. By contrast, a mass arising in the suprasellar region and primarily compressing the chiasm from above (eg a craniopharyngioma) is likely in the early stages to be associated with an inferior quadrantanopia (Fig 21).

Differential diagnosis

The differential diagnosis includes other sellar or parasellar masses, including cysts, craniopharyngioma, meningioma, metastatic, infiltrative or granulomatous disease and lymphocytic hypophysitis.

Treatment

A non-functioning macroadenoma in a patient with pressure symptoms or signs, particularly loss of visual fields, requires urgent surgical debulking (transsphenoidal or occasionally transcranial hypophysectomy). Surgery may lead to partial recovery of anterior pituitary function. Postoperative radiotherapy should be considered if tumour removal is incomplete or subsequently if the tumour recurs.

If there are no pressure symptoms or signs, it may be acceptable in some cases (eg frail, older patients) to adopt an expectant approach. Either way, patients require serial MRIs together with assessment of their visual fields, visual acuity and anterior pituitary function.

Complications

Operative complications include transient diabetes insipidus (DI) in 5–10% of patients, which may persist in 1–5%. Pituitary radiotherapy results in some degree of hypopituitarism in about 50% of patients after 10 years.

Prognosis

Hypopituitarism is associated with an increased mortality rate of at least twice that of the general population (see Section 2.1.8).

2.1.5 Pituitary apoplexy

Aetiology/pathophysiology

Clinically apparent pituitary apoplexy usually results from extensive infarction of a pituitary adenoma with haemorrhage. In ~50% of cases the event is spontaneous and the pathogenesis is not known. A quarter of all cases are associated with arterial hypertension

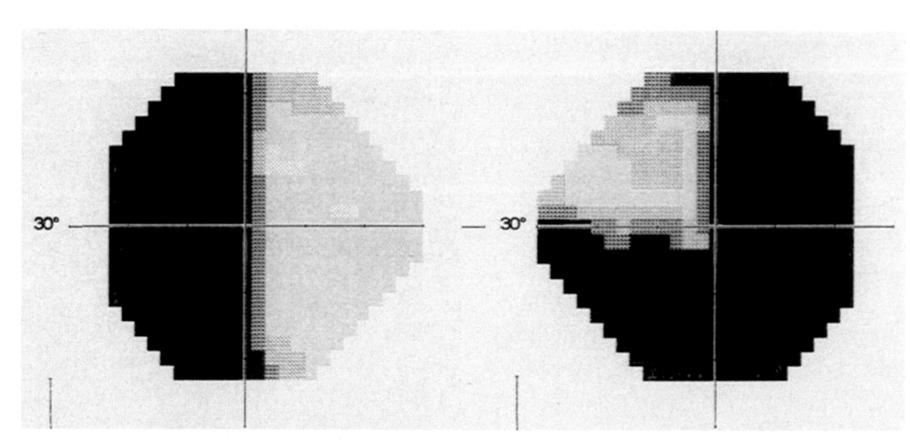

Fig 19 Bitemporal visual field defect. Computerised perimetry provides accurate details regarding visual field loss. In this particular patient there was also loss of the right inferior nasal field.

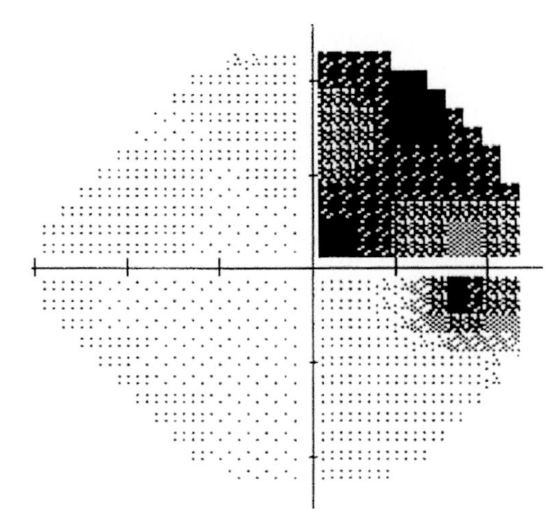

Fig 20 Right superior quadrantanopia. Note the blind spot just below the horizontal meridian.

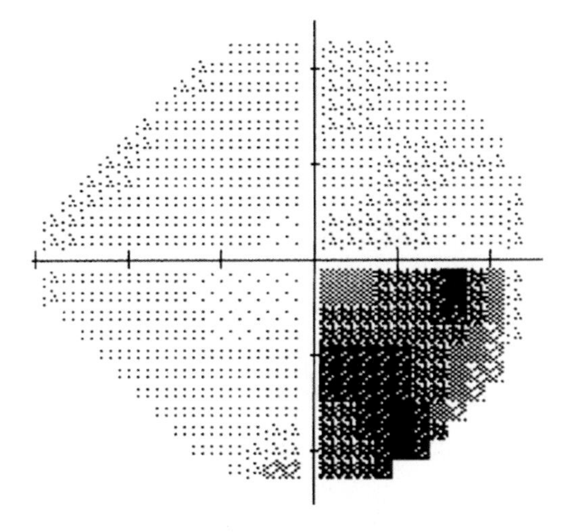

Fig 21 Right inferior quadrantanopia.

and occasionally it is also seen following head trauma or dynamic testing of pituitary function. Patients on anticoagulation are at increased risk, and prolactinomas treated with dopamine agonists often show signs of haemorrhage on follow-up MRI, although many of these episodes are clinically silent.

Epidemiology

The incidence of clinical apoplexy in surgically treated pituitary adenomas has been reported to range from 0.6 to 9.0%. Although it can occur at any age, the mean age at presentation is 45 years.

Clinical presentation

Common

The classical presentation is with a sudden onset retro-orbital headache and visual disturbances, including reduced visual acuity, visual fields, photophobia and ophthalmoplegia (most commonly due to a unilateral third nerve palsy). Symptoms may evolve over hours to days and may be mistaken for those due to subarachnoid haemorrhage.

Uncommon

Occasionally the onset is more insidious with nausea and vomiting, meningism and an altered level of consciousness. Symptoms of hypopituitarism or hyperprolactinaemia, including chronic lethargy, reduced libido, oligomenorrhoea or amenorrhoea, impotence and galactorrhoea may also be present.

Physical signs

Common

Visual field defects and reduced visual acuity, together with ophthalmoplegia (third, fourth or sixth nerve palsies) are common. The conscious level may be reduced.

Uncommon

Signs of underlying pituitary disease (eg acromegaly) are occasionally present.

Investigation

An urgent MRI (or CT) of the pituitary fossa should be performed (Fig 22). If this fails to demonstrate a pituitary haemorrhage, angiography may be necessary to exclude an intracranial aneurysm. There may be elevated numbers of red blood cells in the cerebrospinal fluid or even a frank aseptic meningitic picture. Blood samples for basic tests of anterior pituitary function should be taken, including cortisol, thyroid function tests (TFTs), prolactin, luteinising hormone (LH) and follicle-stimulating hormone (FSH), and oestrogen or testosterone.

Treatment

Emergency

Hazard

Assume adrenal insufficiency

Once the diagnosis of pituitary apoplexy has been considered, anterior pituitary dysfunction must be assumed. Establish venous access (taking bloods for urea and electrolytes, glucose and cortisol) and give IV hydrocortisone (100 mg) immediately prior to establishing on regular replacement (see Section 2.1.8). Fluid and electrolyte balance should be maintained.

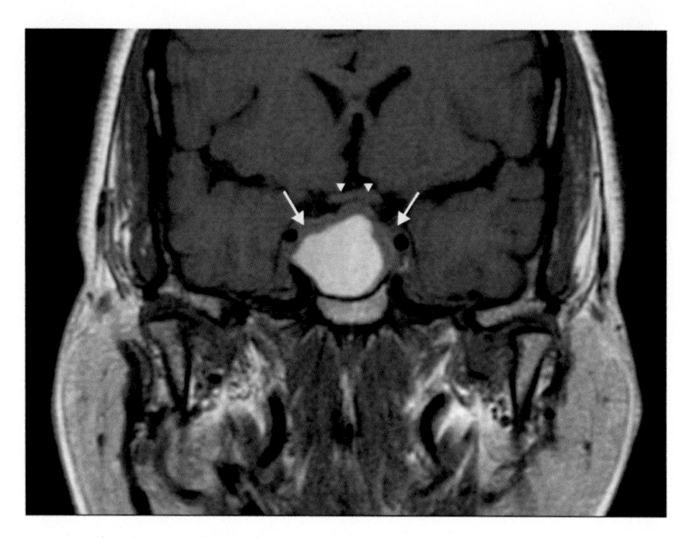

Fig 22 Pituitary apoplexy. Coronal MRI demonstrating extensive haemorrhage (high signal) within a pituitary adenoma in a patient who presented with acute onset of a severe headache and right third and sixth cranial nerve palsies. Note the splaying of the cavernous sinuses (arrows) particularly on the right side. The apex of the tumour abuts the optic chiasm (arrowheads).

Surgery

Urgent decompression is indicated if there is compression of the optic chiasm with visual loss or in patients with reduced consciousness or hemiparesis. In other circumstances a conservative approach may be adopted, particularly if there is no progressive neuro-ophthalmic deficit. Unlike the optic chiasm, the third, fourth and sixth cranial nerves are surprisingly resistant to compression, and spontaneous recovery of function is common even in cases that are managed conservatively.

Hormone replacement

A full endocrine evaluation should be made postoperatively, and appropriate hormone replacement therapies instituted with long-term follow-up (see Section 2.1.8).

Complications

Transient postoperative diabetes insipidus (DI) may occur. Overall mortality rates are not known.

2.1.6 Craniopharyngioma

This tumour, typically comprising both solid and cystic components, arises between the pituitary and hypothalamus.

Aetiology/pathophysiology

The exact origin remains uncertain, but most probably arise from Rathke's pouch. Although histologically benign, local invasion is a frequent finding and many recur after surgery.

Epidemiology

Craniopharyngiomas are estimated to account for between 5 and 12% of all intracranial tumours in childhood and about 1% of brain tumours in adults. The peak incidence is distributed bimodally, with the majority of cases occurring between 5 and 14 years of age, but with a second smaller peak after 50 years of age.

Clinical presentation

Childhood

Although endocrine deficiencies are common, most go unrecognised for years and only come to attention when the child presents with symptoms of raised intracranial pressure (eg headache, nausea and vomiting) or visual disturbance due to the mass effect of an expanding tumour. Growth hormone (GH) deficiency (leading to growth retardation) and diabetes insipidus (DI) are the most commonly encountered endocrine disturbances.

In older children, there may be pubertal delay or arrest as a consequence of gonadotrophin deficiency. Features of hypothalamic dysfunction, including disturbance of appetite or thirst, somnolence and abnormal temperature regulation are sometimes seen.

Adulthood

Endocrine manifestations (including DI) are a more common presenting feature in adulthood, although many cases exhibit symptoms of raised intracranial pressure.

Physical signs

Reduced visual acuity, and visual field defects as a consequence of chiasmal compression, together with papilloedema or optic atrophy (reflecting raised intracranial pressure) may be evident. Careful examination for evidence of pituitary insufficiency should be undertaken.

Investigation

Where possible, initial investigation of suspected cases should include the following.

MRI/CT

MRI (or CT) of the pituitary fossa and hypothalamus. Craniopharyngiomas exhibit a distinctive appearance with mixed solid and cystic components, and heterogeneity of enhancement (Fig 23). Intrasellar or suprasellar calcification is often evident on CT.

Ophthalmological review

To provide a baseline for monitoring the effects of treatment. Remember, that suprasellar craniopharyngiomas often compress the optic chiasm from above, leading to a bilateral inferior quadrantanopia in the first instance, before progressing to a full-blown

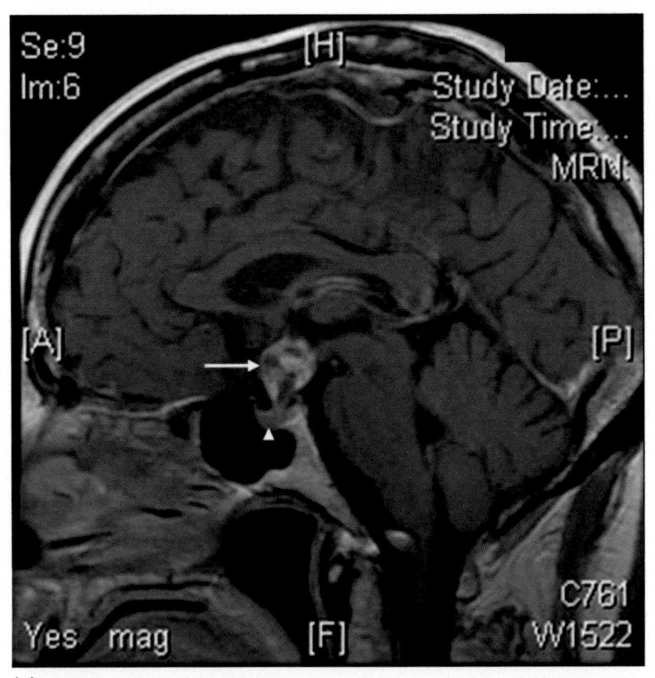

(a)

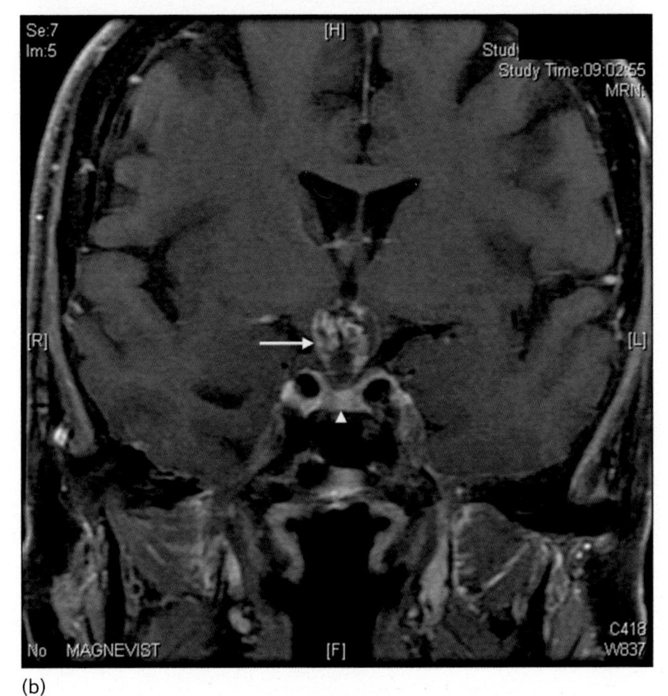

(b)

Fig 23 Craniopharyngioma. Sagittal **(a)** and coronal **(b)** MRIs showing the typical appearances of a craniopharyngioma (arrow) with mixed solid and cystic components. Note the normal pituitary gland (arrowhead), which can be identified separately from the suprasellar mass.

hemianopia. This is the opposite of the situation with a pituitary macroadenoma which compresses the chiasm from below thus leading to a superior quadrantanopia (Figs 19, 20 and 21).

Assessment of hypothalamic–pituitary function

Anterior pituitary function tests and paired urine and plasma osmolalities with serum urea and electrolytes (to look for evidence of DI). Approximately 80% of patients will have pituitary dysfunction at diagnosis.

Treatment

This is a rare condition and ideally patients should be referred to a centre with expertise in pituitary surgery.

Surgery

Up to 50% of cases have evidence of hydrocephalus on initial imaging and one-third require urgent surgical decompression. Transcranial subfrontal surgery may be required to allow full access to the tumour, although complete excision is frequently not possible. The cyst contents are classically said to have the appearance of 'engine/machine oil'.

Key point

Assume adrenal insufficiency

Unless there is clear biochemical evidence to the contrary, assume that all cases have pituitary insufficiency and ensure that adequate steroid cover is given perioperatively (see Section 2.1.8).

Postoperative

Short term

Postoperative care will require combined endocrine, neurological, psychological and ophthalmological input. Since complete surgical resection is usually not feasible, adjunctive radiotherapy is often necessary and has been reported to reduce recurrence rates from 80 to 20%.

Long term

Long-term follow-up is required to detect and treat regrowth of the tumour and any hypothalamic–pituitary dysfunction. Patients and their carers may find contact with The Child Growth Foundation (www.childgrowthfoundation.org/) and The Pituitary Foundation (www.pituitary.org.uk/) useful.

Prognosis

Poor prognostic features include young age and presentation with hydrocephalus. Although non-malignant, craniopharyngiomas often have a worse outcome in childhood than other malignant cerebral tumours.

2.1.7 Diabetes insipidus

Diabetes insipidus (DI) can be defined as the excretion of excessive or 'copious' volumes of urine (traditionally >3 L per 24 hours).

Aetiology/pathophysiology

Classically three types of DI are recognised:

1. Hypothalamic (cranial) DI (HDI) in which there is an absolute deficiency of antidiuretic hormone (ADH – vasopressin).
2. Nephrogenic DI (NDI) which is caused by resistance to the action of ADH in the collecting ducts.
3. Dipsogenic DI (DDI) due to excessive inappropriate fluid intake (ie primary polydipsia (PP)). DDI is sometimes referred to as psychogenic DI, although this term is not appropriate in all cases and is therefore best avoided.

The most common causes of each of these subtypes are shown in Table 22.

Hazard

Do not jump to assumptions

Pituitary adenomas are very rarely associated with DI prior to surgical intervention, hence it is important to keep in mind the other conditions listed in Table 22 when faced with a patient who presents with a pituitary mass and DI.

Table 22 Causes of diabetes insipidus

Condition	Type	Subtype	Examples
Hypothalamic DI	Primary	Idiopathic	–
		Genetic	AD, AR, DIDMOAD
		Developmental	Lawrence–Moon–Biedl syndrome, septo-optic dysplasia
	Secondary	Trauma	Post surgery (TSS, TCS), head injury
		Tumour	Craniopharyngioma, metastasis (especially breast, lung), germinoma
			(Very rarely pituitary macroadenoma)
		Inflammatory	Granulomata (eg sarcoidosis, TB, histiocytosis), meningitis, encephalitis, autoimmune
		Vascular	Aneurysm, infarction, Sheehan's syndrome
Nephrogenic DI	Primary	Idiopathic	–
		Genetic	XR, AR, AD
	Secondary	Chronic renal disease	Obstructive uropathy, tubulointerstitial disease
		Metabolic disease	Hypercalcaemia, hypokalaemia
		Osmotic diuretics	Glucose, mannitol
		Drug induced	Lithium, demeclocycline
		Systemic disorders	Amyloidosis
Dipsogenic DI	Habitual or compulsive water drinking	Occasionally associated with structural/organic hypothalamic disease	Sarcoid, tumours involving the hypothalamus

AD, autosomal dominant; AR, autosomal recessive; DI, diabetes insipidus; DIDMOAD, diabetes insipidus diabetes mellitus optic atrophy deafness; TB, tuberculosis; TCS, transcranial surgery; TSS, transsphenoidal surgery; XR, X-linked recessive.

Epidemiology

Varies according to the underlying cause.

Clinical presentation

Polyuria and polydipsia are the most common presenting symptoms. Nocturia on several occasions is typical; indeed if the patient is able to sleep solidly for 8 hours without needing to get up for the toilet, then it is unlikely that he/she has HDI or NDI. Symptoms of anterior pituitary dysfunction and the underlying disorder may also be present.

Physical signs

Reduced visual acuity, and visual field defects due to chiasmal compression, together with papilloedema or optic atrophy (reflecting raised intracranial pressure) may be evident in cases of HDI. Examine carefully for evidence of pituitary insufficiency. Other clinical signs will be determined by the underlying disorder.

Investigation

Confirming the diagnosis of DI

Having established that the patient is polyuric, an assessment of renal concentrating ability should be undertaken.

Plasma and urine osmolalities

Measurement of paired early morning plasma and urine osmolalities, together with urea and electrolytes, following abstention from / limitation of fluid intake overnight may help to exclude cases in which the index of clinical suspicion is low. The finding of a concentrated early morning urine sample (>750 mosmol/kg; normal range 100–1,000) together with normal plasma osmolality and electrolytes effectively excludes DI. Note, however, that given the unsupervised nature of this test, it should not be used in cases where genuine DI is suspected.

Water deprivation test

For those in whom the overnight test fails to resolve the issue, or in cases with a higher index of suspicion, a formal water deprivation test can be performed, with subsequent assessment of renal concentrating ability in response to exogenous vasopressin (see Section 3.3.2).

Hypertonic saline infusion test

Occasionally, difficulties arise in establishing the diagnosis with fluid deprivation and, moreover, milder forms of HDI, NDI and DDI can not always be differentiated with this type of test. In these circumstances, direct measurement of plasma ADH (also called arginine vasopressin (AVP)) and/or copeptin concentration(s), together with plasma and urine osmolalities, during graded osmotic stimulation (by infusion of hypertonic saline) can accurately diagnose DI and differentiate the various causes. This investigation should only be performed in centres with experience of the test, and must not be undertaken in subjects with cardiac, renal or hepatic impairment, who are likely to become significantly salt overloaded.

Assessment of cause and associated complications in HDI

Assessment of hypothalamic–pituitary function

Evidence of anterior pituitary dysfunction must be sought in all cases of HDI (see Section 2.1.8).

Key point

Remember that cortisol has a permissive effect on free water excretion. Accordingly, DI may be masked in states of cortisol deficiency and only become evident once glucocorticoid replacement has been commenced.

MRI/CT

MRI (or CT) of the pituitary fossa and hypothalamus is mandatory in any patient found to have HDI. The high signal which is normally seen at the site of the posterior pituitary gland is likely to be absent even in the absence of a mass lesion (Fig 24).

Ophthalmological review

To provide a baseline for monitoring the effects of treatment.

Treatment

Wherever possible, treatment should be directed at the underlying disorder.

Hypothalamic (cranial) DI

Desmopressin (DDAVP), a synthetic long-acting vasopressin analogue, is the treatment of choice for patients with HDI. It can be administered via several routes (SC, IM, IV, intranasally or orally). Patients should be treated with the lowest dose necessary to control their polyuria/nocturia and advised of the potential symptoms of over-replacement, especially if they have pre-existing cardiac or renal impairment. Daily weights may help to alert the patient to cumulative over-treatment. In these circumstances, adjustment to the dose/regimen and omission of desmopressin for a short period at regular intervals, perhaps once weekly (to allow break-through polyuria), usually helps to prevent fluid overload.
It is important to monitor plasma electrolytes at regular intervals after commencing treatment and following any dose adjustments.

Nephrogenic DI

NDI due to an acquired metabolic problem is best managed by addressing the underlying cause and maintaining adequate hydration while function recovers. For those patients with congenital NDI or an acquired irreversible defect, various additional measures can be tried including: high-dose desmopressin in cases of partial NDI, thiazide diuretics / amiloride, non-steroidal anti-inflammatory drugs (NSAIDs) or dietary salt restriction.

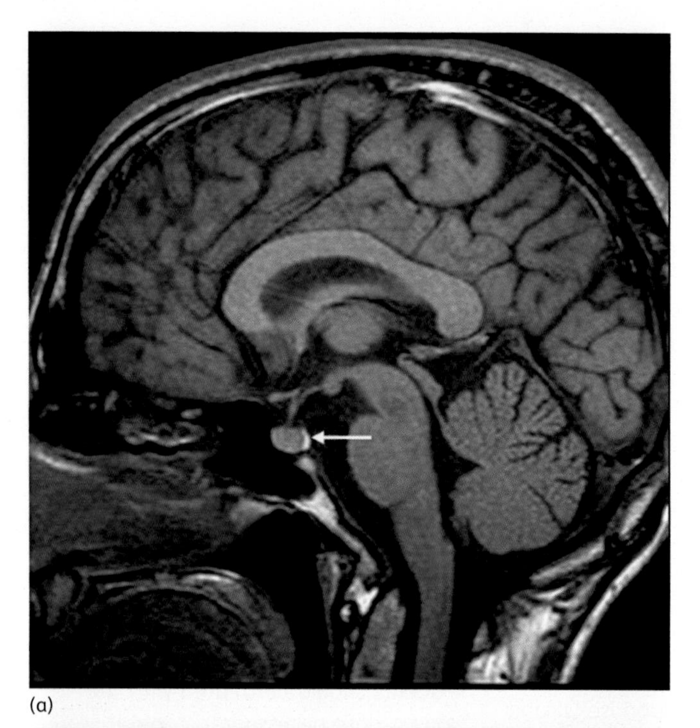

(a)

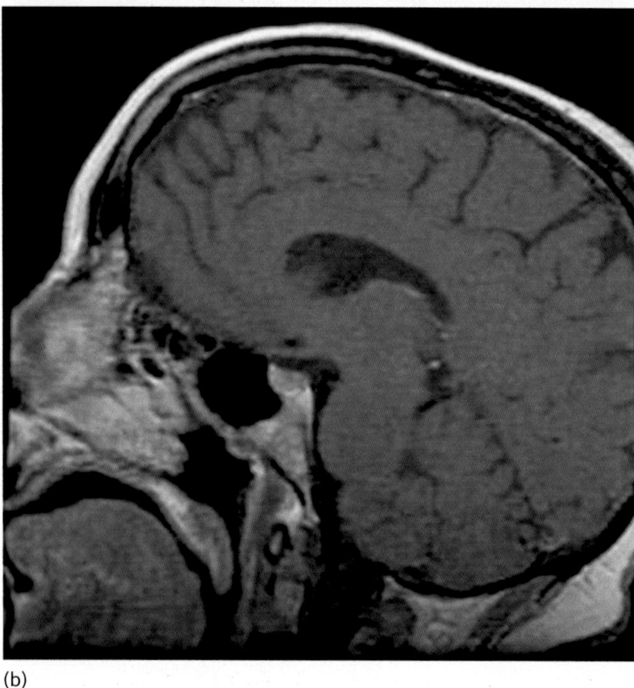

(b)

Fig 24 Absent posterior pituitary signal in HDI. Sagittal MRIs showing **(a)** the normal high signal from the posterior pituitary gland (arrow) and **(b)** loss of signal in a patient with HDI due to pituitary infiltration.

Dipsogenic DI

This is often an extremely challenging condition to manage, especially if the cause is not acknowledged by the patient. Reduction in fluid intake is the only rational treatment. Individuals with persistent DDI are at significant risk of hyponatraemia if given desmopressin.

Prognosis

Prognosis is largely dependent on the underlying disorder.

2.1.8 Hypopituitarism and hormone replacement

Hypopituitarism denotes an insufficiency of one or more of the pituitary hormones.

Aetiology and pathophysiology

Destruction/compression of normal pituitary tissue or a reduction in the blood supply (including the hypothalamic–pituitary portal circulation) account for the majority of cases (Table 23).

Key point

With pituitary tumours, the usual sequence in which pituitary hormone function is lost is:

- growth hormone (GH)
- luteinising hormone (LH) and follicle-stimulating hormone (FSH)
- adrenocorticotropic hormone (ACTH)
- thyroid-stimulating hormone (TSH).

Table 23 Aetiology of hypopituitarism

Frequency	Cause
Common	Pituitary/peripituitary tumours (or as a complication of treatment, including surgery and radiotherapy)
Rare	Vascular (eg pituitary apoplexy, Sheehan's syndrome, intrasellar carotid artery aneurysm)
	Pituitary infiltration (eg metastasis, haemochromatosis, sarcoidosis, histiocytosis, granulomatosis with polyangiitis)
	Infection (eg tuberculosis, pituitary abscess)
	Autoimmune (lymphocytic hypophysitis)
	Traumatic (eg post head injury)
	Congenital (eg isolated or combined pituitary hormone deficiencies)
	Idiopathic

Incidence

The incidence in adults is eight to 10 cases per 1 million people per year.

Clinical presentation

This depends upon the aetiology, the degree of deficiency and the rapidity of onset. For example:

- Chronic hypopituitarism (eg after pituitary radiotherapy) may present with general fatigue and a lack of well-being, symptoms of hypogonadism (sexual dysfunction, loss of libido, oligomenorrhoea/amenorrhoea) and possibly symptoms of hypothyroidism and hypoadrenalism.
- GH deficiency may manifest as reduced exercise performance and quality of life.
- Pituitary apoplexy (see Section 2.1.5).

Physical signs

The physical signs will generally be those of the primary hormone deficiency syndromes (eg hypogonadism, hypothyroidism). Secondary hypoadrenalism may result in postural hypotension and loss of secondary sexual hair, but as the aetiology of the problem is pituitary hormone deficiency, it is not associated with hyperpigmentation. GH deficiency is associated with a reduction in lean body mass and an increase in fat mass (with an increased waist:hip ratio).

Investigation

Once hypopituitarism is suspected:

- complete biochemical assessment of pituitary function
- MRI (or CT) of the pituitary fossa
- formal testing of the patient's visual fields and acuity.

Anterior pituitary function

Growth hormone

The 'gold standard' investigation for possible GH deficiency is the insulin tolerance test (ITT) (see Section 3.1.5). Random GH measurements and serum insulin-like growth factor (IGF)-1 are not reliable means of diagnosing GH deficiency. The glucagon stimulation test and the arginine stimulation test provide alternative provocative tests especially in cases where the ITT is contraindicated.

Gonadotrophins

In women with regular menses, who are not on the combined oral contraceptive pill, further tests are not necessary. Otherwise, LH, FSH and oestradiol (E_2) concentrations should be measured. In men, a testosterone concentration should be checked in conjunction with LH and FSH (and, when indicated, albumin and sex hormone-binding globulin (SHBG) to allow an estimate of free testosterone). Ideally blood samples should be taken at 9am to exclude effects of diurnal variation.

Adrenocorticotropic hormone

Although a 9am cortisol measurement may be informative (eg if the value is very low), random measurements of ACTH and cortisol should not be used to screen for ACTH deficiency. Dynamic assessment of the hypothalamic–pituitary–adrenal axis with an ITT (Section 3.1.5) is the 'gold standard' in this setting. However, in cases where the ITT is contraindicated the short Synacthen test (SST) can be used, providing that the results are interpreted with caution. For example, the SST may fail to identify incipient secondary adrenal failure in the first few weeks after transsphenoidal surgery. If used, the SST should ideally be undertaken at 9am, thereby allowing both the basal and the post-Synacthen cortisol values to be used in the assessment of the axis.

Thyroid-stimulating hormone

Measurement of thyroxine (T4) (ideally free thyroxine (FT4)) with or without triiodothyronine (T3) (ideally free triiodothyronine (FT3)) levels provide the most reliable means of assessing thyroid status in patients with hypothalamic/pituitary disease. TSH levels alone should not be used to screen for secondary/tertiary hypothyroidism.

Prolactin

Deficiency of prolactin is not clinically evident, except postpartum when it is associated with a failure of lactation. Hyperprolactinaemia is a more common finding in the setting of pituitary hormone deficiencies, reflecting stalk compression by an intrasellar mass/infiltration.

Posterior pituitary function

See Section 2.1.7.

Treatment

Hydrocortisone

> Hazard
>
> **Steroid side effects**
>
> It is important to avoid the adverse side effects of long-term treatment with supraphysiological doses of glucocorticoids. For most patients, 15–20 mg hydrocortisone daily is sufficient and is typically given in divided doses (eg 10 mg on waking, 5 mg at lunchtime and 5 mg in the late afternoon; or 15 mg on waking and 5 mg in the late afternoon). The adequacy of replacement can be assessed clinically and, where there is uncertainty, with a cortisol day curve.

> Hazard
>
> **Sick day rules**
>
> Patients must be given written advice about doubling their hydrocortisone dose if they are ill, and seeking early medical help if they are unable to take their tablets. Patients and their relatives should be taught how to administer parenteral hydrocortisone in the event of an emergency. They should also be issued with a steroid card and advised to purchase a MedicAlert bracelet or necklace.

Thyroxine

The T4 dose should be titrated to the FT4 concentration (not the TSH level).

> Hazard
>
> **Replace steroid before thyroid**
>
> Hydrocortisone replacement therapy, if indicated, must be instituted before T4, to avoid the risk of precipitating a life-threatening hypoadrenal crisis.

Sex hormone replacement therapy

Both men and women require sex steroid hormone replacement therapy (HRT) for normal sexual function, to prevent osteoporosis and to maintain body composition.

- Women should be given cyclical oestrogen and progestogen (eg in the form of the combined oral contraceptive pill) or lower dose HRT, especially if over the age of 35, until the time at which a natural menopause would be expected to occur (typically around 50 years). Fertility treatment requires ovulation induction with gonadotrophins.
- Testosterone can be effectively replaced using intramuscular injections, implants or a transdermal gel. Liver function tests and full blood count (haematocrit) should be checked prior to and periodically after starting treatment. Men of an appropriate age should be counselled regarding the pros and cons of prostate surveillance (with periodic digital rectal examination and measurement of serum prostate-specific antigen (PSA)). In men with oligospermia/azoospermia who desire fertility, induction of spermatogenesis with gonadotrophin therapy may be necessary.

> Hazard
>
> **Testosterone replacement needs care**
>
> Restoration of normal serum testosterone levels may not be welcomed by long-term hypogonadal males (or their partners). In these circumstances, or if testosterone replacement is contraindicated for other reasons (eg in men with active prostate carcinoma), consider alternative bone prophylaxis, eg with a bisphosphonate.

Growth hormone

GH replacement therapy is relatively expensive and its use in the UK is subject to National Institute for Health and Care Excellence (NICE) guidelines.

Recombinant human GH is self-administered by subcutaneous injection once a day. The dose is titrated to IGF-1 levels, against the age- and gender-related reference range.

Treatment may increase the patient's lean body mass, bone mineral density (BMD), exercise capacity and quality of life, and improve their lipid profile and insulin sensitivity. The most common side effects of treatment are oedema and arthralgia, which respond to a reduction in dose. There is no evidence to suggest an increase in the risk of new tumour formation or recurrence of a previously treated pituitary tumour in patients receiving GH therapy.

Antidiuretic hormone

See Section 2.1.7.

Prognosis

Hypopituitarism is often associated with reduced psychological well-being and affected subjects have a mortality rate which is at least twice the standardised mortality rate. Both may be related to periods of untreated hypogonadism, excessive glucocorticoid or T4 therapy, inadequate glucocorticoid treatment in times of stress or GH deficiency.

2.2 Adrenal disease

2.2.1 Cushing's syndrome

See Section 2.1.1.

2.2.2 Primary aldosteronism

Primary aldosteronism is an important treatable cause of hypertension in the young to middle aged.

Aetiology

The majority of cases are due to a benign aldosterone-producing adrenal adenoma (so-called Conn's syndrome) or bilateral adrenal nodular hyperplasia. Other rarer causes are shown in Table 24.

Table 24 Aetiology of primary aldosteronism

Subtype	Notes
Aldosterone-secreting benign adrenal adenoma	Classical Conn's syndrome
Idiopathic hyperaldosteronism	Commonly associated with bilateral adrenal hyperplasia
Adrenal carcinoma	–
Familial (hyper)aldosteronism	Includes glucocorticoid-remediable hyperaldosteronism, an autosomal dominantly inherited disorder in which the 11beta-hydroxylase promoter is fused to the aldosterone synthase gene, allowing ACTH-sensitive production of aldosterone in the zona fasciculata
Ectopic aldosterone-producing adenoma/carcinoma	Very rare

ACTH, adrenocorticotropic hormone.

Epidemiology

Although primary aldosteronism was traditionally considered to account for <1% of all cases of hypertension, recent data suggest that it is in fact the most common, potentially curable, cause of secondary hypertension (accounting for 5–10% of all cases of hypertension and 20–25% of those with refractory hypertension). Importantly, when compared with patients with essential hypertension of a similar magnitude, primary aldosteronism is associated with significantly higher rates of cardiovascular disease (ischaemic coronary, cerebrovascular, atrial fibrillation).

Clinical presentation

Most cases come to light during investigation of hypertension or unexplained hypokalaemia. Non-specific symptoms including weakness, lassitude and polyuria may be reported, reflecting potassium depletion.

Physical signs

Mineralocorticoid excess *per se* is often not associated with specific physical signs. The degree of hypertension is variable, ranging from mild to severe, although malignant/accelerated hypertension is exceptionally rare. There may be associated signs of target-organ damage, for example hypertensive retinopathy. Clinical evidence of oedema is rare, except in those with concomitant cardiac disease.

Investigation

Prior to investigation ensure satisfactory dietary sodium intake (>150 mmol/day). Screening tests are traditionally performed having withdrawn agents (eg beta-blockers, spironolactone) that interfere with the renin–angiotensin–aldosterone system in a manner that makes it difficult to interpret renin and/or aldosterone levels. Alternative antihypertensive agents (eg doxazosin and verapamil or diltiazem) may be substituted if necessary. Screening can, however, be undertaken without changes in medication providing that certain precautions are taken when interpreting results (see below).

Screening tests

Urea and electrolytes

The classical picture is one of hypokalaemic alkalosis – the accompanying serum sodium level is usually normal to high. However, many patients subsequently diagnosed with primary aldosteronism are normokalaemic at presentation. This is particularly likely if the patient is not on a potassium-losing diuretic and has a diet with a low sodium content, as urinary potassium excretion is related to the distal nephron sodium load.

Urinary potassium and sodium

Hypokalaemia is associated with inappropriate kaliuresis. Urinary sodium estimation ensures satisfactory dietary intake.

Plasma renin and aldosterone

The hallmark of primary aldosteronism is the excessive autonomous production of aldosterone, which occurs in the face of renin suppression. The ratio of plasma aldosterone to plasma renin (measured either as renin activity or renin mass) is a valid screening test for primary aldosteronism and may be performed without changing antihypertensive medication. An elevated aldosterone:renin ratio is highly suggestive of the diagnosis, but it is important to note that various factors can affect plasma renin and aldosterone, and hence the ratio, eg renin secretion is stimulated by volume or salt depletion (eg as occurs with diuretic treatment) and is suppressed when beta-adrenergic input to the juxtaglomerular apparatus is attenuated (eg with beta-blockers), or if the patient is treated with NSAIDs which promote salt and water retention. Hypokalaemia can impede aldosterone secretion and potassium supplements should be given to correct hypokalaemia before measuring aldosterone levels; similarly, amlodipine and other similar calcium antagonists may suppress aldosterone production leading to a false negative screen in less severe cases.

Note: it is important to ensure that aldosterone:renin ratios are compared with the relevant renin reference range (ie renin activity or renin mass) as these are markedly different in terms of the respective thresholds.

Salt-loading tests

In normal subjects volume expansion due to salt and water retention will suppress plasma renin and aldosterone, whereas in primary aldosteronism further volume expansion does not have the same suppressive effect on aldosterone secretion. Salt loading can be achieved by increasing dietary sodium intake, infusing saline, administering exogenous mineralocorticoid (eg fludrocortisone), or a combination of these, but should only be undertaken under specialist supervision, and not in patients prone to fluid overload (eg those with cardiac failure, renal impairment).

Determining the cause

Plasma renin activity and aldosterone

Look for the following:

- Plasma renin – in normal subjects, adoption of an upright posture for 4 hours stimulates plasma renin when compared with resting supine levels. In patients with primary aldosteronism, supine plasma renin is undetectable and remains suppressed despite ambulation.
- Aldosterone – adrenal adenomas exhibit sensitivity to ACTH, and accordingly aldosterone levels fall in parallel with the circadian cortisol rhythm. By contrast, idiopathic hyperaldosteronism is associated with a lack of ACTH sensitivity, with aldosterone levels typically increasing on ambulation. Aldosterone values must therefore be interpreted in the context of the serum cortisol.

In practice, these tests are now only rarely used. Instead, various imaging modalities are employed to distinguish unilateral from bilateral causes of primary aldosteronism.

CT/MRI of adrenals

Both techniques can be used to identify the cause of primary hyperaldosteronism (Fig 25).

Adrenal vein sampling

Selective venous sampling with comparison of aldosterone:cortisol ratios in the right and left adrenal veins is considered the 'gold standard' for determining whether the patient has a unilateral or bilateral cause of primary aldosteronism. However, the procedure is technically demanding (especially with respect to cannulating the right adrenal vein) and often inconclusive.

Labelled cholesterol scintigraphy / PET-CT

Radionuclide scanning is now rarely used; molecular imaging with tracers (eg ^{11}C-metomidate) which target key enzymes (eg aldosterone synthase) in the steroid biosynthetic pathway may offer an alternative for localising the causative lesion(s) in primary aldosteronism.

Treatment

Spironolactone is the medical treatment of choice because of its ability to block the action of aldosterone at the mineralocorticoid receptor. Treatment is titrated to normalise BP and restore normokalaemia. In patients unable to tolerate spironolactone (most commonly due to the development of gynaecomastia in males), or in whom it is contraindicated, eplerenone and amiloride are useful alternatives.

Thereafter, specific therapy is directed at the underlying cause:

- adrenal adenoma – unilateral adrenalectomy (many centres now routinely offer laparoscopic or retroperitoneoscopic surgery)
- bilateral primary aldosteronism or unsuitable for surgery – long-term spironolactone/eplerenone or amiloride.

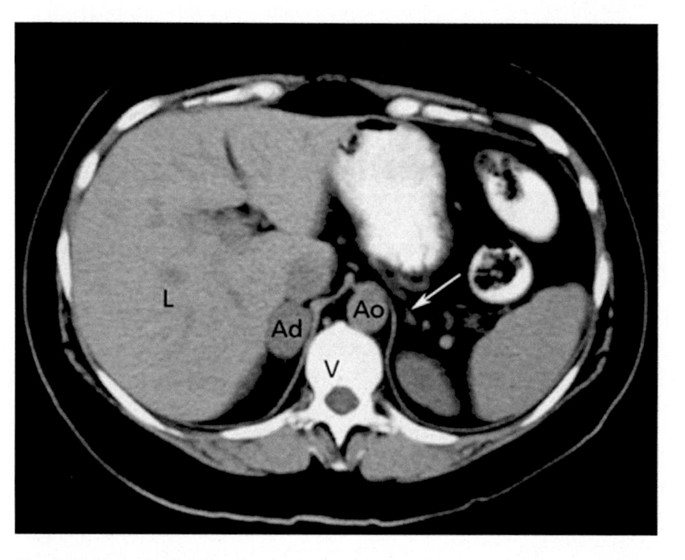

Fig 25 Adrenal adenoma (Ad) in Conn's syndrome. Abdominal CT showing a right-sided adrenal adenoma in a patient with Conn's syndrome. The normal left adrenal gland (arrow) is just visible adjacent to the crus of the diaphragm. Ao, aorta; L, liver; V, vertebral body.

Prognosis

Varies according to the underlying cause. For the majority of cases in whom an adenoma can be identified, excision removes the source of aldosterone but hypertensive end-organ damage may be irreversible. Importantly hypertension may not be cured by removal of the adenoma.

2.2.3 Virilising tumours

Pathophysiology

Virilising tumours may be either adrenal or ovarian in origin. Both are likely to present in middle age, and the greater the tumour size the higher the likelihood of malignancy.

Epidemiology

Very rare, accounting for less than 1% of all causes of androgen excess; however, because of the potential for underlying malignancy, they must be considered in the differential diagnosis of the hirsute/virilised woman.

Key point

Causes of androgen excess in women

- polycystic ovary syndrome (PCOS) (>95% of cases)
- obesity (and associated insulin resistance)
- androgen-secreting tumours (adrenal or ovarian, benign or malignant)
- congenital adrenal hyperplasia
- Cushing's syndrome (ACTH-dependent or adrenocortical carcinoma)
- acromegaly.

Hazard

With large adrenal tumours (>5 cm diameter) the possibility of adrenocortical carcinoma must be considered.

Clinical presentation/physical signs

Presentation is generally later in life compared with the polycystic ovary syndrome (PCOS). Clinical manifestations typically include menstrual irregularity (which can be associated with anovulatory cycles), hirsutism, acne, deepening of the voice, frontal balding (androgenic alopecia), muscle hypertrophy and clitoromegaly. Importantly, a rapid onset of severe symptoms should alert the clinician to the possibility of an underlying androgen-secreting neoplasm.

Abdominal pain with a palpable mass and/or ascites may be present especially if the underlying cause is an adrenocortical carcinoma. Features of Cushing's syndrome should also be sought as some malignant adrenal tumours co-secrete both androgens and cortisol.

Childhood presentations include precocious puberty and/or virilisation.

Investigation

Androgen profiles

One or more serum androgens (dehydroepiandrosterone sulphate (DHEAS), androstenedione, testosterone) are typically raised. DHEAS is synthesised by the adrenal gland, and thus an elevated level indicates an adrenal origin for hyperandrogenism. In contrast, a markedly elevated serum testosterone in a postmenopausal woman with normal DHEAS and androstenedione strongly suggests an ovarian source.

Mildly elevated adrenal androgen levels may be seen in a variety of non-neoplastic conditions. Measurement of DHEAS and androstenedione after the administration of dexamethasone can help to determine which cases require further investigation – adrenal androgen production is ACTH-dependent and failure of exogenous glucocorticoid to suppress circulating levels suggests an autonomous basis for hyperandrogenism. Similarly, gonadotrophin-releasing hormone (GnRH) analogues can be used to 'switch off' non-tumoral ovarian androgen production.

Other endocrine tests

Gonadotrophins

In women with regular menses, who are not on the combined oral contraceptive pill, further investigation is not necessary. Otherwise, luteinising hormone (LH), follicle-stimulating hormone (FSH) and oestradiol (E_2) concentrations should be measured.

17Alpha-hydroxyprogesterone

17Alpha-hydroxyprogesterone (17-OHP) is used to screen for congenital adrenal hyperplasia (see Section 2.2.5).

Urinary free cortisol and/or late night salivary cortisol and/or dexamethasone suppression

If Cushing's syndrome is suspected (see Section 2.1.1).

Radiological imaging

Adrenal CT and/or MRI

An adrenal CT or MRI with contrast should be undertaken if an androgen-secreting adrenal neoplasm is suspected (Fig 26). If adrenal malignancy is considered a possibility, then more extensive imaging (of the chest, abdomen and pelvis) is required to look for evidence of local and distant spread.

Pelvic ultrasound and/or MRI

Ultrasound (especially transvaginal) provides excellent visualisation of most ovarian neoplasms (Fig 27). MRI with contrast is reserved for those cases in which the ovaries are not clearly seen or if malignancy is suspected.

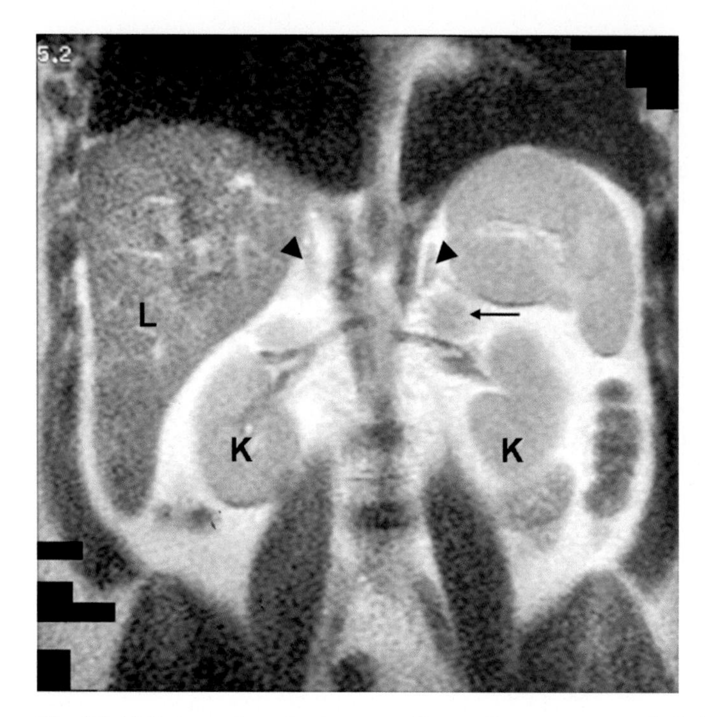

Fig 26 Virilising adrenal adenoma. Coronally reconstructed abdominal MRI showing a left-sided adrenal adenoma in a young female who presented with rapidly progressive virilisation. Although the abnormal mass (arrow) appears to be located just inferior to the left adrenal gland, it was confirmed at surgery to be arising from the tip of the postero-lateral limb. The positions of both adrenal glands are shown by arrowheads. L, liver; K, kidney.

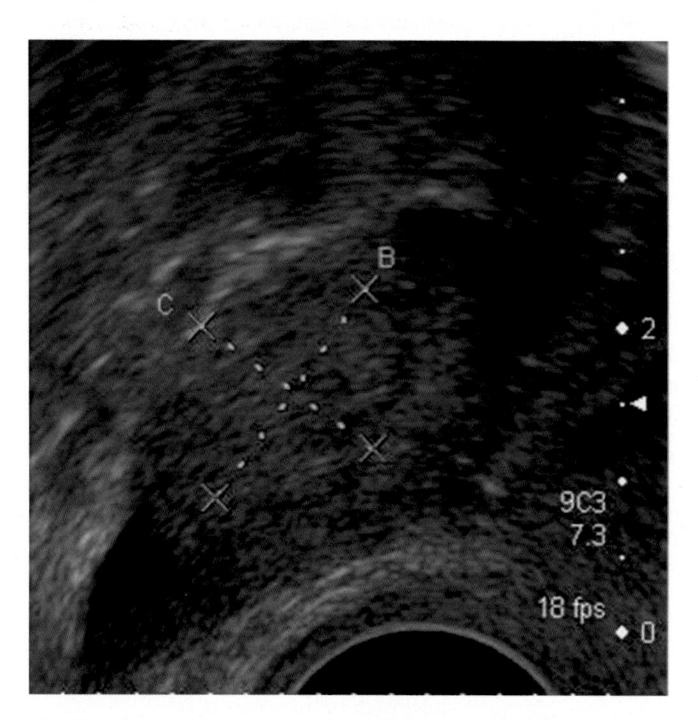

Fig 27 Virilising ovarian tumour. Pelvic ultrasound reveals a right-sided ovarian mass in a 60-year-old female who presented with androgenic alopecia and deepening of the voice, and who was found to have a markedly elevated serum testosterone level. At surgery, a benign Leydig cell tumour was excised.

Treatment

Surgery is the treatment of choice for both benign and malignant adrenal and ovarian neoplasms.

Adjunctive chemotherapy and radiotherapy can be used for malignant tumours, although response rates are often disappointing. Mitotane is the chemotherapeutic agent of choice for adrenocortical carcinoma.

Prognosis

Although surgery cures the majority of patients with benign tumours, some clinical features such as deepening of the voice may persist.

Prognosis for malignant tumours is poor with overall 5-year survival rates less than 40%.

2.2.4 Phaeochromocytoma

Key point

An update on 'well-known facts' about phaeochromocytoma

In adults, phaeochromocytomas were known as the '10% tumour' reflecting approximately:

- 10% extra-adrenal
- 10% bilateral/multiple
- 10% malignant
- 10% familial.

This no longer holds true with, for example, many more cases now identified with an underlying genetic basis (Table 25). In addition, the prevalence of bilateral tumours is greater than 10% in certain familial syndromes (eg multiple endocrine neoplasia type 2 (MEN-2) and von Hippel–Lindau syndrome (VHL)), while in childhood a higher proportion are extra-adrenal and malignancy is more common.

Table 25 Hereditary syndromes associated with phaeochromocytoma and/or paraganglioma

Von Hippel–Lindau syndrome (VHL) *VHL* (tumour suppressor gene) mutations Phaeochromocytomas in ~20%; higher percentage in some kindreds (type 2) ~5% are malignant
Multiple endocrine neoplasia (type 2) syndrome *RET* (proto-oncogene) mutations **Type 2a (Type 2) –** medullary thyroid carcinoma, phaeochromocytomas, hyperparathyroidism **Type 2b (Type 3) –** medullary thyroid carcinoma, phaeochromocytomas, marfanoid habitus, mucosal neuromas
Neurofibromatosis (type 1) *NF* gene mutations Phaeochromocytomas in <5% of cases (20% bilateral)
Hereditary paragangliomas Mutations identified in succinate dehydrogenase complex subunits B, D, C, A, AF2 (ie *SDHB, SDHD, SDHC, SDHA, SDHAF2*) Paraganglioma and/or phaeochromocytoma (PPGL), rare renal cancers, gastrointestinal stromal tumours (GIST); head and neck paragangliomas may occur in addition to, or independent of, abdominal/thoracic PPGL
Familial phaeochromocytomas *TMEM27* mutations – phaeochromocytomas and rare renal cancers *MAX* mutations – mainly PPGL *KIF1B* – phaeochromocytoma and neuroblastoma *EGLN1* – phaeochromocytoma and congenital erythrocytosis *MDH2* – phaeochromocytoma and paraganglioma
Polycythaemia-paraganglioma syndrome *EPAS (HIF2A)* mutations – polycythaemia, PPGL, somatostatinoma
Leiomyomatosis and renal cell cancer Fumarate hydratase (FH) mutations – cutaneous and uterine leiomyomas, type 2 papillary renal carcinoma, rare PPGL

Aetiology/pathophysiology

Originating from the chromaffin cells of the sympathetic nervous system, the majority of phaeochromocytomas arise within the adrenal medulla, with a smaller number derived from sympathetic ganglia. They commonly secrete norepinephrine (noradrenaline) and epinephrine (adrenaline), but in some cases significant amounts of dopamine may be released. As with many other endocrine tumours, the diagnosis of malignancy is dependent upon evidence of local infiltration or distant spread, since histological appearances do not reliably distinguish benign from malignant tumours.

So far, germline mutations in a number of different genes have been found to cause familial phaeochromocytomas (Table 25).

Succinate dehydrogenase (SDH) mutations are a frequent cause of familial phaeochromocytoma and are important as patients with an *SDHB* mutation typically exhibit more aggressive disease with a high incidence of malignancy (Table 25). They are usually extra-adrenal, mainly occurring as paragangliomas in the head, chest and abdomen. *SDHD* mutations are maternally imprinted; thus only carriers who have inherited the mutation from the father develop the disease.

Epidemiology

Rare, accounting for 0.1–0.6% of all cases of hypertension in general outpatient clinics. Many remain occult and are only diagnosed at post-mortem.

Clinical presentation

Cases may come to light during the investigation of poorly controlled hypertension, when direct questioning reveals an array of other manifestations of catecholamine excess. These are frequently reported to occur in an episodic or paroxysmal fashion. Occasional cases present with pregnancy-associated hypertension, myocardial infarction, cardiac dysrhythmias or a dilated catecholamine cardiomyopathy. The incidence in normotensive asymptomatic subjects is 'rising', due to increased use of high-resolution imaging and screening for phaeochromocytoma in subjects with predisposing genetic mutations. About 5% of all adrenal 'incidentalomas' are phaeochromocytomas, with about 25% of all phaeochromocytomas now discovered incidentally during imaging for unrelated disorders.

Key point

Commonly reported symptoms of phaeochromocytoma

- headache
- sweating
- palpitations / forceful heartbeat
- anxiety
- tremor
- nausea and vomiting
- chest and abdominal pain / dyspnoea.

Note that the triad of headache, sweating and palpitations is considered to be highly suggestive of a diagnosis of phaeochromocytoma.

Physical signs

Features of increased sympathetic activity are often present during a paroxysm, eg tachycardia, sweating, pallor (not flushing). Hypertension may be sustained or episodic and approximately 50% of cases exhibit orthostatic hypotension (the latter reflecting intravascular depletion in response to long-standing hypertension).

Investigations

This should be approached in two stages:

- confirm catecholamine excess – through the measurement of their metabolites
- localise the tumour.

Confirm catecholamine excess

Urinary metanephrines

Urinary-fractionated metanephrines (ie normetanephrine and metanephrine measured separately) offer a highly sensitive and specific screening test for the detection of phaeochromocytoma and paraganglioma.

Plasma metanephrines

Plasma free metanephrines (normetanephrine and metanephrine) are a convenient (and slightly more sensitive) alternative to 24-hour urinary collections.

3-Methoxytyramine (a metabolite of dopamine, and measured in urine or plasma) is a potential marker of malignancy.

False positives

There are many causes of false positive biochemical screening. These fall into two groups:

1. true catecholamine excess, due to:
   - drugs (tricyclic antidepressants, phenoxybenzamine, monoamine oxidase inhibitors, levodopa, alpha-methyldopa, sympathomimetics, calcium channel blockers)
   - stimulants (eg coffee, nicotine)
   - anxiety
   - disease states (eg myocardial infarction (MI), heart failure, cardiogenic shock, obstructive sleep apnoea)
2. interference with analytical method (different depending on assay but including coffee, labetalol, levodopa, alpha-methyldopa, paracetamol and sympathomimetics).

Most false positive levels are significantly lower than in phaeochromocytoma. Repeat the test having stopped any interfering medication, and consider an alternative screening method.

Clonidine suppression test

Clonidine acts via presynaptic alpha-adrenoreceptors to block catecholamine secretion and can be used to distinguish increased norepinephrine release due to sympathetic activation from autonomous tumoral secretion. Failure to adequately suppress plasma norepinephrine in response to clonidine is highly predictive of phaeochromocytoma (97%), but a normal test result does not exclude phaeochromocytoma (negative predictive value only 75%). Use of plasma normetanephrine increases the positive and negative predictive values to 100 and 96%, respectively.

Localise the tumour

CT/MRI

CTs of the abdomen and pelvis are commonly used (Figs 28 and 29). T2-weighted MRI with gadolinium enhancement has similar sensitivity and specificity to CT. The tumour typically exhibits a distinctive 'bright white' signal on T2-weighted images.

Radioiodine-labelled metaiodobenzylguanidine scintigraphy / single-photon emission CT (SPECT)

Metaiodobenzylguanidine (^{123}I-MIBG), which is taken up by chromaffin cells, is useful in localising both adrenal and extra-adrenal tumours (Fig 30) and is the first-line nuclear imaging method. Pretreating with potassium iodide blocks thyroidal uptake.

PET-CT

^{18}F-fluorodeoxyglucose (^{18}F-FDG) PET, ^{18}F-fluorodopa PET and ^{18}F-fluorodopamine PET all offer the higher spatial resolution of PET scanning and may allow detection of smaller lesions not readily visualised with ^{123}I-MIBG. ^{18}F-FDG PET has particular use in malignant disease.

Genetic testing

All patients with a phaeochromocytoma/paraganglioma should be considered for genetic testing, first to allow early diagnosis and treatment of other features of the associated hereditary syndrome; secondly to prompt more stringent, lifelong clinical follow-up, as recurrences are more likely in familial phaeochromocytoma/paraganglioma; and thirdly to prompt appropriate family

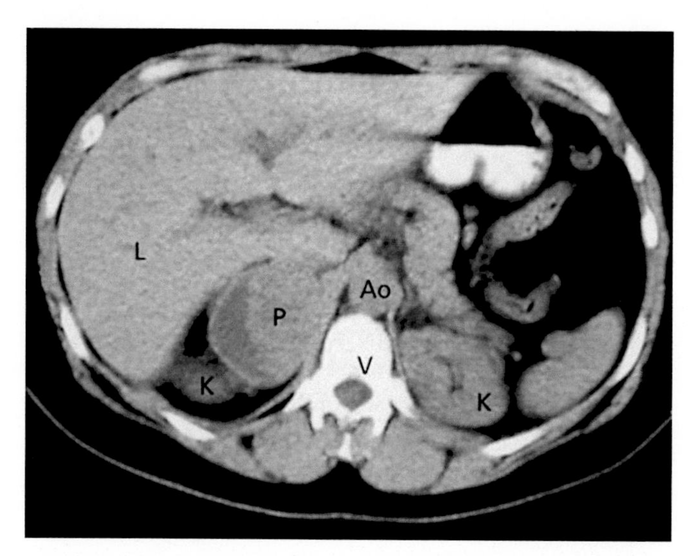

Fig 28 Phaeochromocytoma. Abdominal CT showing a right-sided phaeochromocytoma (P). Ao, aorta; K, kidney; L, liver; V, vertebral body.

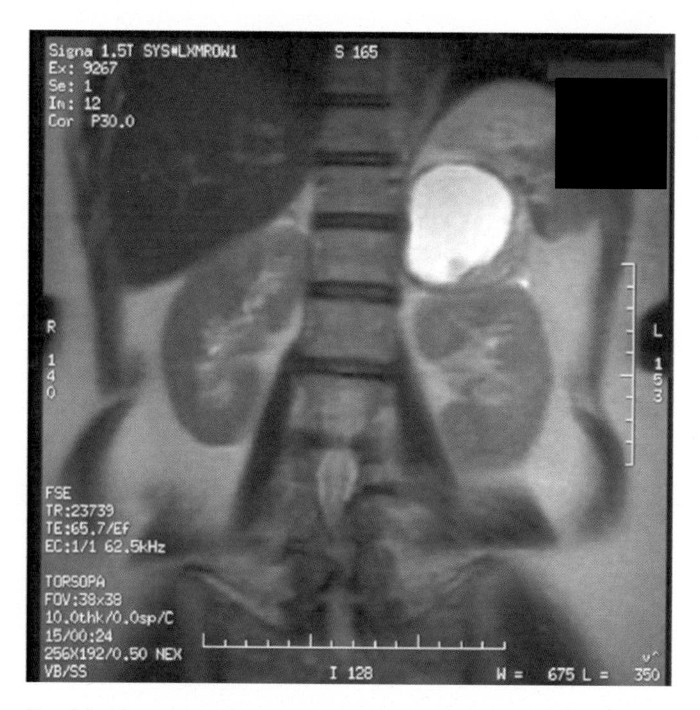

Fig 29 Phaeochromocytoma. Abdominal T2-weighted MRI showing a large left-sided phaeochromocytoma (heterogeneous high signal mass) indenting and compressing the adjacent kidney.

screening. Presently, cost-effective genetic screening is recommended to those with a positive family history or those under 50 years, especially children. Other clues that should be regarded as an indication for genetic testing include bilateral adrenal or multifocal extra-adrenal disease or the association of phaeochromocytoma with other tumours. The clinical picture may direct genetic testing to one of the suspected genes.

Differential diagnosis

Several conditions may present with features of sympathetic overactivity and thus mimic phaeochromocytoma (see Table 3 in Section 1.1.3).

Treatment

Medical therapy

Prior to considering surgical removal, medical treatment must be instituted with the aims of:

- ameliorating symptoms
- normalising BP
- correcting intravascular depletion.

Hazard

Alpha-blockade before beta-blockade

Beta-blockers must not be given to patients with suspected or proven phaeochromocytoma until alpha-blockade has been established, since there is a significant risk of precipitating a life-threatening hypertensive crisis due to unopposed alpha-adrenoceptor activity.

Alpha-blockade

The non-competitive alpha-antagonist phenoxybenzamine is the initial treatment of choice, with escalating dose titration (start with 10 mg twice daily and increase gradually until BP is normalised; most cases require 0.5–2 mg/kg per day in divided doses). The alpha1-antagonist doxazosin provides an alternative for those intolerant of phenoxybenzamine.

Beta-blockade

The non-selective agent propranolol (20–80 mg every 8 hours) is generally preferred, but may not be required in all patients (eg those with a pure noradrenaline-secreting paraganglioma).

Surgical excision

Both traditional and laparoscopic approaches can be used for tumour removal.

extent of end-organ damage is often a key factor in determining long-term outcome.

2.2.5 Congenital adrenal hyperplasia

Congenital adrenal hyperplasia (CAH) is not a single disease entity but encompasses several autosomal recessive disorders (arising as a consequence of inborn errors in adrenal cortical enzyme function), which result in varying degrees of impairment in the synthesis of cortisol and aldosterone.

Pathophysiology

The key stages in the steroid biosynthetic pathway are outlined in Fig 31. Conversion of cholesterol to pregnenolone is the rate-limiting step and a major site of regulation by ACTH. 21-Hydroxylase deficiency is the most common enzyme defect in CAH (~90–95% of all cases), with 11beta-hydroxylase deficiency, 3beta-hydroxysteroid dehydrogenase deficiency and other enzyme deficiencies accounting for a relatively small number of cases.

Reduced cortisol synthesis is the common denominator, with consequent elevation of circulating ACTH levels further stimulating steroidogenesis. Precursors that cannot be metabolised

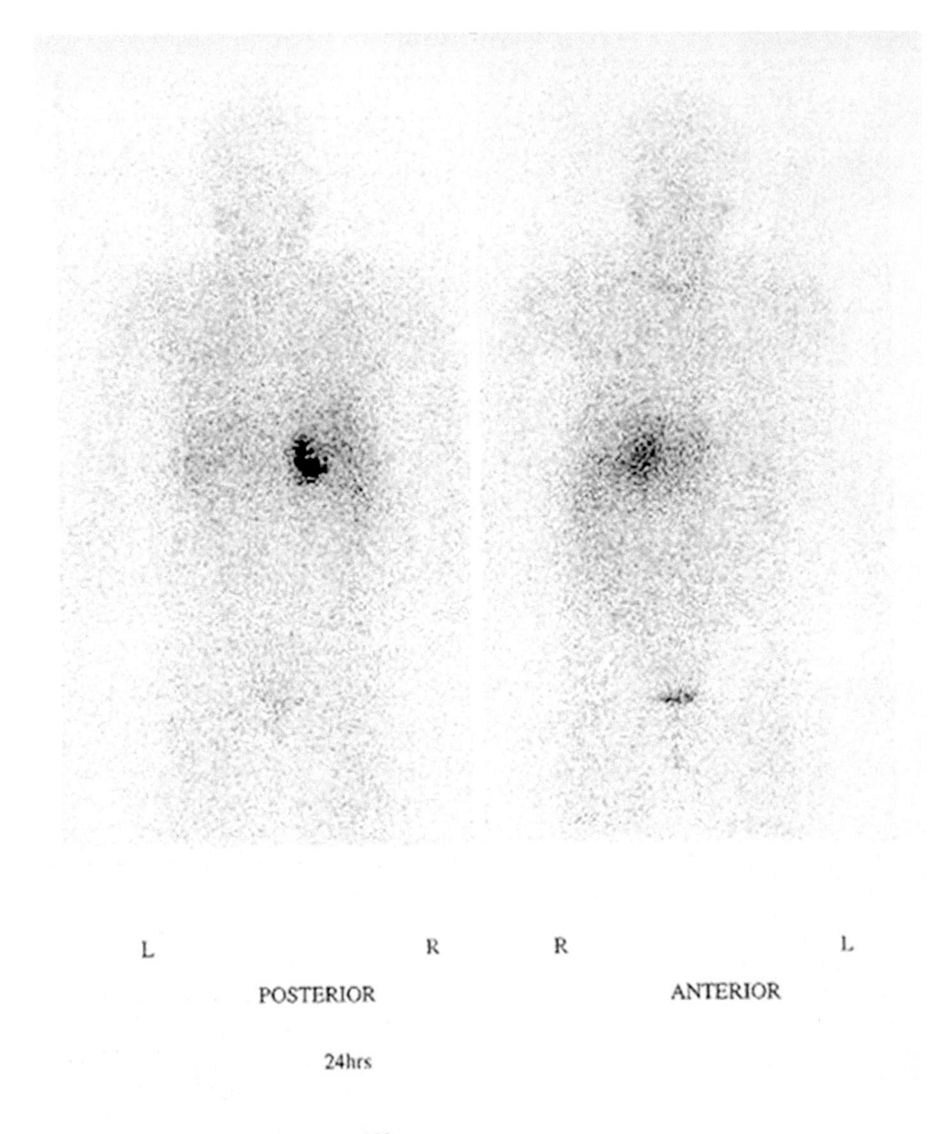

Fig 30 Phaeochromocytoma: ^{123}I-MIBG scan. The right-sided phaeochromocytoma shown in Fig 28 demonstrates avid uptake of MIBG.

Adjunctive therapy for malignant tumours

Options include:

- alpha-methylparatyrosine – which ameliorates symptoms through inhibition of tyrosine hydroxylase, the rate-limiting enzyme in the biosynthetic process
- radioiodine (^{131}I)-labelled MIBG – although large and repeated doses may be necessary.

Prognosis

Even those with malignant tumours frequently survive for many years. The

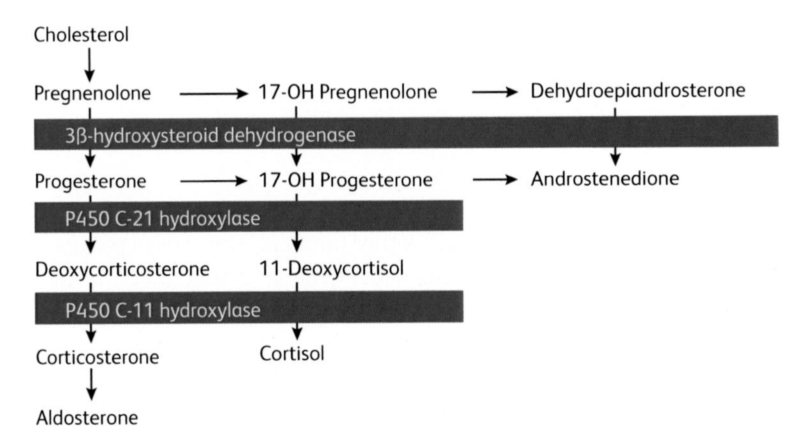

Fig 31 Adrenal cortical steroid biosynthetic pathways.

by the deficient enzyme are then shunted down adjacent pathways, with the resulting clinical phenotype reflecting both hormone deficiency (eg cortisol and aldosterone) and excess (eg androgens).

Epidemiology

Classical 21-hydroxylase deficiency affects approximately one in 14,000 live births in Caucasians. Non-classical 21-hydroxylase deficiency (see below) occurs more frequently (one in 1,000 live births in the general population).

Clinical presentation/physical signs

Both 'classical' and 'non-classical' variants of CAH are recognised. The former denotes a more severe form, predominantly seen in the neonate or young child, while the latter is reserved for milder variants that often only come to light in adulthood. Table 26 indicates typical clinical features according to gender and age at presentation.

Investigation

Depending on the enzyme defect, different steroid precursors/androgens accumulate and can be measured in plasma. In practice most laboratories restrict screening to:

- 17alpha-hydroxyprogesterone (17-OHP) – this precursor accumulates in 21-hydroxylase deficiency. Its ability to discriminate from normal controls in mild non-classical cases is improved following ACTH stimulation with Synacthen (tetracosactide) 250 μg IM, which exaggerates the enzyme block (see Section 3.1.1)
- testosterone, androstenedione and dehydroepiandrosterone sulphate (DHEAS) – elevated in most cases
- plasma ACTH – elevated, although serum cortisol may be low or normal
- plasma renin activity (PRA) – usually elevated in proportion to mineralocorticoid deficiency.

Table 26 Clinical presentations of CAH[1]

Type	Age	Female	Male
Classical	Neonatal	Ambiguous genitalia	Salt wasting
		Virilisation	
		Salt wasting	
	Childhood	—	Precocious puberty
Non-classical	Childhood	Virilisation	Precocious puberty
	Adulthood	Hirsutism	No specific symptoms
		Menstrual irregularities	
		Infertility	

1 Note that symptoms of cortisol deficiency are surprisingly rare, although hypoglycaemia is sometimes seen. However, intercurrent illness is likely to unmask glucocorticoid deficiency and result in a life-threatening adrenal crisis, which is exacerbated by concomitant aldosterone deficiency.

Key point

Screening

Identification of the genes encoding each of the enzymes involved in adrenal steroidogenesis permits screening for mutations. For example, the 21-hydroxylase gene lies on chromosome 6 in close proximity to the major histocompatibility complex, and several common mutations have now been identified. One potential application of this technique is for prenatal diagnosis in families where there is already one affected child.

Treatment

Acute adrenal crisis

Episodes of acute adrenal insufficiency should be managed as outlined in Section 2.2.6, with doses adjusted according to body weight / surface area in neonates.

Routine replacement

Glucocorticoids inhibit ACTH release, restoring androgen levels to the normal range. Dose titration should be performed in relation to 17-OHP and adrenal androgen levels (in particular androstenedione). In childhood this is particularly important as over-treatment is associated with poor growth (through suppression of growth hormone (GH) secretion). Hormone levels should be measured at a consistent time in relation to medication dosing, and used in conjunction with other parameters such as growth measurements and bone age to monitor therapy. Standard steroid sick day rules (see Section 2.1.8) should be observed.

Mineralocorticoid replacement (fludrocortisone) is indicated in salt-wasting forms.

Other issues

Plastic surgery may be required in cases with ambiguous external genitalia.

Psychological support is an important component of the long-term management of patients with CAH.

Prognosis

Salt-wasting forms are potentially life-threatening if unrecognised. Once diagnosed, however, adequate treatment allows most individuals to lead a normal life and retain fertility.

Prevention

In those families in whom there is already one affected child with CAH, treatment of the mother with dexamethasone (which crosses the placenta) from the beginning of all subsequent pregnancies has traditionally been recommended until chorionic villus sampling or amniocentesis is possible, the principal aim being the prevention of excessive fetal androgen production that would lead to virilisation of an affected female fetus. If the fetus is found to be male or an unaffected female, treatment can be stopped. Recently, however, concerns regarding impairment of verbal working memory and increased social anxiety have been reported in some unaffected children exposed to dexamethasone, resulting in debate as to the merit and safety of prenatal treatment of CAH. Isolation and genotyping of fetal DNA in maternal serum may offer a route to earlier diagnosis and thus facilitate targeted treatment in affected female fetuses.

2.2.6 Primary adrenal insufficiency

Adrenocortical insufficiency may be:

- primary – arising as a consequence of destruction or dysfunction of the adrenal cortex, as described by Thomas Addison in 1855
- secondary – occurring secondary to deficient pituitary ACTH secretion (see Section 2.1.8).

Table 27 outlines the main differences between primary and secondary adrenal insufficiency.

This section focuses on primary adrenal insufficiency and the clinical picture resulting from combined cortisol, aldosterone and adrenal androgen deficiency.

Aetiology

Although tuberculosis (TB) probably remains the commonest cause of primary adrenal insufficiency worldwide, in the UK more than 75% of cases are due to immune-mediated destruction of the adrenal glands, and may be associated with other autoimmune glandular hypofunction (see Section 2.7.2).

Key point

Aetiology of primary adrenocortical insufficiency

- autoimmune – isolated or part of a polyglandular syndrome
- infection – TB, histoplasmosis; acquired immune deficiency syndrome (AIDS) (often multifactorial, eg infection with cytomegalovirus, use of drugs such as ketoconazole, adrenal infiltration with Kaposi's sarcoma)
- infiltration – metastatic malignancy/lymphoma (note, however, that despite adrenal metastases being a relatively common finding on imaging, clinically evident adrenal insufficiency is rare), amyloidosis, sarcoidosis, haemochromatosis
- iatrogenic – adrenalectomy, drugs that block adrenal steroidogenesis (eg metyrapone, ketoconazole)
- adrenal haemorrhage – severe sepsis, meningococcaemia
- congenital adrenal hyperplasia
- adrenoleukodystrophy (rare X-linked disorder)
- familial glucocorticoid deficiency including Allgrove (triple A) syndrome (very rare disorder comprising adrenal insufficiency, achalasia, alacrima and, in some cases, autonomic neuropathy).

Table 27 Primary and secondary adrenocortical insufficiency

	Primary	Secondary
Cases	80%	20%
Aetiology	75% autoimmune	Hypothalamic–pituitary disease
ACTH	High	Low
Glucocorticoid	Deficient	Deficient
Mineralocorticoid	Deficient	Preserved
Na^+	Low	Low/normal
K^+	High	Normal
Treatment	Hydrocortisone and fludrocortisone	Hydrocortisone
Associations	Autoimmune polyglandular syndrome	Hypopituitarism

ACTH, adrenocorticotropic hormone.

Epidemiology

Rare: prevalence <0.01% of the UK population, and with female:male ratio of approximately 3:1.

Clinical presentation

The clinical picture varies widely from the acutely ill patient in Addisonian crisis, to the relatively asymptomatic patient with pigmentation. When present, symptoms are often non-specific and the diagnosis is sometimes only made at post-mortem, leading to its description as 'the unforgiving master of non-specificity and disguise' (Brosnan CM and Gowing NF, 1996). Tiredness, weakness, dizziness, anorexia, weight loss and gastrointestinal disturbance are commonly reported. Some patients develop salt craving.

Key point

Clinical features of acute adrenocortical insufficiency

- fever
- nausea and vomiting
- weakness and impaired cognition
- hypotension/shock
- hypoglycaemia.

Physical signs

The more common clinical findings include:

- pigmentation – generalised (Fig 32), palmar creases, scars, buccal mucosa
- postural hypotension
- loss of axillary and pubic hair in females (due to a lack of adrenal sex steroids).

Investigation

Hazard

Treat first, ask questions afterwards

In the acutely ill patient in whom you suspect adrenal insufficiency do not delay treatment:

- Establish venous access (taking blood for urea and electrolytes, glucose and cortisol) and give IV hydrocortisone (100 mg) immediately.
- Set up a 0.9% sodium chloride intravenous infusion.
- Check blood glucose using a finger-prick sample.

In non-emergency cases, consider the following investigations.

Urea, electrolytes and glucose

Note that the classical abnormalities (low sodium, high potassium, high urea and low glucose) are only seen in severe cases. Hypercalcaemia is occasionally reported.

Full blood count

Normochromic normocytic anaemia, neutropenia and eosinophilia are all recognised. The presence of macrocytosis should prompt consideration of possible coexistent pernicious anaemia.

Synacthen test

Short (see Section 3.1.1) and long Synacthen tests. In the short Synacthen test include a basal 9am ACTH measurement (high in primary adrenal failure).

Autoantibodies

Check for adrenal, thyroid and intrinsic factor autoantibodies.

Chest/abdominal radiograph/CT

Look for evidence of TB including adrenal calcification.

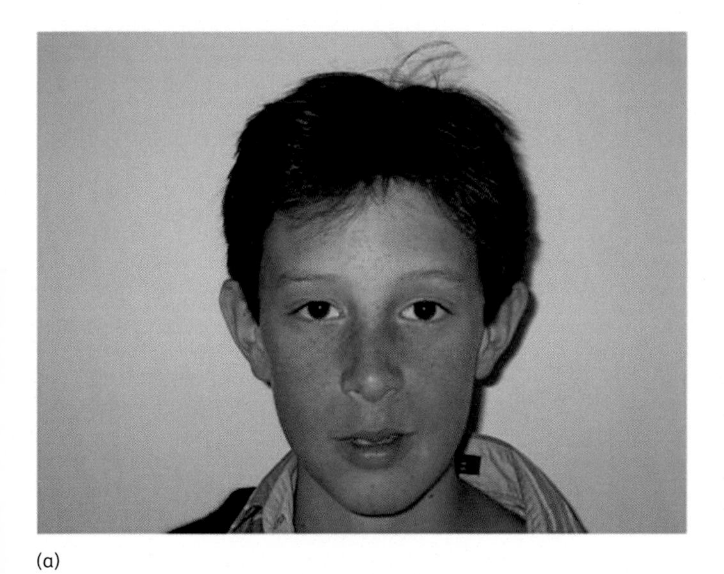

(a)

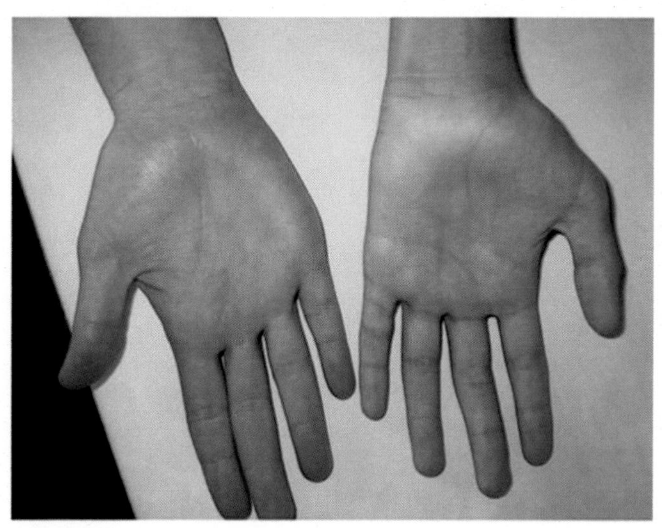

(b)

Fig 32 Addison's disease. **(a)** Generalised hyperpigmentation of the skin and mucous membranes is one of the earliest manifestations of Addison's disease, and is increased in sun-exposed areas. **(b)** Increased pigmentation of the palmar creases (right), compared with an unaffected control subject (left).

Thyroid-stimulating hormone and thyroxine

Ideally free thyroxine (FT4) should be used.

There may be concomitant thyroid dysfunction both in primary (autoimmune thyroid disease) and secondary (TSH deficiency) adrenal insufficiency. Note, however, that in Addison's disease, mild thyroid function abnormalities may revert to normal with satisfactory glucocorticoid replacement.

Treatment

Hypoadrenal crisis

Treat as above, and establish on regular 6-hourly parenteral hydrocortisone (50–100 mg). An intravenous hydrocortisone infusion, which produces more stable replacement than intermittent boluses, may also be used after an initial 100 mg bolus. Investigate and treat any precipitating cause.

Routine replacement

Hydrocortisone

Although most conveniently taken twice daily (eg 15 mg on waking and 5 mg in the late afternoon), thrice daily dosing (eg 10 mg on waking, 2.5–5 mg at midday and 2.5–5 mg in the late afternoon) probably achieves more physiological replacement. Adequacy can be checked with a cortisol day curve. Larger patients and those on enzyme-inducing agents (eg phenytoin, carbamazepine, rifampicin) typically require higher doses of glucocorticoid replacement therapy. The patient must be advised with regards steroid sick day rules and carry a card/bracelet (see Section 2.1.8) (Fig 33).

- Always carry this card with you and show it to anyone who treats you (for example a doctor, nurse, pharmacist or dentist). For one year after you stop the treatment, you must mention that you have taken steroids.
- If you become ill, or if you come into contact with anyone who has an infectious disease, consult your doctor promptly. If you have never had chickenpox, you should avoid close contact with people who have chickenpox or shingles. If you do come into contact with chickenpox, see your doctor urgently.
- Make sure that the information on the card is kept up to date.

STEROID TREATMENT CARD

I am a patient on STEROID treatment which must not be stopped suddenly

- If you have been taking this medicine for more than three weeks, the dose should be reduced gradually when you stop taking steroids unless your doctor says otherwise.
- Read the patient information leaflet given with the medicine.

Name	
Address	
Tel No	
GP	
Hospital	
Consultant	
Hospital No	

Date	Drug	Dose

Fig 33 Generic steroid treatment card. Note a specific steroid replacement therapy alert card has recently been developed by the UK Society for Endocrinology (www.endocrinology.org/adrenal-crisis).

Fludrocortisone

Start with 50–100 μg per day and adjust according to clinical status (postural hypotension, oedema, hypokalaemia) and/or plasma renin. Usual maintenance is with 50–200 μg daily.

Adrenal androgens

Although not routinely given, some evidence suggests that DHEAS may improve well-being in individuals with primary adrenal insufficiency.

Hazard

Avoid precipitating an Addisonian crisis

Thyroid hormone replacement should not be given until glucocorticoid replacement has been established due to the risk of precipitating an Addisonian crisis.

Prognosis

Providing hormone deficiency is adequately corrected, the underlying aetiology is often the most important determinant of outcome.

Patients with Addison's disease and one or more of the other disorders associated with the autoimmune polyglandular syndrome type 2 (eg type 1 diabetes or Hashimoto's thyroiditis – Section 2.7.2) may be at risk of the particularly devastating complication of premature ovarian failure (POF). Depending on the patient it may be appropriate to discuss this to allow them to make an informed decision about the timing of any attempts that they might wish to make to have a family.

2.3 Thyroid disease

2.3.1 Hypothyroidism

Hypothyroidism is the clinical syndrome that results from deficiency of the thyroid hormones thyroxine (T4) and triiodothyronine (T3).

Aetiology/pathogenesis

The causes of hypothyroidism are listed in Table 28. Iodine deficiency remains an important cause worldwide while, in the UK, autoimmune thyroid disease and previous treatment for thyrotoxicosis account for nearly 90% of cases.

Table 28 Aetiology of hypothyroidism

Cause	Frequency	Pathology	Clinical condition
Primary	Common	Autoimmune	Hashimoto's thyroiditis
			Atrophic thyroiditis (primary myxoedema)
		Previous treatment for thyrotoxicosis	Thyroidectomy
			Radioactive iodine
	Less common	Defects of hormone synthesis	Iodine deficiency (or excess)
			Drugs, eg antithyroid agents, lithium, amiodarone
			In-born errors of thyroid hormone synthesis
		Transient hypothyroidism	Subacute thyroiditis
			Postpartum thyroiditis
		Infiltration	Tumour, amyloidosis
		Thyroid hypoplasia/agenesis	
Secondary	—	Hypothalamic or pituitary disease	

The tendency for autoimmune thyroid disease (autoimmune hypothyroidism and Graves' disease) to run in families is strongly suggestive of a significant genetic component, although the nature of the interplay between genetic and environmental factors in their evolution remains to be elucidated.

Hashimoto's thyroiditis is characterised by lymphocytic infiltration of the gland and the presence of thyroid microsomal antibodies. Atrophic thyroiditis also appears to be immune mediated (with lymphocytic infiltration and microsomal antibodies) and is associated with other organ-specific autoimmune disorders.

Epidemiology

Hypothyroidism is common, with a prevalence of 1–2% in the general population. Females outnumber males by ~10:1. Congenital hypothyroidism occurs in about one in 3,500 live births in the UK.

Clinical presentation and physical signs

The classical presenting symptoms and associated physical signs of hypothyroidism are shown in Fig 34.

Other presentations

Myxoedema coma

Patients with unsuspected or inadequately treated hypothyroidism are at risk of developing this rare but life-threatening condition. Coma may complicate an intercurrent illness (eg myocardial infarction, cerebrovascular accident, pneumonia) or be precipitated by certain drugs, particularly sedatives. Hypothermia is accompanied by bradycardia, hypotension, hypoglycaemia, hyponatraemia, hypoxia and hypercapnia.

Congenital hypothyroidism

The introduction of routine neonatal screening in the UK and other countries now permits the early diagnosis of this condition which, if untreated, can lead to short stature, mental retardation and a characteristic puffy appearance of the face and hands (cretinism). It may arise in the setting of:

- placental transfer of thyroid-stimulating hormone (TSH) receptor-blocking antibodies from a mother with autoimmune thyroid disease
- maternal iodine deficiency or treatment with antithyroid agents during pregnancy
- thyroid hypoplasia/agenesis or inborn errors of thyroid hormone synthesis.

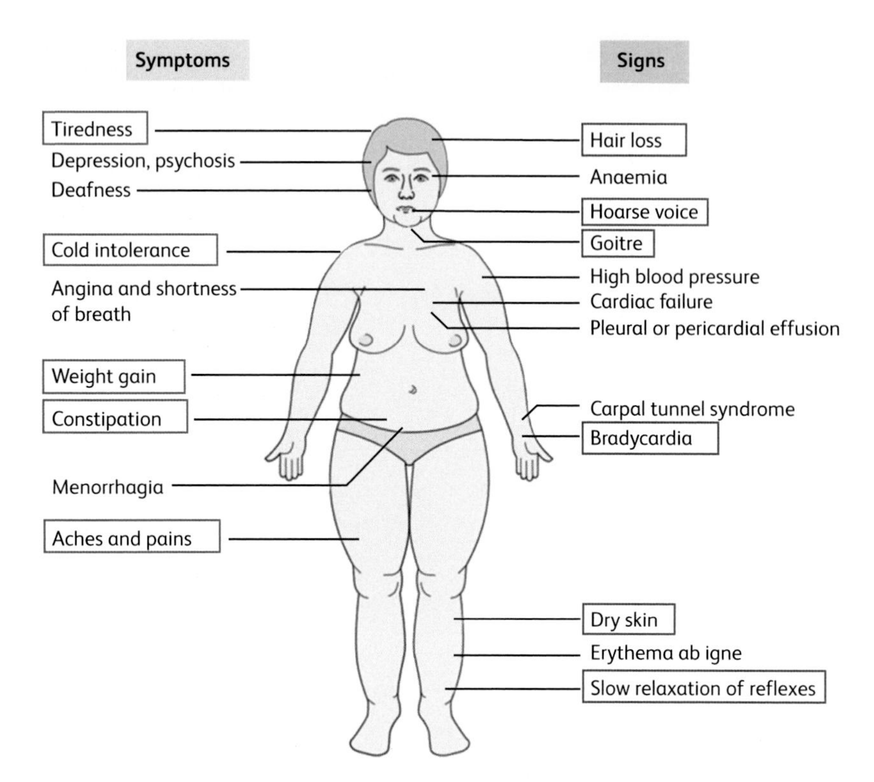

Fig 34 Clinical features of hypothyroidism. The common symptoms and signs are shown in boxes.

Subclinical hypothyroidism

It has been estimated that 10% or more of all females over the age of 50 are affected by this condition, which is characterised biochemically by normal free thyroxine (FT4) and free triiodothyronine (FT3) levels in the presence of a mildly elevated TSH. Although few report specific symptoms of hypothyroidism, hypercholesterolaemia and subtle cardiac abnormalities are recognised, which resolve following normalisation of TSH with exogenous T4. Increasing evidence suggests, however, that in older patients (in their eighth and ninth decades) a mildly raised TSH may actually be associated with increased longevity and therefore not require intervention.

Investigations

Key point

Threshold for considering the diagnosis of hypothyroidism

It is important to have a low threshold for actively excluding hypothyroidism in 'at risk' groups, including those with:

- a goitre
- a history of autoimmune disease
- previously treated thyrotoxicosis
- a family history of thyroid disease

and:

- in older people, in whom the symptoms of hypothyroidism may be mistaken for the normal ageing process.

Thyroid function tests

Table 29 outlines the patterns of thyroid function tests (TFTs) that are typically seen in various hypothyroid states (see Section 3.3.1).

Anti-thyroid peroxidase and anti-thyroglobulin antibodies

Anti-thyroid peroxidase (anti-TPO) (also known as anti-microsomal) and anti-thyroglobulin antibodies are commonly found in Hashimoto's thyroiditis and in atrophic hypothyroidism.

Full blood count

Hypothyroidism can be associated with anaemia:

- normocytic – impaired erythropoiesis
- microcytic – menorrhagia, impaired iron absorption
- macrocytic – vitamin B_{12} or folate deficiency.

Urea and electrolytes

Hyponatraemia may reflect increased antidiuretic hormone (ADH) activity and reduced free water clearance or, if associated with hyperkalaemia, should prompt consideration of coexistent adrenal insufficiency.

Cholesterol and creatine kinase

Both serum cholesterol (total and low-density lipoprotein (LDL)) and creatine kinase are typically elevated, indicating tissue hypothyroidism within liver and muscle, respectively.

Anterior pituitary function

A full assessment of pituitary function should be performed if secondary hypothyroidism is suspected (see Section 2.1.8).

Table 29 Abnormalities of thyroid function in various 'hypothyroid' states

Condition	TSH	FT4/FT3
Primary hypothyroidism	↑↑	↓
Secondary hypothyroidism	↓ or →	↓
Subclinical hypothyroidism	↑	→
Sick euthyroidism	↓ or →	↓ or →
Poor compliance with T4 replacement	↑ or ↑↑	↓ or → or ↑

T3, triiodothyronine; T4, thyroxine; TSH, thyroid-stimulating hormone.

Treatment

Myxoedema coma

Myxoedema coma is a medical emergency, with mortality in some series approaching 50%. Circulatory and ventilatory support are frequently required. Hypoglycaemia must be excluded, hypothermia corrected, and potential precipitating events (eg infection) sought and treated appropriately. Ventilatory support is often required.

Hazard

Don't miss adrenal insufficiency

In the absence of clear evidence to the contrary, it is advisable to assume coexistent adrenal insufficiency and to give hydrocortisone 100 mg IV immediately. Steroid replacement should be continued until normal adrenal function has been demonstrated.

There is some debate as to the best method of starting thyroid hormone replacement. Levothyroxine (L-T4) can be given as a single 500 μg bolus followed by a daily maintenance dose of 50–100 μg. Alternatively, it has been argued that liothyronine (L-T3) should be the preferred mode of replacement due to its rapid onset of action and short half-life, a typical starting dose being 5–10 μg every 6–8 hours. Both can be administered by nasogastric tube. L-T3 can also be given by IV injection. In either case, extreme care must be taken if the patient is suspected/known to have ischaemic coronary disease.

Long-term replacement

Although most cases of hypothyroidism require lifelong replacement with L-T4, occasionally thyroid dysfunction is transient, requiring only temporary treatment, eg subacute or postpartum thyroiditis. If this is suspected, then subsequent withdrawal of treatment should be considered, with repeat TFTs 4–6 weeks later.

The starting dose for L-T4 is typically 50 μg per day. Assessment of adequacy of replacement and adjustments to dose are made on the basis of clinical findings together with measurement of TSH and free thyroid hormone levels, initially checked at 6–8-week intervals. Once stabilised, the patient can be followed up by their GP with annual TFTs.

Hazard

Start with a low dose, and don't forget the adrenals

- Older people and those with ischaemic heart disease may be particularly sensitive to T4, and therefore lower starting doses should be used, eg 25 μg L-T4 per day or on alternate days. If necessary, consider admission to hospital for supervision of replacement with ECG monitoring.
- Always consider the possibility of coexistent adrenal insufficiency, and if in doubt exclude by formal testing (eg with short Synacthen test) prior to initiating T4 replacement.

Key point

Dose titration and combination therapy

- Remember that TSH should not be used to guide L-T4 dose titration in cases of secondary hypothyroidism.
- Some patients and their clinicians advocate combining L-T3 with L-T4 replacement to mimic the natural pattern of hormone release by the thyroid gland. This is not currently routine practice in the UK, and there is little published evidence to support this approach.

Subclinical hypothyroidism

Management is mainly a matter of clinical judgement and each case should be dealt with on its own merits. Epidemiological evidence would suggest that there is high risk of progression to overt hypothyroidism in certain situations, eg in the presence of positive microsomal antibody titres. One suggested strategy for managing such cases is shown in Table 30.

Table 30 Strategy for managing subclinical hypothyroidism		
TSH	**Clinical circumstance**	**Management**
>10 mU/L	Asymptomatic or symptomatic	Treat with T4
5–10 mU/L	Asymptomatic	Observe with repeat TFTs in 6 months
	Symptomatic	Treat with T4
	Antibodies positive	Treat with T4
	Abnormalities of lipids	Treat with T4
	History of radioactive iodine or subtotal thyroidectomy	If asymptomatic, observe with repeat TFTs in 6 months, otherwise treat with T4

T4, thyroxine; TFTs, thyroid function tests; TSH, thyroid-stimulating hormone.

Pregnancy

There is a higher incidence of stillbirths, miscarriages and congenital abnormalities in women with untreated hypothyroidism. In addition, evidence suggests that even mild hypothyroidism may have significant consequences for the long-term intellectual development of the unborn child. Maintenance of TSH within normal limits is therefore important. Dose requirements for T4 may increase by as much as 50–100%, especially during the latter stages of pregnancy. It is important to check TFTs in each trimester and adjust the dose of T4 accordingly.

2.3.2 Thyrotoxicosis

Thyrotoxicosis is the clinical syndrome associated with raised levels of thyroid hormone (T4 and/or T3). Although usually the result of increased production of thyroid hormones (hyperthyroidism), it can also arise when stored hormone is released from a damaged gland (as in subacute thyroiditis) or when exogenous T4 is taken in excess. Secondary hyperthyroidism due to increased TSH secretion is very rare and accounts for less than 1% of all cases.

Aetiology/pathophysiology

The causes of thyrotoxicosis are shown in Table 31.

Graves' disease

Approximately 15% of patients with Graves' disease have a close relative with the same condition, suggesting a significant genetic component in the aetiology of this autoimmune disorder. Sensitisation of T-lymphocytes to antigens within the thyroid gland leads to the production of autoantibodies (from activated B-lymphocytes), which are targeted against these antigens. The development of antibodies, which are capable of binding to and stimulating the TSH receptor, usually correlates with the appearance of thyrotoxic features.

In Graves' ophthalmopathy, infiltration of the extraocular muscles by mononuclear cells is accompanied by an accumulation of glycosaminoglycans (derived from orbital fibroblasts) which promote fluid retention, thereby effectively reducing the available space within the bony orbit. This in turn leads to proptosis, ophthalmoplegia and the other features which typify Graves' eye disease (see below). A similar infiltrative process appears to underlie the skin lesion pretibial myxoedema.

Epidemiology

The prevalence of hyperthyroidism in the UK has been estimated at 1–2%,

Table 31 Aetiology of thyrotoxicosis		
Cause	**Frequency**	**Clinical condition**
Primary	Common	Graves' disease
		Toxic multinodular goitre
	Less common	Toxic adenoma
		Postpartum thyroiditis
		Drug induced, eg amiodarone
		Over-treatment with T4
		Subacute thyroiditis
		Hyperthyroid phase of Hashimoto's thyroiditis ('Hashitoxicosis')
	Rare	Struma ovarii
		Metastatic differentiated follicular thyroid carcinoma
Secondary	Rare	TSH-secreting pituitary adenomas
		Pituitary resistance to thyroid hormone
		Trophoblastic tumours secreting hCG

hCG, human chorionic gonadotrophin; T4, thyroxine; TSH, thyroid-stimulating hormone.

with an incidence of three per 1,000 per year. Females are more commonly affected, especially in Graves' disease (5–10:1), with a peak age of onset in the fourth decade. By contrast, toxic multinodular goitre typically occurs in older patients (>50 years), often in the context of a long-standing non-toxic goitre.

Clinical presentation and physical signs

Fig 35 illustrates the common clinical features seen in thyrotoxicosis.

Key point

Manifestations of thyrotoxicosis

Many of these reflect increased sensitivity to circulating catecholamines, eg tremor, sweating, anxiety. Included among these are the eye signs 'lid lag' and 'lid retraction', which are commonly found in thyrotoxicosis of any cause.

Features specific to Graves' disease

These include:

- eye signs of proptosis/exophthalmos, ophthalmoplegia, chemosis and periorbital oedema (Figs 36 and 37). Interestingly, the development/progression of Graves' ophthalmopathy is independent of thyroid status, although there is a suggestion that it may be exacerbated if the TSH is allowed to rise during treatment. Overall only 3–5% of cases are classified as severe. The condition tends to be more pronounced in smokers
- pretibial myxoedema (Fig 38).

Table 32 summarises the important differences between Graves' disease and toxic multinodular goitre.

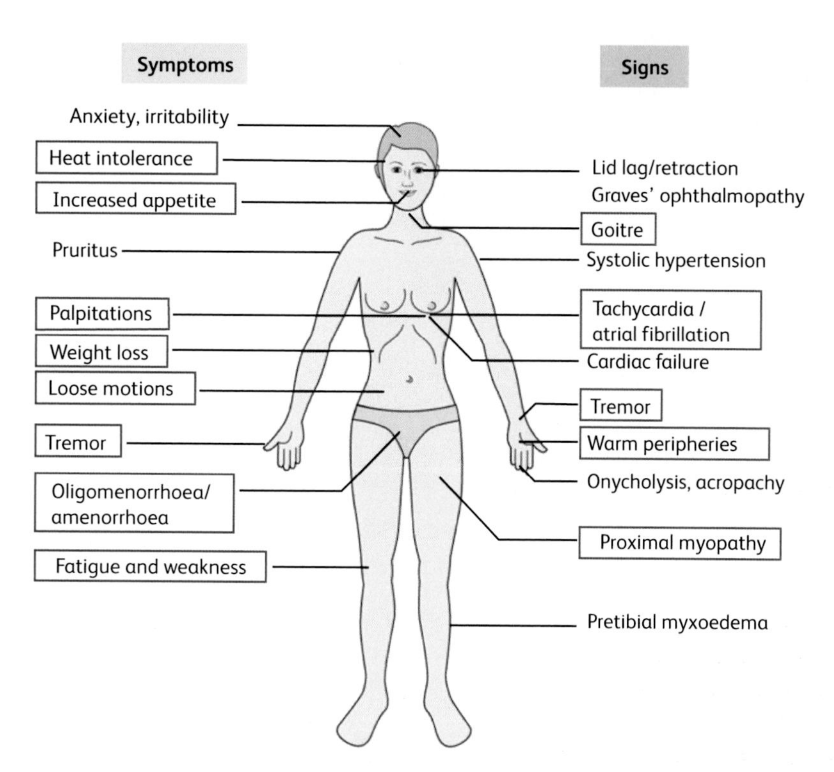

Fig 35 Clinical features of thyrotoxicosis. The common symptoms and signs are shown in boxes.

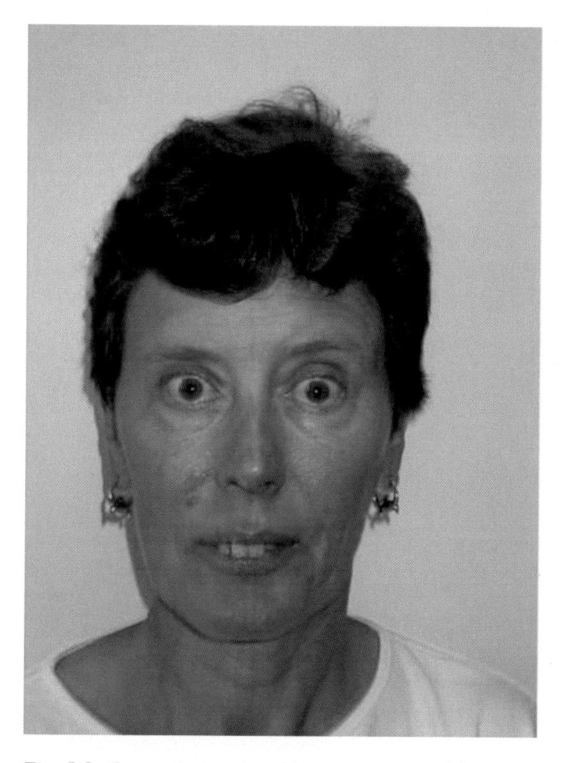

Fig 36 Graves' disease. Note the typical 'staring eyes' with evidence of lid retraction and mild periorbital oedema.

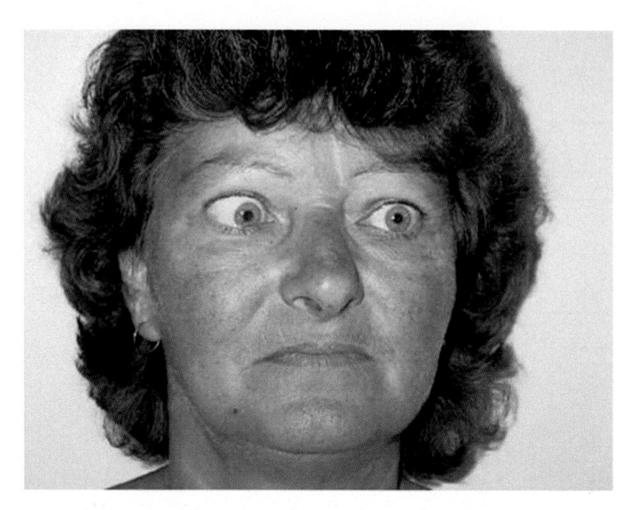

Fig 37 Graves' ophthalmoplegia. This woman with relapsed Graves' disease is trying to look to her left. Her left eye does not abduct. Lid retraction is also evident.

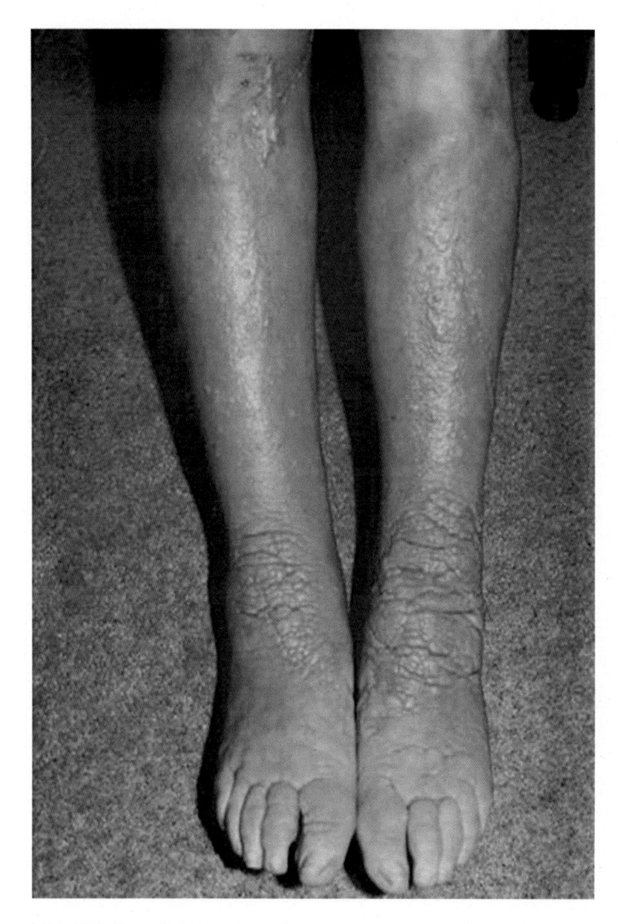

Fig 38 Pretibial myxoedema.

Hazard

Graves' ophthalmopathy requires urgent action

In any patient with suspected Graves' ophthalmopathy it is important to formally assess visual acuity, examine the fundi and to consider checking for loss of colour vision. If there is any concern, or if the patient has evidence of ophthalmoplegia or complains of pain, then urgent referral to an ophthalmologist is required.

Other presentations of thyrotoxicosis

The young and the old

Hyperactivity, increased linear growth and weight gain may occur in children with thyrotoxicosis. Older patients may present with apathy and depression or with symptoms of heart failure, angina or dysrhythmias (so-called apathetic hyperthyroidism). It is therefore important to exclude hyperthyroidism in any patient with atrial fibrillation or heart failure of undetermined aetiology.

Thyroid crisis

Patients with unrecognised thyrotoxicosis or severe poorly controlled disease are at risk of developing a potentially fatal thyroid crisis/storm. Precipitating factors include intercurrent illness, surgery or ^{131}I therapy. Hyperpyrexia, profuse sweating, extreme restlessness, confusion, psychosis, dysrhythmias and features of heart failure are common manifestations. Left untreated, progression to shock, coma and death may occur within hours or days.

Table 32 Clinical features of Graves' disease and toxic multinodular goitre

	Graves' disease	Toxic multinodular goitre
Gender	Female >> male	Female > male
Peak age	20–40 years	>50 years
Goitre	Diffuse, smooth	Multinodular
Eye signs	Lid lag and lid retraction	Lid lag and lid retraction
	Graves' ophthalmopathy	–
Skin	Pretibial myxoedema	–
Nails and fingers	Acropachy, onycholysis	–
Autoantibodies	Usually present	Usually absent

Pregnancy

The child of any mother with Graves' thyrotoxicosis during pregnancy, or with a previous history of Graves' thyrotoxicosis, is at risk of developing fetal or neonatal thyrotoxicosis, since thyroid-stimulating antibodies may persist and cross the placenta.

Close monitoring is essential, especially in those who have previously received definitive treatment in the form of surgery or ^{131}I, and in whom high antibody titres may go undetected because of the lack of clinical signs in the mother. Monitoring of fetal heart rate, growth, and in some centres for evidence of a fetal goitre, may help to identify potential cases.

Neonatal thyrotoxicosis is more common than intrauterine thyrotoxicosis, often becoming clinically apparent 1–2 weeks after delivery. In either case, measurement of TSH receptor-stimulating antibody titres in the mother and infant may help to predict the likelihood/severity of the disorder.

Thyroiditis

Several different forms of thyroiditis are recognised. In some cases there is accompanying thyrotoxicosis, reflecting destruction of thyroid follicles with resultant release of T4 and T3 into the bloodstream (eg subacute thyroiditis). This may be followed by a period of transient hypothyroidism, although in the case of postpartum thyroiditis up to 20% become permanently hypothyroid.

Key point

Differing types of thyroiditis

- acute (suppurative)
- subacute (de Quervain's or granulomatous thyroiditis)
- drug induced (eg amiodarone)
- autoimmune – chronic lymphocytic (Hashimoto's disease)
- atrophic (primary myxoedema), postpartum, juvenile
- Riedel's thyroiditis
- painless (non-postpartum).

Subclinical hyperthyroidism

A normal free thyroid hormone level in the presence of a fully suppressed TSH is a relatively common finding in clinically euthyroid patients with nodule(s) or goitre. It is associated with an increased risk of atrial fibrillation and reduced bone mineral density.

Investigations

Thyroid function tests

- TSH is suppressed unless the cause is a TSH-secreting pituitary tumour.
- FT4 and/or FT3 are raised. T3 thyrotoxicosis (normal FT4 in the presence of signs and symptoms, with a raised FT3 and suppressed TSH) is more commonly associated with toxic adenoma.

Thyroid autoantibodies

- Anti-thyroid peroxidase antibodies are present in some but not all patients with autoimmune hyperthyroidism.
- TSH receptor-stimulating antibodies are usually detectable in Graves' disease. Measurement may be particularly helpful in certain situations, eg pregnancy (see above).

Radioisotope uptake scan

Radioisotope scans (^{99m}Tc or ^{131}I) may be helpful in differentiating between the different causes of thyrotoxicosis (Fig 39):

- In the absence of ophthalmopathy, uniform increased uptake suggests Graves' disease.
- A patchy and irregular appearance is in keeping with toxic multinodular goitre.

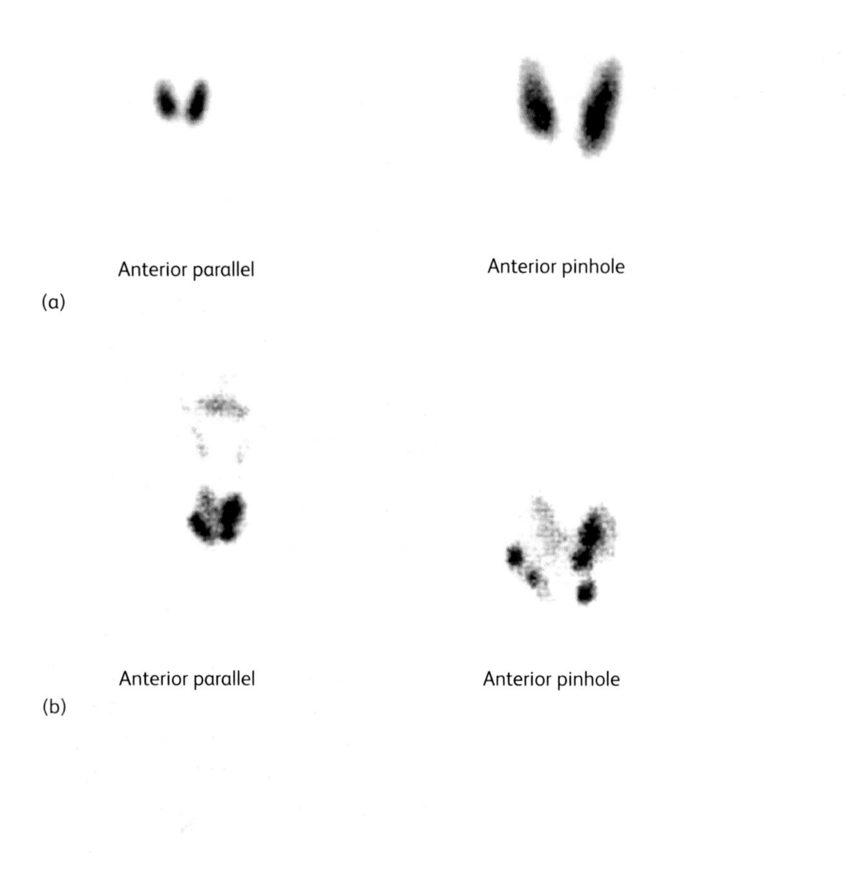

Fig 39 Thyroid isotope scans. Uptake of ^{99m}Tc in **(a)** Graves' disease, **(b)** toxic multinodular goitre and **(c)** solitary toxic adenoma.

- A toxic adenoma will appear as a localised area of increased uptake with suppressed activity elsewhere.
- In thyroiditis the uptake is typically low, although one should also keep in mind the possibility of iodine or T4 ingestion.

Other investigations

Chest radiograph

Tracheal narrowing or deviation may be evident on a chest radiograph (see Fig 5 in Section 1.1.12). Flow–volume loops can help to confirm or exclude extrathoracic obstruction by moderate to large goitres.

ECG and echocardiography

If there is evidence of associated cardiac disease, eg atrial fibrillation.

Treatment

Thyroid crisis

This is a serious and potentially fatal disorder, requiring immediate emergency treatment:

Antithyroid drugs

Give carbimazole (CBZ) (20 mg orally or via nasogastric tube immediately, then every 4–6 hours) or propylthiouracil (PTU) (600 mg orally or via nasogastric tube, then 200 mg every 4–6 hours). PTU may confer additional benefits due to its ability to inhibit conversion of T4 to T3.

Iodide

Sodium iodide (0.5–1 g every 12 hours by IV infusion) or saturated solution of potassium iodide (six to eight drops orally every 6 hours) should be added 1 hour later to prevent additional release of stored thyroid hormone.

> **Hazard**
>
> Iodide must not be started before organification has been blocked with an antithyroid drug due to the risk of providing further substrate for hormone synthesis.

The radiographic contrast agents ipodate and iopanoate may also be used to decrease thyroid hormone release, and have additional beneficial effects including inhibition of peripheral conversion of T4 to T3.

Beta-blockade

Propranolol (0.5–2 mg IV given slowly, followed by 40–80 mg orally every 6–8 hours) blocks many of the peripheral actions of T3 and partially impairs conversion of T4 to T3. Clinically dramatic improvement in cardiovascular performance may follow effective beta-blockade. However, caution is needed in subjects with intrinsic cardiac disease in whom removal of the remaining sympathetic drive to the myocardium may result in rapid decompensation. In these circumstances, the very short-acting agent esmolol is preferred. Alternatively, verapamil (5–10 mg by slow IV injection) may be used if there is a history of asthma or evidence of marked cardiac failure. In either case the patient should be monitored closely in a high-dependency or intensive care unit.

Dexamethasone

A dose of 2 mg orally (or IV) every 6–8 hours helps to reduce peripheral conversion of T4 to T3, and may inhibit further hormone release.

Supportive measures include: oxygen therapy, intravenous fluids and active cooling (with cooling blankets and antipyretic agents, although avoid aspirin because it displaces thyroid hormone from thyroid-binding globulin) are usually required. Diuretics and digoxin may be indicated for cardiac failure. Chlorpromazine (50–100 mg IM) can be used safely as a sedative.

Short- and long-term treatment

Beta-blockers

Non-selective beta-blockers (eg propranolol 10–80 mg tds) are useful for symptomatic relief and rapid control of cardiac toxicity. They can usually be discontinued 3–4 weeks after commencing an antithyroid agent.

Antithyroid drugs

CBZ (40–60 mg per day in divided doses) will render most patients euthyroid within 3–4 weeks. Thereafter, the dose can be reduced in a step-wise fashion to a maintenance level of 5–15 mg given once daily. Alternatively, after initial blockade, a higher dose of CBZ (40 mg per day) can be maintained and T4 replacement added in (starting with 50–100 µg per day) as part of a 'block and replace' regimen, with the dose gradually titrated upwards if necessary. In Graves' disease, treatment is normally continued for 6–18 months, depending on the regimen used. Following cessation of therapy, approximately 50% of patients will relapse, although the timing of this is variable.

PTU is an alternative to CBZ (with 200 mg of PTU equivalent to 20 mg of CBZ). It has a shorter half-life and therefore must be given in a bd or tds regimen, even during the maintenance phase of treatment.

Key point

Monitoring of treatment

The effectiveness of treatment should be monitored clinically and biochemically with periodic measurement of FT4 and/or free T3. Remember that the TSH level often remains suppressed for several months after restoration of euthyroidism.

Hazard

Carbimazole (CBZ) / propylthiouracil (PTU)

Some patients are unable to tolerate CBZ, with rashes the most commonly reported adverse event (up to 5%). In a smaller number of cases (~0.5%), life-threatening agranulocytosis and/or thrombocytopenia occur and require immediate cessation of therapy.

All patients placed on antithyroid drugs should be warned of this potentially serious side effect, and given written instructions advising them to immediately discontinue treatment and attend their GP or emergency department for a full blood count should they develop a sore throat, mouth ulceration or fever.

PTU must *not* be used in patients who have developed agranulocytosis and/or thrombocytopenia in response to CBZ as there is a high risk of recurrence with PTU.

Radioiodine ^{131}I

Offers a safe and effective means of treating thyrotoxicosis. ^{131}I is trapped and organified in the same manner as natural iodine but emits locally destructive beta particles that lead to cell damage and death over a period of several months. It is of particular use in the management of toxic multinodular goitre, toxic adenoma and relapsed Graves' disease. In some instances it is also preferred as first-line treatment for Graves' disease, eg in older people with cardiac disease.

Patients are normally rendered euthyroid prior to treatment, although younger patients with normal cardiac status and mild to moderate thyrotoxicosis can be treated under beta-blockade alone. It is necessary to stop CBZ 5–7 days before administration to allow uptake of the isotope (if PTU is used, then a longer period of withdrawal is required despite its shorter half-life). These can then be restarted 5–7 days after treatment and continued for a further 3 months, at which point residual thyroid status can be assessed. The advantage of this approach is that stable thyroid function is maintained in the peri-radioiodine period. Alternatively, if antithyroid drugs are not recommenced after radioiodine, then earlier review is required. Long-term follow-up is mandatory in all those treated with ^{131}I because of the high risk of subsequent hypothyroidism. Some centres aim to render patients hypothyroid early and treat with thyroxine to minimise the risk of recurrence or missed late hypothyroidism. Many regions operate thyroid registers that facilitate annual recall for TFTs in the community.

Hazard

Radioiodine treatment

- ^{131}I crosses the placenta and is therefore contraindicated in pregnancy, which should also be avoided for at least 6 months after treatment.
- There is ongoing controversy as to whether ^{131}I worsens Graves' ophthalmopathy. Many centres avoid ^{131}I in severe eye disease, but permit treatment in mild to moderate cases under steroid cover (eg prednisolone 30–40 mg per day).

Surgery

Subtotal thyroidectomy is rarely the first-line treatment for uncomplicated thyrotoxicosis. It may be indicated, however, in the presence of:

- relapsing thyrotoxicosis
- compressive symptoms
- multiple allergies to medication or non-compliance with treatment
- toxic adenoma
- personal preference.

Hazard

Patients should be rendered euthyroid prior to surgery to minimise the risks of precipitating dysrhythmias during anaesthesia or of postoperative thyroid storm.

Table 33 outlines the potential complications of thyroid surgery.

Table 33 Potential complications of thyroid surgery

Time course	Complication
Early	Haemorrhage
	Vocal cord paresis
	Hypoparathyroidism (transient or permanent)
Late	Recurrent thyrotoxicosis
	Hypothyroidism

Specific circumstances

Pregnancy

Key point

Interpretation of thyroid function tests in pregnancy

Low TSH values are not uncommon in the first trimester (see Section 3.3.1). FT4 and FT3 levels at this stage are usually normal, but may be mildly elevated. However, as the pregnancy progresses FT4 and FT3 levels can fall below the respective normal population reference ranges. It is therefore important that, whenever possible, trimester-specific reference ranges are used.

Key point

Treatment choices in pregnancy

- ^{131}I therapy is contraindicated (as are radioisotope scans) and accordingly, treatment options are limited to antithyroid drugs or, in some cases, surgery during the second trimester.
- PTU is the drug of choice in the first trimester, when CBZ is generally avoided due to the risk of inducing aplasia cutis; from the second trimester onwards, CBZ is preferred. The lowest possible dose of antithyroid drug should be used at all times, and the block and replace regimen must not be used.

Graves' disease often remits during pregnancy and some patients are able to come off antithyroid treatment completely, but relapse is common during the postnatal period.

TSH receptor antibody titres should be determined early in the third trimester to assess the risk of neonatal thyroid dysfunction.

Thyroiditis

Subacute, postpartum and painless thyroiditis are characterised by destruction of thyroid follicles with release of stored T4 and T3 into the circulation. In the thyrotoxic stage, beta-blockers are the treatment of choice by virtue of their ability to relieve adrenergic symptoms. Antithyroid drugs are of little use. L-T4 replacement may be required subsequently during the hypothyroid phase.

2.3.3 Thyroid nodules and goitre

The term 'goitre' denotes enlargement of the thyroid gland. It may be diffuse or nodular, simple or toxic, benign or malignant and physiological or pathological (Table 34).

Aetiology/pathogenesis

It is likely that an array of different factors interact to stimulate thyroid enlargement / nodule formation. For example, elevated TSH levels in hypothyroid states provide a

Table 34 Classification of goitre and thyroid nodules

	Type	Cause
Diffuse goitre	Physiological	Puberty
		Pregnancy
	Autoimmune	Graves' disease
		Hashimoto's thyroiditis
	Thyroiditis	Subacute (de Quervain's)
		Riedel's disease
	Iodine deficiency	—
	Dyshormonogenesis	—
	Goitrogens	Antithyroid drugs
		Lithium
		Iodine excess
Nodular goitre	Multinodular goitre	Toxic
		Non-toxic
	Solitary nodule	Toxic adenoma
		Benign nodule
		Malignant nodule
		Lymphoma
		Metastasis
	Infiltration (rare)	Tuberculosis
		Sarcoidosis

strong trophic stimulus to the gland; similarly, antibodies directed against the TSH receptor may promote thyroid growth.

Epidemiology

Thyroid nodules and goitre are common; up to 8% of the population have palpable goitres and autopsy series report thyroid nodules in ~50% of people over the age of 40. Women are more commonly affected than men.

Clinical presentation

Many cases are noted incidentally, although there may be features of associated hypothyroidism or hyperthyroidism. Occasionally, thyroid enlargement leads to local pressure symptoms, eg difficulty in breathing (with stridor) or swallowing.

Physical signs

Approaches to the examination of a neck lump and the thyroid gland are outlined below. Remember to check for the presence of lymphadenopathy – enlarged lymph nodes in the cervical chain may be a sinister feature when associated with a thyroid nodule.

Key point

Examination of a neck lump

Determine the following 'S' features:

- Site
- Shape
- Size
- Surface
- Smoothness
- Solid/cyStic
- Surroundings
- pulSatility
- tranSilluminability.

Key point

Examination of the thyroid gland

- Inspect from the front. Does the lump move on swallowing (give the patient a glass of water to help them to do this) or with tongue protrusion? The latter is suggestive of a thyroglossal cyst.
- Stand behind the patient and palpate the gland assessing size, texture, mobility and smoothness. Is the lump solitary? Are there multiple nodules?
- Check for tracheal displacement, tracheal narrowing (ask the patient to open their mouth and breath in and out as fast as they can, listening for stridor as they do so), retrosternal extension (percuss over upper sternum), or a thyroid bruit.
- Assess thyroid status.
- If you have not already done so, check for lymphadenopathy.

Investigations

Blood tests

Thyroid function tests

FT4, FT3 and TSH should be checked to exclude overt thyroid dysfunction.

Thyroid antibodies

The demonstration of positive thyroid antibody titres (anti-thyroid peroxidase, thyroglobulin) may support your suspicions of underlying autoimmune disease. However, it does not exclude coexistent pathology, including malignancy.

Calcitonin

Measurement of basal and stimulated calcitonin levels (see Section 3.1.6) is reserved for cases where medullary thyroid carcinoma (MTC) is suspected. This test was previously used to screen family members of probands with multiple endocrine neoplasia type 2 (MEN-2) or familial MTC, but these individuals should now undergo genetic screening and be offered prophylactic thyroidectomy if they carry the *RET* mutation (see Section 2.7.1). The main clinical indication now for measurement of calcitonin is in monitoring for recurrence or disease progression in individuals with previously resected MTC.

Thyroglobulin

Although thyroglobulin estimation serves as a valuable tumour marker in individuals with differentiated thyroid carcinoma who have undergone completion thyroidectomy, it is of no value in the screening of newly presenting nodules/goitre, since levels are also elevated in several benign conditions.

Imaging

Ultrasonography

Ultrasound is helpful in distinguishing between solid, cystic or mixed nodules. It is now considered the 'gold standard' imaging modality in all patients with a thyroid nodule/enlargement (with the exception of those in whom there is clear biochemical evidence of thyrotoxicosis). It is typically combined with fine-needle aspiration cytology (FNAC) (see below). Ultrasonographic features that are suggestive of malignancy in a thyroid nodule are hypoechogenicity, irregular margins / infiltration, microcalcification and increased central vascularity. Findings are graded on a scale U1–5 covering a spectrum from normal to malignant. Cervical lymphadenopathy is also readily detected with ultrasound.

^{99m}Tc scintigraphy

Radioisotope scans are not routinely used in the evaluation of thyroid nodules since the identification of a 'cold' or 'hot' lesion does not necessarily correlate with the presence of a malignant or benign lesion, respectively. However, it may be indicated in a patient with clear biochemical evidence of thyrotoxicosis (eg when the TSH receptor antibody titre is not elevated).

Key point

- Less than 20% of cold nodules are malignant. The remainder are benign (colloid nodules, Hashimoto's thyroiditis, haemorrhage).
- The presence of a 'warm' or 'hot' nodule does not exclude malignancy.
- On ultrasound, a solid nodule is more likely to be malignant than a cystic lesion. However, the majority of solid nodules are benign, while some cystic lesions are malignant.

Plain radiographs / CT

Radiographs of the chest and thoracic inlet may demonstrate retrosternal extension of a goitre and/or compression of surrounding structures which can be confirmed on CT examination (Fig 40). Flow–volume loop studies may be helpful in such cases.

FNAC / ultrasound-guided biopsy

Due to the lack of sensitivity and specificity of clinical examination and routine radiology in the differentiation of benign from malignant solitary/ dominant thyroid nodules, FNAC remains an important first-line investigation in many patients. Results are typically reported as either non-diagnostic (indicating a need for repeat aspiration) or on a spectrum from benign to malignant. In the UK, the Thy1–5 classification is preferred for grading:

- Thy1
- non-diagnostic (action: repeat FNAC)
- Thy2
- non-neoplastic/benign (action: repeat FNAC at 3–6 months – similar findings allow the lesion to be classified as non-neoplastic)
- Thy3
- follicular lesion / suspected follicular lesion
- Thy3 is divided in to 3a (atypical – requiring repeat cytology and/or surgery) and 3f (which requires surgery); in the first instance, lobectomy allows a formal histological diagnosis to be made and guides further intervention (eg completion thyroidectomy / lymph node dissection) if malignant
- Thy4
- suspicious for malignancy (action: refer for surgery)
- Thy5
- diagnostic of malignancy (action: refer for surgery).

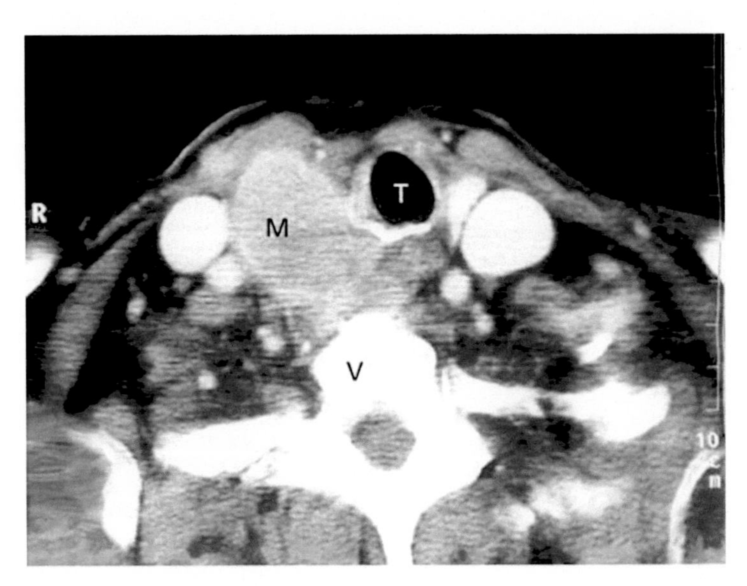

Fig 40 Thyroid carcinoma. CT of the neck showing a large right-sided thyroid mass (M) displacing the trachea (T) to the left and extending posteriorly to the vertebral body (V).

Treatment

Wherever possible, the underlying condition should be treated appropriately, eg T4 replacement in hypothyroidism associated with Hashimoto's thyroiditis; thyroidectomy for suspicious or frankly malignant nodules. Surgery may also be indicated for single benign nodules or non-toxic multinodular goitre associated with local pressure effects.

2.3.4 Thyroid malignancy

Thyroid malignancy represents the commonest of the endocrine cancers. Mutations have been described in proto-oncogenes (eg the *PTC/RET* mutation in some cases of papillary carcinoma) and tumour suppressor genes (eg p53 mutations in anaplastic carcinoma). Tumours can be considered according to their cell of origin (eg papillary, follicular, Hürthle cell and anaplastic cancers are derived from thyrocytes; medullary thyroid cancer from parafollicular C-cells; lymphoma from thyroidal lymphocytes). Table 35 outlines the important clinical aspects of this disorder. See also the *Oncology* book of Medical Masterclass.

2.4 Reproductive disorders

2.4.1 Delayed growth and puberty

Definition

The average age of onset of puberty is 11 years in girls and 12 years in boys. In general, investigations should be initiated if there are no secondary sexual characteristics by $13^1/_2$ years in girls and 14 years in boys, and/or if the child's height falls below the third centile and is inappropriate for the height of the parents. Remember, however, that up to 3% of children exhibit constitutional pubertal delay.

Assessment of pubertal development

The Tanner staging system (Tables 36 and 37) allows for an objective assessment of sexual maturity. In recognition of the differing actions of adrenal androgens and gonadal steroids, it distinguishes between genital and pubic hair development in boys and breast and pubic hair development in girls.

Aetiology/pathophysiology

Causes of pubertal delay and/or short stature are shown in Table 38.

Clinical presentation

Patients may present with short stature, failure to develop secondary sexual characteristics or primary amenorrhoea. It is important to determine whether there is a family history of delayed growth and puberty or a history of other childhood illnesses.

During the initial assessment it is useful to consider the following points:

- Are data showing the time course of growth failure available, eg child health records that include growth charts (see Fig 4 in Section 1.1.7)? Enquire about birth weight and problems at delivery since low birth weight is associated with short stature.
- Is there a history of chronic illness, eg asthma, cystic fibrosis, Crohn's disease or chronic renal disease? Consider also occult coeliac disease. All of these conditions can be associated with short stature.
- Is there a family history of short stature or delayed puberty?

Table 35 Clinical aspects of thyroid malignancy

Type of thyroid malignancy	Epidemiology	Clinical features/spread/metastases	Treatment/prognosis
Papillary	About 70–80% of all cases ♂:♀ ~1:3 Peak incidence during the fourth decade of life	Considered to be the slowest growing of the thyroid cancers. Although local spread to cervical lymph nodes is common at presentation, distant metastases are rare	Total thyroidectomy is recommended for all but the smallest of tumours, and is followed by an ablative dose of radioactive iodine in many patients. This in turn is followed by suppressive T4 therapy (although this is no longer automatically life long). In these circumstances thyroglobulin acts as a useful tumour marker. Cancer-related death occurs in only ~10% of cases during 20 years' follow-up
Follicular	About 10–15% of all cases ♂:♀ ~1:2.5 Peak incidence during the fifth decade of life	More aggressive than papillary carcinoma. Spread may occur by local invasion of lymph nodes or by blood vessel invasion with distant metastases to lung and bone	Follicular carcinoma is treated along the same lines as papillary carcinoma. However, TSH suppression is typically life long. Tyrosine kinase inhibitors (eg sorafenib) may be tried in advanced/inoperable cases. Cancer-related deaths occur in a higher proportion of patients (20–60%) during 20 years' follow-up
Hürthle cell	Rare	Typically more aggressive behaviour	Total thyroidectomy and central compartment lymphadenectomy are advised. Radioactive iodine is less efficacious
Anaplastic	<10% of all cases ♂:♀ ~1:1 Peak incidence between 65 and 70 years of age	An aggressive form of thyroid cancer, which typically presents with a painful rapidly expanding thyroid mass	Despite combined treatment with surgery, radiotherapy and in some cases chemotherapy, the prognosis is poor, with few patients surviving more than 6 months
MTC	<5% of all cases ♂:♀ ~1:1 Sporadic MTC has a peak incidence in the fourth to fifth decades, while hereditary MTC is often detected at a much earlier age	More aggressive than papillary or follicular carcinoma, but less so than anaplastic tumours. Locally invasive with distant spread via lymphatics and blood. Associated with the MEN-2 syndromes	Total thyroidectomy may be curative in the early stages, hence the rationale for screening relatives of affected individuals in MEN kindreds. Radiotherapy and chemotherapy are usually of little benefit. Long-term survival is variable
Lymphoma	<1% of all cases	May arise as a primary in the thyroid or as part of a generalised lymphoma	Variable prognosis and response to radiotherapy

MEN, multiple endocrine neoplasia; MEN-2, multiple endocrine neoplasia type 2; MTC, medullary thyroid carcinoma; T4, thyroxine; TSH, thyroid-stimulating hormone.

- Is there any evidence of nutritional deficiency or disorders such as anorexia nervosa?
- What are the social circumstances? Emotional stress can have adverse effects on growth.

Physical signs

A thorough examination is necessary, looking for signs of systemic illness, eg chronic lung disease. You should also make a note of:

- height, weight and arm span – this will help to determine whether growth failure is uniformly distributed
- pubertal stage, using the Tanner staging scheme
- the presence or absence of testes within the scrotal sac; testicular volume should be assessed with an orchidometer (Fig 41)
- features suggesting a specific diagnosis such as Kallmann's syndrome, Klinefelter's syndrome, Turner's syndrome or other genetic, endocrine (eg hypothyroidism, Cushing's syndrome) or dysmorphic disorders.

Table 36 Tanner pubertal stages in boys

Area of development	Stage	Description
Genital	1	Pre-adolescent: testes, scrotum and penis are of about the same size and proportion as in early childhood
	2	Enlargement of scrotum and testes. Skin of scrotum reddens and changes in texture. Little or no enlargement of the penis at this stage
	3	Enlargement of the penis, which occurs at first mainly in length. Further growth of testes and scrotum
	4	Increased size of penis with growth in breadth and development of glans. Testes and scrotum larger; scrotal skin darkened
	5	Genitalia adult in size and shape
Pubic hair	1	Pre-adolescent: the vellus over the pubes is not further developed than that over the abdominal wall, ie no pubic hair
	2	Sparse growth of long, slightly pigmented downy hair, straight or slightly curled, chiefly at the base of the penis
	3	Considerably darker, coarser and more curled. The hair spreads sparsely laterally
	4	Hair now adult in type, but the area covered is still considerably smaller than in the adult. No spread to medial surface of the thighs
	5	Adult in quantity and type

Table 37 Tanner pubertal stages in girls

Area of development	Stage	Description
Breast	1	Pre-adolescent: elevation of papilla only
	2	Breast bud stage: elevation of breast and papilla as small mound. Enlargement of areolar diameter
	3	Further enlargement and elevation of breast and areola, with no separation of their contours
	4	Projection of areola and papilla to form a secondary mound above the level of the breast
	5	Mature stage: projection of papilla only, due to recession of the areola to the general contour of the breast
Pubic hair	1	Pre-adolescent: the vellus over the pubes is not further developed than that over the abdominal wall, ie no pubic hair
	2	Sparse growth of long, slightly pigmented downy hair, straight or slightly curled, chiefly along labia
	3	Considerably darker, coarser and more curled. The hair spreads sparsely over the junction of the pubes
	4	Hair now adult in type, but the area covered is still considerably smaller than in the adult. No spread to medial surface of the thighs
	5	Adult in quantity and type

Table 38 Aetiology of delayed growth and puberty

Frequency	Cause
Commonest causes of delayed growth and puberty	'Constitutional delay', a non-pathological condition, commoner in boys, which is often familial. Bone age is typically less than chronological age and the child usually achieves their predicted adult height
	Chronic/severe illness (eg coeliac disease, hypothyroidism, renal tubular acidosis, eating disorders and psychosocial deprivation)
Rarer causes of short stature	Chromosomal abnormalities (eg Down's syndrome, Turner's syndrome)
	Single-gene defects (eg the skeletal dysplasias such as achondroplasia)
	Dysmorphic syndromes (eg Prader–Willi syndrome)
	Endocrine disorders (eg growth hormone deficiency or resistance, pituitary disease and glucocorticoid excess)
Rarer causes of delayed puberty	Hypogonadotrophic hypogonadism (eg idiopathic, Kallmann's syndrome, pituitary dysfunction)
	Hypergonadotrophic hypogonadism (eg Turner's syndrome, Klinefelter's syndrome, gonadal dysgenesis, previous cytotoxic treatment or radiotherapy, trauma/orchitis in males, androgen insensitivity (testicular feminisation))
	Androgen excess (eg CAH, adrenal or ovarian tumours, Cushing's syndrome)

CAH, congenital adrenal hyperplasia.

Investigation

Initial investigations

Routine blood tests / urinalysis

Initial evaluation should include screening for underlying disorders with:

- a full blood count (anaemia)
- urea and electrolytes (chronic renal impairment)
- glucose
- C-reactive protein (CRP) and/or erythrocyte sedimentation rate (ESR) (systemic disorders)
- thyroid-function tests (TFTs) (free thyroxine (FT4) and thyroid-stimulating hormone (TSH))
- anti-tissue transglutaminase antibodies and IgA (coeliac disease)
- plasma bicarbonate and urinalysis (renal tubular acidosis).

Gonadotrophins (luteinising hormone (LH), follicle-stimulating hormone (FSH)) and oestradiol (E_2) or testosterone: While hypergonadotrophic hypogonadism (ie high LH and FSH with low E_2/testosterone) suggests primary gonadal failure, hypogonadotrophic hypogonadism (ie low LH and FSH with low E_2/testosterone) does not distinguish between constitutional delay (ie prepubertal levels) and secondary gonadal failure.

Key point

Bone age

Bone age (determined by plain radiograph, typically of the wrist) can be compared with chronological age to aid in the diagnosis of pubertal delay and allow predictions regarding potential future growth. For example:

- Low gonadotrophins and a more advanced bone age are suggestive of underlying pathology.
- Low gonadotrophins and a relatively delayed bone age are more likely in the long term to be associated with normal pubertal development.

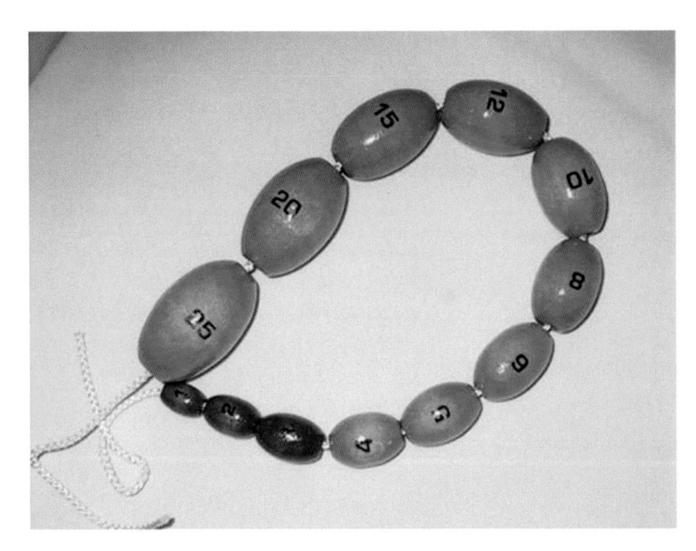

Fig 41 Prader orchidometer.

Karyotype analysis

The karyotype of all girls with delayed puberty and short stature should be checked, as the diagnosis of Turner's syndrome is not always clinically apparent (one in 1,500–2,500 of live-born females – see Section 2.4.4). Analysis may be necessary using DNA extracted from a second tissue (eg skin fibroblasts) in cases of mosaicism, where lymphocyte DNA is normal.

Males with delayed puberty should be screened for possible Klinefelter's syndrome.

Further investigations

Depending on the results of the initial investigations, more complex tests of pituitary function (eg a gonadotrophin-releasing hormone (GnRH) test, see Section 3.1.4; assessment of growth hormone (GH) status, see Section 2.1.8) may be indicated, together with structural studies, eg MRI of the pituitary fossa, visual field assessment and pelvic ultrasound.

Treatment

The choice of treatment will be directed by the underlying aetiology. Most children with constitutional delay of puberty, especially if mild, require only simple reassurance (they are normal, but their 'body clock' is starting later than that of their friends). Occasionally, psychological pressures are such that intervention may be indicated to 'start things off'. This typically involves the use of short-term (<6 months) low-dose sex steroids, eg oestrogen treatment in girls (5–10 μg ethinyloestradiol per day) or testosterone injections (starting at 50 mg IM every 4 weeks) in boys. In both sexes, once treatment is discontinued the child's own pubertal development takes over in cases of constitutional delay.

Complications

The main problems associated with constitutional delay of growth and puberty are psychological and social. It is important to define the worries of the patient, their parents and you (as their doctor): these may be different. Adolescence is a difficult time anyway, and short stature and sexual infantilism will exacerbate the usual problems. The child's behaviour may become immature or aggressive and antisocial. Parents may not allow the child the independence appropriate for their age, and may be inclined to 'baby' them. There may be bullying or teasing at school, with delays in developing social skills if they feel unable to start 'dating' at the same time as their peers. Contact with The Child Growth Foundation may be useful.

2.4.2 Male hypogonadism

A small proportion of patients presenting with delayed puberty and poor growth, and with a prepubertal hormone profile (ie low LH and FSH and low E_2 or testosterone) prove on follow-up to have true hypogonadotrophic hypogonadism, ie they fail to enter puberty spontaneously as the years advance or, conversely, fail to progress through puberty after a small priming dose of sex steroids, as outlined in Section 2.4.1. In girls this typically presents with primary amenorrhoea (see Section 2.4.3), while in boys there is failure to acquire secondary sexual characteristics.

Men may also present with loss of secondary sexual characteristics later in life, and again, determination of paired gonadotrophins and testosterone is critical in directing further investigation.

Aetiology/pathophysiology

Hypothalamic/pituitary disease, whether due to tumour, inflammation, infiltration or to previous surgery/radiotherapy, may present with hypogonadotrophic hypogonadism (indeed, the hypothalamic–pituitary–gonadal axis is among the most sensitive of the hormonal axes to damage), and these disorders must be excluded. In the case of true isolated hypogonadotrophic hypogonadism, the aetiology is often not apparent, but genetic advances continue to define single gene defects which produce the phenotype. Traditionally, patients with hyposmia/anosmia were considered to form a separate group defined as Kallmann's syndrome (see below). However, it is now clear that there is considerable overlap between Kallmann's syndrome and other forms of so-called idiopathic hypogonadotrophic hypogonadism (IHH), and both entities have even been described in the same family. Identification of specific genetic defects is likely to rationalise this diagnostic classification. Affected genes discovered to date include the *KAL1* gene (see below) and those encoding the GnRH receptor, the fibroblast growth factor receptor (FGFR), and the G protein coupled receptor 54 (GPR54). Some of the syndromes produced by these defects have characteristic associated features as outlined in Section 2.4.3. A retrospective clue to the diagnosis is a history of cryptorchidism, often bilateral, reflecting failure of the perinatal activation of the hypothalamic–pituitary–testicular axis.

In later onset hypogonadism, the finding of a hypogonadotrophic hormone profile should prompt a careful search for more generalised hypothalamic or pituitary disease.

Moderate to severe obesity and/or severe insulin resistance may also be associated with apparent mild hypogonadism (typically with normal LH and FSH levels), as these conditions are associated with suppression of sex hormone-binding globulin (SHBG), and hence total testosterone levels, but with relative preservation of free testosterone as gauged by calculation of the free testosterone index.

Where gonadotrophin levels are elevated primary testicular failure is present, which may be due to a range of infective, traumatic or ischaemic insults, and more rarely as a consequence of excess iron deposition in the context of haemochromatosis (see Section 2.5.3). Klinefelter's syndrome is an important congenital cause of hypergonadotrophic hypogonadism (see the following 'Key point' box).

Key point

Kallmann's syndrome

Kallmann's syndrome is a congenital disorder characterised by isolated gonadotrophin deficiency and hypoplasia of the olfactory lobes with consequent hyposmia/anosmia, due to a range of genetic defects which interfere with normal migration of neurones from the olfactory placode during development. Associated abnormalities in some patients include gynaecomastia, mirror movements, midface abnormalities such as cleft lip/palate, renal agenesis, hearing loss and ataxia. Inheritance may be autosomal dominant, X-linked recessive or, rarely, autosomal recessive. Genes implicated to date include *KAL1* on the X chromosome, and those encoding fibroblast growth factor receptor (FGFR1) and prokineticin receptors (PROKR1 and 2).

Klinefelter's syndrome

Klinefelter's syndrome is a congenital disorder associated with one or more supernumerary X chromosomes (karyotype 47,XXY in 80–90% of cases). It is the commonest chromosomal abnormality leading to hypogonadism in men. It is characterised by small firm testes, small phallus, eunuchoid proportions and gynaecomastia. Case control studies have suggested an associated mild degree of learning impairment. The most common presentations are in late teenage or adult life with gynaecomastia or infertility. Azoospermia is the norm, reflecting seminiferous tubule dysgenesis. Testosterone production is variable, leading to differing degrees of sexual development. Psychosocial problems are commonly seen, and there is also an excess incidence of mitral valve prolapse which should be screened for.

Clinical presentation

Androgen status

Ask about:

- frequency of shaving and beard growth
- axillary and pubic hair development
- deepening of the voice
- libido, erectile function (and where appropriate fertility).

Enquire further about:

- problems with sense of smell (hyposmia or anosmia in Kallmann's syndrome)
- colour vision (also sometimes impaired in Kallmann's syndrome)
- undescended testes in infancy (and timing of corrective surgery)
- history of cleft palate/lip (a rare feature of FGFR mutations)
- features suggesting other pituitary hormone deficiencies (see Section 2.1.8)
- headaches / visual problems (hypothalamic/pituitary space-occupying lesion)
- galactorrhoea (hyperprolactinaemia)
- testicular trauma or bilateral orchitis in the past (eg due to postpubertal mumps)
- gynaecomastia
- diabetes, arthritis or liver disease (haemochromatosis – see Section 2.5.3).

Physical signs

Check for the presence of the following:

- the distinctive facial appearance of long-standing hypogonadism, especially in older men, in whom the poverty of facial hair and lack of temporal recession is most noticeable (Fig 42)
- other secondary sexual characteristics
- testicular volumes using an orchidometer (see Fig 41 in Section 2.4.1)
- an absent or impaired sense of smell (Kallmann's syndrome)
- eunuchoid habitus (ie span greater than height and heel to pubis distance greater than pubis to crown), which is common in those in whom hypogonadism precedes puberty, eg Klinefelter's syndrome
- mirror movements (eg the tendency of the contralateral side to mimic unilateral hand movements)
- gynaecomastia – indicates a decrease in the androgen:oestrogen ratio
- features suggestive of a pituitary tumour, eg bitemporal hemianopia, hypopituitarism, galactorrhoea (hyperprolactinaemia).

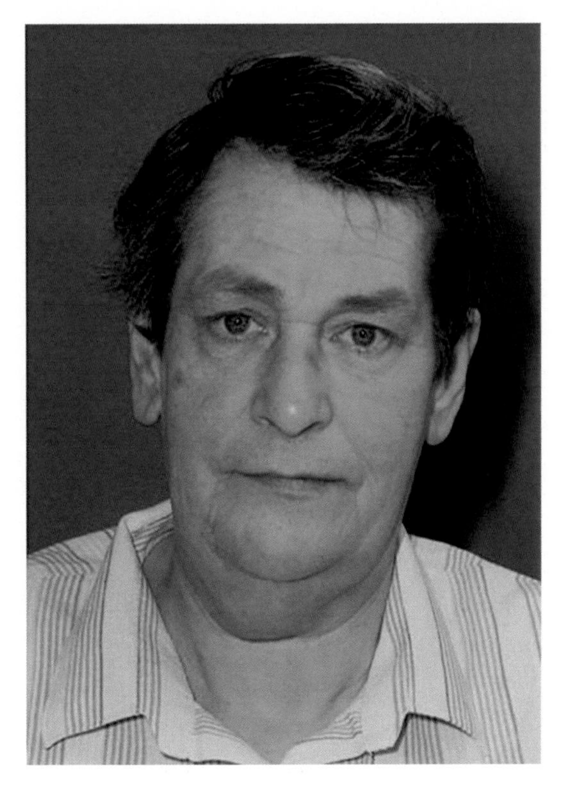

Fig 42 Hypogonadal male. Note the absence of facial hair and fine wrinkles around the corners of the eyes and mouth.

> Hazard
>
> **Cryptorchidism**
>
> Cryptorchidism (unilateral or bilateral absence of the testes from the scrotum) is an important clinical finding since it indicates a significant risk of malignant transformation in the affected gonad(s) and further investigation is mandatory (see below).

Investigation

Initial investigations

Routine blood tests

Unless the clinical features suggest a specific underlying disorder, some simple screening tests should be performed including: full blood count (anaemia), urea and electrolytes (chronic renal impairment), fasting glucose, thyroid function, prolactin, liver biochemistry and serum transferrin saturation / iron studies (haemochromatosis).

Gonadotrophins (LH, FSH), testosterone and SHBG (allows estimation of free testosterone)

To distinguish primary (hypergonadotrophic) and secondary (hypogonadotrophic) hypogonadism.

Specific investigations

These will be guided by clinical impression and preliminary screening tests, but may include:

- karyotype analysis – to exclude Klinefelter's syndrome
- assessment of pituitary function / MRI pituitary fossa – in cases of secondary hypogonadism / hyperprolactinaemia (see Section 2.1.8)
- ultrasound of the testes – the clinical finding of cryptorchidism must be investigated further to try and identify the site of the undescended/ maldescended tissue
- genetic screening for haemochromatosis (see Section 2.5.3)
- semen analysis – including assessment of sperm number, morphology and motility
- human chorionic gonadotrophin (hCG) stimulation – hCG is able to mimic the ability of LH (with which it shares a common alpha-subunit) to stimulate testosterone synthesis and secretion, and therefore may help to differentiate primary and secondary gonadal failure
- bone densitometry (dual-energy X-ray absorptiometry (DXA)) – testosterone is required for maintenance of normal bone mineral density (BMD) in men. Bone densitometry may help to identify those at significant risk of fracture, and is particularly useful in older men who decline testosterone replacement, when alternative treatment may be required, eg bisphosphonate.

Management

The general principles governing management of the hypogonadal male include:

- patient and sympathetic explanation
- treatment of any underlying disorder
- replacement of hormone deficiency
- referral for specialist fertility advice if appropriate.

Various formulations of testosterone replacement are available and are discussed in more detail in Section 2.1.8. Safety monitoring should include screening for liver dysfunction, polycythaemia, dyslipidaemia, obstructive sleep apnoea and (where appropriate) prostate neoplasia. Testosterone therapy should only be used with extreme caution in men with a history of venous thromboembolic disease.

2.4.3 Oligomenorrhoea/ amenorrhoea and premature menopause

Amenorrhoea is traditionally subdivided into:

- primary amenorrhoea: lack of menses by the age of 16 years
- secondary amenorrhoea: absence of menstrual periods for 6 months or more after cyclical menses have been established.

Oligomenorrhoea indicates lighter/ irregular periods.

Aetiology/pathophysiology

In practice, there is considerable overlap between primary and secondary amenorrhoea, as a number of conditions can give rise to either (Table 39). A small number of disorders are, however, specifically associated with primary amenorrhoea, including anatomical defects of the female reproductive tract and Turner's syndrome (see Section 2.4.4).

Table 39 Causes of amenorrhoea

Cause	Condition
Physiological	Pubertal delay
	Pregnancy
	Lactation
	Postmenopausal
Pathological	PCOS
	Hypothalamic–pituitary dysfunction (including excessive weight loss or exercise, stress, pituitary tumours/infiltration, hyperprolactinaemia)
	Turner's syndrome
	POF
	CAH
	Adrenal/ovarian neoplasms
	Congenital anomalies of the female reproductive tract

CAH, congenital adrenal hyperplasia; PCOS, polycystic ovary syndrome; POF, premature ovarian failure.

Key point

'Post-pill amenorrhoea' is not a satisfactory diagnosis

Most clinicians agree that 'post-pill amenorrhoea' does not exist, and that an underlying cause should be sought in such cases.

Clinical presentation

Common

- oligomenorrhoea/amenorrhoea
- impaired fertility
- hirsutism or acne.

Uncommon

Menopausal symptoms including:

- hot flushes
- night sweats
- vaginal dryness with or without dyspareunia.

Rare

If there is a space-occupying pituitary lesion:

- visual symptoms
- headache
- features of other pituitary hormone deficiency or excess.

Physical signs

Common

- extremes of BMI (>30 or <20 kg/m^2)
- mild hirsutism or acne.

Rare

- virilisation (marked hirsutism, muscle development in a male pattern, clitoromegaly) (see Section 2.2.3)
- bitemporal hemianopia (suggestive of a pituitary tumour).

Investigation

Key point

Always consider pregnancy!

Patients should be fully evaluated at initial presentation: subfertility is always an urgent concern, and prolonged low oestrogen levels may lead to osteopaenia and osteoporosis. However, before embarking on more complex investigations the possibility of pregnancy must be considered to prevent embarrassment for all concerned at a later date.

Once pregnancy has been excluded, baseline investigations should include measurement of:

- gonadotrophins – FSH and LH
- E_2
- prolactin.

Together with the clinical features, these preliminary screening tests will guide subsequent investigations (Table 40), which may include:

- thyroid function tests (TFTs) (ideally free thyroxine (FT4) and TSH to distinguish primary and secondary thyroid dysfunction)
- dynamic assessment of pituitary reserve, eg insulin tolerance test (see Section 3.1.5)
- testosterone and dehydroepiandrosterone sulphate (DHEAS) (if there are any signs of androgen excess)
- 17alpha-hydroxyprogesterone (17-OHP) (late onset congenital adrenal hyperplasia (CAH) may present in adulthood with oligomenorrhoea) (see Section 2.2.5)
- a progestogen (eg medroxyprogesterone or norethisterone) challenge/withdrawal test. In non-pregnant patients, medroxyprogesterone at a dose of 10 mg daily is administered for 5–10 days. If a withdrawal bleed occurs within 10 days, the endometrium must have been exposed to oestrogen, and it is likely that oestrogen levels

Table 40 Differential diagnosis of oligomenorrhoea/amenorrhoea according to gonadotrophins and prolactin

Cause	Condition
Hypogonadotrophic	Excessive weight loss, exercise or stress, pubertal delay, Kallmann's syndrome, idiopathic hypogonadotrophic hypogonadism, pituitary disease/treatment
Normogonadotrophic	PCOS, CAH, androgen-secreting tumour, anatomical defects, androgen insensitivity
Hypergonadotrophic	Turner's syndrome, POF
Hyperprolactinaemia	Prolactinoma, stalk disconnection syndrome, drugs (eg dopamine antagonists)

CAH, congenital adrenal hyperplasia; PCOS, polycystic ovary syndrome, POF, premature ovarian failure.

- are sufficient to protect against osteopaenia/osteoporosis even if she is amenorrhoeic
- a mid-luteal phase (day 21 for a 28-day cycle) progesterone. In menstruating patients, a level of more than 30 nmol/L suggests that ovulation has occurred during that cycle
- karyotype analysis (Turner's syndrome)
- radiological imaging of the pituitary, adrenals or ovaries, depending on the biochemical pattern of results
- bone densitometry.

Treatment

General

Specific treatment should be directed at the underlying disorder. Weight adjustment may be effective in hypogonadotrophic hypogonadism and polycystic ovary syndrome (PCOS) but is often very difficult for the patient to achieve.

Prevention/amelioration of osteopaenia/osteoporosis

Oestrogen therapy (with a cyclical progestogen unless the patient has had a hysterectomy) is indicated to prevent osteoporosis if the progestogen challenge test is negative. This can be given in the form of postmenopausal hormone replacement therapy (HRT) (which would not prevent conception, however unlikely) or the combined oral contraceptive pill (COCP).

Fertility

Hypogonadotrophic hypogonadism may respond to specialist treatment with gonadotrophins or GnRH. In women with premature ovarian failure (POF), *in vitro* fertilisation (IVF) using a donated oocyte is the only option (see Section 2.4.8).

Complications

- osteopaenia, with the subsequent risk of osteoporotic fractures, due to oestrogen deficiency
- psychological problems linked to impaired fertility or hirsutism.

Disease associations

POF may be associated with other autoimmune endocrine disorders such as type 1 diabetes, hypothyroidism and Addison's disease (see Section 2.7.2).

2.4.4 Turner's syndrome

Turner's syndrome commonly presents as primary amenorrhoea in a girl with short stature. The classical stigmata of Turner's syndrome include a webbed neck, low hairline, widely spaced nipples, and cubitus valgus (Fig 43). Remember, however, that the clinical features may be less marked if there is only partial X chromosome deletion or alternatively mosaicism (see the *Genetics and molecular medicine* book of Medical Masterclass).

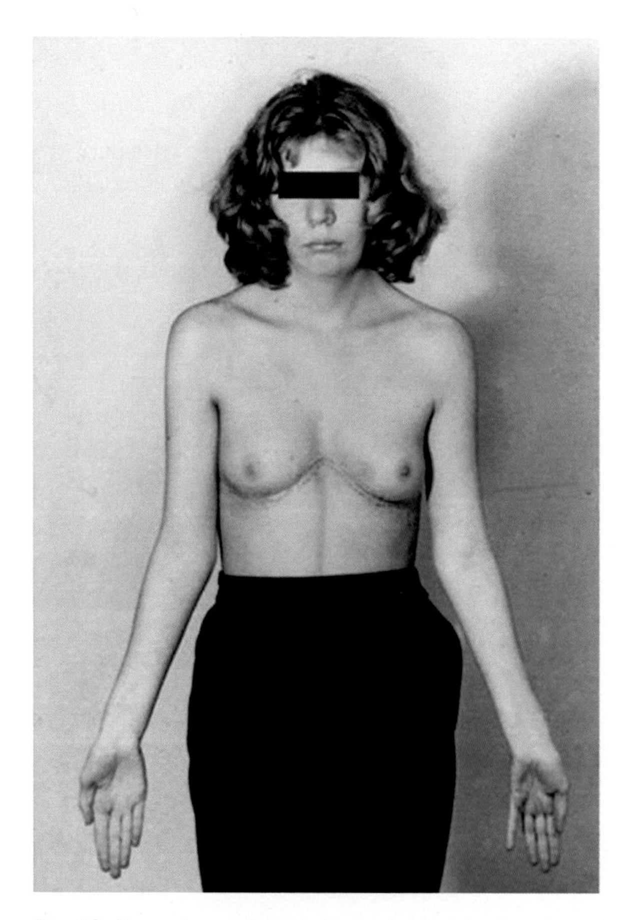

Fig 43 Turner's syndrome. Note the webbed neck and wide carrying angle, which are typical of classical Turner's syndrome. In addition, there is a visible thoracotomy scar from a previous atrial septal defect repair.

Patients with classical Turner's syndrome usually exhibit:

- low/undetectable E_2 with high levels of LH and FSH (hypergonadotrophic hypogonadism)
- 45,XO karyotype.

Further investigations in confirmed cases of Turner's syndrome are discussed below.

Specific management

There are many issues, both physical and psychological, that need to be addressed in the management of women with Turner's syndrome.

Hormone replacement therapy

A natural oestrogen will promote the development of secondary sexual characteristics. Treatment should be started with a low dose of oestrogen alone and gradually increased. After 1–2 years, maintenance treatment with cyclical combined oestrogen and progestogen therapy can be substituted.

Key point

Gonadal replacement therapy in Turner's syndrome

The timing and dose of oestrogen replacement is critical. Use of a low dose in the early stages of treatment helps to maximise growth and final height, especially in those receiving concomitant growth hormone (GH) therapy (see below). In addition, although traditionally oral preparations have been favoured, there is increasing interest in the use of transdermal oestrogen therapy (as oral oestrogens may antagonise the effect of GH through inhibition of hepatic insulin-like growth factor (IGF)-1 synthesis).

Osteoporosis

Women with Turner's syndrome are at an increased risk of developing osteoporosis. In addition to oestrogen replacement therapy, their diet should be checked to ensure an adequate supply of calcium, and regular weight-bearing exercise encouraged.

Ischaemic heart disease

A threefold excess mortality from ischaemic heart disease (IHD) probably reflects an increased incidence of insulin resistance / type 2 diabetes and hypertension. Both of these conditions should therefore be sought and treated, and the benefits of hormone replacement therapy (HRT), weight control and exercise reiterated.

Structural cardiac and renal abnormalities

Echocardiography, cardiac MRI and renal ultrasonography may reveal structural abnormalities. A bicuspid aortic valve is the commonest cardiac abnormality and may be associated with progressive aortic root dilatation. Good BP control is essential.

Hypothyroidism

Turner's syndrome is associated with an increased incidence of primary autoimmune hypothyroidism (Hashimoto's thyroiditis) and thyroid function tests (TFTs) should be monitored on a regular basis, even in asymptomatic patients.

Cryptic Y chromosome material

Karyotyping may reveal cryptic Y chromosome material (45,XO/46,XY). This predisposes to gonadoblastoma and is an indication for prophylactic gonadectomy (or close observation).

Fertility

Between 2 and 5% of women with Turner's syndrome have spontaneous menstrual periods, although only 0.5% have ovulatory cycles, and an early menopause is likely. Contraceptive advice and genetic counselling are important in this subgroup, since there is an approximately 30% risk that their offspring will have a congenital anomaly. For the majority of cases, however, specialist fertility input is required if they wish to conceive by *in vitro* fertilisation (IVF) or gamete intrafallopian transfer (GIFT) using a donor ovum. Prepregnancy cardiovascular and renal screening is imperative.

Intelligence

Intelligence is generally normal, although hand–eye coordination and visuospatial skills may be impaired. Lower social competence has also been reported.

Short stature

Although children with Turner's syndrome are not GH deficient, treatment with recombinant human GH (either alone or in combination with anabolic agents such as oxandrolone) may increase their final adult height.

Hearing loss

Recurrent middle-ear infections occur commonly during the first decade of life, and there may be a history of glue ear requiring ventilation tubes. Unfortunately, many adult women with Turner's syndrome are left with a significant hearing loss and, accordingly, all should be referred for formal audiological assessment.

Key point

Turner's syndrome – ethical issues and communication

There are many important psychological issues to consider in caring for women with Turner's syndrome. Most importantly, to quote from literature produced by the Turner's Syndrome Support Society (www.tss.org.uk/), 'women with Turner's syndrome should have no doubt of their femininity: physically, behaviourally and sexually'. A number of the management issues outlined above may be self-evident to a physician, but confusing to the patient unless fully explained:

- the need for gonadectomy if there is cryptic Y material, even though the ovaries are non-functioning
- the need for 'periods' (rather than unopposed oestrogen therapy)
- that 'periods' are actually withdrawal bleeds and do not represent restored fertility
- why the patient is prescribed the low-dose combined oral contraceptive pill even though she is infertile.

2.4.5 Polycystic ovary syndrome

Polycystic ovary syndrome (PCOS) describes the association of ovarian hyperandrogenism with chronic anovulatory cycles in females with polycystic ovaries.

Aetiology/pathophysiology

Although the aetiology of PCOS is unclear, there is evidence to suggest that it is a complex disorder reflecting interplay between genetic susceptibility and environmental factors. It is now recognised that decreased peripheral insulin sensitivity with consequent hyperinsulinaemia are key features of the metabolic derangement that is typical of PCOS. In addition, retention of insulin sensitivity by the ovary has been suggested to contribute to ovarian thecal androgen production (in response to insulin and IGF-1).

The risk of developing type 2 diabetes is approximately sixfold higher in women with PCOS than in the general population, and they frequently exhibit dyslipidaemia typical of the metabolic syndrome.

Epidemiology

PCOS is estimated to affect approximately 5% of women of reproductive age.

Clinical presentation

The symptoms of PCOS usually date from menarche and develop gradually. The most common presentation is with features of hyperandrogenism (hirsutism/acne) and menstrual irregularity (oligomenorrhoea or amenorrhoea).

Physical signs

Obesity and hirsutism (but not virilisation) are common findings. About 5% of women exhibit acanthosis nigricans (Fig 44), which is a sign of insulin resistance.

Investigations

The choice of investigations should be guided by the clinical presentation:

LH and FSH

The ratio of LH to FSH may be increased to >2 (reflecting anovulatory cycles and a lack of progesterone to inhibit LH release). However, gonadotrophins are normal in a significant number (30–50%) of women who meet the other diagnostic criteria for PCOS.

Testosterone

Testosterone is often slightly increased (although usually <5 nmol/L, thereby distinguishing PCOS from most androgen-secreting tumours).

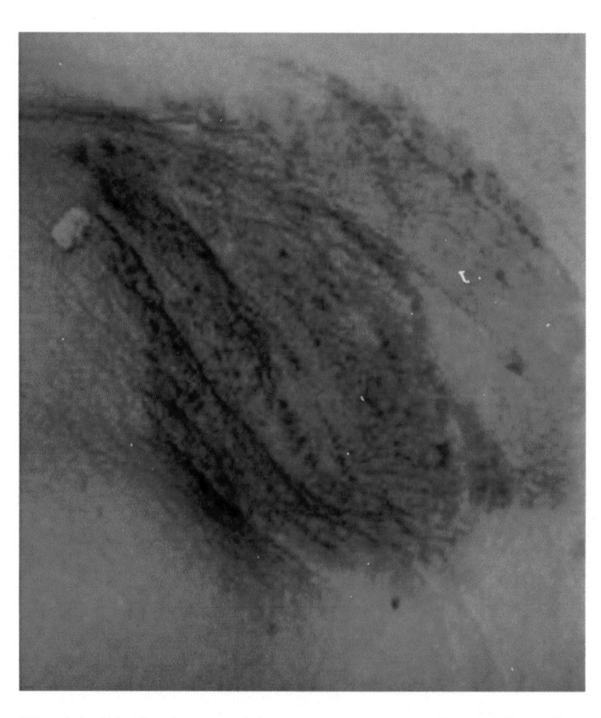

Fig 44 Marked acanthosis nigricans in the axilla of a patient with severe insulin resistance.

Prolactin

Between 10 and 20% of cases have mildly elevated prolactin levels.

Fasting glucose / oral glucose tolerance test / lipid profile

Check for evidence of impaired glucose tolerance / frank diabetes mellitus and the dyslipidaemia of the metabolic syndrome.

Progestogen withdrawal bleed

PCOS is not an oestrogen deficient state and therefore a withdrawal bleed typically follows progesterone treatment.

Pelvic ultrasonography

A pelvic ultrasound scan (preferably transvaginal) may reveal the typical ovarian appearance of multiple peripherally sited follicles ('string of pearls') with increased central stroma. However, note that the presence of polycystic ovaries does not in itself indicate that the woman has PCOS (approximately 20% of all women have polycystic changes on ultrasound, although only one-third of these have PCOS).

Further investigations

Other tests may be considered to help distinguish between PCOS and:

- adult onset congenital adrenal hyperplasia (CAH) (17alpha-hydroxyprogesterone) (see Section 2.2.5)
- ovarian or adrenal tumours (dehydroepiandrosterone sulphate (DHEAS), androstenedione) (see Section 2.2.3)
- Cushing's syndrome (see Section 2.1.1)
- monogenic causes of insulin resistance (especially in slim women: check paired fasting glucose and insulin).

Treatment

Weight loss

Key point

Weight loss will help patients with PCOS

There is good evidence to suggest that if patients manage to lose weight this will ameliorate many of the features of PCOS.

Hirsutism/infertility

Approaches to the management of hirsutism and infertility are outlined in Sections 2.4.6 and 2.4.8, respectively.

Metformin treatment

Several studies have suggested that metformin treatment (eg 500 mg tds) in obese women with PCOS can regularise menses, reduce the frequency of anovulatory cycles and perhaps improve hirsutism. However, this is not yet a licensed use for metformin, and there remain questions about the optimum dose and safety in early pregnancy. Larger studies are awaited, both with metformin and other insulin sensitisers including the thiazolidinediones (TZDs) (eg rosiglitazone, pioglitazone).

Other cardiovascular risks

In women with the metabolic form of PCOS, risk factors for coronary heart disease should be addressed, including type 2 diabetes, hypertension, hyperlipidaemia and smoking.

Prognosis

Epidemiological data are still sparse with regards the anticipated increase in the risk of coronary heart disease or cerebrovascular disease in women with PCOS.

Prevention

It has been suggested that if patients are targeted when they first present with mild hirsutism and oligomenorrhoea, and strongly encouraged to lose weight and engage in regular aerobic exercise using whatever support systems are available, the progression of the syndrome to infertility can be avoided.

2.4.6 Hirsutism

Hirsutism is excessive terminal hair growth in an androgen-dependent (or male pattern) distribution, and is a very common presenting complaint in endocrine practice. It should be discriminated from hypertrichosis, in which hair growth occurs in a non-androgen-dependent distribution. A visual scale developed by Ferriman and Gallwey can be used to make an objective assessment of the extent and severity of hirsutism, using a score of 1 (a few scattered hairs) to 4 (complete cover) for each of eleven body areas (Table 41).

Aetiology/pathophysiology

Excessive androgen-dependent hair growth can reflect high levels of circulating free androgens of adrenal or ovarian origin, or enhanced sensitivity of the hair follicles to androgens due to variations in local androgen metabolism or androgen receptor sensitivity. There is only a relatively poor correlation between levels of total testosterone and degree of hirsutism, although most women with a testosterone level more than twice the upper limit of normal will exhibit some degree of excess hair growth. Other women with high testosterone will show features of hyperandrogenism (seborrhoea, acne, male pattern alopecia) but without significant hirsutism. Furthermore, some women with apparently normal serum

Table 41 The Ferriman–Gallwey scoring system[1]

Site	Grade	Definition
Upper lip	1	Few hairs at outer margin
	2	Small moustache at outer margin
	3	Moustache extending halfway from outer margin
	4	Moustache extending to midline
Chin	1	Few scattered hairs
	2	Scattered hairs with small concentrations
	3	Light complete cover
	4	Heavy complete cover
Chest	1	Circumareolar hairs
	2	Additional midline hairs
	3	Fusion of these areas with three-quarter cover
	4	Complete cover
Upper back	1	Few scattered hairs
	2	Rather more, but still scattered
	3	Light complete cover
	4	Heavy complete cover
Lower back	1	Sacral tuft of hair
	2	With some lateral extension
	3	Three-quarter cover
	4	Complete cover
Upper abdomen	1	Few midline hairs
	2	Rather more, but still midline
	3	Half cover
	4	Full cover
Lower abdomen	1	Few midline hairs
	2	Midline streak of hair
	3	Midline band of hair
	4	Inverted V-shaped growth
Upper arm	1	Sparse growth affecting not more than one-quarter of limb surfaces
	2	More than this, but cover still incomplete
	3	Light complete cover
	4	Heavy complete cover
Forearm	1–4	Complete cover of dorsal surface, 2 grades of light and 2 grades of heavy growth
Thigh	1–4	As for arm
Leg	1–4	As for arm

1 Adapted with permission from Ferriman D and Gallwey JD. Clinical assessment of body hair growth in women. *J Clin Endocrinol Metab* 1961; 21:1440–7.

testosterone actually have elevated free testosterone: this is generally a consequence of reduced levels of sex hormone-binding globulin (SHBG), the main binding protein, which is very hormonally responsive, being suppressed by the hyperinsulinaemia of insulin resistance, by androgens themselves, and by hypothyroidism. However, a significant number of women with hirsutism have no elevation of androgens, and their condition is often called idiopathic hirsutism. This is believed to be due to genetic variation in genes encoding the androgen receptor and in enzymes such as 5alpha-reductase which is responsible for local activation of testosterone to the more potent dihydrotestosterone (DHT). Causes of hirsutism are shown in Table 42.

Epidemiology

Using the cut-off score of 8 on the Ferriman–Gallwey scale, a prevalence of hirsutism of around 5% is estimated in women of reproductive age, although there is significant ethnic and familial variation.

Clinical presentation and history

The presentation is almost always with cosmetically distressing hirsutism, often in association with oligomenorrhoea. Assessment of the patient should be strongly guided by: (1) the need to identify the small proportion of patients with an underlying virilising tumour; and (2) an appreciation of the importance of the subjective distress caused by the excess hair growth. Thus the time course of the development of hirsutism should be established: onset and gradual progression after puberty, often with progressive weight gain, is most common. A short history of rapid hair growth or sudden onset in adulthood are important clues to a possible underlying tumour. The extent and frequency of cosmetic measures taken to control hair growth also give a useful idea of the extent of the problem. Deepening of the voice in association with hair growth is sinister as it implies very high levels of androgens, with virilisation due to their action on androgen-responsive tissues other than hair follicles. The history should also be directed towards eliciting symptoms suggestive of diabetes (see Section 2.6) or Cushing's syndrome (see Section 2.1.1), and should document the presence and degree of menstrual disturbance. The drug history should concentrate on any preparations with androgenic activity, and the desire for fertility and use of contraception are important in deciding upon the therapeutic strategy.

Because in most cases anxiety caused by the cosmetic appearance of hirsutism is the main problem, it is also important to pay attention to the degree of psychological distress and extent of lifestyle disturbance produced by the excessive hair growth.

Table 42 Causes of hirsutism

Frequency	Condition
Common	Idiopathic
	Racial/familial
	PCOS
Less common	CAH (non-classical)
	Adrenal or ovarian androgen-secreting tumours
	Cushing's syndrome
	Hypothyroidism
	Other severe insulin resistance states
	Drugs, eg glucocorticoids, anabolic steroids

CAH, congenital adrenal hyperplasia; PCOS, polycystic ovary syndrome.

Physical signs

Using the Ferriman–Gallwey visual scale, hirsutism may be graded and given a numerical score for future comparative purposes. Signs of virilisation (deep voice, masculine body habitus and muscularity, clitoromegaly) should be sought, as well as alopecia, acne and seborrhoea. Features suggestive of insulin resistance (obesity, acanthosis nigricans), Cushing's syndrome or other endocrinopathy should also be noted, and the abdomen palpated for masses.

Investigation

Opinions differ as to the extent to which women with hirsutism should be investigated. A practical approach based on clinical findings is shown in Table 43.

The presence of obesity or clinical features of polycystic ovary syndrome (PCOS) / insulin resistance should prompt measurement of fasting glucose and lipids. Clinical suspicion of endocrinopathy such as hypothyroidism or Cushing's syndrome necessitates appropriate investigation.

Treatment

In general, the evidence base for the treatment of hirsutism is fragmented, and individual physicians' experience and preferences still inform treatment advice significantly. Specific causes of hirsutism should be treated appropriately, eg using glucocorticoids to suppress adrenal hyperandrogenism in non-classical congenital adrenal hyperplasia (CAH). Because of the long hair-growth cycle, it is important to emphasise to patients that effective systemic therapies may not show clinical benefit until they have been used for 6–9 months.

Reassurance and lifestyle advice

Reassurance that there is no sinister underlying problem (in most cases) and explanation of the cause of the excess hair growth is a very important part of management. In the large proportion of patients with PCOS or features of insulin resistance, dietary advice should be given, and aerobic exercise and weight loss, where relevant, encouraged.

Cosmetic and topical measures

After reassurance and explanation of the condition, mild or moderate hirsutism may often be managed to the satisfaction of the patient with local cosmetic measures including waxing, plucking, bleaching, depilatory creams or shaving. A topical preparation of the cell cycle inhibitor eflornithine improves facial hirsutism in some patients. Laser therapy and electrolysis to individual hair follicles may also be very effective in selected patients, though they are uncomfortable, repetitive and costly to patients, with a paucity of large-scale clinical evidence to support their use.

Suppression of ovarian function

As the most common cause of elevated circulating androgens is ovarian hyperproduction, approaches aimed at suppressing ovarian function are logical. Most commonly prescribed combined oral contraceptive preparations (COCPs) can be used, in particular those with low androgenic activity. Particularly popular is Dianette (co-cyprindiol), containing cyproterone acetate, which has some antagonistic activity at the androgen receptor. A common limitation of COCPs is exacerbation of weight gain, as well as other common complications of exogenous oestrogens including migraines and increased thromboembolic risk. In intractable cases of ovarian hyperandrogenism, chemical ablation of ovarian function is achieved with potent gonadotrophin-releasing hormone (GnRH) agonists such as leuprorelin, although this renders the patient oestrogen deficient and at an increased risk of unduly rapid bone loss.

Antiandrogens

Androgen receptor antagonists (eg spironolactone, cyproterone acetate, flutamide) have been used successfully to treat hirsutism in small-scale clinical trials. However, none of these agents are licensed for this clinical indication and flutamide is generally avoided due to rare but occasionally fatal hepatotoxicity. Because of their antiandrogenic activity,

Table 43 Strategy for the investigation of hirsutism

Clinical presentation	Likely diagnosis	Investigation
Mild long-standing hirsutism with regular menses	Idiopathic	None (if the patient is concerned, LH, FSH and testosterone can be checked for reassurance)
Moderate hirsutism with long-standing irregular menses	Idiopathic, PCOS, CAH	LH, FSH, testosterone, SHBG, DHEAS, 17alpha-hydroxyprogesterone (± ACTH stimulation), ± ovarian ultrasound
Severe hirsutism / rapid onset of symptoms / virilisation / testosterone >5 nmol/L	CAH, adrenal/ovarian tumour	LH, FSH, testosterone, SHBG, DHEAS, 17alpha-hydroxyprogesterone (± ACTH stimulation), ultrasound/CT/MRI of adrenals and/or ovaries

ACTH, adrenocorticotropic hormone; CAH, congenital adrenal hyperplasia; CT, computed tomography; DHEAS, dehydroepiandrosterone sulphate; FSH, follicle-stimulating hormone; LH, luteinising hormone; MRI, magnetic resonance imaging; PCOS, polycystic ovary syndrome; SHBG, sex hormone-binding globulin.

all of these agents are potentially teratogenic and should not be prescribed without reliable contraception or sterilisation. 'Additional' cyproterone acetate may be given during the first 10 days of each menstrual cycle, often in conjunction with the low-dose cyproterone-containing preparation Dianette (co-cyprindiol). Spironolactone is used at doses of 50–200 mg daily, except in the presence of liver or kidney disease. The 5alpha-reductase inhibitor finasteride (which blocks the conversion of testosterone to DHT) may also be tried (5 mg daily), although again it is unlicensed in this setting.

2.4.7 Erectile dysfunction

Aetiology and pathophysiology

Erectile dysfunction can be conveniently classified according to pathophysiology (Table 44).

Key point

Many patients have more than one cause of erectile dysfunction

Several different factors (eg diabetes, medication and anxiety) may contribute to the erectile dysfunction in any one patient. Furthermore, the psychological response to 'organic' impotence can be difficult to distinguish from primary psychogenic erectile dysfunction.

Epidemiology

General population

Impotence is estimated to affect 5% of men aged 40–50 years, 15% aged 50–60 years, 25% aged 60–70 years and 40% aged 70–80 years.

Men with diabetes

For men who were less than 30 years old when their diabetes was diagnosed, 45–50% will be impotent by 50 years of age and 60–70% will be impotent by 60 years of age.

Clinical presentation and physical signs

Erectile dysfunction should be distinguished from premature ejaculation or reduced libido. Penile curvature suggests Peyronie's disease. If the patient experiences masturbatory or early morning erections, this effectively excludes organic pathology and suggests a psychogenic basis.

In all other cases, take a detailed history and perform a careful clinical examination bearing in mind those conditions listed in Table 44. Check femoral pulses, examine for evidence of a peripheral neuropathy and consider performing a digital rectal examination of the prostate in men of an appropriate age.

Key point

The importance of asking the question

Men may not volunteer the symptom of impotence. It is therefore important to ask 'at risk' groups, including those with diabetes, hypertension, atherosclerotic disease and hypopituitarism.

Investigation

The availability of the phosphodiesterase inhibitors, the prototype of which is sildenafil (Viagra), has changed the investigation and management of erectile dysfunction.

Where applicable, a psychological evaluation should be arranged, and medication that could be causally related changed. It may then be appropriate to institute a therapeutic trial of a phosphodiesterase inhibitor (see below) without further investigation, when the aetiology of the problem is clear (eg in a man with long-standing diabetes mellitus). Otherwise, a screen for systemic disease should be carried out, including full blood count, urea and electrolytes, glucose, cholesterol and possibly prostate-specific antigen (PSA). Prolactin and testosterone levels should also be checked.

Table 44 Classification of erectile dysfunction

Category	Examples
Psychogenic	Anxiety, depression, relationship problems
Drug induced	Beta-blockers, thiazides, many recreational drugs, alcohol
Neurogenic	Post-CVA, Parkinson's disease, spinal cord injury, pelvic surgery
Vascular	Hypertension, atherosclerosis, DM
Hormonal	Hypogonadism, hyperprolactinaemia
Chronic/systemic illness	Chronic renal failure, DM

CVA, cerebrovascular accident; DM, diabetes mellitus.

If the testosterone level is below the normal range, it should be repeated (at 9am), together with measurement of sex hormone-binding globulin (SHBG), luteinising hormone (LH) and follicle-stimulating hormone (FSH) concentrations.

- If the testosterone concentration remains low (less than 8 nmol/L) (normal range for males 9.0–35.0) with an appropriately raised LH and FSH, a trial of androgen replacement therapy may be instituted for primary gonadal failure.
- If the pattern is that of hypogonadotrophic hypogonadism (low testosterone with low LH and FSH), assessment of anterior pituitary function together with imaging of the pituitary fossa should be considered (see Section 2.1.8).

Treatment

An approach to the management of erectile dysfunction is shown in Fig 45.

Phosphodiesterase inhibitors

Inhibitors of phosphodiesterase type 5 such as sildenafil produce increased

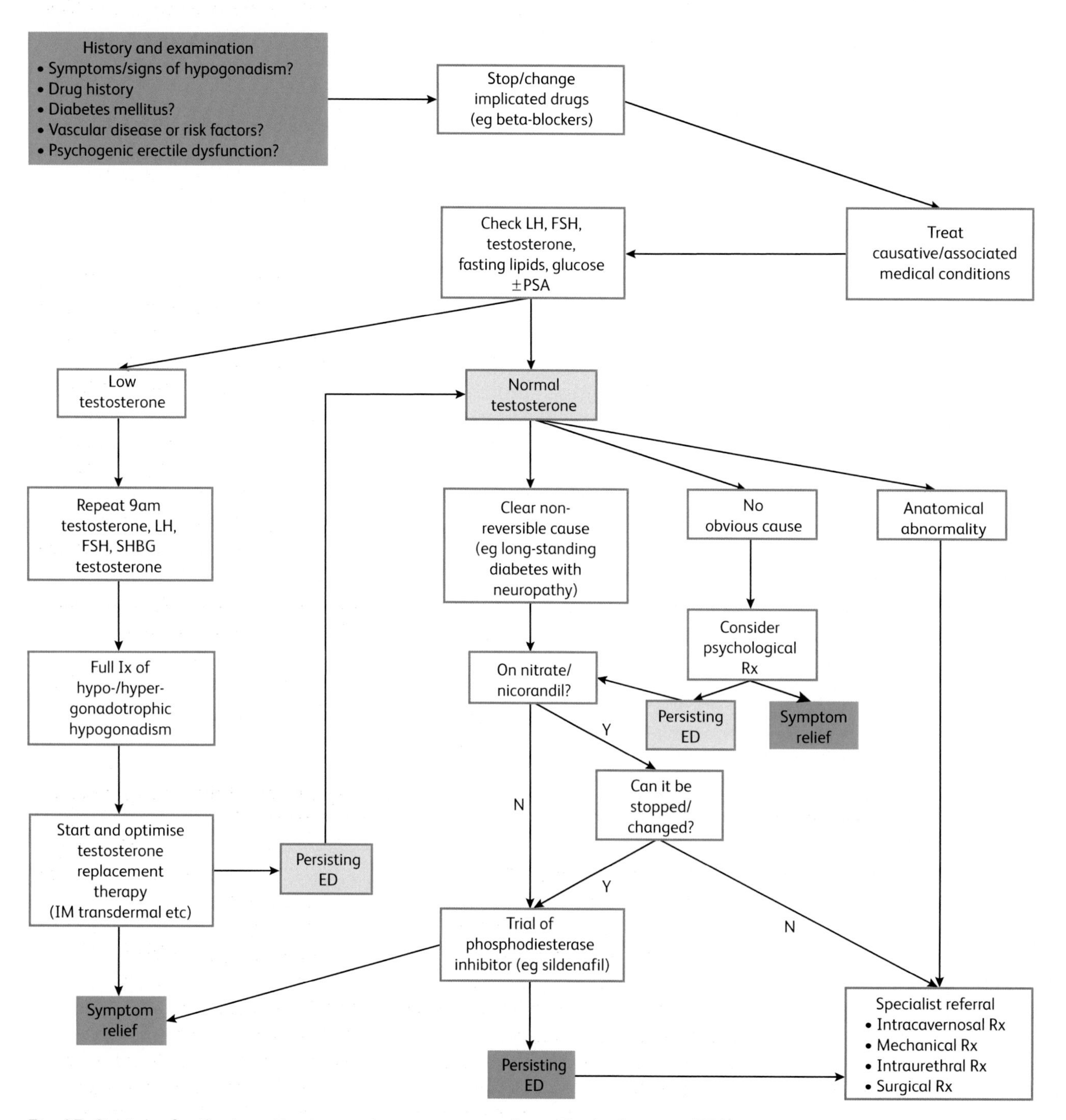

Fig 45 Strategy for the investigation and management of erectile dysfunction (ED).

cyclic guanosine monophosphate (cGMP) concentrations in the glans penis, corpus cavernosum and corpus spongiosum, mimicking the effect of parasympathetically-induced nitric oxide (NO) release, and leading to increased smooth muscle relaxation and an improved erection. During clinical trials, 60% of attempts at intercourse were successful following sildenafil compared with 20% following placebo. Tadalafil and vardenafil have subsequently followed sildenafil into clinical use, with the same mechanism of action, but variations in pharmacokinetics.

Key point

Action of phosphodiesterase inhibitors

Phosphodiesterase inhibitors augment the erectile response to sexual stimulation, but do not cause an erection to occur by itself. It is important that the patient understands that sexual activity must be attempted before the treatment is considered a failure.

Headache and flushing are the most commonly experienced side effects. Contraindications to the use of phosphodiesterase inhibitors include nitrate therapy (risk of severe hypotension), significant cardiovascular disease and retinitis pigmentosa (phosphodiesterase type 6 is strongly expressed in the retina, and current phosphodiesterase inhibitors also inhibit this enzyme). Phosphodiesterase inhibitors should also be used with care in those with Peyronie's disease and in subjects with a predisposition to prolonged erection (eg in sickle cell disease, leukaemia).

Urological treatment

Urologists may institute treatment with alprostadil (a synthetic form of prostaglandin E_1) either by intracavernosal injection or intraurethral application. Papaverine (a non-specific phosphodiesterase inhibitor) and phentolamine (alpha-adrenoceptor antagonist) may also be given by intracavernosal injection, often in combination or with alprostadil. Some men prefer the use of mechanical devices, such as vacuum constrictors. Various surgical treatments are available including penile prostheses and attempts at revascularisation.

Androgen replacement

Where indicated, testosterone replacement should be instituted (see Section 2.1.8).

Prognosis

Erectile dysfunction can have a considerable impact on a patient's quality of life, although one should not assume that all men (or all relationships) require sexual activity. Importantly, it may also be an important surrogate marker of cardiovascular risk, and overall cardiovascular disease risk should be carefully assessed and managed as appropriate.

Prevention

Prevention of erectile dysfunction, particularly in patients with diabetes mellitus, is dependent on achieving optimal hypertensive and glycaemic control, correction of dyslipidaemia, cessation of smoking and avoidance of excessive alcohol consumption.

2.4.8 Infertility

Infertility is defined as a failure to conceive despite regular unprotected sexual intercourse for 2 years, in the absence of known reproductive pathology. The cumulative probability of conception in the general population under these circumstances is 84% after 1 year, and 92% after 2 years. It is estimated that around one in six couples seek medical advice at some stage due to failure to conceive. In part because of the expensive technology involved in some forms of assisted conception, and because of its high media and political profile, there is an extensive evidence base for many aspects of assisted conception, which has been the subject of extensive guidelines from the National Institute for Health and Care Excellence (NICE). Much of the management of infertility occurs in specialist reproductive medicine clinics, but because many endocrine disorders can compromise fertility, there is close liaison with endocrinologists and often an integrated multidisciplinary approach involving both specialties.

Aetiology/pathophysiology

Infertility may be due to dysfunction at any level of the hypothalamic–pituitary–gonadal axis in either men or women, as well as to anatomical, infective or inflammatory disorders affecting the reproductive tracts. Among the most common endocrine causes for reduced fertility are polycystic ovary syndrome (PCOS) with reduced or absent ovulation, hypogonadotrophic hypogonadism in either male or female, and primary gonadal failure, whether acquired or due to underlying genetic disorders (eg Turner's syndrome, Klinefelter's syndrome). In a significant proportion of cases, no clear cause for impaired fertility is discovered.

Clinical assessment

A key principle of the assessment and management of infertility is that it is couple-centred. Assessment often begins after 1 year with no conception despite regular unprotected sexual intercourse. The history should concentrate on identifying predisposing factors for infertility, including the woman's age being >35 years, amenorrhoea, oligomenorrhoea, pelvic inflammatory disease, or undescended testes. Prior treatment for cancer, infection with HIV, hepatitis B or C should also be documented. Clinical examination should note body weight, signs of PCOS (see Section 2.4.5) or hypogonadism (see Section 2.4.2), and features of syndromes such as Klinefelter's syndrome.

Investigation

Initial investigation:

- Semen analysis should be carried out with reference to World Health Organization (WHO) standards. Repeat at 3 months if abnormal, or immediately if grossly abnormal.
- Day 21 progesterone (assuming a 28-day cycle) to look for evidence of ovulation.

Guided by these results, further investigation may include:

- LH, FSH, testosterone/oestradiol
- prolactin
- screening for *Chlamydia trachomatis*
- hysterosalpingogram or pelvic ultrasound (if no history of pelvic disease)
- laparoscopy and dye (if history of pelvic disease).

These investigations will allow identification of several types of problem, which may be grouped as follows:

- hypogonadotrophic hypogonadism (male or female)
- gonadal failure
- ovarian dysfunction due to PCOS
- obstructive azoospermia
- tubal occlusion
- no clear explanation.

Treatment

At the first assessment of couples concerned by delays in conception, care should be taken to explain the cumulative probability of conception over 2 years, and the marked decline in female fertility in women from 35 years onwards. Simple lifestyle advice should be given:

- sexual intercourse every 2–3 days
- reduce/abstain from alcohol consumption
- smoking cessation
- aim for a body mass index (BMI) between 19 and 29.

Advice about drugs (both prescribed and recreational) should be given, and appropriate preconception measures such as folic acid, rubella and cervical screening recommended.

Medical management will be guided by the nature of any underlying problem, and should be undertaken under specialist supervision. Options include:

- Ovulation induction – using agents such as clomiphene, a non-steroidal selective oestrogen receptor modulator, which enhances gonadotrophin release among other actions. Treatment with clomiphene should be supervised using ovarian ultrasound to assess follicular development. Where ovulation is not achieved, adjunctive therapy with metformin, FSH or ovarian drilling may be used.
- Intrauterine insemination – may enhance chances of conception with clomiphene by overcoming the hostile cervix induced by the anti-oestrogenic action of clomiphene. It may also be used in mild male factor infertility, after treatment of tubal disease, and in unexplained infertility.
- Gonadotrophin or pulsatile gonadotrophin-releasing hormone (GnRH) therapy (for hypogonadotrophic hypogonadism).

In cases of bilateral tubal occlusion, azoospermia or persisting infertility despite the above measures various different techniques using *in vitro* fertilisation (IVF) may be tried:

- Sperm recovery – may be used in cases of obstructive azoospermia, with recovered cells subsequently used for IVF.
- Ovulation induction / oocyte maturation / oocyte retrieval – produces oocytes for fertilisation.
- Intracytoplasmic sperm injection (ICSI) – may be required to achieve IVF in cases with severe semen quality defects or azoospermia.
- Donor insemination or oocyte donation – may be required where defects in spermatogenesis or oogenesis are irremediable (eg premature ovarian failure, Klinefelter's syndrome).
- Ultrasound-guided embryo transfer – is used to introduce no more than two embryos to the uterus.
- Luteal support – with exogenous progesterone may additionally be required.

Complications

The main complications of ovulation induction therapy are the occurrence of multiple pregnancy and ovarian hyperstimulation syndrome (OHSS). Both these risks should be explained prior to treatment.

The clinical symptoms and signs of OHSS may range from transient lower abdominal discomfort, mild nausea, vomiting, diarrhoea and abdominal distention through to rapid weight gain with tense ascites, postural hypotension, tachycardia, tachypnoea and oliguria. These features result from extravasation of protein-rich fluid and contraction of the vascular volume, compounded by mechanical effects of tense ascites. Complications of OHSS which may be life-threatening include renal failure, acute respiratory distress syndrome (ARDS), haemorrhage from ovarian rupture and thromboembolism.

Mild OHSS can be managed as an outpatient using only oral analgesia and counselling regarding the signs and symptoms of progressing illness. Treatment of more severe OHSS requires antiemetics and more potent analgesics, with careful evaluation including frequent physical and ultrasound examinations (to detect increasing ascites), daily weight measurements and serial determinations of haematocrit, electrolytes and serum creatinine. Hospitalisation may be required based on severity of symptoms, analgesic requirements and social considerations. Such patients may require IV volume expansion with careful monitoring of electrolytes and clinical state, diuretics and sometimes ultrasound-guided paracentesis. Thromboembolic deterrent (TED) stockings and prophylactic heparin are important. Surgery is occasionally required for ovarian rupture or ectopic pregnancy.

Units who offer assisted reproduction technologies should have protocols in place for management of OHSS, but occasionally patients do present to hospital in the context of unselected medical takes.

2.5 Metabolic and bone diseases

2.5.1 Disorders of lipid metabolism (dyslipidaemia/ hyperlipidaemia)

Definitions

Simple and complex lipids

Lipids in the circulation include simple lipids (cholesterol and saturated, monounsaturated and polyunsaturated fatty acids) and complex lipids (cholesterol esters, triglycerides and phospholipids).

Cholesterol and cholesterol ester

Cholesterol is essential to the membrane fluidity of all cells and is also required for the synthesis of bile acids in the liver and steroid hormones in various endocrine organs. The free cholesterol molecule is only minimally soluble in aqueous solutions such as plasma. Esterification of cholesterol with fatty acid renders the molecule (cholesterol ester) completely lipid soluble.

Triglycerides and phospholipids

Triglycerides serve as a source of energy for cells when fats are oxidised. The fatty acid chains of triglycerides vary in length and saturation, but they make their triglyceride molecule essentially lipid soluble. Substitution of a phosphate group in place of one of the chains creates the phospholipid, another component of cell membranes, with the strong polar nature of the phosphate group meaning that phospholipids are hydrophilic at one end.

Lipoproteins

Lipid molecules cannot circulate freely in plasma. Instead, they are packaged into aggregate particles known as lipoproteins: a collection of phospholipids and free cholesterol with their water-soluble ends facing the outer aqueous environment of plasma and the lipid-soluble ends facing into the particle's interior. Cholesterol esters and triglycerides reside in the core of the particle, protected from the aqueous environment.

Apolipoproteins

Every lipoprotein has at least one apolipoprotein. This polypeptide serves many critical functions for the lipoprotein: they identify the species of the lipoprotein particle, facilitate interactions with specific receptors, provide stability and may serve as cofactors for enzymes to carry out the particle's critical functions. The different circulating lipoproteins differ in size, due to their widely varying compositions as well as in the apolipoproteins that they carry (Table 45).

Physiology

Exogenous lipid pathway

The basic role of the exogenous lipid pathway is to deliver dietary absorbed cholesterol to the liver, and fatty acids to the liver, skeletal and adipose tissue. This is channelled through the use of large particles called chylomicrons.

The pathway for circulation of dietary derived (exogenous) lipids begins with the production of chylomicron particles in the intestinal epithelial cells. These large particles are then packaged with apolipoprotein (Apo)B48 and, after initial release into the lymphatic system, are eventually circulated into the bloodstream.

Throughout the circulation, they are acted upon by lipoprotein lipase (LPL) which reside on the surface of endothelial cells. LPL remove triglycerides from these chylomicron particles liberating fatty acids for use by tissues such a skeletal muscle and adipose tissue wherein they can be stored as re-esterified triglycerides or used as a source of energy. The remaining modified chylomicron remnants are ultimately removed from the circulation by the liver through a variety of pathways involving ApoE.

Endogenous lipid pathway

The endogenous pathway deals with the circulation of liver-derived (endogenous) lipids in the post-absorptive state.

This begins with the production of very low density lipoprotein (VLDL) particles, which are packed with ApoB100 and are very rich in triglycerides. VLDL are modified by LPL to form intermediate-density lipoprotein (IDL), which serves as ligand for LDL receptor-related protein (LRP) and the LDL receptor (LDLR).

Ultimately, the end product of triglyceride hydrolysis is cholesterol-rich low-density lipoprotein (LDL), which is linked to ApoB-100 (serves as a ligand to facilitate uptake of LDL by the liver via the LDLR).

Table 45 Characteristics of the major circulating lipoprotein particles

	CM and CM remnants	VLDL	IDL	LDL	HDL
Particle diameter (nm)	70–600	30–70	10–30	20–25	7–10
Density (g/mL)	<0.94	<1.006	1.006–1.019	1.019–1.063	1.063–1.21
Composition					
Cholesterol	5%	20%	40%	50%	20%
Triglyceride	90%	60%	35%	10%	5%
Phospholipid	4%	15%	20%	20%	30%
Protein	1%	5%	5%	20%	45%
Major core component	Triglycerides	Triglycerides	Triglycerides cholesterol esters	Cholesterol esters	Cholesterol esters
Major apolipoproteins	ApoB48 ApoCI/CII/CIII ApoE ApoAI/AII/AIV	ApoB100 ApoCII/CIII ApoE	ApoB100 ApoE	ApoB100	ApoAI/AII/AIV ApoCI/CII/CIII ApoE

Apo, apolipoprotein; CM, chylomicrons; HDL, high-density lipoprotein; IDL, intermediate-density lipoprotein; LDL, low-density lipoprotein; VLDL, very low density lipoprotein.

Other pharmacologically important pathways

- *Reverse cholesterol transport pathway*: involves the circulation of cholesterol from peripheral tissues back to the liver and is mediated by high-density lipoprotein (HDL). One of the more important exchanges that takes place is the transfer of cholesterol esters from HDL (in exchange for triglycerides from VLDL) into IDL and LDL, mediated by the enzyme cholesterol ester transfer protein (CETP), which is a target for several novel therapies.
- *Intrahepatic cholesterol metabolism*: involves uptake of LDL particles by the LDLR, which is then recycled back to the cell membrane. The important rate-limiting step of the *de novo* cholesterol synthesis pathway is mediated by enzyme 3-hydroxy 3-methoxyglutaryl coenzyme A (HMG-CoA). Statins work by inhibiting this enzyme.
- *Other scavenger pathways*: mostly mediated by cells of the reticuloendothelial system (eg monocytes, macrophages), which respond to various chemotactic signals.

Key point

PCSK9 – a novel therapeutic target

The proprotein convertase subtilisin-like kexin type 9 (PCSK9) is a newly discovered serine protease which is involved in the degradation of LDLRs in liver, and thereby regulates the level of LDL in plasma. Human mutations that increase PCSK9 activity cause hypercholesterolemia and ischaemic heart disease (IHD); in contrast, mutations that inactivate PCSK9 have the opposite effect, lowering LDL levels and reducing IHD. This protease has therefore become a novel therapeutic target to lower plasma levels of LDL and prevent IHD.

Classification

Traditionally, lipid disorders were classified according to the Fredrickson system of lipoprotein electrophoresis patterns.

Although, this remains the most accurate classification, most clinical laboratories do not perform ultracentrifugation or electrophoresis routinely, and instead measure total cholesterol, triglycerides and HDL cholesterol, with LDL cholesterol calculated using the Friedewald formula. Hence, it is more useful to have a working classification of dyslipidaemia into predominant hypercholesterolaemia, predominant hypertriglyceridaemia or mixed dyslipidaemia.

Furthermore, dyslipidaemia can also be classified as either primary (monogenic/organic) or secondary. Table 46 provides an example of such a hybrid classification.

Table 46 Combined classification of dyslipidaemia based on predominant biochemical phenotype, lipoprotein abnormality (Fredrickson classification) and aetiology

Biochemical phenotype	Lipoprotein abnormality	Fredrickson classification	Primary causes	Secondary causes
Predominant hypercholesterolaemia	↑ LDL	IIa	Familial hypercholesterolaemia	Hypothyroidism
			Polygenic hypercholesterolaemia	Obstructive jaundice
				Corticosteroids
				Anorexia nervosa
Predominant hypertriglyceridaemia	↑ CM	I	Lipoprotein lipase deficiency	Diabetes
			Apo-CII deficiency	Oral contraceptive pill
	↑ VLDL	IV	Familial combined hyperlipidaemia	Alcohol excess
			Familial hypertriglyceridaemia	Thiazide diuretics
	↑ CM, ↑ VLDL	V	Lipoprotein lipase deficiency	
			Apo-CII deficiency	
Mixed dyslipidaemia	↑ Remnants	III	Familial dysbetalipoproteinaemia	Diabetes
				Obesity
	↑ VLDL, ↑ LDL	IIb	Familial combined hyperlipidaemia	Nephrotic syndrome
				Renal failure
				Glycogen storage disease
				Paraproteinaemia

Apo, apoprotein; CM, chylomicrons; LDL, low-density lipoproteins; VLDL, very low density lipoproteins.

Two of the monogenic dyslipidaemias warrant specific mention:

- The molecular defect in familial hypercholesterolaemia involves the LDL receptor. In homozygotes there is minimal LDL uptake, with high (~20 mmol/L) levels of total and LDL cholesterol and a greatly increased risk of atherosclerosis. Heterozygotes have an intermediate phenotype.
- Type III dyslipidaemia is a classic example of gene–environment interaction; apo-E_2 homozygosity is required, but in combination with an 'environmental' factor (such as diabetes, obesity, hypothyroidism) to produce the characteristic lipid profile and clinical features.

Key point

LDL cholesterol

Current management guidelines focus on LDL cholesterol as the main target. LDL is actually a spectrum of particles, with LDL cholesterol values usually calculated based on the direct measurement of other fractions using the Friedewald equation (mmol/L) as below:

LDL cholesterol (mmol/L) = Total cholesterol – [HDL cholesterol + (Triglycerides ÷ 2.2)]

Epidemiology

Several large-scale studies, eg the Multiple Risk Factor Intervention Trial (MRFIT), Framingham studies, the Seven Countries Study and the Prospective Cardiovascular Münster (PROCAM) study, have demonstrated the significant links between dyslipidaemia and IHD. Similarly, large-scale intervention studies in subjects without known cardiovascular disease have demonstrated the efficacy of lipid lowering for the prevention of new cardiovascular events. The Lipid Research Clinics Coronary Primary Prevention Trial (LRC-CPPT), the Helsinki Heart study, the West Of Scotland Coronary Prevention Study (WOSCOPS) and the Air Force/Texas Coronary Atherosclerosis Prevention Study (ACAPS/TexCAPS) have all shown the benefit of primary prevention by lowering cholesterol levels.

Key point

Lipid abnormalities and risk of IHD

Epidemiological evidence suggests:

- an association between high levels of total and LDL cholesterol and risk of IHD
- the relationship between cholesterol and risk of IHD is curvilinear, a 10% increase in cholesterol conferring a 20% increase in risk
- an inverse relationship between HDL cholesterol and IHD risk
- a weak relationship between hypertriglyceridaemia and IHD risk, which has not been confirmed in all studies, although high levels of triglycerides do seem to confer an increased risk in the presence of hypercholesterolaemia.

Clinical presentation

Hyperlipidaemia may present with IHD (eg myocardial infarction or angina) or other vascular disease (eg stroke or peripheral arterial disease). Alternatively, it may be uncovered in an asymptomatic patient screened either because of a positive family history of premature IHD, the presence of other risk factors for IHD, the existence of a known secondary cause of hyperlipidaemia, or because he/she exhibits the characteristic stigmata of one of these disorders (see below).

Relevant points in taking the history from a hyperlipidaemic patient include:

- assessment of lifestyle factors – diet, exercise, smoking, alcohol consumption
- family history of hyperlipidaemia, hypertension, premature IHD
- past history of vascular disease, diabetes, thyroid disease, liver/renal failure, myeloma
- drug history.

Physical signs

Some of the stigmata of hyperlipidaemia are given in Fig 46.

The examination of the hyperlipidaemic patient should include a search for evidence of vascular disease (eg carotid or femoral bruits, diminished peripheral pulses), features of other disorders associated with secondary hyperlipidaemia (eg diabetes mellitus, hypothyroidism, liver or renal failure) and an assessment of other risk factors (eg obesity or hypertension).

Investigation

Initial laboratory assessment should include a full blood count and erythrocyte sedimentation rate (ESR) (with or without serum electrophoresis – to exclude myeloma), tests of renal, liver and thyroid function, fasting glucose and a baseline creatine kinase. A resting ECG may not be as useful as an exercise test. In all cases a full fasting lipid profile (with measurement of total and HDL cholesterol and triglycerides and calculation of LDL cholesterol) should be obtained.

Treatment

Given the high prevalence of IHD and the fact that many people who develop IHD appear to be at a relatively low risk, it is sensible to offer lifestyle advice to all (see Section 1.1.15).

Secondary causes of hyperlipidaemia and other risk factors must be managed appropriately and subjects at high risk of IHD should be started on aspirin.

There is now abundant evidence that lipid-lowering drug therapy (with statins or fibrates) reduces IHD risk and overall mortality in patients with IHD (secondary prevention) or in subjects at high risk of developing IHD (primary prevention). Current Joint British Societies' guidelines recommend in people with established cardiovascular disease, people with diabetes, and those asymptomatic individuals at high cardiovascular risk (10 years IHD risk exceeding 20%), total and LDL cholesterol targets of <4.0 mmol/L and <2.0 mmol/L, respectively, or a 25% reduction in total cholesterol and a 30% reduction in LDL cholesterol, whichever gets the person to the lowest absolute value. Note that these targets are more stringent than previous recommendations (total cholesterol <5.0 mmol/L, LDL cholesterol <3.0 mmol/L) which are still in use in some areas of practice. Convenient tables or computer programs for estimating 10-year risk based on age, sex, total:HDL cholesterol ratio, BP, diabetes and smoking status are now widely available.

Failure to achieve target (LDL cholesterol <2.0 mmol/L, HDL cholesterol >1.0 mmol/L and triglycerides <2.0 mmol/L) with monotherapy is an indication for referral to a lipid clinic.

Management

Therapy for lipid disorders should *always* begin with modification of nutritional and lifestyle factors. Ongoing adherence to such modifications remain important, even when pharmacological intervention is required, and regular reinforcement should be provided.

Pharmacotherapy

When an adequate trial of Therapeutic Lifestyle Change of at least 12 weeks has not resulted in achievement of treatment targets, pharmacological intervention is then indicated. Table 47 shows a list of currently licensed lipid-lowering agents.

Primary and secondary prevention of cardiovascular disease

Risk calculators

Risk assessment calculators are recommended by both NICE (clinical guideline 181 (July 2014)) and JBS3 (Joint British Societies' (JBS) consensus recommendations for the prevention of cardiovascular disease, 2014). They should not be used in patients at high cardiovascular risk. Both calculators are unsuitable for assessing risk in those aged 85 years and over.

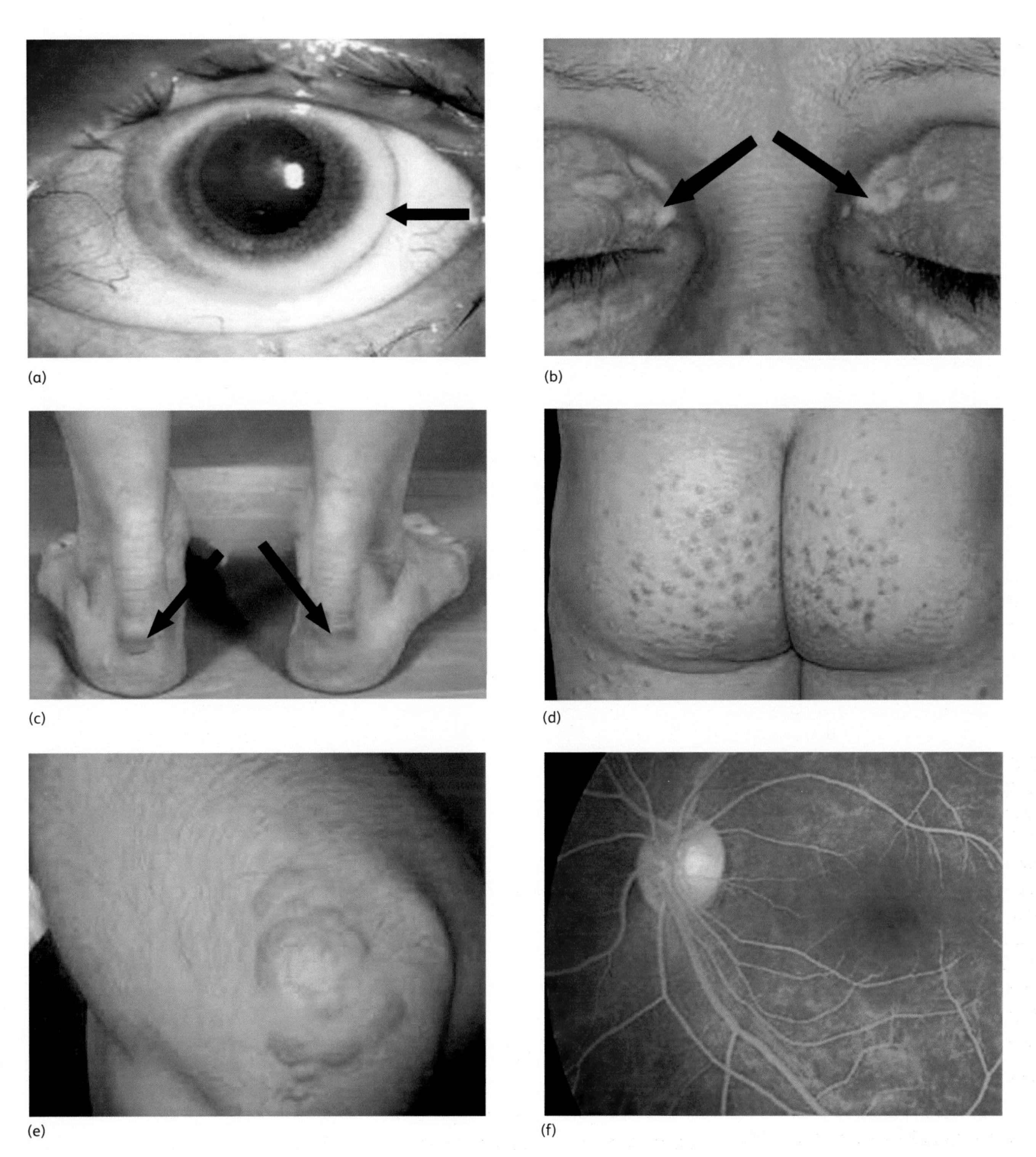

Fig 46 Stigmata of hyperlipidaemia. **(a)** Corneal arcus – note the circumferential nature of this advanced arcus; in less advanced cases the upper eyelid may need to be retracted to expose the arcus. **(b)** Xanthelasma – sharply demarcated yellowish deposit of fat underneath the skin, usually on or around the eyelids. **(c)** Tendon xanthoma – over the extensor tendons of a patient with homozygous familial hypercholesterolaemia. **(d)** Eruptive xanthoma – clinically characterised by small, yellowish-orange to reddish-brown papules that appear all over the body. **(e)** Tuberous xanthoma over the knees of a patient with mixed hyperlipidaemia. **(f)** Lipaemia retinalis – note the milky appearance of all the retinal vessels, both arteries and veins. (Copyright Dr S Sharma.)

Table 47 Important lipid-modulating drugs currently licensed for use in the UK

Class of drugs	Drug	Dosage range	Efficacy	Side effects
Bile acid sequestrants *(resins)*	Cholestyramine Colestipol Colesevelam	4–16 g daily 5–20 g daily 2.6–3.8 g daily	LDL-C ↓15–30% HDL-C ↑3–5% TG ↔	GI upset Constipation Retards absorption of other medications
Nicotinic acid derivatives	Niacin Extended – release (Niaspan)	1.5–3 g daily 1–2 g daily	LDL-C ↓ 5–25% HDL-C ↑15–35% TG ↓ 15–30%	Flushing Hyperglycaemia Hyperuricaemia/gout Hepatotoxicity
HMG-CoA reductase inhibitors *(statins)*	Pravastatin Simvastatin Fluvastatin Atorvastatin Rosuvastatin	20–40 mg daily 20–80 mg daily 20–80 mg daily 10–80 mg daily 5–40 mg daily	LDL-C ↓ 18–55% HDL-C ↑ 5–15% TG ↓ 7–30%	Hepatotoxicity Myopathy
Fibric acid derivatives *(fibrates)*	Fenofibrate Bezafibrate Gemfibrozil	160–267 mg daily 400–600 mg daily 0.9–1.2 g daily	LDL-C ↓ 5–20% HDL-C ↑ 10–20% TG ↓ 20–50%	Dyspepsia Gallstones Hepatotoxicity Myopathy
Cholesterol absorption inhibitor	Ezetimibe	10 mg daily	LDL-C ↓ 5–20% HDL-C ↑ 5–15% TG ↓ 2–10%	Fatigue GI disturbance
MTP inhibitor	Lomitapide	5–60 mg daily	LDL-C ↓ 15–30% HDL-C ↑ 5–10% TG ↓ 5–10%	Abdominal pain Abnormal LFTs
Omega-3 acid ethyl esters	Eicosapentaenoic Docosahexaenoic acid ethyl esters	1–4 g daily	LDL-C ↑ 5–8% HDL-C ↑ 5–10% TG ↓ 20–40%	Dyspepsia Nausea
PCSK9 inhibitors	Alirocumab Evolocumab	75–150 mg 2-weekly 140–420 mg 2-weekly	LDL-C ↓ 45–65% HDL-C ↑ 25–45% TG ↓ 20–50%	Rhinorrhea Pruritus Oropharyngeal pain

GI, gastrointestinal; HDL-C, high-density lipoprotein cholesterol; HMG-CoA, 3-hydroxy 3-methoxyglutaryl coenzyme A; LDL-C, low-density lipoprotein cholesterol; LFTs, liver function tests; MTP, microsomal triglyceride transfer protein; PCSK9, proprotein convertase subtilisin-like kexin type 9; TG, triglycerides; VLDL, very low density lipoproteins.

The QRISK®2 risk calculator is recommended by NICE (clinical guideline 181), and the JBS3 risk calculator is endorsed by JBS. Cardiovascular disease risk is underestimated in those who are already taking antihypertensive or lipid-regulating drugs, and in those who have recently stopped smoking.

Primary prevention

Individuals at high risk of developing cardiovascular disease include those who have diabetes mellitus, chronic kidney disease (estimated glomerular filtration rate (eGFR) <60 mL/minute/1.73 m^2) and/or albuminuria, and those with familial hypercholesterolaemia. The risk also increases with age; those aged 85 years and over are at particularly high risk, especially if they smoke or have hypertension. Individuals with a 10-year risk of cardiovascular disease of ≥10% stand to benefit most from drug treatment.

For primary prevention, NICE clinical guideline 181 recommends that atorvastatin, prescribed at a dose of at least 20 mg/day, be offered to those with a 10-year risk of cardiovascular disease of ≥10%; patients aged ≥85 years benefit from atorvastatin to reduce the risk of non-fatal myocardial infarction.

Secondary prevention

For secondary prevention, atorvastatin is also recommended. Patients taking a low- or medium-intensity statin should discuss the benefits and risks of switching to a high-intensity statin at their next medication review.

2.5.2 Porphyria

The porphyrias are a group of metabolic disorders resulting from defects in the enzymes of the haem synthetic pathway with consequent accumulation of various precursors. Clinically they may be divided into the acute and non-acute porphyrias (Table 48).

Table 48 Classification of the porphyrias	
Type	**Conditions**
Acute porphyrias	Acute intermittent porphyria
	Variegate porphyria
	Hereditary coproporphyria
Non-acute porphyrias	Porphyria cutanea tarda
	Congenital porphyria
	Erythropoietic protoporphyria

Pathophysiology

The haem synthetic pathway is shown in outline in Fig 47.

- In both acute and non-acute porphyrias the reduced production of haem results in increased activity of delta-amino laevulinic acid (δ-ALA) synthetase as a consequence of impaired negative feedback.
- In the acute porphyrias there is accumulation of δ-ALA and porphobilinogen.
- In the non-acute porphyrias, however, increased porphobilinogen deaminase activity means there is no accumulation of δ-ALA or porphobilinogen.

The acute porphyrias are all dominantly inherited.

Clinical presentation

Acute porphyrias

Presentation is typically in early adult life with intermittent episodes characterised by:

- acute abdominal pain and vomiting
- sensorimotor neuropathy, respiratory muscle weakness, coma, seizures
- psychiatric disturbance
- sinus tachycardia, hypertension and occasionally left ventricular failure.

Attacks may be precipitated by alcohol, sex steroids and a wide variety of drugs, especially barbiturates and other enzyme inducers. In variegate porphyria and hereditary coproporphyria (but not acute intermittent porphyria) these features are accompanied by the cutaneous features of porphyria cutanea tarda.

Non-acute porphyrias

The clinical features of each disorder include:

- porphyria cutanea tarda – a bullous photosensitive rash that heals by scarring, hepatomegaly, haemochromatosis
- congenital porphyria – a scarring bullous photosensitive rash, dystrophic nails, tooth discoloration, anaemia, splenomegaly
- protoporphyria – presentation in childhood, photosensitivity, peripheral paraesthesiae, hepatic dysfunction.

Investigation

During an attack of acute porphyria, porphyrin can usually be detected in fresh urine (red/brown on standing). Porphobilinogen in fresh urine can be detected by the development of a characteristic pink/red colour on mixing with Ehrlich's reagent, which is not absorbed out by chloroform or other organic solvents.

Elevated bilirubin and alanine aminotransferase (ALT) levels are also often present during an acute episode.

Family members should be offered screening (ideally genetic, but failing that biochemical) to detect latent cases.

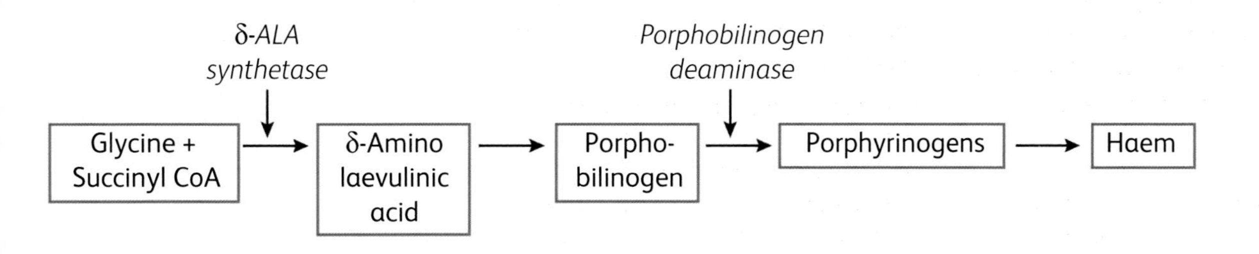

Fig 47 Key steps in the haem synthetic pathway.

Treatment

Acute attacks are treated with supportive measures, a high carbohydrate intake with or without parenteral haem administration. Beta-blockers (eg propranolol), chlorpromazine, certain opioids (eg codeine, morphine, diamorphine) and diazepam are safe treatments.

Key point

Avoidance of acute attacks

- Following recovery, patients should be advised to abstain from alcohol, and given a list of drugs to be avoided (including oral contraceptives).
- An up-to-date list of agents that are considered safe for use in the acute porphyrias can be found on several websites (including: www.wmic.wales.nhs.uk/specialist-services/drugs-in-porphyria/ and www.drugs-porphyria.org/languages/UnitedKingdom/index.php).

Specific treatments for some types of porphyria

- Porphyria cutanea tarda – venesection to reduce iron overload; alcohol should be avoided.
- Congenital porphyria – may be helped by low-dose chloroquine.
- Protoporphyria – can be helped by beta-carotene and bile acid sequestrants.

2.5.3 Haemochromatosis

Aetiology

The term haemochromatosis was introduced by von Recklinghausen in 1889 to describe the pathological accumulation of iron in a wide range of tissues producing organ dysfunction. It is most frequently due to a recessively inherited genetic disorder (adult, juvenile and neonatal forms), but may also complicate repeated blood transfusion, chronic iron ingestion and some forms of anaemia (thalassaemia, chronic haemolytic and dyserythropoietic anaemias).

Pathophysiology

Adult hereditary haemochromatosis (HH) is usually due to mutations in a novel major histocompatibility complex (MHC) class 1-type gene, originally called *HLA-H* and now termed *HFE*, on chromosome 6 (which is close to, and in linkage disequilibrium with, the gene for human leukocyte antigen (HLA)-A3). Approximately 90% of cases are homozygous for the C282Y mutation (tyrosine replacing cysteine at residue 282). The mutated protein, unlike wild-type HFE protein, cannot bind beta2microglobulin and hence is unable to bind to the transferrin receptor (TfR). Another mutation H63D (aspartate substituting for histidine at codon 63) has been identified in 6% of subjects (who harbour either one or two copies of the mutated gene), while 4–7% of patients with HH are C282Y/H63D compound heterozygotes. How these mutations lead to pathological iron accumulation is incompletely understood, but the current model proposes that mutations in *HFE* may impair TfR-mediated uptake of transferrin-bound iron into crypt cells, providing a false signal that iron stores are low.

Iron is involved in oxygen transport and redox reactions, but the mechanism of its cellular toxicity is not known. In haemochromatosis excess iron is found in almost all tissues, accompanied by cell loss and marked fibrosis, with the liver, pancreas, spleen, heart and several endocrine organs (anterior pituitary, testes and parathyroids) particularly affected. A similar pattern is seen in the other (secondary) causes of haemochromatosis.

Epidemiology

HH is the commonest known inherited disease among Caucasians of northern European descent, with a homozygote prevalence of between 0.1 and 0.5% and an overall gene frequency of 3–10%. Penetrance is incomplete with one large series reporting an incidence of clinical disease of less than 1% in patients with homozygous C282Y *HFE* mutations identified by population screening. This might be due to the need for a concomitant mutation in a second gene (eg the transferrin receptor 2 gene) for full disease expression. Males are more likely to develop disease than females, presumably reflecting protection by menstrual losses. Accumulation of iron and associated tissue damage takes years to develop, with 70% of cases presenting between 40 and 70 years of age.

Clinical presentation

The classical triad of diabetes mellitus (DM), cirrhosis and skin hyperpigmentation (bronzed diabetes) occurs relatively late, usually when total body iron stores exceed 20 g. A variety of other organ systems may be involved, as described below. However, increasingly patients are picked up prior to clinical presentation with evidence of iron overload on routine biochemistry or when screening is performed because a relative has HH.

Liver disease

- cirrhosis – abdominal pain, fatigue, bruising.

Endocrine disease

- DM – polyuria, polydipsia, weight loss
- hypogonadism – hair loss, diminished libido, impotence
- hypoparathyroidism – weakness, tetany.

Cardiac disease

- dilated cardiomyopathy – fatigue, breathlessness.

Arthritis

- large joints with chondrocalcinosis
- small joints resembling rheumatoid arthritis (particularly second and third metacarpophalangeal (MCP) joints).

Arthritis occurs in about half of all cases, as does hypogonadism (usually hypogonadotrophic, but sometimes hypergonadotrophic), while cardiac disease occurs in approximately one-third.

Physical signs

The clinical signs of haemochromatosis include:

- hyperpigmentation (due to a combination of iron and melanin)
- hepatomegaly with other stigmata of chronic liver disease
- testicular atrophy
- diminished body hair
- arthritis – especially second and third metacarpophalangeal joints and wrists
- splenomegaly
- cardiac disease – cardiomegaly, signs of biventricular failure.

Investigation

Who to screen?

Symptomatic patients with:

- liver disease
- DM, particularly with hepatomegaly/ stigmata of chronic liver disease, atypical cardiac disease or early onset sexual dysfunction
- early onset atypical arthropathy, cardiac disease and male sexual dysfunction.

Asymptomatic patients:

- first-degree relatives of a confirmed case of HH
- individuals with unexplained elevation of liver enzymes or the incidental finding of asymptomatic hepatomegaly or radiologic detection of enhanced attenuation of the liver on CT.

As treatment is more effective the earlier it is initiated, the aim is to identify subjects before they become symptomatic. Most centres recommend concurrent measurement of iron status and genetic screening for relatives of HH probands. While population screening is probably not currently cost-effective, some centres make a case for biochemical screening of all patients with DM, in whom a prevalence of approximately five times that in the general population has been described.

Basic blood tests and radiology

Routine haematology and biochemistry should be sent, including liver function tests, clotting screen, and alpha-fetoprotein if hepatocellular carcinoma is suspected. Radiology may show deposition of calcium pyrophosphate (chondrocalcinosis) in large joints such as the knee.

Iron status

Iron overload can be assessed by transferrin saturation, plasma (or serum) iron concentration and plasma ferritin. A fasting transferrin saturation >60% in men or >50% in women detects about 90% of patients with homozygous HH. Many centres, however, use a 'cut-off' value of 45% for both sexes, leading to fewer missed diagnoses at the expense of an increased false positive rate. Increased plasma ferritin provides supporting evidence but, compared with transferrin saturation it is generally less specific (as it is also an acute phase reactant) and less sensitive (as higher levels of iron overload are required to increase ferritin concentration). The definitive test for iron overload is liver biopsy.

In a patient where plasma indices indicate iron overload and genetic analysis demonstrates a homozygous C282Y *HFE* mutation, the diagnosis of HH is secure. If the patient is under 40 years with normal liver enzymes, cirrhosis is unlikely and therefore liver biopsy is not always necessary. Non-invasive imaging studies, such as CT and MRI have become increasingly accurate for determining both hepatic and cardiac iron deposition.

Treatment

Genetic haemochromatosis is best treated by venesection on a weekly basis until iron depletion is demonstrated by normalisation of serum ferritin and transferrin saturation and the development of a mild anaemia. Thereafter, the frequency of venesection can be reduced to 1–2 monthly to prevent reaccumulation of iron stores.

Venesection has been shown to reduce the early mortality associated with untreated haemochromatosis, particularly cardiac or hepatic failure, but does not appear to reduce the risk of hepatocellular carcinoma or the severity of diabetes or arthritis. Given the efficacy of venesection, especially when instituted early in the course of the disease, identification of a case of haemochromatosis should be followed by screening of the relatives.

Diabetes (see Section 2.6), hypogonadism (see Sections 2.4.2 and 2.4.3) and hypoparathyroidism (see Section 2.5.9) are managed according to standard guidelines.

The iron-chelating agent desferrioxamine may be used in the prevention/treatment of secondary haemochromatosis.

Complications

Haemochromatosis carries an approximately threefold increased risk of premature death due to hepatocellular carcinoma (32%), other malignancy (14%), cirrhosis (20%), DM (6%) or cardiomyopathy (6%). Patients must be kept under regular surveillance to allow early detection and treatment of these complications.

2.5.4 Osteoporosis

Osteoporosis has been defined as 'a disease characterised by low bone mass and microarchitectural deterioration of the tissue, leading to enhanced bone fragility and a consequent increase in fracture risk'.

More pragmatic definitions of osteoporosis rely on measurement of bone mineral density (BMD), as it has been shown that a bone mass 1 SD (one standard deviation) below the mean peak bone mass of young adults carries a 1.5–2.5-fold increased risk of fracture. BMD is therefore compared with the average BMD of a person of the same gender at age 30 years to yield a *T* score. In certain circumstances (eg young adults), comparison is made with the age-adjusted bone mass (*Z* score).

Pathophysiology

Bone mass increases during growth and adolescence, peaks in the third decade and declines with age thereafter, with an increased rate of loss after the menopause in women. A number of factors influence bone mass including:

- genetic/racial, eg African-Caribbean people are much less likely to develop osteoporosis than Caucasian people
- sex hormones – risk factors for osteoporosis include early menopause in women and hypogonadism in men
- environmental – inadequate calcium intake, physical inactivity, cigarette smoking and alcohol abuse
- drugs – especially corticosteroids and long-term heparin
- in addition, osteoporosis may arise secondary to a large number of other medical conditions (Table 49).

Key point

Fracture risk

Bone mass is not the only determinant of fracture risk, which also depends on the quality and geometry of the bone, previous history of fracture and frequency of falls.

Epidemiology

It has been estimated that one-half of women and one-third of men in the UK will suffer an osteoporotic fracture in their lifetime, and that 22.5% of women and 5.8% of men aged over 50 years in the UK have a BMD greater than 2.5 SD below the sex-adjusted mean peak BMD.

Clinical presentation

Osteoporosis typically presents with a low trauma fracture. Although any bone may be affected, the hip, vertebrae and distal forearms are classically involved. Relevant features to note in the history include:

- past medical history of major illness or any secondary cause of osteoporosis (including low body mass index (BMI), ie <19 kg/m^2)
- timing of puberty and menopause in females, history of prolonged oligomenorrhoea or amenorrhoea
- average calcium intake
- exercise level
- current and previous drug treatment
- family history of osteoporotic fractures
- symptoms of gastrointestinal disease or malabsorption.

Physical signs

If left untreated, osteoporosis leads to progressive loss of height with increased kyphosis as a result of successive vertebral fractures.

Investigation

The principal objectives of investigation are to determine the overall risk of fracture and to identify any treatable cause of secondary osteoporosis.

Blood tests

Key point

Blood tests in osteoporosis

Osteoporosis is not a disorder of calcium metabolism, and therefore serum calcium, phosphate and alkaline phosphatase are usually normal. Following fracture, alkaline phosphatase may be elevated.

Table 49 Secondary causes of osteoporosis

Cause	Condition
Gastrointestinal disease	Coeliac disease, Crohn's disease, ulcerative colitis, gastrectomy, primary biliary cirrhosis
Endocrine disease	Cushing's syndrome, hyperparathyroidism, hypogonadism, hyperthyroidism, hypopituitarism, DM
Psychological disorders	Anorexia nervosa, exercise-induced amenorrhoea
Others	Myeloma, mastocytosis, osteogenesis imperfecta, Gaucher's disease

DM, diabetes mellitus.

Biochemical markers of bone turnover (reflecting the processes of bone formation and bone resorption) are finding increasing use in predicting individuals at risk of osteoporosis and in monitoring the effect(s) of drugs used in treatment. Bone-specific osteoblastic (eg osteocalcin and procollagen type 1 N-terminal propeptide (P1NP)) and osteoclastic (eg N-terminal or C-terminal cross-linking telopeptides of type 1 collagen (NTX, CTX)) markers are preferred. A key advantage is the more rapid change (within 3–6 months of intervention) in biochemical markers when compared with bone densitometry (changes may take up to 18–24 months).

Radiology

- Plain radiographs may demonstrate a fracture or vertebral collapse (Fig 48).
- BMD, measured by dual-energy X-ray absorptiometry (DXA), is usually determined at the spine and hip (Fig 49).

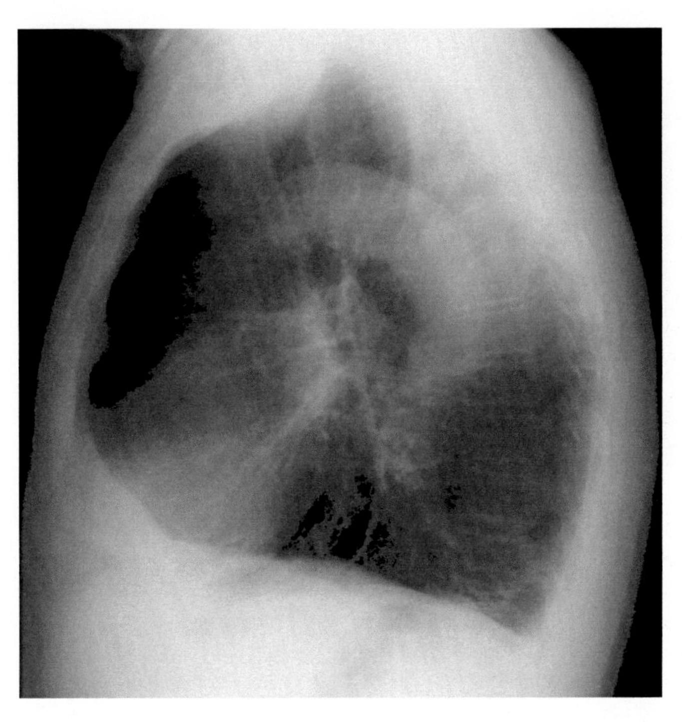

Fig 48 Osteoporotic vertebral fractures. Lateral chest X-ray demonstrating loss of vertebral height and anterior wedging at several levels within the thoracic spine, leading to kyphosis. Preferential loss of trabecular over cortical bone gives rise to characteristic 'picture-frame' vertebrae.

Treatment

Reduce fracture risk

In addition to appropriate pain relief in the event of an acute fracture, the main aim of treatment is to reduce the risk of fracture. Several agents are licensed for use in the UK, although not all have proven efficacy in terms of reducing vertebral and/or non-vertebral fractures. Drugs either inhibit bone resorption (the most common mode of action) or stimulate bone formation, and may be used for primary or secondary prevention.

Who should be offered treatment?

Key point

Postmenopausal women with a previous fragility fracture should be considered for treatment without further need for risk assessment.

For groups other than postmenopausal women who have had a fragility fracture, risk factor calculators, eg QFracture® (www.qfracture.org) or FRAX® (www.sheffield.ac.uk/FRAX/), are useful tools in helping to determine who should receive intervention. These integrate clinical risk factors, with or without femoral neck BMD, to calculate the 10-year probability of hip fracture or a major osteoporotic fracture (clinical spine, hip, forearm or proximal humerus). Current NICE recommendations for the treatment of osteoporosis can be found at www.nice.org.uk.

Treatment for women

Treatment options include:

- Exercise – regular exercise reduces fracture risk, but the magnitude of benefit is relatively small and requires a committed, maintained exercise regime.
- Calcium supplementation – decreases cortical bone loss and rates of fracture. Total calcium intake should be about 1,500 mg per day, often requiring supplements of 500–1,000 mg, combined with vitamin D (400–800 IU/day) (although not a true cause of osteoporosis, vitamin D deficiency and osteomalacia may compound bone fragility in older people).
- Bisphosphonates – increase BMD and decrease fracture risk, with a magnitude of benefit similar to hormone replacement therapy (HRT) (see below). They are particularly useful in steroid-induced bone loss. All the bisphosphonates have low bioavailability when given orally and should be taken on an empty stomach, in the upright position (oesophageal irritation/ulceration occasionally limits the use of these agents). Alendronic acid and risedronate sodium are given either daily or, more commonly, as a once-a-week preparation.

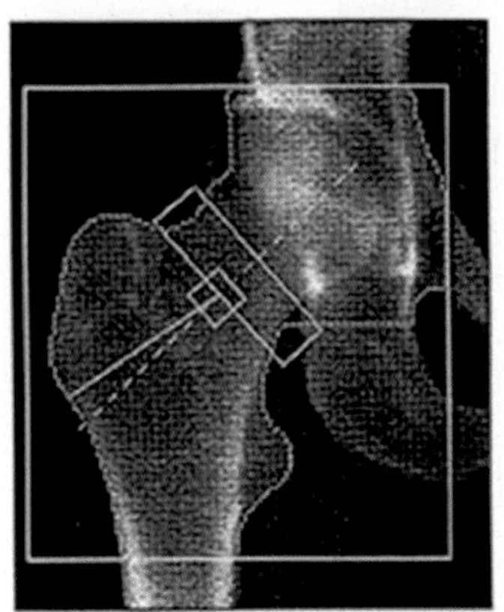

-30.Nov.1998 16:46 (113 × 122)
Hologic QDR-4500A (S/N 45208)
Right Hip V8.20a:3

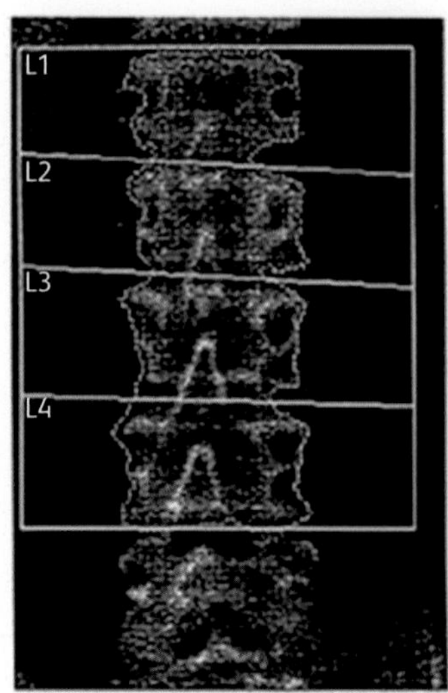

-30.Nov.1998 16:07 (116 × 138)
Hologic QDR-4500A (S/N 45208)
Lumbar Spine V8.20a:3

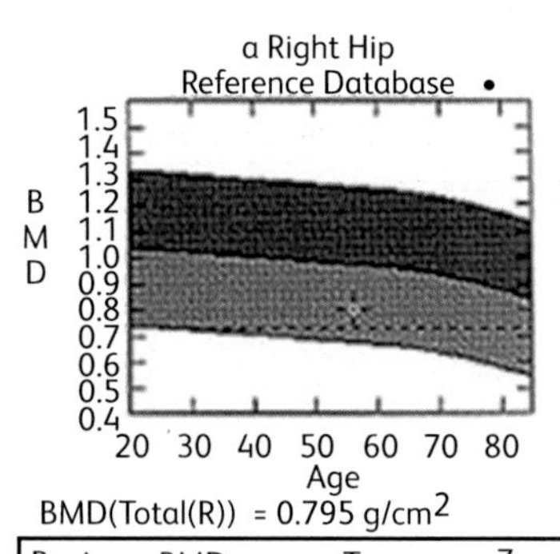

Region	BMD	T	Z
Neck	0.656	−2.01 71% (25.0)	−1.14 81%
Troch	0.647	−1.03 83% (25.0)	−0.72 88%
Inter	0.902	−1.62 75% (25.0)	−1.34 79%
TOTAL	0.795	−1.58 77% (25.0)	−1.18 82%
Ward's	0.548	−1.68 70% (25.0)	−0.19 95%

• Age and sex matched
T = peak BMD matched
Z = age matched NHA 01 Feb 91

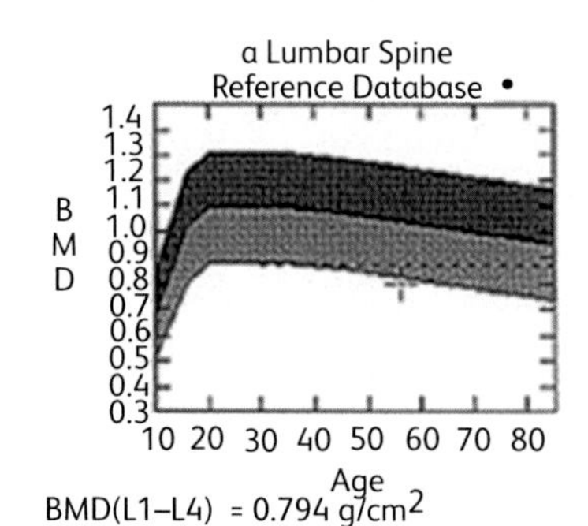

Region	BMD	T(30.0)	Z
L1	0.702	−2.70 70%	−2.30 74%
L2	0.797	−2.70 73%	−2.18 77%
L3	0.830	−2.48 75%	−1.95 79%
L4	0.825	−2.91 72%	−2.37 76%
L1–L4	0.794	−2.70 73%	−2.19 77%

• Age and sex matched
T = peak BMD matched
Z = age matched TK 04 Nov 91

Fig 49 Bone densitometry. DXA bone mineral density scan in a man with osteoporosis of the lumbar spine secondary to long-standing hypogonadism. Values for the hip and lumbar spine are shown with both T and Z scores calculated for each site. The World Health Organization (WHO) defines osteoporosis as a bone density ≥2.5 SD below the mean peak bone density in youth.

Ibandronic acid may be given orally once monthly or intravenously every 3 months. Zoledronic acid is given by intravenous infusion every 12 months, typically for three doses in the first instance.

- Denosumab (a monoclonal antibody targeting RANK ligand to inhibit osteoclast formation, function and survival) is given by subcutaneous injection every 6 months. Following cessation of treatment, a rebound increase in bone turnover is often observed and alternative therapy may therefore be needed to prevent a sudden decline in bone mass.
- Selective oestrogen receptor modulators (SERMs), eg raloxifene – exhibit oestrogen-like agonist activity in some tissues, eg bone, while acting as antioestrogens in others, eg breast. Raloxifene has been linked with an increased risk of venous thromboembolic disease and does not prevent menopausal hot flushes.
- Teriparatide (recombinant parathyroid hormone (PTH) given by daily subcutaneous injection) may be used in patients with severe osteoporosis who have failed to respond to, or are intolerant of, standard antiresorptive therapy. It is given for up to 2 years.
- Strontium ranelate – by increasing bone formation and decreasing bone resorption, strontium increases BMD and decreases fracture rates. However, following various safety alerts, and with diminishing clinical use, the major manufacturer of this drug ceased production in the UK and worldwide in 2017.
- Intranasal calcitonin is also no longer available for use in osteoporosis (risk of cancer).

Hazard

Side effects of bisphosphonates

Although the bisphosphonates have a good safety record, there have been reports of potentially serious side effects in some contexts. Osteonecrosis of the jaw is mainly seen in those with poor dentition receiving intravenous therapy. More commonly, atypical femoral fractures (eg subtrochanteric or femoral shaft) may complicate continuous long-term treatment. Accordingly, current guidelines recommend that oral therapy should be used for up to 5 years, and intravenous therapy for up to 3 years, in the first instance. The decision to continue treatment beyond this should be taken by a metabolic bone expert after careful review of the individual case.

Hazard

Hormone replacement therapy (HRT)

HRT has previously been used as a treatment for osteoporosis. However, the risks of treatment (increased breast cancer, thromboembolic and cardiovascular disease) must be balanced against benefits in relation to BMD. Accordingly, HRT is no longer routinely recommended for the prevention or treatment of osteoporosis in postmenopausal females, but it remains an important step in reducing the risk of osteoporosis in women <50 years of age who have undergone an early/premature menopause.

Treatment for men

Exercise, calcium/vitamin D supplementation and medications such as bisphosphonates, denosumab and teriparatide are also central to the prevention and management of osteoporotic fractures in males. Testosterone replacement is reserved for hypogonadal patients.

Prophylaxis with corticosteroid therapy

Patients who require prolonged treatment with high doses of glucocorticoids (equivalent to $\geq$7.5 mg of prednisolone per day) should receive calcium/vitamin D supplementation and be considered for treatment with a bisphosphonate for at least the duration of the corticosteroid therapy.

Secondary osteoporosis

Where possible the underlying cause should be treated appropriately.

2.5.5 Osteomalacia

Osteomalacia is the result of defective bone mineralisation, leading to weakness and an increased propensity to fracture with subsequent deformity. If this occurs during childhood before fusion of the epiphyseal plates, it is known as rickets.

Pathophysiology

The formation of bone is a two-stage process involving the deposition of unmineralised matrix and its subsequent mineralisation in a vitamin D-dependent process, requiring normal osteoblast function. The metabolic pathways leading to the synthesis of the active form of vitamin D (1,25-dihydroxy-D_3) are shown in Fig 50.

Table 50 lists the causes of osteomalacia; by far the commonest is reduced cutaneous production of

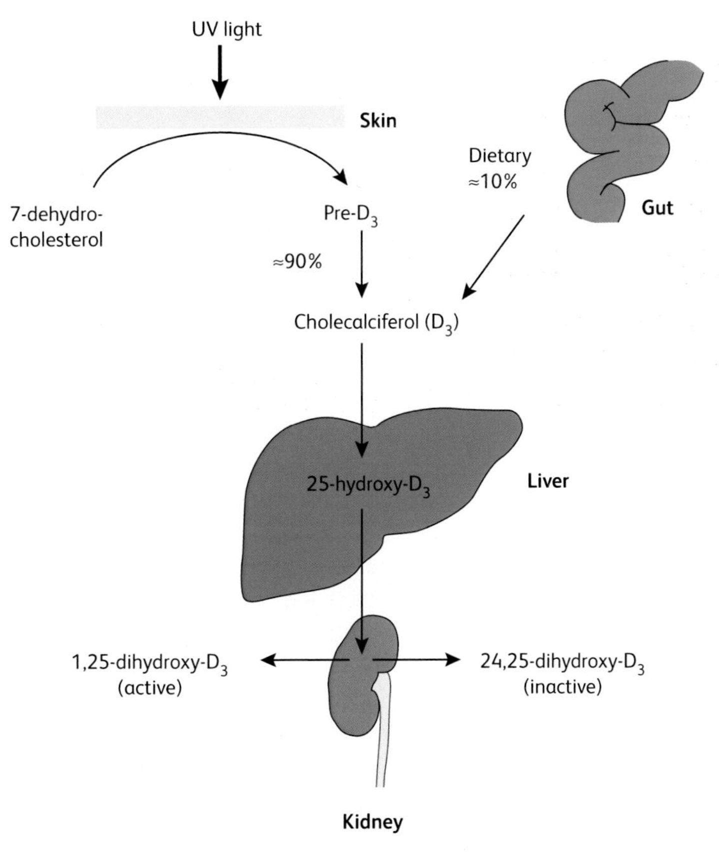

Fig 50 Key steps in vitamin D metabolism.

Table 50 Causes of osteomalacia

	Mechanism	Cause
Vitamin D deficiency	↓ Production	↓ Sunlight exposure
		↓ Dietary intake
		Malabsorption, eg coeliac disease, intestinal resection
		Liver disease, eg primary biliary cirrhosis
	↑ Clearance	Enzyme inducers, eg anticonvulsants
	↓ 1-Hydroxylation	Renal failure
		Vitamin D-dependent rickets type I (AR)[1]
	↓ Action	Vitamin D-dependent rickets type II (AR)[2]
Hypophosphataemia	↓ Intake	Antacids (phosphate binding)
	↑ Loss	Hypophosphataemic rickets (vitamin D-resistant rickets, XLD)
		Fanconi syndrome
		Renal tubular acidosis
		Oncogenous osteomalacia
Defective mineralisation		Hypophosphatasia
		High-dose etidronate
Defective bone matrix		Fibrogenesis imperfecta ossium

1 Renal 25-hydroxyvitamin D 1alpha-hydroxylase deficiency.
2 Absent or defective vitamin D receptor.
AR, autosomal recessive; XLD, X-linked dominant.

vitamin D, which declines with age and is often exacerbated by reduced sunlight exposure and poor dietary intake. It is also more frequent following migration to a cooler climate, eg among Asian immigrants in the UK, where dietary consumption of phytates additionally impairs calcium absorption.

Epidemiology

Definitive diagnosis of osteomalacia depends on bone histology, so an accurate estimate of its prevalence is not readily available. The biochemical features of osteomalacia are present in about 5% of the older population and up to 10–20% of patients with hip fractures.

Clinical presentation and physical signs

The presentation of osteomalacia is often vague and insidious with a gradual onset of generalised muscle aches and pains. A history of immigration, long-term anticonvulsant use, gastric surgery, coeliac disease or other malabsorption should prompt consideration of the diagnosis. Proximal myopathy may occur and manifest as difficulty rising out of a chair or in climbing stairs (see Section 1.4.5). Features of hypocalcaemia may be present (see Section 2.5.9). Many patients presenting with a pathological fracture have underlying osteomalacia.

In childhood the characteristic features are of rickets with short stature, bowed legs and widened metaphyses (seen as 'rickety rosary' of the ribs).

Investigation

Although a definitive diagnosis of osteomalacia can only be made on bone biopsy, this is rarely indicated and most centres rely on biochemical and radiological evidence including the following.

Bone chemistry

- low or low-normal serum calcium
- low or low-normal serum phosphate (except in renal failure)

- elevated serum alkaline phosphatase
- vitamin D levels – if measured, 1,25-dihydroxyvitamin-D_3 levels are often normal, albeit inappropriately so in the face of hypocalcaemia, hypophosphataemia and secondary hyperparathyroidism. Vitamin D-dependent rickets type II is an exception to the rule.

Key point

Biochemical findings in osteomalacia

Many of these are attributable to progressive secondary hyperparathyroidism.

Radiographs

- vertebrae – 'cod-fish' appearance due to ballooning of intervertebral disc
- pelvis, long bones, ribs – Looser's zones or 'pseudofractures', ie areas of low density representing unmineralised osteoid (Fig 51)
- rickets produces characteristic widening of the epiphyses with widening and cupping of the metaphyses.

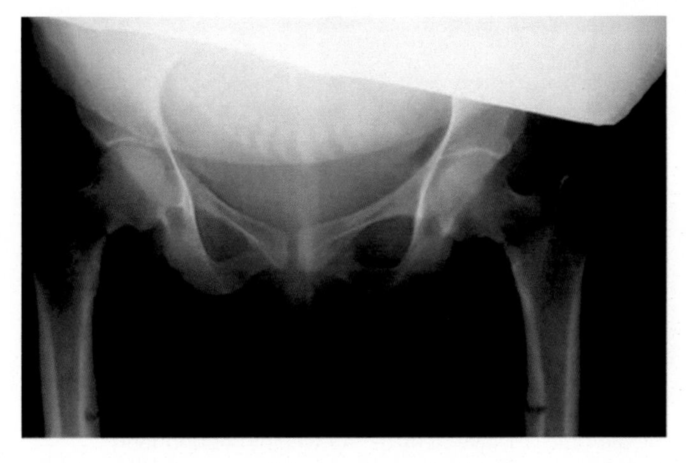

Fig 51 Looser's zones. Pelvic radiograph showing pseudofractures (Looser's zones – areas of low density) in a patient with severe osteomalacia (seen in the medial cortex of both femurs close to the bottom of the image).

Treatment

Multiple formulations of vitamin D and its metabolites are available. The choice of formulation and dosage depend on the underlying aetiology. Serum calcium must always be monitored, especially in those receiving larger (pharmacological) doses and activated forms.

Key point

Different preparations of 'vitamin D'

- ergocalciferol = calciferol = vitamin D_2
- c(h)olecalciferol = vitamin D_3
- alfacalcidol = 1alpha-hydroxycholecalciferol
- calcitriol = 1,25-dihydroxycholecalciferol.

Both alfacalcidol and calcitriol are considered 'activated' forms of vitamin D.

- Mild insufficiency – 400–800 units (IU)/day (of ergocalciferol or colecalciferol) may suffice.
- Clear deficiency – the recommended treatment is based on fixed loading doses of vitamin D (ergocalciferol or colecalciferol – up to a total of 300,000 IU) given either as weekly or daily split doses, followed by lifelong maintenance treatment (typically 800 IU/day).
- Severe malabsorption states / chronic liver disease – pharmacological doses (eg 40–50,000 IU/day of ergocalciferol) may be required.

The treatment of rickets secondary to phosphate wasting disorders requires oral supplementation sufficient to balance renal losses. Co-administration of vitamin D is often required to prevent hypocalcaemia. Any underlying disorder, eg coeliac disease should be managed appropriately.

Prognosis

With treatment, hypocalcaemia, hypophosphataemia and any accompanying symptoms, including proximal myopathy, typically improve over several weeks. Alkaline phosphatase and parathyroid hormone (PTH) levels may take up to 6 months to normalise, during which time the bone remains weak and liable to fracture.

2.5.6 Paget's disease

Paget's disease of bone was first described by Sir James Paget in 1879 as 'osteitis deformans'. It is characterised by grossly disordered bone formation giving rise to deformity and pain.

Aetiology/pathophysiology

The cause of Paget's disease remains incompletely understood. Evidence suggests both genetic and environmental influences. The most well-characterised genetic links are mutations affecting the *SQSTM1* gene, which encodes p62 (sequestosome-1), an important regulator of RANK-mediated nuclear factor kappa B (NF-κB) signalling in osteoclasts.

The primary disorder appears to reflect an increase in the number and activity of osteoclasts, possibly as a consequence of exposure to a viral pathogen (although the latter remains contentious). This is followed by imperfect osteoblast-mediated bone repair. Thus, the normal regulation of bone resorption and new bone formation is lost, with the subsequent production of hypertrophied, osteosclerotic bone. Bone deformity and pain are common, together with partial and pathological fractures. The disease process mainly affects the axial skeleton, skull and long bones, and frequently results in secondary osteoarthritis and nerve root entrapment.

Epidemiology

Paget's disease of bone is the second commonest metabolic bone condition after osteoporosis, with approximately 1% of European and North American Caucasians aged 40 years or over affected. It is less common in other ethnic groups.

Clinical presentation

Paget's disease is not infrequently an incidental radiological finding, or comes to light during the investigation of an elevated alkaline phosphatase noted on routine blood tests in an otherwise asymptomatic individual. Bone pain may reflect disease activity, which is often localised but multicentric, although it can also arise as a result of partial or complete fractures. The deformed bone places abnormal stresses on adjacent joints with subsequent osteoarthritis. The characteristic bony deformities (bowing of long bones and thickening of the skull) may be noticed by the patient. Nerve root entrapment can affect any of the cranial nerves (classically the eighth nerve resulting in deafness) or spinal nerve roots. Occasionally enlargement of the base of the skull (platybasia) leads to paraplegia or aqueductal stenosis and hydrocephalus.

Physical signs

Bony deformities

- enlargement of the skull with frontal bossing
- bowing of long bones, especially the tibia
- kyphosis of the skeleton.

Increased vascularity

- warmth over affected bones
- prominence of superficial temporal arteries
- high cardiac output (bounding pulse, cardiac failure).

Nerve entrapment

- deafness.

Investigation

Biochemistry

- Alkaline phosphatase is usually raised, but without abnormalities of serum calcium or phosphate (except following prolonged immobility when hypercalcaemia may occur).
- Other markers of bone resorption may provide evidence of increased bone turnover.

Radiology

Plain radiographs

Plain radiographs may show localised enlargement of bone with cortical thickening and localised areas of both sclerosis and osteolysis (Fig 52).

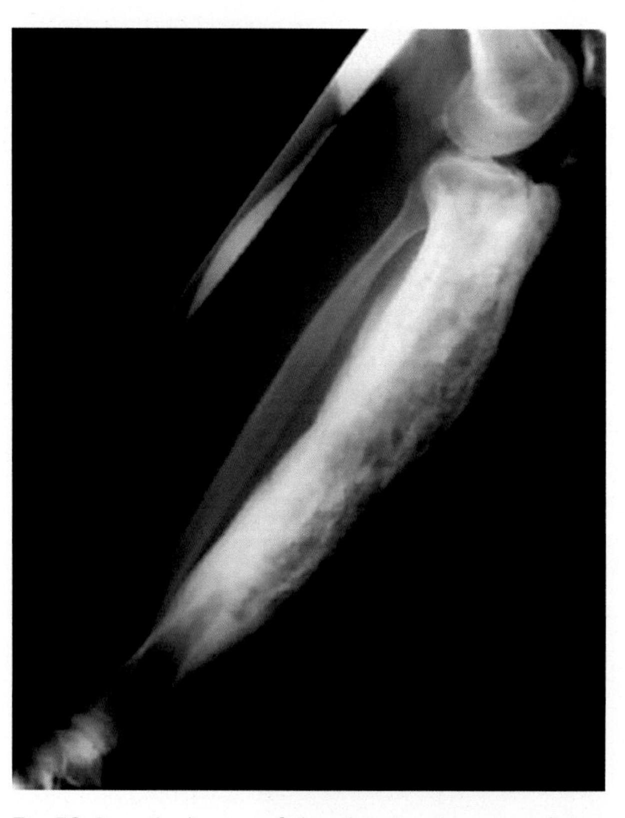

Fig 52 Paget's disease of the tibia. Involvement of the weight-bearing long bones leads to bowing, particularly of the femur and, as shown here, the tibia ('sabre' tibia), which bow anteriorly and laterally. Note that the fibula is spared.

Radioisotope scanning

Bone scintigraphy allows demonstration of the full extent of bone involvement.

Treatment

Bisphosphonates are the mainstay of treatment for symptomatic Paget's disease, and produce a prolonged, marked reduction of bone resorption by inhibiting osteoclast activity, with intravenous zoledronic acid demonstrating the greatest efficacy. Administration is followed by decreased uptake on bone scanning, reduction in alkaline phosphatase, stabilisation of hearing loss and improvement in other neurological dysfunction. The role of bisphosphonates in asymptomatic patients remains unclear, and further trials are awaited.

As a potent inhibitor of osteoclastic RANK ligand, denosumab would appear to be an attractive alternative in patients intolerant of bisphosphonates, although clinical experience to date is limited.

Accompanying arthritis requires suitable analgesia and knee or hip replacement as indicated.

Complications

In addition to the neurological (nerve entrapment), rheumatological (osteoarthritis) and cardiac (high-output cardiac failure) complications, osteosarcoma occurs in ≤1% of cases; it is not yet known whether the risk is reduced by bisphosphonates.

> **Hazard**
>
> In a patient with Paget's disease, soft tissue swelling, increased pain or a rapidly rising alkaline phosphatase level should alert the clinician to the possibility of a developing osteosarcoma.

2.5.7 Hyperparathyroidism

Pathophysiology

There are normally four parathyroid glands, closely related to the thyroid, although occasionally there may be extra glands, eg ectopically sited in the superior mediastinum. Hyperparathyroidism means over-production of parathyroid hormone (PTH). Conventionally this is classified as primary, secondary or tertiary, although some clinicians argue that secondary and tertiary should be grouped together. *Primary* hyperparathyroidism refers to production of PTH in a physiologically inappropriate manner which is not entrained to serum calcium levels. It is most frequently the result of a single adenoma, but in about 20% of cases there are multiple adenomata or diffuse hyperplasia of all four glands. Parathyroid carcinoma is rare (~1% of cases). *Secondary* hyperparathyroidism refers to hyperplasia and hypersecretion of PTH as part of the homeostatic response to chronically low serum calcium (eg in the context of renal disease with deficiency of activated vitamin D). This PTH hypersecretion generally restores serum calcium levels to normal, at the expense of bone mineral loss. Screening for this and intervening with activated vitamin D at the appropriate stage of chronic renal disease is important both to preserve bone mineral density, and to prevent autonomous parathyroid adenomas arising from the hyperplastic parathyroid glands. Once this occurs, with an attendant rise in serum calcium, *tertiary* hyperparathyroidism is said to have developed.

The excess PTH produces hypercalcaemia through three routes:

- increased osteoclastic bone resorption
- increased renal calcium reabsorption (although note that the increase in serum calcium usually overwhelms the resorptive capacity of the tubules, and hence hypercalciuria is the norm in hyperparathyroidism)
- increased intestinal calcium absorption (mediated through increased vitamin D activity).

Epidemiology

The prevalence is estimated to be approximately 0.1–0.2%, affecting females twice as frequently as males.

Clinical presentation and physical signs

Asymptomatic hypercalcaemia, discovered on routine biochemical testing, is now most commonly the first indication of the diagnosis. A smaller number of cases present with hyperparathyroid renal disease (urolithiasis, nephrocalcinosis) or hyperparathyroid bone disease, leading to bone pain, especially once osteoporosis is established. Other features of hypercalcaemia may also be present (see Section 2.5.8).

Investigation

Routine biochemistry

Hypercalcaemia is an almost universal finding in patients with primary hyperparathyroidism. The serum phosphate level is usually low-normal or low, reflecting the effects of PTH in promoting urinary phosphate excretion. Alkaline phosphatase levels are typically normal or mildly elevated. Urea and electrolytes and glomerular filtration rate (GFR) should be determined.

A 24-hour collection for estimation of urinary calcium excretion should be performed, which will help to discriminate hyperparathyroidism from familial hypocalciuric hypercalcaemia (FHH), an asymptomatic trait caused by loss-of-function mutations in the parathyroid calcium sensing receptor. Measurement of a spot urinary calcium: creatinine excretion ratio is another helpful way of distinguishing primary hyperparathyroidism and FHH.

Parathyroid hormone levels

Confirmation of the diagnosis can be made by determining the intact PTH level in a two-site assay (using monoclonal antibodies directed against both ends of the full-length PTH molecule), which fails to detect the smaller fragment PTH-related peptide (PTHrP). The finding of an elevated or normal PTH level is inappropriate in the setting of hypercalcaemia.

Radiology

Manifestations of hyperparathyroidism

The radiological hallmark of hyperparathyroid bone disease (osteitis fibrosa cystica) is the subperiosteal erosion, most easily seen in the distal phalanges of the fingers. A similar process in the skull results in the so-called 'pepper-pot' appearance. Occasionally osteolytic lesions are seen, suggesting the presence of bone cysts or 'brown tumours'. Long-standing hyperparathyroidism leads to generalised osteoporosis, which may be evident on plain radiographs. Nephrocalcinosis and urolithiasis are sometimes identified on plain abdominal radiographs or ultrasound examination of the renal tract (Fig 53).

Localisation of tumours

It has been argued by many that preoperative imaging is unnecessary prior to initial surgical exploration in an uncomplicated case, and that an experienced surgeon should be able to determine the aetiology and effect the appropriate treatment for primary hyperparathyroidism. However, with the advent of minimally invasive parathyroid surgery (see below) and in cases of surgical re-exploration, localisation studies including ultrasonography, ^{99m}Tc-sestamibi (Fig 54), CT/MRI and/or venous sampling may be useful.

Treatment

Emergency/short term

Hypercalcaemia should be treated as outlined in Section 2.5.8.

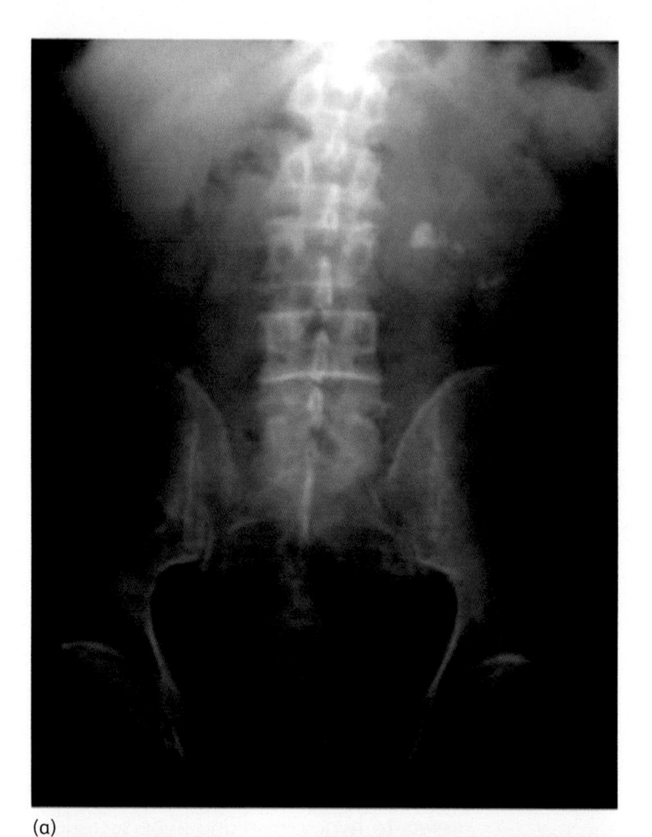

(a)

(b)

Fig 53 Renal involvement in primary hyperparathyroidism. Plain abdominal radiographs demonstrating nephrolithiasis **(a)** and nephrocalcinosis **(b)** in the setting of primary hyperparathyroidism.

Fig 54 Parathyroid adenoma. ^{99m}Tc-sestamibi scan showing a parathyroid adenoma (arrow) in close proximity to the inferior pole of the right lobe of the thyroid gland.

Long term

Key point

Surgery remains the definitive treatment for primary hyperparathyroidism.

Indications for surgery

The US National Institutes of Health (NIH), recognising (1) the changing presentation of primary hyperparathyroidism (with increasing numbers of younger patients being detected), (2) the potential for long-term adverse sequelae in untreated cases (especially renal, bone and cardiovascular (hypertension) complications), and (3) improved surgical techniques, has issued revised guidance as to which patients with 'apparently asymptomatic disease' should be referred for surgery (those with symptoms should be automatically referred):

- all patients who are <50 years of age
- when the serum corrected calcium level is >0.25 mmol/L above the upper limit of the reference range
- when the 24-hour urine calcium excretion is persistently >10 mmol/day
- in the presence of impaired renal function (eg eGFR <60 mL/minute/ 1.73 m^2)
- in the presence of nephrolithiasis or nephrocalcinosis
- in the presence of skeletal involvement (eg osteoporosis as defined by WHO DXA criteria or when there is evidence of a vertebral fracture)
- in patients with demonstrable proximal weakness, hyperreflexia or ataxia.

When surgery is not undertaken, regular monitoring (clinical, biochemical, radiological) is required to check for disease progression / development of complications.

Surgical technique

Many centres now offer minimally invasive parathyroid day-case surgery, in which preoperative localisation of single/ipsilateral double adenomas is used to guide the surgeon to the site of the adenoma(s), thus avoiding more extensive neck exploration. Intraoperative PTH measurement can help to confirm complete excision prior to closure, by virtue of the short half-life of PTH. Patients with suspected bilateral disease should be considered for conventional full neck exploration.

Medical treatments

Calcimimetics (eg cinacalcet) mimic the effect of calcium on the parathyroid calcium-sensing receptor and so decrease the synthesis and/or secretion of PTH. They may provide an alternative treatment strategy for selected cases, including in patients:

- with recurrent/relapsing disease
- deemed unsuitable for surgery
- with refractory secondary/tertiary hyperparathyroidism
- with parathyroid carcinoma failing primary surgery.

Disease associations

Primary hyperparathyroidism occasionally occurs as part of the multiple endocrine neoplasia (MEN) syndromes (see Section 2.7.1). In such cases there is usually four-gland hyperplasia rather than a single adenoma, and thus conventional rather than minimally invasive surgery is required.

Important information for patients

Where primary hyperparathyroidism is an incidental finding, the indications for and complications of surgery must be carefully discussed with the patient. The requirement for follow-up, particularly if surgery is not initially undertaken, should also be stressed, and the patient advised to maintain adequate hydration (especially in hot weather) and to avoid thiazide diuretics.

2.5.8 Hypercalcaemia

Aetiology/pathophysiology

Regulation of calcium metabolism

The vast majority of body calcium is found in bone and teeth, with only about 1% in extracellular fluid and within cells. Of the extracellular calcium, approximately half is bound to protein (mainly albumin) or complexed to anions (phosphate, citrate and bicarbonate), with the other half existing as free ionised calcium (the bioavailable fraction).

Hormonal control of extracellular calcium is exerted mainly by parathyroid hormone (PTH) and vitamin D (Fig 55). Broadly speaking, the role of PTH is to act rapidly to maintain extracellular free calcium, while the actions of vitamin D are directed towards preserving skeletal calcium levels, both to act as structural support and as a reservoir of calcium.

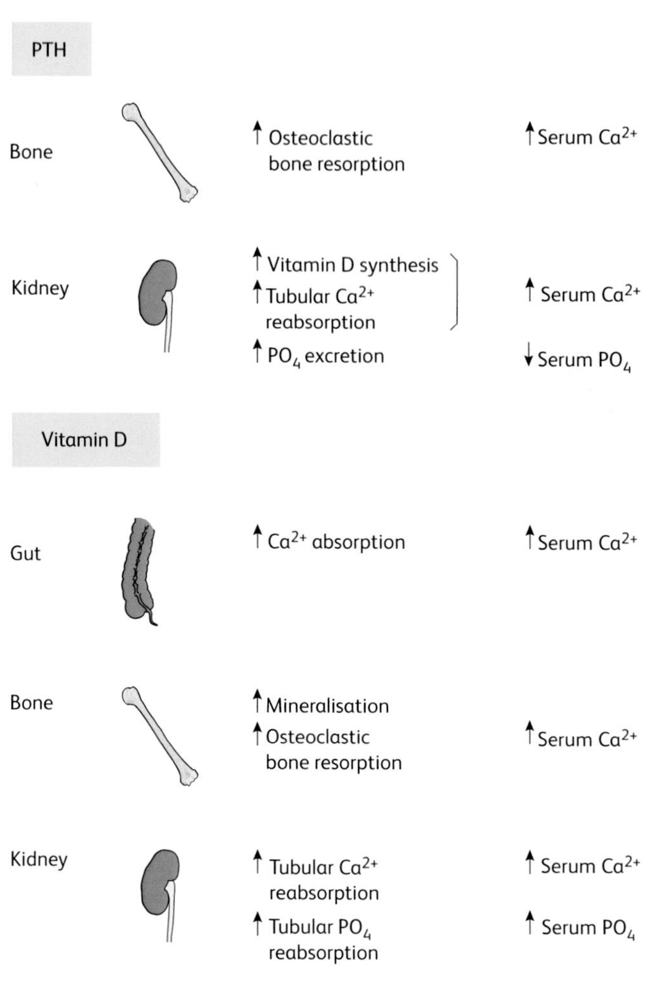

Fig 55 Calcium homeostasis.

Clinical features of hypercalcaemia

Hypercalcaemia is often an incidental finding in an otherwise apparently asymptomatic individual. In others, symptoms and signs are varied and are often remembered according to the mnemonic 'stones, bones, abdominal groans and psychic moans':

- stones – renal colic (urolithiasis), polyuria and polydipsia (nephrogenic diabetes insipidus (DI)), nephrocalcinosis
- bones – arthritis and bone pain
- abdominal groans – nausea and vomiting, anorexia, constipation, peptic ulcer, pancreatitis
- psychic moans – lethargy, fatigue, depression, confusion, psychosis.

In addition, chronic hypercalcaemia may be associated with corneal calcification (band keratopathy). In all cases a thorough physical examination should be undertaken, looking for features which suggest an underlying cause, especially malignancy.

Causes of hypercalcaemia

The major causes of hypercalcaemia are listed in Table 1 (see Section 1.1.1). The two most important and prevalent groups are hyperparathyroidism and malignancy. Hyperparathyroidism is dealt with in detail in Section 2.5.7. Malignancy can lead to hypercalcaemia via a number of direct and paraneoplastic mechanisms including:

- osteolytic bone metastases (eg breast, bronchus, kidney or thyroid cancer)
- production of PTH-related peptide (PTHrP) with PTH-like effects (eg squamous cell lung cancer)
- production of cytokines (eg osteoclast activating factor (OAF)) with bone resorbing activity, eg multiple myeloma
- production of vitamin D (eg lymphoma – rare).

The hypercalcaemia associated with some granulomatous disorders, particularly sarcoidosis, is thought to be due to 1alpha-hydroxylation of vitamin D by granulomata. It is thus classically aggravated by exposure to sunlight, producing summertime rises in the incidence of sarcoidosis-related hypercalcaemia. Vitamin D intoxication is an occasional cause of hypercalcaemia.

Investigation

See Section 1.1.1.

Treatment

Mild hypercalcaemia (<3.0 mmol/L)

When detected as the result of routine biochemistry in an otherwise asymptomatic patient, mild hypercalcaemia may require no specific immediate treatment. Such cases should, however, be investigated to establish the underlying cause. The need for adequate hydration, especially in hot weather, and avoidance of thiazide diuretics should be stressed.

Moderate hypercalcaemia (3.0–3.5 mmol/L)

Although chronic hypercalcaemia of this magnitude can appear relatively asymptomatic, these patients are at significant risk of developing severe hypercalcaemia (eg during intercurrent illness) and treatment is therefore required. However, the extent and aggressiveness of the intervention should be determined based on symptoms, comorbidities, magnitude of hypercalcaemia and underlying cause (see below for management options).

Emergency / short term

Emergency management of severe hypercalcaemia is described in Section 1.4.2.

Long term

The long-term management of hypercalcaemia is directed at the underlying condition. Where such treatment fails to control hypercalcaemia, repeated therapy with bisphosphonates may be indicated. Calcimimetics may also play an important role (see Section 2.5.7).

Complications

Long-standing hypercalcaemia can result in ectopic calcification. Renal stones and nephrocalcinosis are both well described, as is widespread calcification of the medial layer of arterial walls. Hypercalcaemia is also a recognised cause of a shortened QT interval on the ECG.

Prognosis

In general, the prognosis is dictated by the underlying disease.

2.5.9 Hypocalcaemia

Aetiology/pathophysiology

The causes of hypocalcaemia are listed in Table 51.

Key point

'Corrected' and ionised serum calcium

Since albumin is the principal calcium-binding protein in blood, hypoalbuminaemic states may be associated with apparent hypocalcaemia by virtue of reducing total calcium levels. Ionised calcium, however, remains unchanged. Accordingly, most laboratories routinely issue a 'corrected' calcium result, which includes an adjustment up or down from the measured level depending on whether the recorded albumin is below or above a defined 'normal' set-point, respectively.

The balance between total and ionised calcium is affected by acid–base balance and occasionally by the presence of anions such as citrate, such that a low ionised calcium, with the clinical features of hypocalcaemia, may occur in alkalosis and following extensive blood transfusion, even though the measured serum level lies within the normal range.

Hypoparathyroidism

In hypoparathyroidism PTH deficiency leads to:

- increased renal loss of calcium and retention of phosphate
- reduced bone resorption
- reduced calcium absorption (as a consequence of impaired 1-hydroxylation of 25-hydroxyvitamin D_3).

Serum phosphate levels are therefore high and alkaline phosphatase low.

Hypoparathyroidism most commonly arises in the setting of previous neck surgery, eg thyroidectomy. A period of transient hypocalcaemia may follow removal of a parathyroid adenoma, pending restoration of PTH secretion by the remaining intact glands. Occasionally this can be severe, reflecting avid uptake of calcium and phosphate by bone which has been chronically stimulated by PTH ('the hungry bone syndrome'). Idiopathic (acquired) hypoparathyroidism may occur as an isolated finding or is sometimes seen in the setting of the polyglandular endocrinopathies (see Section 2.7.2).

Pseudohypoparathyroidism

Pseudohypoparathyroidism is a rare disorder resulting from target organ resistance to the action of PTH. The clinical and biochemical features of hypoparathyroidism are frequently accompanied by a characteristic somatic phenotype including short stature, a rounded face and short fourth and fifth metacarpals (Fig 56). PTH levels are high. Interestingly, other family members may exhibit the somatic features without evidence of disordered calcium metabolism, so-called pseudopseudohypoparathyroidism.

Clinical presentation

Hypocalcaemia causes tetany, cramps, paraesthesiae of the extremities and muscle spasms precipitated by exercise or hypoxia. Seizure threshold is reduced and fits may occur. Chronic hypocalcaemia produces lethargy/malaise, and may mimic psychosis.

Physical signs

- In hypocalcaemia latent tetany can be provoked by inflating a sphygmomanometer cuff to 10–20 mmHg greater than systolic BP for 3 minutes. Carpopedal spasm results in the hand adopting a characteristic posture referred to as *main d'accoucher* (Trousseau's sign).

Table 51 Causes of hypocalcaemia

Mechanism	Examples
Hypoparathyroidism	Post surgery
	Idiopathic/acquired
	Congenital
'Resistance' to action of PTH	Renal failure
	Drugs that impair osteoclastic bone resorption, eg bisphosphonates, calcitonin
	Pseudohypoparathyroidism
Vitamin D deficiency/resistance	
Acute pancreatitis	
Hypomagnesaemia	Proton-pump inhibitor therapy
	Alcoholism
	Gastrointestinal losses
Hyperphosphataemia	Rhabdomyolysis
	Excessive phosphate administration
Malignant disease	

PTH, parathyroid hormone.

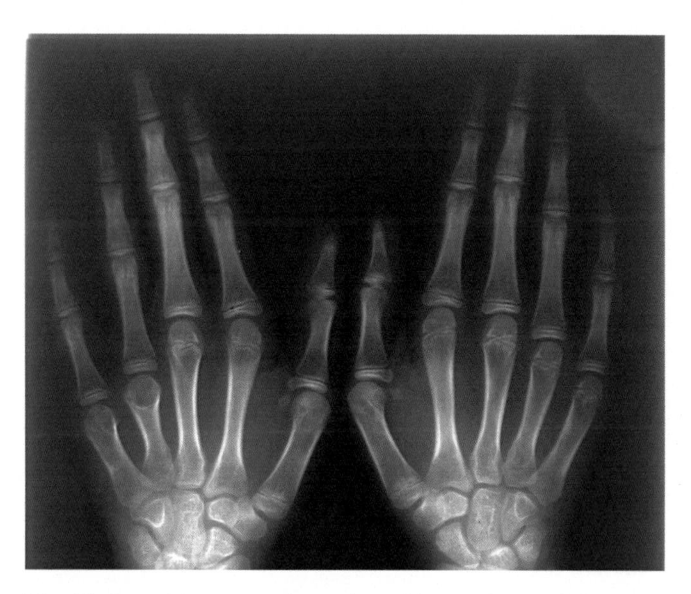

Fig 56 Pseudohypoparathyroidism. Plain radiograph demonstrating the classical short fourth and fifth metacarpals of pseudohypoparathyroidism in the left hand compared, in this case, with normal appearances on the right.

- Tapping the facial nerve in front of the ear may induce a brief contraction of the facial muscles on that side (Chvostek's sign).

Other manifestations of chronic hypocalcaemia include dystrophic nails, alopecia, subcapsular cataracts, papilloedema and occasionally movement disorders (reflecting basal ganglia calcification). Signs of other autoimmune endocrine failure (eg hypothyroidism, hypoadrenalism) may also be present.

Investigation

Relevant blood tests include urea and electrolytes (checking for renal failure), liver function tests (including albumin and alkaline phosphatase), serum calcium and phosphate. Arterial blood gases may be needed to confirm an underlying alkalosis. Further tests may include determination of 25-hydroxyvitamin (OH)-D_3 (the most reliable indicator of total body stores of vitamin D) and PTH levels, while a failure to increase urinary cAMP in response to infused PTH (the Ellsworth–Howard test) may be used to confirm resistance to PTH action in pseudohypoparathyroidism.

Treatment

Emergency

Hazard

Acute, severe symptomatic hypocalcaemia

IV calcium, given as 10 mL of 10% calcium gluconate over 5–10 minutes, should be followed by a maintenance infusion – see the *British National Formulary* (BNF) for guidelines. Oral calcium and vitamin D should be commenced as soon as possible.

Key point
Refractory hypocalcaemia

If hypocalcaemia proves refractory to treatment, serum magnesium levels should also be checked.

Long term

Specific underlying causes require appropriate management. As treatment with PTH is not routinely available, hypoparathyroidism is commonly managed using a combination of alfacalcidol (1alpha-hydroxycholecalciferol) or calcitriol (1,25-dihydroxycholecalciferol) together with calcium supplements as required. The dose must be carefully titrated, aiming to keep the serum calcium level in the low-normal range (thereby reducing the risk of nephrolithiasis and nephrocalcinosis).

Table 52 Classification of diabetes mellitus (adapted from American Diabetes Association, 2018)

Type of diabetes	Subtypes
Type 1 diabetes (~10%) *(absolute insulin deficiency due to beta cell destruction)*	A Immune-mediated B Idiopathic
Type 2 diabetes (~85%) *(predominantly insulin resistance with relative insulin deficiency)*	
Other specific types (<5%)	A Genetic defects: MODY (types 1–14), transient or permanent neonatal diabetes, mitochondrial diabetes B Genetic defects in insulin action: type A insulin resistance, leprechaunism, Rabson–Mendenhall syndrome, lipoatrophic diabetes C Diseases of the exocrine pancreas: pancreatitis, trauma/pancreatectomy, neoplasia, cystic fibrosis, haemochromatosis D Endocrinopathies: acromegaly, Cushing's syndrome, glucagonoma, phaeochromocytoma, hyperthyroidism, somatostatinoma E Drug or chemical induced: pentamidine, glucocorticoids, thiazide diuretics, thyroid hormones, diazoxide F Infections: congenital rubella, cytomegalovirus G Uncommon forms of immune-mediated diabetes: stiff-man syndrome, anti-insulin receptor antibodies H Other genetic syndromes sometimes associated with diabetes: Down's, Turner, Klinefelter's, Lawrence–Moon–Biedl, Prader–Willi, myotonic dystrophy
Gestational diabetes	

MODY, maturity onset diabetes of the young.
Diagnosis of Diabetes: Standards of Medical Care in Diabetes – 2018: *Diabetes Care* 2018;41(Suppl 1): S13–S27.

2.6 Diabetes mellitus

Diabetes mellitus (DM) is one of the most common metabolic diseases with a complex, multifactorial aetiology and varied clinical and biochemical manifestations. It is caused by inadequate secretion and/or impaired action of insulin on target tissues. Table 52 outlines the current classification of this disorder.

Aetiology

See Table 53.

Type 1 diabetes

In genetically susceptible individuals, one or more environmental factors trigger immune-mediated destruction of islet beta cells (insulitis) leading to a complete deficiency of insulin.

Type 2 diabetes

In the vast majority of patients with type 2 diabetes the principal abnormality is one of insulin resistance. In the very early phase of the disease increased insulin production may mitigate the effects of insulin resistance. However, if insulin secretion is insufficient to compensate, impaired glucose tolerance or frank diabetes results. This typically occurs as a result of beta cell exhaustion.

In maturity onset diabetes of the young (MODY), which can be caused by several different genetic defects (eg mutation

Table 53 Aetiology and pathogenesis of diabetes mellitus

	Type 1	Type 2 and other specific types of diabetes
Genetics	Polygenic. *IDDM-2* is the insulin gene locus present on chromosome 11p and is also linked with diabetes	High identical twin concordance (60–100%), familial aggregation and varying prevalence in different ethnic populations suggest a strong genetic component. In only about 2% of cases has the genetic mutation been identified, eg MODY types 1 (*HNF 4alpha* gene), 2 (glucokinase gene) and 3 (*HNF 1alpha* gene); MELAS syndrome (mitochondrial DNA mutations)
	Most (90%) people with type 1 diabetes have no family history of the condition	
	Several susceptibility loci have been identified (*IDDM-1*, *IDDM-2*, etc). *IDDM-1* is the major susceptibility locus, associated with HLA class II genes, situated on chromosome 6p	
	HLA-DR3 and/or *DR4* are found in >90% of type 1 diabetics	
	HLA-DQ (a variant of *HLA-DQ beta* gene) is more closely associated with diabetes	
Aetiology	Evidence of autoimmunity: HLA genes on chromosome 6 are closely linked to immune modulation; association of type 1 diabetes with other autoimmune diseases; immunosuppressants can prolong beta cell survival	Insulin resistance: whole body insulin resistance is present in type 2 diabetes Increased secretion of insulin can limit hyperglycaemia but patients with coexisting beta cell dysfunction are likely to develop diabetes
	Mechanism of autoimmunity: probably T-cell-mediated as there is a mononuclear cell infiltrate in the islets (insulitis)	Defects of insulin secretion: in type 2 diabetes insulin levels are low relative to the degree of hyperglycaemia, with blunting of the acute first phase and other abnormalities of stimulated insulin secretion. Diabetes results if insulin secretion can no longer compensate for the degree of insulin resistance present
	Autoantibodies associated with type 1 diabetes: ICA are present in around 90% of people with newly diagnosed type 1 diabetes. Other antibodies present include GAD, tyrosine phosphate antibodies and IAA	
Environmental factors	Viruses: coxsackie, rubella, mumps, CMV, EBV, etc	Strongly associated with obesity. BMI >35 kg/m^2 incurs a 40-fold increase in risk as compared with BMI <23 kg/m^2. Obesity is present in more than two-thirds of type 2 patients and associated with insulin resistance
	Dietary constituents: BSA in cow's milk, especially if infants are fed on it	
	Nitrosamines in certain foods	

BMI, body mass index; BSA, bovine serum albumin; CMV, cytomegalovirus; EBV, Epstein–Barr virus; GAD, glutamic acid decarboxylase; HLA, human leukocyte antigen; IAA, insulin autoantibodies; ICA, islet cell antibodies; IDDM, insulin-dependent diabetes mellitus; MELAS, myopathy, encephalopathy, lactic acidosis, stroke-like episode; MODY, maturity onset diabetes of the young.

of the glucokinase gene), insulin sensitivity is normal but production by pancreatic beta cells is reduced leading to hyperglycaemia.

Epidemiology

The estimated diabetes prevalence for adults between the ages of 20 and 70 worldwide in 2015 was 415 million, and it is expected to affect one person in 10 by 2040, ie 642 million. It is estimated globally that one in two adults with type 2 diabetes are undiagnosed.

The International Diabetes Federation (IDF) estimated that in 2015 seven countries had more than 10 million people with diabetes: China, India, the USA, Brazil, the Russian Federation, Mexico and Indonesia.

The IDF also reported that in 2015 the 10 countries with the highest diabetes prevalence in the adult population were Tokelau (30.0%), Nauru, Mauritius, Cook Islands, Marshall Islands, Palau, Kuwait, Saudi Arabia, Qatar and New Caledonia (19.6%).

Type 1 diabetes

- incidence increasing; high prevalence in Caucasians (Europe, North America and Australia)
- the UK has one of the highest rates of type 1 diabetes in the world with

the incidence increasing by about 4% each year, particularly in children under 5, with a fivefold increase in this age group in the last 20 years. Prevalence 0.5% in the UK

- typically young age at presentation. Peak incidence: 9–14 years of age.

Type 2 diabetes

- prevalence varies in different countries but increasing markedly, especially in developing countries. The UK average prevalence is 6.2% in adults, and ranges between 1.7% in Caucasians to 8.9% in South Asian ethnicities
- strongly linked with the rising prevalence of obesity
- predominantly affects older people, with a peak incidence between 50 and 70 years of age.

Clinical presentation

The classic triad of diabetic symptoms consists of:

- polyuria
- increased thirst (polydipsia)
- weight loss.

In type 1 diabetes, these features (Table 54) typically manifest in either acute (days to weeks) or subacute (few weeks) fashion. Patients with type 2 diabetes often give a history of chronic progressive non-specific symptoms, predominantly tiredness. Due to the length of duration between disease onset and presentation it is not uncommon for complications to be present at the time of diagnosis or to define the presenting complaint, including opportunistic fungal (eg *Candida*) or bacterial (eg staphylococcal) infections.

Key point

Emergency presentations of diabetes

Patients with both type 1 and type 2 diabetes can present for the first time as medical emergencies:

- diabetic ketoacidosis (DKA) – up to 20% of presentations of type 1 diabetes
- hyperosmolar hyperglycaemic syndrome (HHS) – sometimes (rare) in those with type 2 diabetes.

Table 54 Clinical features of diabetes mellitus (DM): features of underlying conditions may be present in other specific types (eg pancreatitis)

Type 1	Type 2
Usually sudden or subacute onset; can present with DKA	Mostly gradual onset
Usually lean individuals	Mostly obese individuals
Polyuria (++)	Polyuria (+)
Polydipsia (++)	Polydipsia (+)
Weight loss (+++)	Weight loss (+/–)
Tiredness (++)	Tiredness (+)
Blurred vision (++)	Blurred vision (+/–)
Balanitis, thrush, pruritus vulvae (+)	Balanitis, thrush, pruritus vulvae (++)
Neuritis (++)	Neuritis (+)
Presentation with DKA (not uncommon)	Presentation with HHS (rare)
Presentation with diabetic complications (rare)	Presentation with diabetic complications (common)
Absent C-peptide	C-peptide present
Markers of autoimmunity, eg anti-GAD or ICA usually present in 60–80%	Markers of autoimmunity usually absent

DKA, diabetes ketoacidosis; GAD, glutamic acid decarboxylase; HHS, hyperosmolar hyperglycaemic syndrome; ICA, islet cell antibodies.

Physical signs

In younger type 1 patients there may be evidence of recent weight loss, due to dehydration, as well as loss of muscle and fat mass. In 20% of patients, the first presentation may be with features of DKA. There may also be signs of opportunistic infections (eg balanitis, thrush).

In type 2 diabetes, the presentation is typically gradual in onset, but few patients present more acutely, eg with macrovascular and microvascular end-organ damage, opportunistic infections (fungal and/or bacterial) or HHS (typically precipitated by an intercurrent illness).

Those with secondary diabetes may have obvious features of the primary pathology (eg Cushing's syndrome, acromegaly, bronzing due to haemochromatosis).

Drowsiness/coma, dehydration and hypotension are common findings in both DKA and HHS. Kussmaul respiration (indicating ketosis and acidosis) is usually limited to DKA. It is important to examine for evidence of a precipitating cause, eg infection or myocardial infarction, although this is only found in only approximately one-third of cases.

Diagnostic investigations

Diagnostic criteria currently recommended by the World Health Organization (WHO), the IDF and the American Diabetes Association (ADA) are shown in Table 55.

Based on the above criteria, subjects can also be classified as normal, borderline states and diabetes as shown in Table 56.

Table 55 Diagnostic criteria for DM

Test	Description	Diagnostic cut-off
HbA_{1c}[1]	Test to be performed in a laboratory using a standardised method	≥6.5% (48 mmol/mol)
OR		
Fasting plasma glucose[1]	Fasting is defined as no calorie intake for at least 8 hours	≥7 mmol/L
OR		
Two-hour plasma glucose during an OGTT[1]	This test should be performed using a glucose load containing the equivalent of 75 g anhydrous glucose dissolved in water	≥11.1 mmol/L
OR		
Random plasma glucose	This test is advised for people with classic symptoms of hyperglycaemia or hyperglycaemic crisis	≥11.1 mmol/L

1 In the absence of symptoms/unequivocal hyperglycaemia, each of these criteria should be confirmed by repeat testing.
HbA_{1c}, glycated haemoglobin A_{1c}; OGTT, oral glucose tolerance test.

Table 56 Various categories of DM based on biochemical testing

Test	Normal	Borderline states	Diabetes
HbA_{1c}	<5.7% (<38 mmol/mol)	Prediabetes: 5.7–6.4% (38–47 mmol/mol)	≥6.5% (≥48 mmol/mol)
Fasting plasma glucose	<6.1 mmol/L	IFG: 6.1–6.9 mmol/L	≥7 mmol/L
Two-hour plasma glucose during OGTT	<7.8 mmol/L	IGT: 7.8–11.0 mmol/L	≥11.1 mmol/L

HbA_{1c}, glycated haemoglobin A_{1c}; IFG, impaired fasting glycaemia; IGT, impaired glucose tolerance; OGTT: oral glucose tolerance test.

Key point

Borderline states

Impaired fasting glycaemia (IFG) and impaired glucose tolerance (IGT) are metabolic states between normal glucose homeostasis and diabetes. Both (especially IFG) are predictors of the risk of progression to diabetes, and both (particularly IGT) are associated with higher risk of future cardiovascular disease. Depending on duration, they may be associated with microvascular complications. Both IFG and IGT can revert to normal with appropriate lifestyle interventions.

Urinalysis

Urinalysis is of limited use in the diagnosis of diabetes mellitus (DM). Glycosuria (ie positive test on Glucostix™) may suggest the presence of diabetes but may not be diagnostic and requires further confirmation with blood tests. The presence of glucose in urine is dependent on tubular maximal reabsorption capacity, and hence its absence does not exclude the diagnosis of diabetes.

Other urine dipstick measurements commonly include tests for ketones, blood, protein, nitrites and leukocytes. The presence of ketones in urine does not necessarily equate with a diagnosis of ketosis and needs further investigation/assessment.

2.6.1 Management of diabetic emergencies

Emergencies associated with diabetes can be broadly classified into hyperglycaemic and hypoglycaemic emergencies:

2.6.1.1 Hyperglycaemic emergencies

Hyperglycaemic diabetic emergencies are of two types: diabetic ketoacidosis (DKA) and hyperglycaemic hyperosmolar syndrome (HHS) (see Table 57). Although the basic principles of management for DKA and HHS are similar, there are some important pathophysiological differences, which are reflected in important distinctions between their presentations and management.

Presentations

Diabetic ketoacidosis

This commonly occurs in type 1 diabetes and is due to absolute lack of insulin. The cause in 30–40% of cases is increasing insulin requirement precipitated by stress, including sepsis. In 25% of patients it is associated with non-compliance with treatment (ie missed or inadequate insulin dosages). In 10–20% of cases it may be the presentation as a disease defining illness, while in 10–15% of cases it may be attributable to inappropriate alterations in insulin (ie errors by patient or healthcare professional). The predominant features of DKA are related to increased ketone production (ketonaemia), which in turn leads to acidosis.

Although DKA is relatively uncommon in type 2 diabetes, in patients with poorly controlled diabetes, major stressful precipitating factors (eg pneumonia, stroke or myocardial infarction) can lead to DKA.

Hyperosmolar hyperglycaemic syndrome

This is more common in type 2 diabetes, where there is residual insulin secretion which is overwhelmed in the presence of major intercurrent illness. In HHS, glucose levels are typically much higher than in DKA, leading to hyperosmolarity and dehydration. Mild ketonaemia can be seen, but is not severe enough to produce the degree of acidosis typically seen in DKA.

Table 57 Salient features and differences between DKA and HHS

	DKA	HHS
Plasma glucose	Usually >13.3 mmol/L	Usually >33.3 mmol/L
Arterial pH	pH <7.3	pH >7.3
Serum bicarbonate	<15 mmol/L	>15 mmol/L
Anion gap	>12	Varies
Serum osmolality	Usually <320 mosmol/kg	Usually >340 mosmol/kg
Demographics of patient	Usually type 1 DM(children, young people)	Usually type 2 DM(older people, physically impaired)
Pathophysiology	Absolute insulin deficiency	Relative insulin deficiency
Expected mortality	1–4%	10–20%

DKA, diabetic ketoacidosis; DM, diabetes mellitus HHS, hyperglycaemic hyperosmolar syndrome.

Investigations

The following investigations are mandatory for all patients with diabetes-related hyperglycaemic emergencies:

- laboratory blood glucose – to confirm hyperglycaemia
- urea and electrolytes – potassium (K^+) status; any renal impairment?
- arterial blood gases / venous bicarbonate – to determine degree of acidosis
- blood ketone levels
- serum osmolality – can also be calculated as (serum [Na^+] + serum [K^+]) × 2 + serum urea + plasma glucose
- full blood count – neutrophilia is common in DKA or HHS due to margination of leukocytes; elevated C-reactive protein (CRP) is a more dependable marker of infection
- urinalysis – for ketones.

Depending on clinical status and the precipitating factor consider:

- septic screen (blood cultures, chest radiograph and midstream urine)
- ECG and cardiac enzymes
- CT head.

Hazard

Don't delay treatment of hyperglycaemic emergencies

Remember that prompt treatment is required. Do not waste time performing unnecessary tests.

Treatment

Both conditions carry a significant mortality (1–4% in DKA and up to 20% in HHS) and hence appropriate management should be instituted promptly. Appropriate management of obvious precipitating factors should be carried out in parallel with management of the DKA/HHS.

The broad pillars of management of DKA or HHS comprise of IV hydration, insulin replacement, potassium replacement, and supportive care to maintain airway, breathing and circulation.

IV hydration

The degree of dehydration in DKA is 48 L, while in HHS it is 8–12 L, and this must be corrected as a matter of priority.

Key point

Fluid management in DKA

- Aim to give 5–6 L within the first 24 hours (eg 1 L over 1 hour, followed by 1 L over 2 hours, then 1 L over 4 hours, with 1 L every 4–8 hours thereafter), but bear in mind the clinical setting, eg a fit 20-year-old is likely to tolerate more aggressive fluid replacement than an older patient with a history of cardiac disease. Consider central venous pressure (CVP) monitoring in the latter group.
- Begin replacement with 0.9% sodium chloride intravenously (0.45% sodium chloride is preferred if the serum sodium level exceeds 155 mmol/L, but this must be accompanied by frequent (every 1–2 hours) monitoring of the serum sodium and osmolality to prevent a precipitous decline with consequent cerebral oedema).
- When the blood glucose falls below 14 mmol/L, commence intravenous 10% dextrose alongside the 0.9% sodium chloride infusion.

Insulin administration

In DKA, start a continuous fixed rate intravenous insulin infusion (FRIII) via an infusion pump. This is made of 50 units of human soluble insulin (eg Actrapid®) made up to 50 mL with 0.9% sodium chloride solution. Ideally this should be provided as a ready-made infusion:

- Infuse at a fixed rate of 0.1 unit/kg/hour (ie 7 mL/hour if weight is 70 kg, see Table 58).
- Only give a bolus (stat) dose of intramuscular (IM) insulin (0.1 unit/kg) if there is a delay in setting up an FRIII.
- If the patient normally takes a long-acting basal insulin like Insulatard®, Lantus®, Levemir® or Tresiba® subcutaneously, continue this at the usual dose and usual time.
- Insulin may be infused in the same line as the intravenous replacement fluid provided that a Y connector with a one-way, anti-siphon valve is used and a large-bore cannula has been placed.

The recommended targets are:

- reduction of the blood ketone concentration by ≥0.5 mmol/L/hour
- increase of venous bicarbonate by ≥3.0 mmol/L/hour
- maintain serum potassium between 4.0 and 5.5 mmol/L.

If these rates of change of ketones and bicarbonate are not achieved, then the FRIII rate should be increased.

Key point

The goals of emergency treatment

Resolution of DKA is defined as:

- bicarbonate >15.0 mmol/L and venous pH >7.3
- blood ketone level <0.3 mmol/L.

Note: Do not rely on bicarbonate alone to assess the resolution of DKA. The presence of hyperchloraemic acidosis (secondary to the large volumes of infused sodium chloride solution) lowers serum bicarbonate and thus leads to difficulty in assessing whether the ketosis has resolved.

Key point

The reason for giving insulin

Remember that insulin is being given first and foremost to switch off ketosis, and normalisation of blood glucose is not the priority. If blood glucose falls to <14 mmol/L, commence intravenous dextrose and maintain the insulin infusion at a rate sufficient to suppress ketosis and therefore acidosis.

Hazard

Hyperosmolar hyperglycaemic syndrome

Patients with HHS are often very insulin sensitive and may need only small amounts of insulin to lower their blood glucose satisfactorily – aim for a fall of 3 mmol/L/hour. A reduction in plasma glucose levels will occur automatically as osmolality is corrected, so insulin is not normally advised in the early phase of treatment unless significant ketonaemia (>1 mmol/L) is present. Thereafter, an FRIII is recommended, but at reduced dose (0.05 units/kg/hour) compared with DKA management.

Potassium replacement

Hypokalaemia and hyperkalaemia are life-threatening conditions and are more common in DKA than HHS. Serum potassium is often high on admission (although total body potassium is low) but falls precipitously upon treatment with insulin. Regular monitoring at 2-hourly intervals initially is mandatory with replacement as shown in Table 59.

Table 58 Calculation of the insulin dose while initiating FRIII as per body weight (kg)

Weight (kg)	Insulin infusion rate (mL(units)/hour)
60–69	6
70–79	7
80–89	8
90–99	9
100–109	10
110–119	11
120–129	12
130–139	13
140–149	14
>150	15 (maximum rate)

FRIII, fixed rate intravenous insulin infusion.

Table 59 Guide to potassium replacement

Potassium level on first presentation (mmol/L)	Potassium replacement in mmol/L of infusion solution
>5.5	Nil
3.5–5.5	40
<3.5	Senior review as additional potassium needs to be given

Hazard

Beware of hypokalaemia

Hypokalaemia may develop rapidly. Insulin drives potassium inside cells, and total body potassium levels are low. Do not wait for the serum potassium to reach low levels before commencing replacement.

Many hospitals have formal guidelines for the management of both DKA and HHS.

Other considerations

- broad-spectrum intravenous antibiotics if there is any suspicion of an infectious precipitant
- insertion of a nasogastric tube to prevent aspiration if the conscious level is depressed. Remember acidosis delays gastric emptying

- systemic anticoagulation (therapeutic dose as per body weight) in all cases of HHS, which is a hypercoagulable state
- bicarbonate should not be given routinely as it may exacerbate intracellular acidosis. Adequate fluid and insulin therapy will resolve the acidosis in DKA and the routine use of bicarbonate is not indicated. It should be reserved for very sick patients with severe acidosis (pH <7.0), and ideally within the intensive care / high-dependency unit setting. Excessive bicarbonate may cause a rise in the CO_2 partial pressure in the cerebrospinal fluid (CSF) and lead to a paradoxical increase in CSF acidosis. There is some evidence to suggest that bicarbonate treatment may be implicated in the development of cerebral oedema in children and young adults.

Transition to subcutaneous insulin / oral agents

Continue insulin infusion until the ketosis/acidosis is controlled. This is usually reflected by lowering of blood glucose to <14 mmol/L, improvement of bicarbonate to >15 mmol/L and reduction of blood ketone levels to <0.3 mmol/L, in a patient who is eating a normal oral diet.

If the patient normally takes a long-acting basal insulin, this should be continued throughout the management of DKA/HHS so as to make the transition to subcutaneous insulin easier and reduce the risk of rebound ketosis.

Patients with pre-existing type 1 diabetes can often be re-established on their original regimen (or this can be altered to prevent further recurrences of DKA), while newly diagnosed patients should be started on either a twice daily biphasic regimen of premixed insulins or a multiple daily injection (MDI) (also referred to as a 'multiple dose injection') regimen (see below).

In some patients with HHS and no evidence of ketonuria, it may be possible to start/recommence oral hypoglycaemic agents, while others may need insulin.

Patients must be reviewed by a diabetes specialist nurse and dietician prior to discharge, who will be able to follow up by providing much-needed telephone support. Further follow-up should be in a specialist diabetes clinic.

2.6.1.2 Hypoglycaemic emergencies

Hypoglycaemia is a known metabolic complication arising in diabetes patients who are either treated with insulin and/or certain oral hypoglycaemic agents including sulfonylureas. Most insulin-treated patients can expect to experience hypoglycaemic episodes at some time, with up to one in seven having a more severe episode each year and 3% suffering recurrent episodes. Those at particular risk are older patients and patients with renal impairment.

Pathogenesis

Hypoglycaemia in diabetes is fundamentally iatrogenic, the result of pharmacokinetically imperfect treatment with an insulin secretagogue (eg a sulfonylurea) and/or exogenous insulin. It results from the interplay of relative or absolute therapeutic insulin excess with compromised physiological and behavioural adaptations to falling plasma glucose concentrations.

Signs and symptoms of hypoglycaemia

The features of hypoglycaemia can be divided into two main groups: autonomic symptoms and neuroglycopaenic symptoms as shown in Table 60. Autonomic symptoms usually occur first (when the blood glucose is <3.6 mmol/L), but some drugs such as non-selective beta-blockers and alcohol may mask these autonomic symptoms leading to progressive depletion of cerebral glucose, which culminates in neuroglycopaenic symptoms (typically when blood glucose falls to <2.6 mmol/L).

Diagnosis

Hypoglycaemia is defined as a blood glucose of <4 mmol/L. Severe hypoglycaemia is defined as an episode of hypoglycaemia which needs third-party help (ie someone else to help the patient to recover from that episode).

Management

Mild episodes of hypoglycaemia (in the conscious patient) – oral carbohydrate (20–30 g) is often sufficient to resolve the problem. This can be given in the form of

Table 60 Signs and symptoms of hypoglycaemia

Autonomic	Neuroglycopaenic
Sweating	Tiredness
Pallor	Lack of concentration
Anxiety	Headache
Nausea	Dizziness
Tremor	Confusion
Shivering	Incoordination
Palpitations	Drowsiness
Tachycardia	Aggression
Hunger	Coma

rapid-acting carbohydrates (eg five to six dextrose tablets or a glass of orange juice) for immediate correction of hypoglycaemia, followed by slow-release carbohydrate (eg two digestive biscuits) to maintain euglycaemia.

Severe episodes of hypoglycaemia (eg in a confused patient) – a buccal gel preparation (eg containing 40% glucose gel) can be tried, but should not be used in an unconscious patient due to the risk of aspiration. In the latter, 50–100 mL of 20% dextrose should be given intravenously followed, if necessary, by an infusion of 5% or 10% dextrose. Glucagon 1 mg IM or by deep subcutaneous injection is another option for severe hypoglycaemia.

It is important to ensure adequate management steps are put in place to prevent recurrent hypoglycaemic episodes. Re-education of patients with advice about alcohol, exercise and snacks is very important for prevention. Monitoring of renal function is equally important.

Key point

Hypoglycaemic unawareness

In patients with long-standing diabetes (type 1 more commonly than type 2), classical autonomic symptoms of hypoglycaemia may be impaired or absent and hence neuroglycopaenia can occur without any prior warning, so-called hypoglycaemic unawareness. This is related to a reduced threshold for counter-regulatory hormone release and autonomic nervous system activation.

Hazard

Hypoglycaemia in chronic kidney disease

Renal impairment is an important contributing factor to recurrent hypoglycaemic episodes. Hypoglycaemia due to sulfonylureas on a background of renal impairment can last for several hours and hence blood glucose needs to be actively monitored after initial management of hypoglycaemia.

2.6.2 Management of diabetes

Key point

Principal objectives of diabetes management

- educate patients and empower them to be more engaged with their self-management
- relieve symptoms and improve quality of life
- monitor diabetes control, rationalise drug options and prevent side effects
- reduce risk factors
- prevent and treat complications.

General approach

The management of diabetes requires a multidisciplinary team approach, involving doctors (physicians, GPs, orthopaedic and vascular surgeons, ophthalmologists and urologists), nurses (diabetes specialist nurses, practice and district nurses), dietitians, chiropodists and psychologists, all of whom work as a team around the main protagonist – the patient.

A thorough history and examination should be carried out at the patient's first visit. Record details of presenting symptoms, past medical history (including hypertension and dyslipidaemia), family history and check for features suggestive of vascular disease. Ask about tobacco and alcohol use. Examine the cardiovascular (BP, peripheral pulses, etc), and peripheral nervous systems, and assess the eyes, feet and skin. Where possible, arrange for the patient to see the diabetes specialist nurse and dietitian at the same visit, and consider referral for chiropody, retinal screening and vascular assessment.

Glycaemic control

Several large prospective randomised controlled trials have shown that good glycaemic control reduces the risk of developing complications in diabetes (see below). Home monitoring (preferably finger-prick testing) of blood glucose, together with periodic measurement of the glycated haemoglobin (HbA_{1c}) (which reflects glycaemic control over the preceding 10–12 weeks) will indicate the level of diabetic control and the need for adjustment to therapy.

There are varying opinions as to what constitutes good or adequate glycaemic control. In general, pre-meal blood glucose levels of 4–8 mmol/L are likely to correlate with a satisfactory HbA_{1c} (<53 mmol/mol). However, bear in mind the clinical setting: eg while it is important to aim for tight control in a young type 1 patient, it may be necessary to accept more modest control in an older patient with type 2 diabetes who lives alone, and in whom it is important to avoid hypoglycaemia.

Key point

Landmark trials in diabetes

The following landmark clinical trials have strongly influenced clinical practice in diabetes.

Diabetes Control and Complications Trial – 1995

The Diabetes Control and Complications Trial (DCCT) ran from 1983 to 1993 and examined the value of intensive/tight versus conventional control in 1,441 patients with type 1 diabetes. Tight diabetic control with intensive insulin therapy (mean HbA_{1c} ~7%, ie 53 mmol/mol) reduced diabetes complications over a 7-year period in a cohort of type 1 patients. Risk of retinopathy was reduced by 60%, nephropathy by 30% and neuropathy by 20%. A twofold to threefold increased risk of severe hypoglycaemia was observed in the intensively treated group.

United Kingdom Prospective Diabetes Study – 1998

The United Kingdom Prospective Diabetes Study (UKPDS) examined the effect of intensifying glucose control on the subsequent development of complications in type 2 patients, and assessed the relative benefits of specific therapies in a cohort of 5,102 patients followed between 1977 and 1991. Good glycaemic control (median HbA_{1c} of 7% over a 10-year period) reduced the risk of microvascular complications, while tight BP regulation decreased the risk of both microvascular and macrovascular complications.

The Action to Control Cardiovascular Risk in Diabetes study – 2006

The Action to Control Cardiovascular Risk in Diabetes (ACCORD) study, which involved ~10,000 patients with type 2 diabetes, randomised patients to an intensive glycaemic control strategy (target HbA_{1c} <6.0%, ie 42 mmol/mol) versus standard therapy (target HbA_{1c} 7.0–7.9%, ie 53–63 mmol/mol). The unexpected primary finding of the trial – that mortality was higher in the intensively treated group – led to its premature termination in 2009, with the suggestion that some patients with type 2 diabetes (ie high-risk patients with multiple cardiovascular risk factors and heart disease such as those recruited to ACCORD) might benefit most from focused management of other risk factors (BP, lipids), rather than stringent glycaemic control.

Action in Diabetes and Vascular Disease: Preterax and Diamicron MR Controlled Evaluation trial – 2009

The Action in Diabetes and Vascular Disease: Preterax and Diamicron MR Controlled Evaluation (ADVANCE) trial demonstrated in over 10,000 patients with type 2 diabetes that an intensive strategy with conventional agents could achieve mean HbA1c levels of 6.5% safely, with no increase in mortality. This had no significant effect in reducing macrovascular disease, but reduced diabetes-related nephropathy by 20%.

Empagliflozin, Cardiovascular Outcomes, and Mortality in Type 2 Diabetes – 2016

The Empagliflozin, Cardiovascular Outcomes, and Mortality in Type 2 Diabetes (EMPA-REG) study examined the effects of empagliflozin on cardiovascular morbidity and mortality in patients with type 2 diabetes who were at high risk for cardiovascular events. A total of 7,020 patients were randomised to receive 10 or 25 mg of empagliflozin or placebo once daily. Those who received empagliflozin, as compared with placebo, had a lower rate of the primary composite cardiovascular outcome and of death from any cause when the drug was added to standard care.

LEADER study – 2016

The LEADER study investigated cardiovascular safety of liraglutide over a period of up to 5 years in 9,340 patients with type 2 diabetes who were randomised to receive liraglutide or placebo. It demonstrated that the Liraglutide-treated group had a statistically lower risk of the primary outcomes, which included death from cardiovascular causes, non-fatal myocardial infarction (MI) or non-fatal stroke.

Table 61 Diet and lifestyle advice for diabetics

Category	Advice
Carbohydrates (45–50% of total calories)	Starchy carbohydrates with high fibre content and low glycaemic index, in which release occurs in a slow and uniform fashion
Fats (30–35% of total calories)	Polyunsaturates <10%, saturates <10% and monounsaturates >10% of the total
Proteins (15–20% of total calories)	If urinary albumin normal, 15–20% of total calories, if abnormal <10% of total calories[1]
Sweeteners	Aspartame and saccharin based are recommended
'Diabetic'-branded food	Can be high in calories, expensive and confer no advantage
BMI	Weight reduction: aim for BMI <25 kg/m^2
Alcohol	Moderate consumption (1 unit/day for women and 1–2 units/day for men), especially of wine
Exercise	Regular exercise is important to help reduce and maintain weight, to reduce insulin resistance and to improve BP and lipid control
Smoking	Stop smoking

1 Some clinicians consider protein restriction unnecessary and indeed it may even be deleterious in certain circumstances, eg in adolescence.
BMI, body mass index; BP, blood pressure.

Diet and lifestyle modifications

Table 61 outlines key dietary and lifestyle issues for patients with diabetes.

Insulin

Types of insulin

Table 62 describes the major classes of insulin currently in use, which are also depicted in Fig 57 on the basis of onset and duration of action.

Suitable patients for insulin therapy

These include:

- all patients with type 1 diabetes
- type 2 patients where oral therapy fails due to progressive beta cell exhaustion
- newly diagnosed type 2 patients who present with high blood glucose levels and show suboptimal response to oral medications due to glucotoxicity
- patients with type 2 diabetes during acute illness / surgery
- patients with secondary diabetes due to pancreatic failure / pancreatectomy
- gestational diabetes where dietary or oral therapy is inadequate.

Table 62 Types of insulin currently available for administration

Type	Origin	Action	Onset	Peak	Duration[1]	Examples ®
Ultra-rapid acting	Analogue	Very rapid	2–5 minutes	90 minutes	4 hours	Fiasp (faster acting aspart)
Rapid acting	Analogue	Rapid	15–30 minutes	2 hour	4 hours	Humalog (lispro) NovoRapid (aspart) Apidra (glulisine)
Soluble	Human or animal	Short	30 minutes	2–3 hours	6–8 hours	Actrapid Humulin S Hypurin
Isophane	Human or animal	Intermediate	2 hours	4–6 hours	8–12 hours	Insulatard Humulin I
Long acting	Analogue	Intermediate	2–3 hours 2–3 hours 2–3 hours 3–4 hours	Peakless Peakless Peakless Peakless	12–16 hours 16–20 hours 24 hours 40 hours	Levemir (detemir) Lantus (glargine) Toujeo (glargine U-300) Tresiba (degludec)
Biphasic (pre-mixed)	Isophane + analogue in fixed ratios	Rapid	15–30 minutes	2–3 hours	8–12 hours	NovoMix 30 Humalog Mix 25/50 Humulin M3
Inhaled insulin	Analogue	Rapid	10–20 minutes	1–2 hours	4 hours	Afrezza

1 Effective duration in plasma.

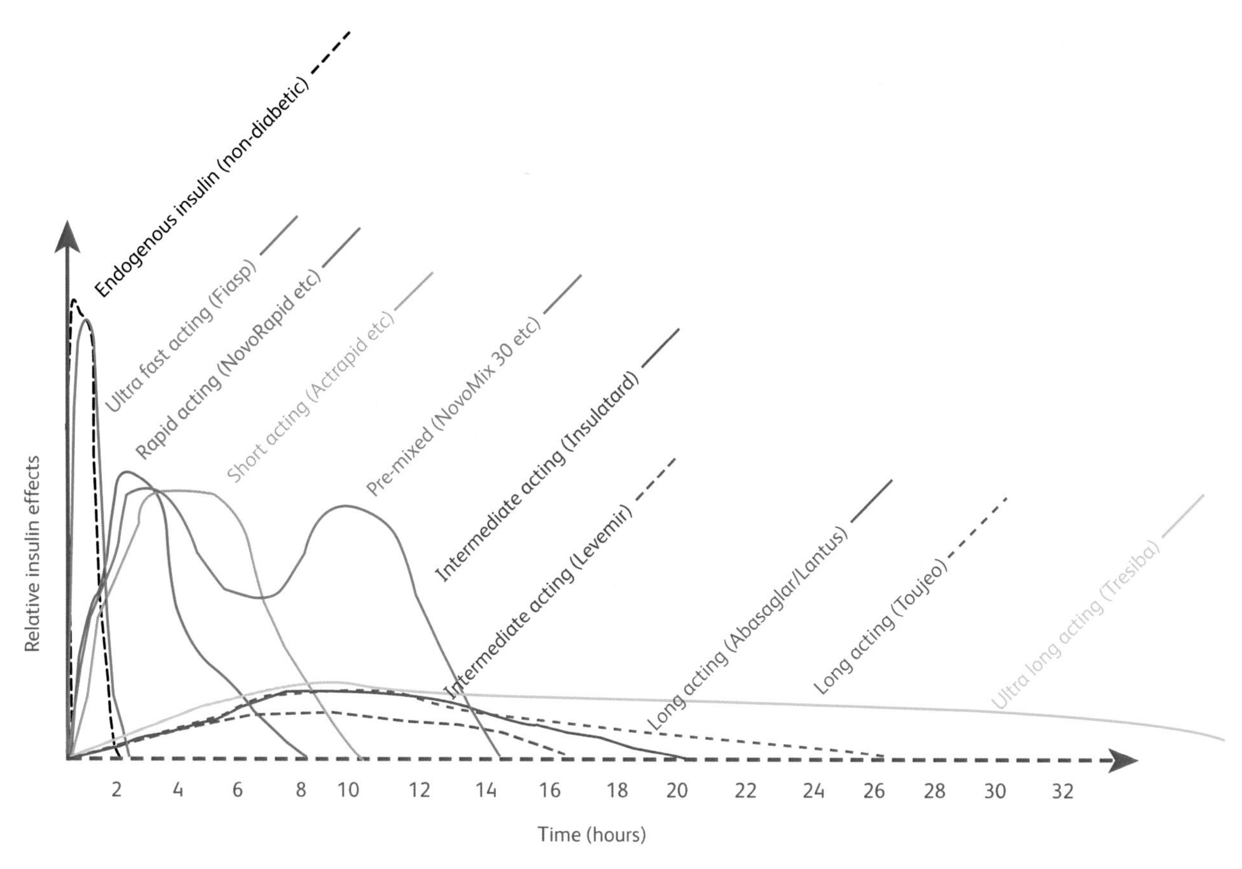

Fig 57 Onset and duration of action of different insulins and insulin analogues. (Copyright Dr S Sharma.)

Which insulin?

Irrespective of type of diabetes, most patients who are severely ill at diagnosis should be initially managed as hospital inpatients on an intravenous insulin regimen (see management of DKA/HHS in Section 2.6.1.1). Following initial management, the choice of therapy depends on several factors.

Most type 1 diabetes patients should ideally be managed on a multiple daily injection (MDI) regimen comprising of one or two basal (long/intermediate) insulin injections and three mealtime rapid-acting bolus insulins. This is termed as 'basal-bolus' regimen. Occasionally, in some patients (eg paediatric or needle phobic) a biphasic regimen can be used initially with a plan to change to an MDI regimen later.

Key point

Starting treatment with insulin

A phase of transient remission, referred to as the 'honeymoon period', sometime occurs shortly after starting treatment in patients with type 1 diabetes. Stopping insulin in this period is discouraged (although sometimes necessary) as the need for insulin will recur.

Whichever regimen is chosen, start cautiously! Aim to avoid hypoglycaemia that adversely affects the patient's confidence and makes your job harder in the long run.

In some newly diagnosed type 2 patients, oral therapy (see below, under the heading 'Drugs for management of type 2 diabetes') might not be fully effective due to glucotoxicity, reflecting the fact that the pancreatic beta cells do not release insulin adequately due to inhibition by high levels of circulating plasma glucose. In such patients, an intermediate-acting insulin (eg Isophane) or a biphasic insulin may be used for 2–3 months and then gradually withdrawn as the beta cells begin to function more adequately.

Long-standing type 2 patients frequently show suboptimal response to oral therapy due to beta cell exhaustion, and therefore require insulin for optimisation of control. It is estimated that every year 5% of those with type 2 diabetes need to be commenced on insulin, and up to 50% require insulin after 10 years.

Some patients on insulin show brittle control with frequent hypoglycaemic episodes despite multiple changes in their insulin regimens. In such patients rapid-acting insulin can be delivered by a continuous subcutaneous insulin infusion (CSII) using a small pump, which may be worn clipped to a belt. However, the current usage of CSII in the UK is restricted by the National Institute for Health and Care Excellence (NICE) guidance to patients with type 1 diabetes.

Hazard

Driving

Insulin-induced hypoglycaemia presents a specific challenge for those who drive. All insulin users should be educated (and reminded on a regular basis) to test their capillary blood glucose levels (CBG) immediately prior to driving and to ensure that is at least 5 mmol/L. If the journey is more than 1 hour, then the CBG needs to be checked at hourly intervals.

Rapid-acting carbohydrates, eg glucose tablets, should be readily available while driving.

In the UK it is legally compulsory for all patients to inform the Driver and Vehicle Licensing Agency (DVLA) following insulin initiation.

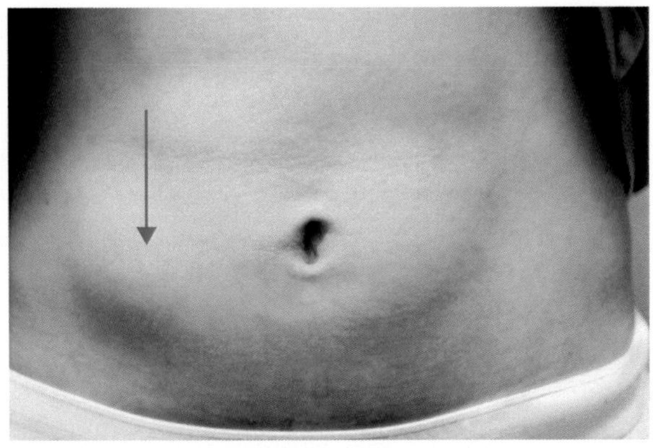

(a)

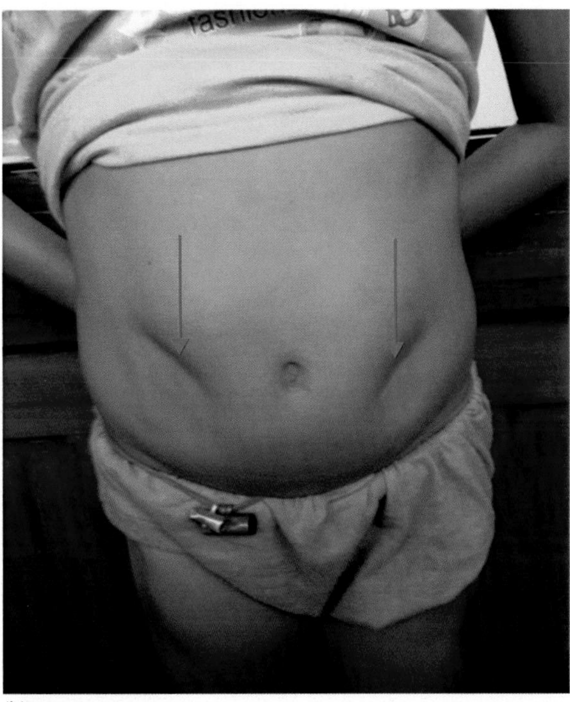

(b)

Fig 58 Insulin-induced lipohypertrophy **(a)** and lipoatrophy **(b)**. (Fig 58a Copyright Dr S Sharma. Fig 58b reproduced with permission from the American Diabetes Association: Singha A, Bhattarcharjee R, Ghosh S *et al.* Concurrence of Lipoatrophy and Lipohypertrophy in Children With Type 1 Diabetes Using Recombinant Human Insulin: Two Case Reports, *Clinical Diabetes* 2016;34:51–53. Copyright and all rights reserved.)

Side effects and complications

These may include:

- visual blurring on starting insulin therapy – this is due to frequent changes in plasma glucose levels leading to osmolality changes within the lens in the eye. It is usually transient
- lipohypertrophy (fatty lumps) at injection sites, especially if repeated in the same area (Fig 58a)
- lipoatrophy, although this is less common since the introduction of purified insulins (Fig 58b)
- hypoglycaemia
- weight gain.

Drugs for management of type 2 diabetes

Pharmacologic therapy of type 2 diabetes has changed dramatically in the last 10 years, with new drugs and drug classes becoming available (Table 63 and Fig 59). These drugs allow for the use of combination oral therapy, often with improvement in glycaemic control that was previously beyond the reach of medical therapy.

Management of cardiovascular risk factors in patients with type 2 diabetes

Individuals with type 2 diabetes mellitus, compared with non-diabetics, have increased cardiovascular

Table 63 Medical agents used in the management of type 2 diabetes

Agent	Examples	Action	Notes
Biguanides	Metformin	Reduces hepatic glucose production and improves peripheral insulin sensitivity	First line of treatment especially in obese type 2 diabetes Does not cause weight gain; reduces HbA_{1c} by 9–17 mmol/mol (ie 0.8–1.5%) It should be avoided in renal, liver and cardiac failure because of the risk of lactic acidosis Side effects include nausea, vomiting, bloating, diarrhoea and a metallic taste Slow-release preparations can be used in intolerant patients (with GI side effects)
Sulfonylureas	Gliclazide Glipizide Glibenclamide Glimepiride	Act (via the SU receptor) to close beta cell potassium channels, with subsequent calcium channel activation and insulin secretion	Often used as the first-line agent in non-obese people who have type 2 diabetes Reduces HbA_{1c} by up to 22 mmol/mol (ie 2%) Shorter-acting agents are preferred (eg gliclazide, glipizide) All can cause weight gain and hypoglycaemia
Meglitinide derivatives	Repaglinide Nateglinide	Prandial glucose regulators – act via the SU receptor	Rapid onset of action allowing them to be taken with each meal Reduces HbA_{1c} by up to 17 mmol/mol (ie 1.5%)
Thiazolidinediones	Pioglitazone	PPARγ agonist; act as insulin sensitiser	Mainly used as second-line agent, given in combination with metformin and/or SU Increasingly being used with insulin. Contraindicated in heart failure and renal insufficiency as may cause fluid retention and weight gain. Reduces HbA_{1c} by 7–17 mmol/mol (ie 0.6–1.5%)
DPP-4 inhibitors	Alogliptin Sitagliptin Linagliptin Saxagliptin Vildagliptin	DPP-4 inhibitors prolong the action of incretin hormones – GLP-1 and GIP	Stimulate insulin release in response to increased blood glucose levels following meals Used second line with metformin or third line in addition to SU Weight neutral; can be used with insulin Reduces HbA_{1c} by 7–13 mmol/mol (ie 0.6–1.2%)
Sodium-glucose transporter-2 inhibitors	Empagliflozin Dapagliflozin Canagliflozin Ertugliflozin	Lowers the renal threshold for glucose, thereby increasing urinary glucose excretion	Used second line with metformin or third line in addition to SU. Can be used with insulin as a sparing agent. Predisposes to DKA in poorly controlled type 2 patients. Recently, canagliflozin has been associated with increased minor amputations. HbA_{1c} reduction up to 22 mmol/mol (ie 2%) with weight loss up to 10 kg. UTI and genitourinary infections occur in 6–8%
GLP-1 analogues and GLP-1 receptor agonists	Liraglutide Dulaglutide Exenatide Albiglutide Semaglutide	Mimic the endogenous incretin GLP-1 stimulating glucose-dependent insulin release and reducing glucagon release	Subcutaneous injection. Used second line with metformin or third line in addition to SU Powerful agents that can reduce HbA_{1c} up to 27 mmol/mol (ie 2.5%) with associated weight loss up to 15 kg. Nausea is common in 10% of cases. Both dulaglutide and semaglutide are used once weekly
Alpha-glucosidase inhibitors	Acarbose	Reduces carbohydrate absorption from the gut	Modest effect with frequent GI side effects limiting its wider use. HbA_{1c} reduction up to 7 mmol/mol (ie 0.6%)

DKA, diabetic ketoacidosis; DPP-4, dipeptidyl peptidase IV; GI, gastrointestinal; GIP, glucose-dependent insulinotropic peptide; GLP-1, glucagon-like peptide-1; HbA_{1c}, glycated haemoglobin A_{1c}; PPARγ; peroxisome proliferator-activated receptor gamma; SU, sulfonylurea; UTI, urinary tract infection.

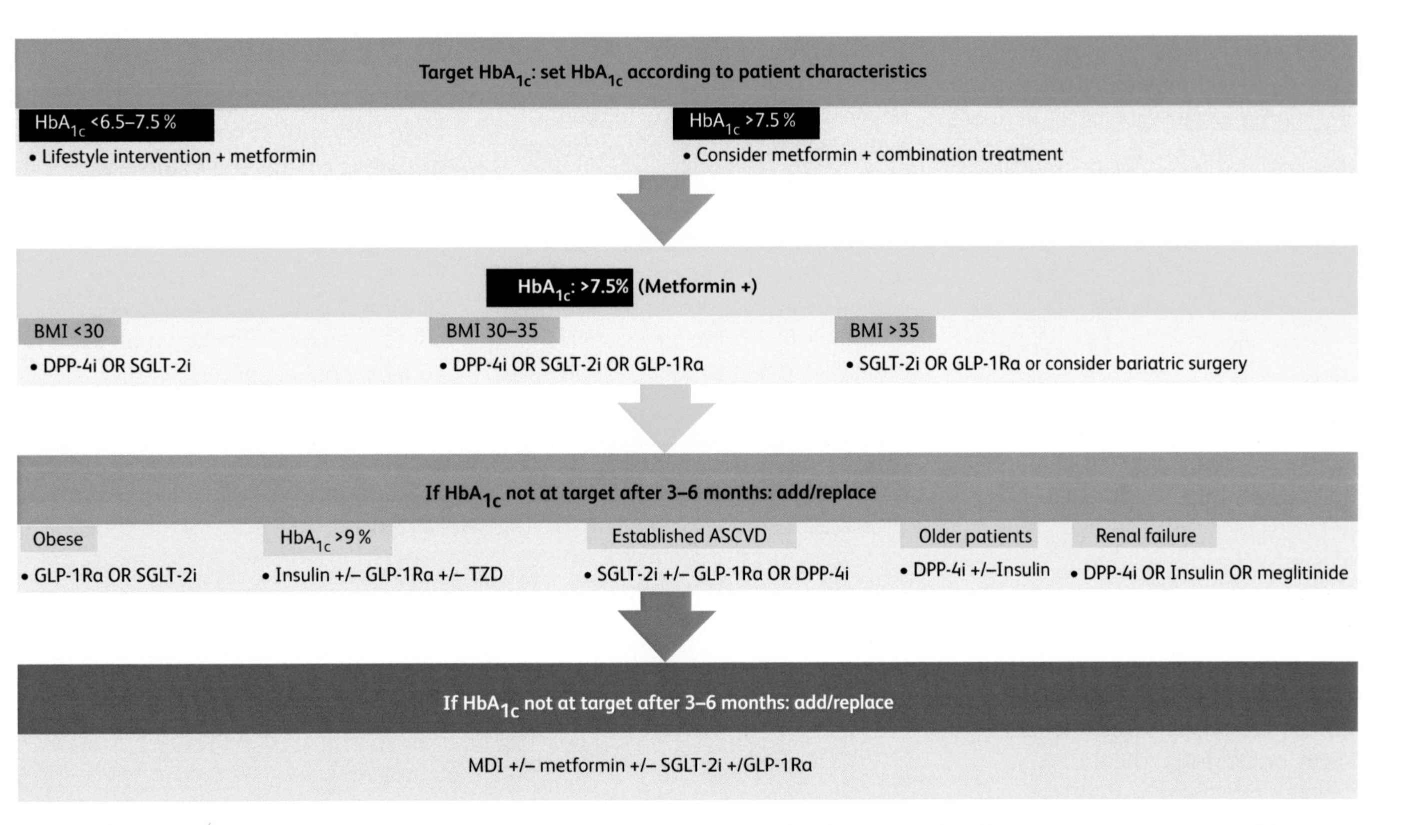

Fig 59 A simplified approach to the management of type 2 diabetes. ASCVD, atherosclerotic cardiovascular disease; DPP-4i, dipeptidyl peptidase IV inhibitor; GLP-1Ra, GLP-1 receptor agonist; MDI, multiple daily injections; SGLT-2i, sodium-glucose transporter-2 inhibitor; TZD, thiazolidinedione. (Copyright Dr S Sharma.)

morbidity and mortality. Diabetic vascular disease is associated with a twofold to fourfold increase in the incidence of coronary heart disease and stroke, and two to eight times the risk of heart failure. Part of this excess risk is associated with a higher prevalence of risk factors in these patients, such as obesity, dyslipidaemia and hypertension.

Key point

Treatment of cardiovascular risk factors is very important in reducing the risk of cardiovascular disease (CVD) in patients with type 2 diabetes mellitus.

Obesity

Obesity has been linked to insulin resistance and defects in insulin secretion. Obesity also leads to the production of proinflammatory cytokines that cause an inflammatory state, contributing to the development of atherosclerotic lesions.

The primary approach to weight management is a change of lifestyle, which can produce a 3–5% rate of weight loss. Low-fat and low-carbohydrate diets are effective for improving glycaemia and CVD risk factors. Bariatric surgery is the most effective treatment for weight loss and improves comorbidities for patients with morbid obesity, or in those with BMI $\geq$35 kg/m^2 who have multiple comorbidities and do not respond to standard treatment.

Hypertension

It is important to control BP at an early stage. Current recommendations suggest that the target BP for patients with type 2 diabetes is <140/90 mmHg. The target BP should be lowered to 130/85 mmHg if there is evidence of proteinuria. Angiotensin-converting enzyme (ACE) inhibitors and angiotensin II receptor blockers (ARBs) are considered to be the first-line therapy in diabetes. Thiazide-like diuretics (eg indapamide) are also effective, especially in combination with ACE inhibitors or ARBs. Calcium channel antagonists, alpha-blockers and other diuretics are also useful.

Dyslipidaemia

There is a threefold excess risk of macrovascular disease associated with diabetes. Elevated low-density lipoprotein cholesterol (LDL-C) is identified as the primary target of lipid-lowering therapy. Many trials of lipid-lowering agents suggest that patients with diabetes appear to benefit at least as much, if not more, than their non-diabetic counterparts from treatment with 3-hydroxy 3-methoxyglutaryl coenzyme A (HMG-CoA) reductase inhibitors, ie statins.

Ezetimibe is a useful adjunct to statin therapy and works by inhibiting the absorption of cholesterol from the intestine. Fibric acid derivatives are another class of agents used selectively to reduce raised triglycerides in blood.

Lipid targets in type 2 diabetes include LDL-C <2 mmol/L, total cholesterol: high-density lipoprotein (HDL) ratio <4 and triglycerides <1.7 mmol/L.

Smoking

Smoking acutely elevates circulating free fatty acid levels, with negative consequences for insulin-mediated glucose uptake. It is possible that nicotine also impairs insulin sensitivity directly or indirectly. There is a relationship between risk and the number of cigarettes smoked, and various studies have shown that smokers have an increased risk of myocardial infarction or sudden death.

Aspirin

Low-dose aspirin (75 mg) is recommended for patients with a 10-year CVD risk of ≥10%, provided they are not considered to be susceptible to gastrointestinal bleeding. However, aspirin should not be recommended for routine atherosclerosis prevention in adults with diabetes who are considered to be at low cardiovascular risk.

Follow-up

The frequency of follow-up will vary depending on the clinical context. However, even well-controlled patients should be reviewed every 4–6 months in a diabetes clinic (either in secondary care or in an appropriate primary care centre) to aid early detection and treatment of complications.

In addition to assessing glycaemic control, it is important to enquire about symptoms of vascular disease (ischaemic heart disease (IHD), cerebrovascular disease (CVD), peripheral vascular disease (PVD)), check for other macrovascular risk factors (especially smoking, hypertension, dyslipidaemia) and ask about features of neuropathy, including erectile dysfunction in males. Prepregnancy counselling should be considered if appropriate. Table 64 details those parameters which should be recorded at each visit and Table 65 outlines targets for management.

2.6.3 Complications

Diabetic complications (Fig 60) are more likely with in patients with poor glycaemic control and in those with long-standing diabetes. They are broadly classified as macrovascular, affecting larger calibre vessels eg coronary and cerebral arteries, or microvascular, affecting small calibre blood vessels eg renal and retinal capillaries.

Table 64 Diabetic follow-up: interim visits and annual review

Follow-up	Review and action
Check at each visit	Home monitoring record, HbA_{1c}, BMI, waist circumference, urinalysis, BP. Continue education and assessment. Review and adjust treatment
Check once a year (ie annual review)	Clinical assessment: pulses, BP, feet, visual acuity, fundi, injection sites
	Biochemical assessment: HbA_{1c}, urea and electrolytes, lipid profile, thyroid function, urinalysis, albumin: creatinine ratio (or other indicator of microalbuminuria)

BMI, body mass index; BP, blood pressure; HbA_{1c}, glycated haemoglobin.

Table 65 Targets in the management of diabetic patients

Domain	Targets
Advice	Education, self-management, ensure compliance with treatment; special focus on smoking cessation, diet, physical activity and weight reduction
Blood pressure	<140/80 mmHg; may require a combination of ACE inhibitor / ARB, diuretics and a calcium channel antagonist
Cholesterol	Total cholesterol <4.0 mmol/L, LDL-C <2.0 mmol/L and preferably triglycerides <1.7 mmol/L with HDL-C >1.0 mmol/L in men and >1.2 mmol/L in women
Diabetes control	Target HbA_{1c} 48–58 mmol/mol (ie 6.5–7.5%); metformin is increasingly the agent of first choice for type 2 diabetes. Early escalation to multiple therapies and insulin if targets are not reached (see Fig 59); avoidance of hypoglycaemic episodes
Eye care	Annual digital photography is recommended with appropriate ophthalmological referral when needed
Foot care	Annual examination with appropriate referral as required
Guardian drugs	ACE inhibitor / ARB therapy is indicated when there is microalbuminuria, proteinuria or diabetic nephropathy
	Therapy with a statin to achieve total and LDL-C targets is appropriate for most patients with diabetes

ACE, angiotensin-converting enzyme; ARB, angiotensin receptor blocker; HbA_{1c}, glycated haemoglobin; HDL-C, high-density lipoprotein cholesterol; LDL-C, low-density lipoprotein cholesterol.

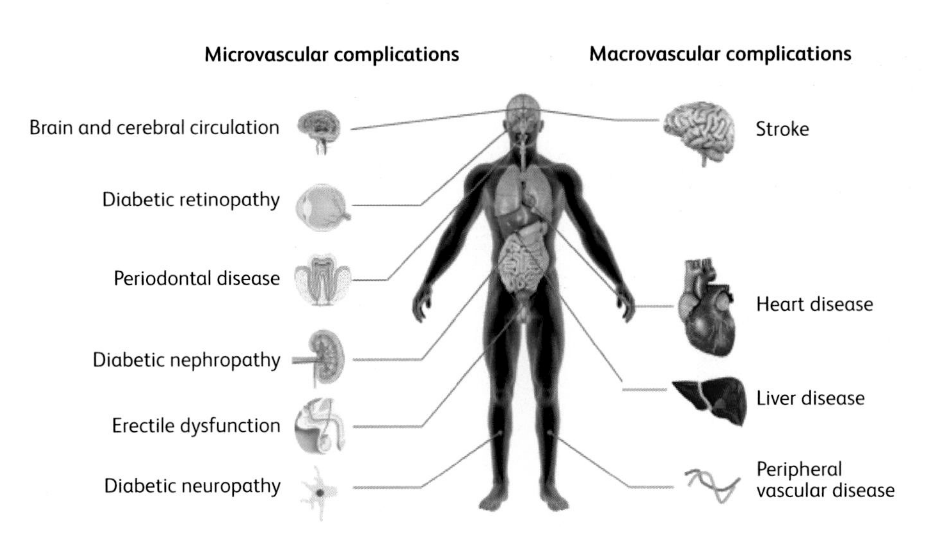

Fig 60 List of complications associated with diabetes. (Copyright Dr S Sharma.)

Table 66 Diabetic eye disease

Complication	Type	Clinical feature
Retinopathy (R)	Background (R1)	Microaneurysms
		Dot and blot haemorrhages
		Hard exudates
		Occasional (<5) cotton-wool spots
	Preproliferative (R2)	Venous beading/looping
		Multiple haemorrhages
		Multiple cotton-wool spots
		IRMA
	Proliferative (R3)	Neovascularisation around the disc
		Neovascularisation elsewhere
Maculopathy (M)		Exudate within a DA of fovea
		Microaneurysm or haemorrhage within DA of fovea
		Oedema
Advanced diabetic eye disease		Preretinal or vitreous haemorrhage
		Retinal detachment
Cataracts		

DA, disc area; IRMA, intraretinal microvascular abnormalities.

Atherosclerosis

Diabetes is a major risk factor for the development of the macrovascular complication of atherosclerosis and is associated with a high incidence of myocardial infarction, stroke and amputation. The presence of other risk factors such as smoking, dyslipidaemia, hypertension and obesity compound the risk. Management follows the same principles as in patients without diabetes, with rigorous control of other risk factors and appropriate use of antiplatelet agents, angiotensin-converting enzyme (ACE) inhibitors / angiotensin II receptor blockers (ARBs) and beta-blockers.

Diabetic eye disease

Retinopathy is the commonest microvascular complication, affecting almost all patients with long-standing type 1 diabetes, and evident in ~20% of those with type 2 diabetes at presentation. The classification of diabetic eye disease is shown in Table 66.

Routine screening aims to detect eye disease before visual symptoms develop. Every diabetes subject must therefore undergo yearly examination including:

> visual acuity
> fundoscopy (through dilated pupils, providing that there is no contraindication to tropicamide, eg glaucoma), preferably with retinal photography.

Key point

Examination of the retina in diabetes

Microaneurysms and haemorrhages are most easily seen with the green lamp of the ophthalmoscope.

Background retinopathy

If background retinopathy is present (Table 66 and Fig 61), assessment should be repeated in 6 months. Review glycaemic control, check for evidence of microalbuminuria and treat hypertension. ACE inhibitors can reduce the progression of retinopathy, even in normotensive diabetic patients.

Preproliferative retinopathy

Multiple cotton-wool spots indicate retinal ischaemia, and together with venous beading/looping and intraretinal microvascular abnormalities (IRMA) (intraretinal new vessels which, unlike 'classical' new vessels, do not lead to haemorrhage) constitute the changes of preproliferative retinopathy (Fig 62). Prompt referral to an ophthalmologist is necessary for consideration of panretinal photocoagulation. Glycaemic control needs to be reviewed urgently, and other risk factors like hypertension, smoking and dyslipidaemia need to be controlled.

Proliferative retinopathy

If left unchecked, preproliferative changes may progress rapidly with the development of new retinal vessels, which are fragile and prone to haemorrhage, threatening vision (proliferative retinopathy) (Fig 63). Urgent referral to an ophthalmologist is necessary for laser treatment. Review glycaemic control; hypertension and microalbuminuria/nephropathy are likely to be present.

Maculopathy

Maculopathy is the commonest threat to vision in type 2 diabetes. It is often difficult to diagnose, although macular ischaemia should be suspected in the presence of circinate macular exudates ('macular star') (Fig 64). Refer promptly to an ophthalmologist for consideration for macular grid laser therapy. Again, address poor glycaemic control and hypertension.

Advanced diabetic eye disease

In advanced diabetic eye disease (Fig 65) widespread neovascularisation and haemorrhage may lead to traction retinal detachment, with preretinal or vitreous haemorrhage, presenting as sudden loss of vision.

Cataracts

Cataracts are more common and occur at an earlier age in diabetes. They present with an insidious decline in visual acuity. Occasionally 'snow-flake' cataracts may complicate acute hyperglycaemia, and these transiently worsen with imposition of good glycaemic control.

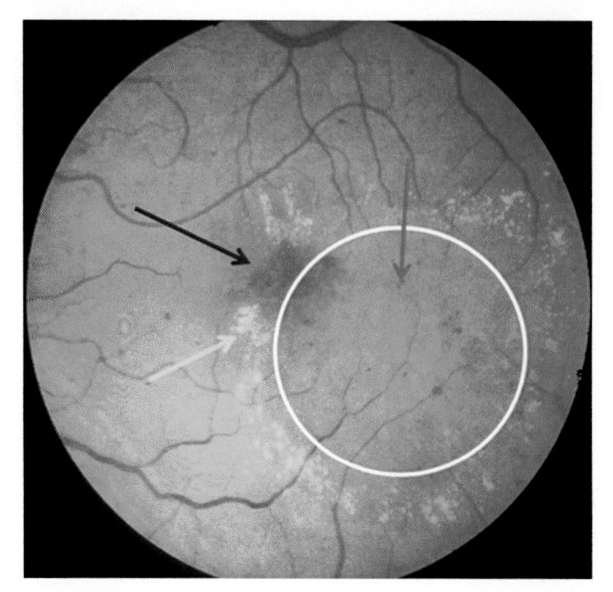

Fig 61 Background diabetic retinopathy. Note the scattered red 'dots and blots' (microaneurysms and haemorrhages) and hard exudates (inferiorly): dot haemorrhage (red arrow); Blot haemorrhage (blue arrow); hard exudate (yellow arrow). (Copyright Dr S Sharma.)

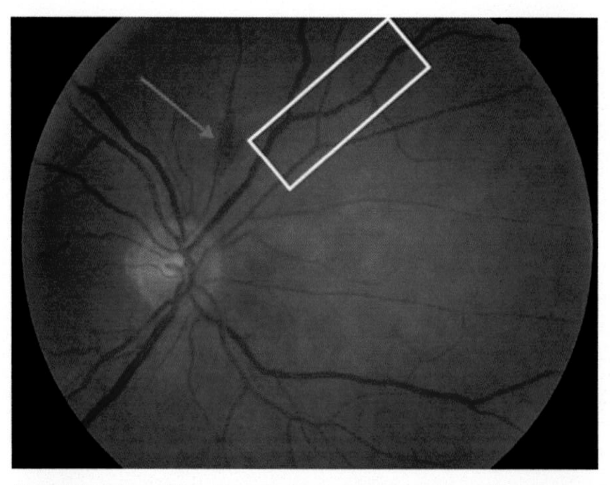

Fig 62 Preproliferative diabetic retinopathy. Note the venous irregularity and beading (white box). The red arrow denotes a haemorrhage. (Copyright Dr S Sharma.)

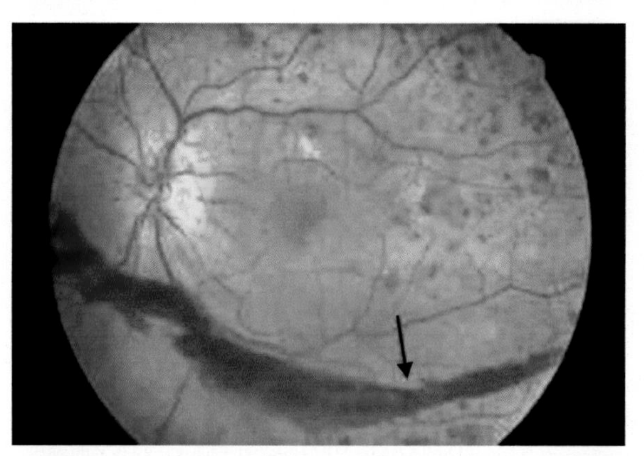

Fig 63 Proliferative diabetic retinopathy. Note the leashes of new vessels and multiple haemorrhages. The black arrow indicates absorbing vitreous haemorrhage. (Copyright Dr S Sharma.)

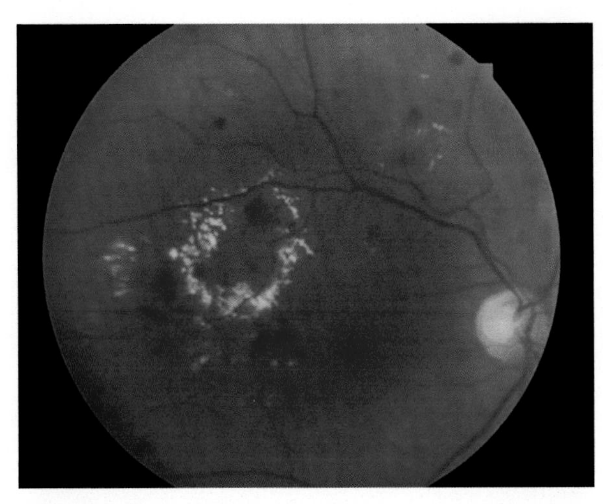

Fig 64 Diabetic maculopathy. Note the ring of hard exudates encroaching on the macula. (Copyright Dr S Sharma.)

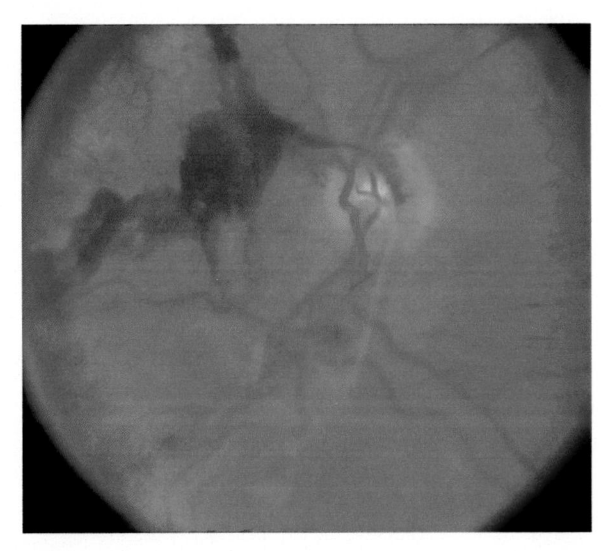

Fig 65 Advanced retinopathy. Retinal detachment complicating extensive neovascularisation and haemorrhage. (Copyright Dr S Sharma.)

Key point

Glycaemic control and retinopathy

Rapid improvement of glycaemic control may occasionally precipitate new retinopathy or worsening of existing retinopathy.

Diabetes nephropathy – now termed as diabetic kidney disease

This overall increase in the number of people with diabetes has had a major impact on development of diabetic kidney disease (DKD), one of the most frequent complications of both types of diabetes. DKD is the leading cause of end-stage renal disease (ESRD), accounting for 25–50% of cases in the developed world.

Definition

DKD is defined as albuminuria (albumin excretion rate of >300 mg/24 hours which equates to a 24-hour urinary protein of >0.5 g (normal threshold <0.2 g)) and declining renal function in a patient with known diabetes who does not have urinary tract infection, heart failure or any other renal disease. This is usually associated with systemic hypertension, diabetes retinopathy or neuropathy, and in the absence of diabetes retinopathy the diagnosis needs to be carefully evaluated.

Epidemiology

DKD develops in about 30% of patients with type 1 diabetes, around 25% of Caucasians with type 2 diabetes, but up to 50% of patients of Asian and African-Caribbean origin with type 2 diabetes, reflecting the earlier age of onset of diabetes and increased prevalence of hypertension in these ethnic groups. End-stage renal failure now occurs in fewer than 20% of those with type 1 diabetes, mainly because of aggressive treatment of hypertension.

Aetiology/pathogenesis

It has been suggested that the elevated glomerular filtration rate (GFR) seen at the onset of diabetes may predispose to the later development of renal disease, which is characterised by thickening of the glomerular basement membrane. Microalbuminuria (see below) is the earliest detectable change in the urine and progresses to intermittent and then persistent proteinuria. This is accompanied by mesangial expansion and then nodular sclerosis (Kimmelstiel–Wilson nodules). Eventually, glomeruli are replaced by hyaline material.

Natural history of DKD

Table 67 shows the natural history of DKD and the various stages of development with associated changes in the estimated glomerular filtration rate (eGFR), albumin excretion and BP.

Key point

Diabetic kidney disease and GFR

Serum creatinine and eGFR can remain normal in early stages of DKD. After 5 years of continuous proteinuria, creatinine begins to rise and eGFR begins to fall.

Table 67 Natural history of DKD

	Designation	Characteristics	eGFR changes	Albumin excretion	Blood pressure	Chronology
Stage 1	Hyper function and hypertrophy	Glomerular hyper filtration	Increase in type 1 and type 2	May be increased	Type 1 normal Type 2 normal or hypertensive	Present at time of diagnosis
Stage 2	Silent stage	Thickened basement membrane, extended mesangium	Normal	Type 1 normal Type 2 may be less than 30–300 mg/day	Type 1 normal Type 2 normal or hypertensive	First 5 years
Stage 3	Incipient stage	Microalbuminuria	eGFR begins to fall	30–300 mg/day (ACR: male 2.5–30, female 3.5–30 mg/mmol)	Type 1 increased Type 2 normal or hypertensive	6–15 years
Stage 4	Overt diabetic nephropathy	Macroalbuminuria	eGFR below normal	>300 mg/day (ACR >30 mg/mmol)	Hypertension	15–25 years
Stage 5	Uraemia	ESRD (CKD stage 5)	0–15 mL/minute/ 1.73 m^2	Decreasing	Hypertension	25–30 years

ACR, urinary albumin:creatinine ratio; CKD, chronic kidney disease; eGFR, estimated glomerular filtration rate; ESRD, end-stage renal disease.

Clinical presentation / physical signs

Nephropathy is usually detected during routine screening and patients are usually asymptomatic from the renal perspective at the time of presentation. Symptoms of uraemia may develop when eGFR falls to <15 mL/min (chronic kidney disease (CKD) stage 5).

Physical signs may include the pallor of anaemia, oedema from fluid overload, excoriations and associated features such as high BP or retinopathy.

Screening and diagnosis of DKD

Table 68 shows the various abnormalities of urinary albumin excretion in diabetes and their definitions based on the methods of collection.

Patients with diabetes should be screened annually for DKD. Initial screening should commence:

- 5 years after the diagnosis of type 1 diabetes, or
- from the time of diagnosis of type 2 diabetes.

Screening should include:

- measurement of urinary albumin: creatinine ratio (ACR) in a spot urine sample; and
- measurement of serum creatinine and estimation of eGFR
- an elevated ACR should be confirmed in the absence of urinary tract infection, with two additional first-void specimens collected during the next 3–6 months: microalbuminuria is defined as an ACR between 2.5 mg/mmol for males (3.5 mg/mmol for females) and 30 mg/mmol; macroalbuminuria is defined as an ACR >30 mg/mmol; two of three samples should fall within the microalbuminuric or macroalbuminuric range to confirm classification.

In most patients with diabetes, CKD is likely to be attributable to diabetes if:

- microalbuminuria or macroalbuminuria is present
- diabetes retinopathy is present
- patient has had type 1 diabetes of at least 10 years duration.

Other causes of CKD should be considered in the presence of any of the following circumstances,

Table 68 Definitions of abnormalities of albumin excretion[1]

Category	Spot collection of urine (mg/mmol creatinine)	24-hour collection of urine (mg/24 hours)	Timed collection of urine (µg/min)
Normoalbuminuria	<2.5 (male), <3.5 (female)	<30	<20
Microalbuminuria	2.5(3.5)–30	30–300	20–200
Macroalbuminuria	>30	>300	>200

1 Because of variability in urinary albumin excretion, at least two specimens, preferably first morning void, collected within the 3–6-month period should be abnormal before considering a patient to have crossed one of these diagnostic thresholds. Exercise within 24 hours, infection, fever, congestive heart failure, marked hyperglycaemia, pregnancy, marked hypertension, urinary tract infection and haematuria may increase urinary albumin above baseline values.

although the diagnosis may still turn out to be DKD:

- absence of diabetic retinopathy
- low or rapidly decreasing GFR
- rapidly increasing proteinuria or nephrotic syndrome
- refractory hypertension
- presence of active urinary sediment (haematuria in addition to proteinuria)
- signs or symptoms of other systemic disease
- more than 30% reduction in eGFR within 2–3 months after initiation of ACE inhibitor or ARB (consider renovascular disease).

Exclusion of other causes – consider investigations to exclude other causes of proteinuria and renal impairment. Such investigations include midstream urine (haematuria), blood tests (calcium, urate, plasma and urinary protein electrophoresis, screen for autoimmune / vasculitic conditions), imaging (urinary tract ultrasound to assess renal size and symmetry, and check for evidence of obstruction, magnetic resonance angiography if renal artery stenosis suspected) and renal biopsy (rarely required).

Hazard

Contrast-induced nephrotoxicity

Radiological investigations using contrast agents can precipitate acute kidney injury in patients with diabetes, especially in the presence of dehydration or eGFR <30 mL/min/1.73 m^2. Pre-hydration with 0.9% saline or 1.26% sodium bicarbonate may prevent contrast-induced nephrotoxicity.

Treatment

Established nephropathy

Once the urinary albumin excretion rate exceeds 300 mg per day, effective BP management is the mainstay of treatment, using ACE inhibitors or ARBs (not in combination) along with other antihypertensives to keep BP <135/75 mmHg. Diuretics may be needed for fluid overload and oedema.

Drugs that are longer acting and predominantly renally excreted (eg glibenclamide) should be avoided. Metformin is contraindicated in renal failure (eGFR <30 mL/min/1.73 m^2) due to the risk of lactic acidosis.

End-stage renal failure

Patients with advanced DKD are best managed in a joint diabetic–renal clinic. Dialysis or renal transplantation is typically required at lower creatinine levels (around 500–550 μmol/L) than in non-diabetics. The preferred option is renal transplantation if comorbidities permit.

Diabetic neuropathy

Diabetic neuropathy can be defined as peripheral neuropathy, either clinically evident or subclinical, arising in the setting of diabetes mellitus and without other cause. It can manifest in the somatic and/or autonomic parts of the peripheral nervous system, and is classified according to clinical criteria. Table 69 shows the common types of diabetes-related neuropathy.

Pathogenesis

Both metabolic and vascular changes have been aetiologically implicated. Pathologically, there is distal axonal loss with focal demyelination and attempts at nerve regeneration. The vasa nervorum often shows basement membrane thickening, endothelial cell changes and some occlusion of its lumen. This results in slowing of nerve conduction velocities or a complete loss of function. The unmyelinated C and thinly myelinated A-δ fibres are first affected, resulting in subclinical small fibre neuropathy, before progression to affect the A-α and A-β large fibres, culminating in sensory and/or motor loss.

Common types of diabetes neuropathy

Distal symmetrical polyneuropathy (peripheral neuropathy)

This is the most common type of diabetic neuropathy, occurring in up to 50% of patients with diabetes, and typically affects long peripheral nerves.

Clinical presentation – most patients present with slowly developing sensory loss with occasional hyperaesthesia, but they can present acutely as foot ulceration due to undetected trauma. More than 50% remain asymptomatic and are detected on their annual screen. Sensory fibre involvement causes 'positive' sensory symptoms such as paresthesia, dysesthesia, numbness and pain, in addition to 'negative' symptoms such as reduced sensation.

Physical signs – diminished or absent vibration sense and ankle jerks, together with an inability to feel the 10 g monofilament, are usually the earliest signs. Motor symptoms and signs (eg muscular weakness and wasting) are late features.

Investigations – diagnosis is clinical, but can be confirmed by nerve conduction studies.

Treatment – the mainstay of treatment is good diabetic control. Hyperglycaemia and dyslipidaemia play an important role in progression, which can also be affected by hypertension and smoking.

Further complications – these include wasting of the small muscles of the hand (diabetic cheiroarthropathy), high arched feet with clawing of toes (hammer toes), neuropathic joints (Charcot's joints) and neuropathic ulcers leading to sepsis.

Prevention – preventative advice regarding foot care and hygiene are important to prevent ulceration, and patients should undergo regular review

Table 69 Classification of diabetic neuropathy

Characteristic features	**I Progressive neuropathy** › Gradual onset › No recovery › Associated with increasing duration of diabetes › Associated with other chronic diabetes complications	**II Reversible neuropathy** › Sudden onset › Spontaneous recovery › No association with duration of diabetes › Not associated with chronic diabetes complications	**III Pressure palsies** › Onset varies › Recovery is usually complete › No association with duration of diabetes › Not associated with chronic diabetes complications
Subtypes	A *Distal symmetrical polyneuropathy* › Predominant sensory › Autonomic involvement common (but mostly asymptomatic) › Clinical motor involvement very rare	A *Mononeuropathy* › Femoral (amyotrophy) › Cranial nerve palsy (third, fourth) › Truncal radiculopathy › Mononeuritis multiplex	A *Medial nerve palsy* (eg carpal tunnel syndrome) B *Ulnar nerve palsy* C *Lateral popliteal nerve palsy*
	B *'Small-fibre' neuropathy* › Autonomic involvement common › Symptomatic	B *Acute diffuse painful neuropathy* (stocking distribution) – may start after insulin injections (acute insulin neuritis)	

by a chiropodist. Screening for peripheral neuropathy is essential as it is often asymptomatic.

Diabetes painful neuropathy

Acute painful neuropathy has been described as a separate clinical entity, preferentially affecting the small calibre nerve fibres A-δ and C fibres. It is encountered infrequently in patients with type 1 and type 2 diabetes, presenting with continuous burning pain, particularly of the soles of the feet ('like walking on burning sand'), with nocturnal exacerbation.

Clinical presentation – a characteristic feature is cutaneous, contact discomfort with clothes and sheets, which can be objectified as hypersensitivity to tactile (allodynia) and painful stimuli (hyperalgesia). Depression and erectile dysfunction are commonly associated features. Autonomic neuropathy is usually present but typically asymptomatic.

Physical signs – motor function is preserved, and sensory loss may be only slight, being greater for thermal than vibration sensation.

Investigations – diagnosis is clinical but can be further proved by tests directed at small fibres, including laser Doppler imaging and confocal microscopy.

Treatment – this is mostly symptomatic. Commonly used drugs include amitriptyline, duloxetine, pregabalin and gabapentin. Some patients might need opioids due to severity of pain.

Prognosis – in 50% of patients the condition may be self-limiting, with pain and discomfort becoming less severe after a median of 2–3 years, and replaced by sensory loss characteristic of distal diabetes polyneuropathy; in 50% the pain often remains debilitating with loss of quality of life.

Diabetes autonomic neuropathy

Diabetes autonomic neuropathy is a common and serious complication of diabetes, associated with an increased risk of cardiovascular mortality.

Clinical presentation – the clinical manifestations are shown in Table 70.

Investigations – these depend on the organ systems involved:

- cardiovascular system – lying and standing BP, tilt table test, ECG monitoring (loss of sinus arrhythmia, loss of heart rate response to Valsalva manoeuvre), BP response to sustained hand grip
- pupillary system – pupillary response to light
- gastrointestinal system – radionuclide meal test (for gastroparesis).

Table 70 Clinical manifestations of diabetic autonomic neuropathy

System	Manifestation
Cardiovascular system	Resting tachycardia, orthostatic hypotension, sudden death, malignant arrhythmia
Respiratory system	Sleep apnoea, reduced ventilatory drive to hypercapnia
Pupillary system	Pupillary reflex dysfunction, reduced dark adaptation
Gastrointestinal tract	Oesophageal dysmotility, gastroparesis, diabetic enteropathy, colonic hypomotility
Urogenital system	Erectile dysfunction, cystopathy, female sexual dysfunction
Thermoregulation	Sudomotor dysfunction, hypohidrosis/anhidrosis, arteriovenous shunting, peripheral oedema
Neuroendocrine system	Hypoglycaemia associated autonomic failure, postural hypotension, defective counter-regulation

Treatment – is based on specific symptoms:

- for postural hypotension – review diuretics, vasodilators and tricyclic antidepressants; mechanical measures such as support stockings; adequate salt intake; drugs (eg fludrocortisone and midodrine)
- for erectile dysfunction – exclude other conditions (eg hypogonadism and Peyronie's disease), review medications (eg beta blockers and thiazides), phosphodiesterase type 5 (PDE-5) inhibitors (eg vardenafil and sildenafil), intraurethral and intracavernosal alprostadil, vacuum devices
- for gastroparesis – erythromycin for motilin receptors in the gut, domperidone and metoclopramide for increasing lower oesophageal tone.

Key point

Relatively uncommon but important types of diabetes neuropathies

- cranial mononeuropathies:
  - typically affect the third, fourth or sixth nerves
  - pupillary responses are spared in diabetic third nerve palsy
- meralgia paresthetica:
  - entrapment neuropathy of the lateral cutaneous nerve of the thigh
  - loss of cutaneous sensation of the front of the thigh
- diabetes amyotrophy
  - typically affects middle-aged men with long-standing type 2 diabetes, who present with asymmetrical painful wasting of the quadriceps muscles on one side
  - it is often associated with anorexia and weight loss; symptoms gradually abate with time, although a significant number are left with residual disability
- radiculopathies
  - may involve any nerve roots, especially those affecting the trunk
- acute insulin neuritis:
  - insulin neuritis is a historical term for an acute neuropathy affecting patients with diabetes who achieve rapid re-establishment of previously poor glycaemic control
  - it presents with neuropathic pain, symptoms of autonomic dysfunction or a combination of both
  - the management focuses on controlling the symptoms while they gradually improve with time and takes 6–18 months to remit completely.

2.6.4 Other specific diabetic complications

The diabetic foot

Foot problems are very common and give rise to significant morbidity and mortality, accounting for most hospital admissions in those with diabetes. Proper education and early detection can prevent many of the problems encountered.

Risk factors for foot ulcer development

- Peripheral neuropathy – present in up to 80% of diabetes patients with foot ulcers. It reduces awareness of pain and trauma caused by footwear, and foreign bodies (eg nails) are not infrequently found in shoes.
- Peripheral vascular disease – present in up to 10–15% of patients. An ankle:brachial pressure index (ABPI) <0.8 suggests arterial disease, while >1.0 suggests normal flow, although values >1.4 suggest calcified arteries. Microvascular circulatory disease also contributes to local ischaemia and increased risk of ulcer formation.
- Autonomic neuropathy – leads to anhidrosis and dry skin which subsequently cracks and provides a portal of entry for infections.
- Motor neuropathy – results in a variety of foot abnormalities including altered foot muscle tone, wasting of small muscles, alteration of longitudinal and transverse pedal arches, and clawing of toes, all of which predispose to callus and ulcer formation.
- Presence of other microvascular complications – including concomitant presence of diabetic kidney disease (DKD) and retinopathy are also important risk factors for development of foot ulceration.
- Duration of diabetes – is a risk factor in those with type 1 diabetes, while foot ulceration can be the presenting problem in type 2 diabetes.
- Previous ulceration – is associated with further foot ulceration in up to 50% of cases.
- Ethnicity and sex – men have a 1.6-fold increase in ulcers, and various epidemiological studies have shown that some ethnic groups are more susceptible to foot ulceration.

Key point

Prevention is crucial in the management of diabetic foot lesions

All the risk factors listed above should be evaluated in every patient with diabetic foot disease.

Classification of diabetes foot lesions

The University of Texas classification system is widely used (Table 71).

Clinical features and management

Table 72 outlines the major clinical features and approach to the investigation and management of the neuropathic and neuroischaemic foot.

Table 71 University of Texas ulcer classification system

Stage	Grade 0	Grade 1	Grade 2	Grade 3
A (no infection or ischaemia)	Pre- or post-ulcerative lesion completely epithelialised	Superficial wound not involving tendon, capsule or bone	Wound penetrating to tendon or capsule	Wound penetrating to bone or joint
B	Infection	Infection	Infection	Infection
C	Ischaemia	Ischaemia	Ischaemia	Ischaemia
D	Infection and ischaemia	Infection and ischaemia	Infection and ischaemia	Infection and ischaemia

Table 72 Clinical features, investigations and management of the diabetic foot

	Neuropathic foot (Fig 66)	Neuroischaemic foot (Fig 67)
Presentation	Numbness, pain, calluses, ulcers, swelling	In addition to the features of neuropathy, patients may complain of intermittent claudication and/or rest pain
Physical signs	Evidence of sensory loss, absent ankle jerk, neuropathic oedema; calluses and ulcers at major pressure points, eg under the first and fifth metatarsal heads. Abscess and cellulitis. Good pulses	Cold foot with dependent rubor. Absence of pulses and trophic changes. Ulcers over the heel, dorsum of the foot and toes (often related to ill-fitting shoes). Gangrene or pre-gangrenous changes may be present
Investigations	Ulcer swab, blood cultures, blood glucose, blood count, CRP. Radiograph of the foot is usually adequate but MRI of the foot is occasionally indicated	Doppler ultrasound to measure ABPI (normal <1.0; significant arterial occlusive disease is suggested by values <0.8). Arterial duplex is often necessary followed by either CT angiogram or MR angiogram. Other investigations are as per neuropathic ulcer
Treatment	Remove callus, clean and debride. Antibiotics for infection. If osteomyelitis, cellulitis, abscess or sepsis present, arrange hospital admission for intravenous antibiotics and review of glycaemic control. Consider surgical/orthopaedic referral for drainage, debridement or amputation	Depending on the pathology involved, DSA with angioplasty may be indicated, while in others a bypass graft will need to be considered. General supportive care remains the same as in neuropathic foot ulcers
Complications	Trauma, infection, gangrene, amputation, Charcot's joint	Similar to those of the neuropathic foot, but with an increased risk of amputation if severe arterial disease is present
Example	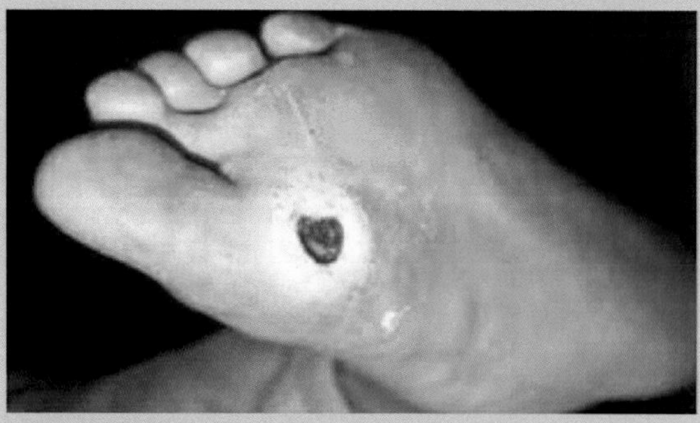 **Fig 66** Neuropathic ulcer. Typical 'punched-out' neuropathic ulcer in heavily callused skin underlying the first metatarsal head. (Copyright Dr S Sharma.)	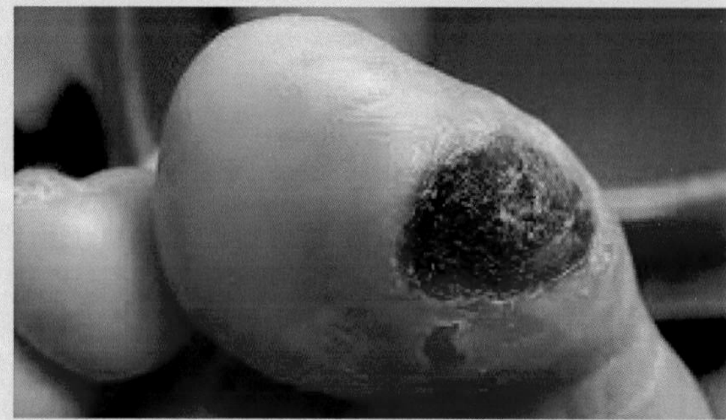 **Fig 67** Neuroischaemic foot. Classical ulceration reflecting both sensory neuropathy and vascular insufficiency. (Copyright Dr S Sharma.)

ABPI, ankle:brachial pressure index; CRP, C-reactive protein; DSA, digital subtraction angiography.

Neuropathic joint (Charcot's neuroarthropathy)

Aetiology

Charcot's neuroarthropathy is a non-infective arthropathy that occurs in a well-perfused insensate foot. Although the exact mechanism remains unclear, the problem commonly occurs in a neuropathic foot due to the presence of abnormal mechanical stresses (including trauma, infection, surgery) which stimulate the osteoclasts via the RANKL/osteoprotegerin pathway. There is associated increased blood flow due to sympathetic nerve loss.

Clinical presentation

Typically with a warm/hot, swollen and often uncomfortable foot (Fig 68), which may be indistinguishable from cellulitis and gout. Peripheral pulses are invariably present and peripheral neuropathy is clinically evident. There may or may not be a local rise in skin temperature. The most likely sites include the tarsometatarsal region or the metatarsal-phalangeal joints.

> Hazard
>
> **Charcot's neuroarthropathy can be difficult to diagnose**
>
> Diagnosis is often missed in early or subtle cases, which can lead to inappropriate treatment as cellulitis or even investigation for deep-vein thrombosis. Plain radiographs can be normal in the early phase, and if measures to avoid weight-bearing are not instituted appropriately, the softened bones become progressively deformed, with subsequent ulceration and even limb loss.

Investigation

Radiographs of the foot may be normal in the early stages, but soon become abnormal with destruction and disorganisation, particularly of the ankle and tarsometatarsal regions. MRIs are useful in early cases to differentiate from infection by demonstrating bone marrow oedema. Occasionally isotope bone scans may be required to detect new bone formation.

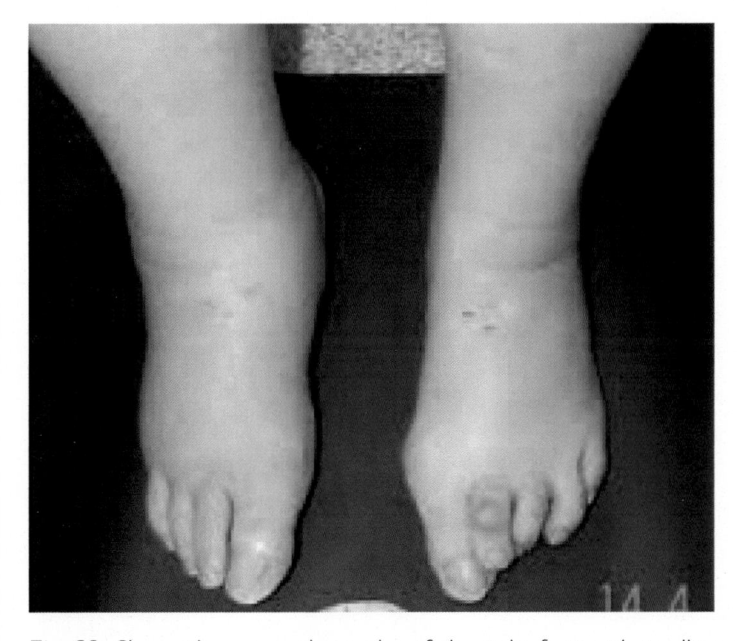

Fig 68 Charcot's neuroarthropathy of the right foot with swelling and loss of the normal arches. (Copyright Dr S Sharma.)

Treatment

The mainstay of treatment of Charcot's neuroarthropathy is immobilisation with the use of a total contact cast until the swelling and local rise of temperature has completely subsided. Occasionally, MRI of the foot may be required to demonstrate absence of any marrow oedema prior to cast removal. Patients need to be followed up long term to prevent/detect foot ulceration. There is no role for intravenous bisphosphonates in the management of Charcot's neuroarthropathy.

Diabetic foot skin lesions

In addition to leg ulcers and fungal or bacterial infections of the skin, patients with diabetes may develop several other characteristic conditions as follows.

Granuloma annulare

A cluster of small papules that typically form a ring on the back of hands or feet (Fig 69). Usually recovers spontaneously, but cryotherapy or steroid injections may be used.

Necrobiosis lipoidica diabeticorum

A patch of erythematous skin with a central yellow area of atrophy that may ulcerate. The shin is the most commonly affected site (Fig 70). The lesions are chronic and rarely resolve. Topical steroids or injection may be used but are not of proven benefit.

Cheiroarthropathy

Also termed as diabetic limited joint mobility, this presents as tightness and thickening of the skin and periarticular connective tissue of the fingers, resulting in a painless loss of joint mobility. Initial involvement of the distal interphalangeal joints of the fifth digit usually progresses proximally to involve all fingers. Larger joints of the elbow, knee and foot may be affected. The actual joint space, however, remains uninvolved, so that the condition is not a true arthropathy. The characteristic clinical sign is the 'prayer sign', which is an inability to approximate the palmar surfaces and interphalangeal joint

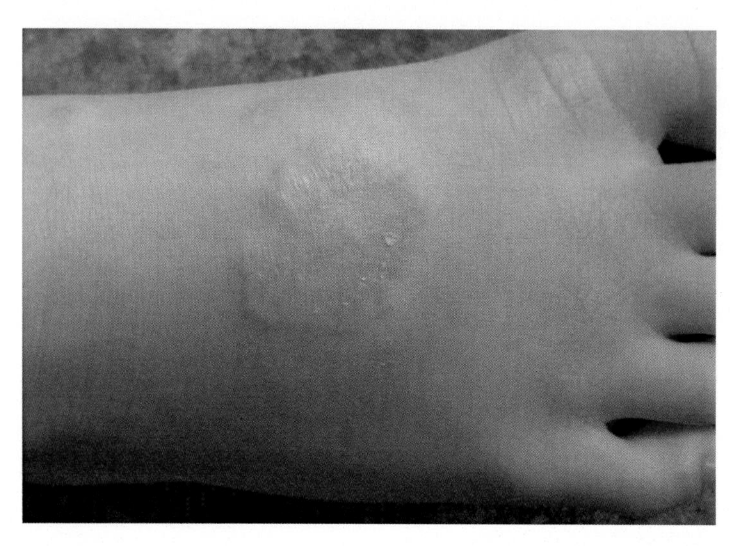

Fig 69 Granuloma annulare in the dorsum of the foot. (Copyright Dr S Sharma.)

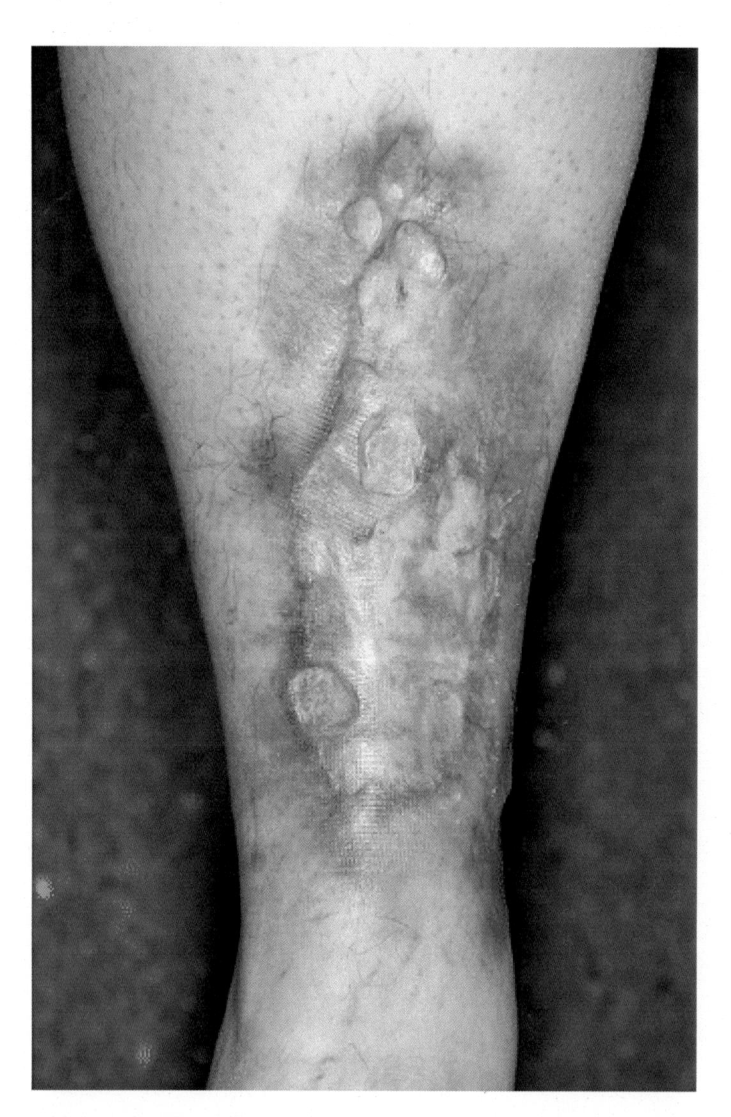

Fig 70 Necrobiosis lipoidica diabeticorum. (Copyright Dr S Sharma.)

spaces with the hands pressed together and fingers separated (Fig 71). In addition to joint contractures, the skin may appear thickened, waxy and smooth with apparent loss of adnexa, resembling skin changes in scleroderma.

2.6.5 Pregnancy and diabetes mellitus

Approximately 700,000 women give birth in England and Wales each year, and up to 5% of these women have either pre-existing diabetes or gestational diabetes. Of women who have diabetes during pregnancy, about 87.5% have gestational diabetes (which may or may not resolve after pregnancy), 7.5% have type 1 diabetes and 5% have type 2 diabetes. The prevalence of type 1 diabetes, and especially type 2 diabetes, has increased in recent years. The incidence of gestational diabetes is also increasing as a result of higher rates of obesity in the general population and more pregnancies in older women.

Diabetes in pregnancy is associated with risks to the woman and to the developing fetus. Miscarriage, pre-eclampsia and preterm labour are more common in women with pre-existing diabetes. In addition, diabetic retinopathy can worsen rapidly during pregnancy. Stillbirth, congenital malformations, macrosomia, birth injury, perinatal mortality and postnatal adaptation problems (such as hypoglycaemia) are more common in babies born to women with pre-existing diabetes.

Preconception planning and care

All women with diabetes who are planning to become pregnant should be given the following advice:

- aim for a target glycated haemoglobin A_{1c} (HbA_{1c}) of $\leq$48 mmol/mol (ie $\leq$6.5%). To achieve this HbA_{1c} target, a fasting plasma glucose of 5–7 mmol/L on waking and a plasma glucose of 4–7 mmol/L before meals at other times of the day is necessary

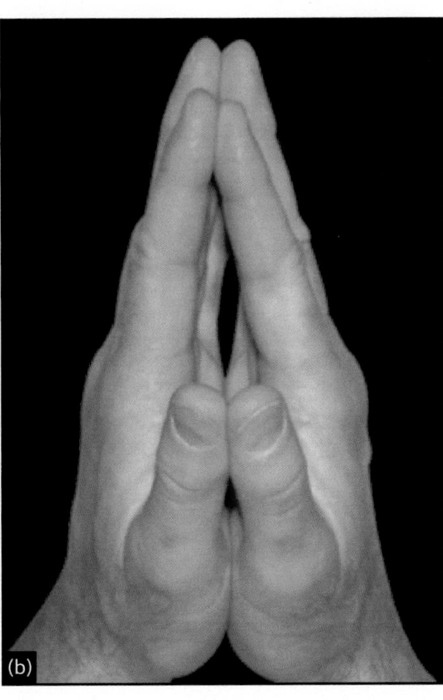

Fig 71 Diabetic cheiroarthropathy. The patient is unable to approximate the palmar surface of the proximal and distal interphalangeal joints with palms pressed together (known as the 'prayer sign'). **(a)** Ulnar view; only fingertips are approximated. **(b)** Radial view; straining to press palms together. (Copyright Dr S Sharma.)

- take folic acid (5 mg once daily) for at least 3 months prior to conception
- discontinue potentially teratogenic agents (eg ACE inhibitors, statins) and stop oral hypoglycaemic agents (except metformin)
- stop smoking
- advice about diet and lifestyle should be reinforced
- risks associated with pregnancy (both to the mother and fetus) should be discussed.

Gestational diabetes

The term 'gestational diabetes' refers to diabetes detected for the first time during pregnancy, hence some patients with type 2 diabetes that has not been previously recognised may initially be labelled as having this condition.

The diagnosis of gestational diabetes is controversial. Current National Institute for Health and Care Excellence (NICE) guidance (NG3 (published February 2015; last updated August 2015)) recommends risk-based screening using a 75 g oral glucose tolerance test (OGTT), with the following groups being considered to be at risk:

- first-degree relative with diabetes mellitus
- previous gestational diabetes
- previous macrosomia (>4.5 kg)
- maternal body mass index (BMI) >30 kg/m^2
- minority ethnic family origin.

Patients deemed to be at risk should be offered a 75 g OGTT at 24–28 weeks, with the exception of women with previous gestational diabetes who should be screened at 16 weeks (and repeated at 24–28 weeks if the first OGTT is normal). Current NICE diagnostic thresholds are: fasting plasma glucose ≥5.6 mmol/L, 2-hour post-75 g OGTT plasma glucose ≥7.8 mmol/L.

Antenatal care for women with diabetes

All pregnant women with diabetes should be reviewed in a joint diabetes antenatal clinic in secondary care. NICE guidance NG3 provides a clear schedule for antenatal care.

All pregnant women with diabetes should perform capillary blood glucose testing aiming for the following targets: fasting plasma glucose <5.3 mmol/L; 1 hour after meals <7.8 mmol/L and/or 2 hours after meals <6.4 mmol/L.

Intrapartum care for women with diabetes

Pregnant women with pregestational diabetes and no other complications should be offered induction of labour or caesarean section between 37^{+0} weeks and 38^{+6} weeks gestation. Pregnant women with gestational diabetes should be advised to give birth no later than 40^{+6} weeks.

It is important to maintain good glycaemic control throughout the labour process to reduce the risk of fetal hypoglycaemia. Joint British Diabetes Societies' guidelines provide advice on intrapartum glucose management.

Key point

Planning for after delivery

It is essential that women with pregestational diabetes should have a postnatal insulin plan documented in their antenatal notes as insulin requirements fall back to prepregnancy levels immediately following delivery.

Postnatal care

For women diagnosed with gestational diabetes whose blood glucose levels return to normal after birth:

- offer lifestyle advice (including weight control, diet and exercise)

- arrange a fasting plasma glucose test 6–13 weeks after the birth to exclude diabetes
- if a fasting plasma glucose test has not been performed by 13 weeks, offer a fasting plasma glucose test or HbA_{1c} measurement
- do not routinely offer a 75 g 2-hour OGTT.

Offer annual screening (either fasting plasma glucose or HbA_{1c}) to women with previous gestational diabetes.

Hazard

Effects of diabetes on pregnancy

Poor diabetic control at conception and in early pregnancy can lead to congenital malformations (twice the background risk), and later in pregnancy to excessive fetal growth (50% risk) and late intrauterine death.

2.6.6 Important information for patients

Sick day rules

Stress increases insulin resistance and hepatic glucose production. Accordingly, patients with type 1 diabetes need more insulin, and those with type 2 diabetes may require short-term insulin, under conditions of severe or acute stress. Patients must be advised never to stop or even reduce their insulin. Indeed, in intercurrent illness the insulin requirement may increase by 10–20%. Meals may be substituted with frequent snacks and drinks, especially in the presence of anorexia or nausea. Frequent monitoring of blood glucose is necessary.

Hazard

Sick day rules for patients with diabetes

- Never stop or even reduce your insulin; illness usually increases your insulin requirement.
- People with type 1 diabetes need to continue their basal insulin and make changes to their mealtime insulin when they are not eating normally.
- Seek help if you are unwell, especially with vomiting or diarrhoea and if you cannot keep food or fluid down. If your blood sugar rises above 20 mmol/L or remains above 15 mmol/L for 24 hours, or if your blood test is positive for ketones, seek urgent medical help.

Surgery

Most hospitals have protocols for the management of patients with diabetes undergoing procedures that require a period of fasting, eg colonoscopy through to major abdominal surgery. The Joint British Diabetes Societies have produced consensus guidelines.

Adolescence

Many physiological, behavioural and psychosocial factors complicate the management of diabetes during adolescence. Ideally, young people with diabetes should attend a dedicated clinic, with psychology input, where they can experience mutual support away from the delays and obvious complications on view in the adult clinic. Patient-sensitive education and encouragement are vital. Long-term complications and emergencies should be explained in a realistic but non-threatening fashion. Contraceptive advice is essential.

Younger patients may benefit from diabetes camps where informal education is provided and practical techniques are taught.

Driving

Key point

Hypoglycaemia is the major factor that impacts on driving.

In the UK, patients with diabetes treated with tablets and/or diet may hold a 'car/motorcycle' group 1 licence and need not inform the Driver and Vehicle Licensing Agency (DVLA) unless they have complications (see below for specific rules relating to hypoglycaemia), but they must inform their insurance company. The DVLA (and insurance company) must be notified once a patient commences insulin therapy. Those treated with insulin will be given a group 1 entitlement licence for 1, 2 or 3 years depending upon the quality of their glycaemic control, the regularity of medical surveillance and the extent of complications.

Patients with type 2 diabetes not requiring insulin may be issued with a 'till 70' licence, unless they have complications of their diabetes.

Recent changes to DVLA regulations mean that it is now possible for a patient receiving insulin to hold a group 2 (large goods vehicle (LGV)), passenger-carrying vehicle (PCV)) licence, with review on an annual basis, but a series of strict medical criteria must be met, in particular with respect to hypoglycaemia (preserved awareness, regular recorded testing, no episodes requiring third party rescue, etc), absence of complications, and annual review by an independent consultant diabetologist.

The onus is on the driver to prove they are fit to drive, and they should test at times relevant to driving. A capillary blood glucose (CBG) should be recorded on a memory meter, with time and date set correctly, within 2 hours of driving. CBG must be 5 mmol/L or above ('five to drive').

Hypoglycaemia is the major factor that impacts on driving in all categories. Patients must be able to effectively recognise and treat hypoglycaemia. The DVLA advises that patients should check their blood glucose at times relevant to driving. Patients must carry glucose tablets (or equivalent) to treat hypoglycaemia, as well as their glucometer, and they are expected to stop and test their glucose level every 2 hours on a long journey. If a hypoglycaemic episode occurs while driving, they should pull over, remove the keys from the ignition and move to the passenger side, so they are no longer in charge of the vehicle. They must wait an appropriate time (45 minutes) after correcting any hypoglycaemia before recommencing their journey. Hypoglycaemia requiring third-party rescue is considered a major concern and will lead to even a group 1 licence being revoked if it has occurred on more than one occasion in the preceding 12 months.

Employment

The Equality Act 2010 applies in England, Wales and Scotland, while the Disability Discrimination Act 1995 applies in Northern Ireland. Prior to these acts, some occupations, eg the fire service, denied entry to those with insulin-treated diabetes. However, since the introduction of these acts, the blanket bans have been lifted in the emergency services for people with type 1 diabetes and people with type 2 diabetes who use insulin. The armed forces are exempt from these acts.

Exercise

Regular exercise is helpful in reducing BP, weight and lipid levels, and increases insulin sensitivity. Regular exercise for 20–30 minutes, three to five times a week, should be encouraged. Individuals with diabetes are advised to carry sugar with them when exercising and to take a snack or meal high in complex carbohydrates afterwards, although those who regularly undertake exercise should be able to reduce their pre-exercise insulin dose, to avoid additional carbohydrate requirement.

2.7 Other endocrine disorders

2.7.1 Multiple endocrine neoplasia

There are several multiple endocrine neoplasia (MEN) syndromes, each characterised by autosomal dominant inheritance. Endocrinopathies develop in several glands which undergo hyperplastic or neoplastic transformation, usually associated with hyperfunction.

Table 73 outlines the key features of the more common types (MEN-1–MEN-3). MEN-4 is rare and is characterised by parathyroid and pituitary tumours, in possible association with tumours of the adrenals, kidneys and reproductive organs; it is caused by mutations in a cyclin-dependent kinase inhibitor (*CDNK1B*).

Management

The individual components of the MEN syndromes are managed along standard guidelines, with certain caveats. In contrast to sporadic cases, multiple lesions are common. Four-gland parathyroid hyperplasia is more common than a single adenoma, hence minimally invasive surgery is generally not appropriate. Pancreatic tumours are also often multiple, recurrence is common and surgical cure rates are lower than in sporadic cases. There are also other challenges, eg it is important to first exclude/treat a phaeochromocytoma prior to embarking on thyroid or parathyroid surgery. For these reasons MEN cases should be managed at specialist centres.

Screening

Genetic testing, which raises important ethical and legal issues, has now replaced biochemical screening in the identification of affected members of MEN kindreds.

- MEN-1 – genetic screening has clear benefits for unaffected individuals, who can be discharged without the need for long-term biochemical/radiological surveillance, while affected individuals can be enrolled into appropriate screening programmes.
- MEN-2 and familial medullary thyroid carcinoma (MTC) kindreds – identification of *RET* proto-oncogene mutations is particularly important as affected individuals should undergo prophylactic thyroidectomy to prevent MTC. There is a well-recognised genotype–phenotype correlation, with some *RET* mutations being associated with particularly aggressive MTC of very early onset. The timing of thyroidectomy is therefore determined by the mutation, but should in general be performed in childhood (before 5 years of age) or in infancy (before 6 months) for the most aggressive mutations.

Table 73 An overview of MEN

	Type		
	MEN-1 (Wermer syndrome)	**MEN-2a (Sipple syndrome) (sometimes denoted as MEN-2)**	**MEN-2b (sometimes denoted as MEN-3)**
Components	Parathyroid hyperplasia (~80%)	MTC (~100%)	Mucosal neuromas (~100%)
	Pancreatic tumours (~75%)	Phaeochromocytoma (~50%)	MTC (~90%)
	Pituitary tumours (~65%)	Parathyroid hyperplasia (~40%)	Marfanoid habitus (~65%)
			Phaeochromocytoma (~45%)
			(Parathyroid hyperplasia – rare)
Genetic locus	Chromosome 11 – loss-of-function mutations of the *MENIN* tumour suppressor gene	MEN-2a and MEN-2b are both associated with activating mutations in the *RET* proto-oncogene (alpha-receptor tyrosine kinase) on chromosome 10	
Clinical notes	Hyperparathyroidism is the most common presenting feature Gastrinomas (~50%) and insulinomas (~30%) form the bulk of pancreatic tumours Prolactinomas and non-functioning tumours are the most common pituitary lesions	MTC in the setting of MEN-2b is particularly aggressive Phaeochromocytoma may be bilateral Hyperparathyroidism is much more common in MEN-2a than MEN-2b	
		Familial MTC without the other features of MEN-2a also occurs with certain mutations in the *RET* proto-oncogene	Mucosal neuromas most commonly affect the oral cavity and gastrointestinal tract

MEN, multiple endocrine neoplasia; MTC, medullary thyroid carcinoma.

2.7.2 Autoimmune polyglandular endocrinopathies

Two major polyglandular syndromes have been described in which autoimmune-mediated dysfunction of two or more endocrine glands is frequently associated with other non-endocrine autoimmune disorders. Table 74 describes the main features of each condition.

- Type I, also referred to as the autoimmune polyendocrinopathy–candidiasis–ectodermal dystrophy (APECED) syndrome is a rare autosomal recessive disorder due to mutations in the autoimmune regulator (*AIRE*) gene on chromosome 21q22.3, the product of which appears to be a nuclear transcription factor. Hypoparathyroidism or chronic mucocutaneous candidiasis is usually the first manifestation.
- Type II (Schmidt's syndrome) is much more prevalent and primary adrenal insufficiency is its principal manifestation. Approximately 50% of cases are familial, with several modes of inheritance (autosomal recessive, autosomal dominant and polygenic) reported. Women are affected up to three times more often than men, with most cases occurring between age 20 and 40 years.

2.7.3 Ectopic hormone syndromes

Some tumours (both benign and malignant) may be associated with ectopic hormone production and the development of a clinical syndrome due to hormone excess. Several examples are shown within Table 75.

Table 74 Autoimmune polyglandular syndromes

Type	Type I	Type II (Schmidt's syndrome)
Epidemiology	Rare, autosomal recessive Childhood onset	Autosomal dominant, recessive or sporadic Young adults: females > males
HLA association	–	*DR3*, *DR4*
Common endocrinopathies	Hypoparathyroidism Adrenal insufficiency	Adrenal insufficiency Hypothyroidism or hyperthyroidism Type 1 DM
Less common endocrinopathies	Gonadal failure Hypothyroidism or hyperthyroidism Type 1 DM	Gonadal failure
Non-endocrine manifestations	Mucocutaneous candidiasis Chronic active hepatitis Pernicious anaemia Vitiligo Alopecia	Myasthenia gravis Pernicious anaemia Vitiligo Alopecia

DM, diabetes mellitus.

Table 75 Ectopic hormone secretion by benign and malignant tumours and their associated clinical syndromes

Hormone	Clinical syndrome	Tumours
ACTH	Cushing's syndrome	Small-cell bronchial carcinoma
		Bronchial carcinoid
		Pancreatic neuroendocrine tumour
		Thymic carcinoid
ADH	SIADH	Small-cell bronchial carcinoma
PTHrP	Hypercalcaemia	Squamous cell bronchial carcinoma
OAF	Hypercalcaemia	Multiple myeloma
		Leukaemia
hCG	Clinical syndromes rare, but may include: precocious puberty, gynaecomastia, menstrual irregularity	Testicular germ cell tumour
		Hepatocellular carcinoma
		Gastrointestinal tumour
		Choriocarcinoma
Erythropoietin	Polycythaemia	Renal cell carcinoma
		Cerebellar haemangioblastoma
		Uterine fibromas

ACTH, adrenocorticotropic hormone; ADH, antidiuretic hormone; hCG, human chorionic gonadotrophin; OAF, osteoclast activating factor; PTHrP, parathyroid hormone-related peptide; SIADH, syndrome of inappropriate antidiuretic hormone secretion.

3 Investigations and practical procedures

3.1 Stimulation tests

3.1.1 Short Synacthen test

Principle

The principle behind the short Synacthen test (SST) is administration of tetracosactrin (synthetic adrenocorticotropic hormone (ACTH) or 'synACTHen') allows the acute adrenal response to ACTH to be assessed. In addition to promoting cortisol secretion, it also increases the production of other ACTH-dependent steroids (eg androgens) in the biosynthetic pathway and hence can be used to exacerbate the enzyme block in differing types of congenital adrenal hyperplasia (CAH) (see Section 2.2.5), thereby helping to confirm/exclude the diagnosis in patients with equivocal basal values.

Indications

- diagnosis of primary (and secondary) adrenal insufficiency
- diagnosis of CAH (especially non-classical).

Contraindications

Known allergy to Synacthen; poorly controlled asthma.

Practical details

Before investigation

In patients already on hydrocortisone replacement, the morning dose on the day of the test should be withheld until the test has been completed. Some centres also omit the evening dose on the day before the investigation. In subjects taking supraphysiological glucocorticoid therapy (>30 mg hydrocortisone or >7.5 mg prednisolone per day) Synacthen testing should, where possible, be deferred until the dose has been weaned to a more physiological level.

The investigation

1. 9am.

   Take blood for serum cortisol and plasma ACTH; give Synacthen 250 μg IM (or IV).

2. 9.30am.

   Take blood for serum cortisol.

3. 10am.

   Take blood for serum cortisol – however, not all centres routinely measure a 60-minute response.

- ACTH samples should be taken on ice to the laboratory for immediate processing.
- Low-dose Synacthen (1 μg) is advocated by some as a more sensitive test of adrenocortical function, especially if the SST is being used to screen for secondary adrenal insufficiency. However, there remain problems with accurate dosing (currently the 250 μg vial must be diluted) and the validity of the test remains to be proven.
- For suspected CAH, measurement of 17alpha-hydroxyprogesterone (17-OHP) is also required.

After investigation – interpretation

Adrenal insufficiency

There is variation between laboratories as to the exact cut-off for a normal response, but a serum cortisol level of >500 nmol/L at 30 minutes is generally taken to exclude primary adrenal failure. A subnormal response following Synacthen suggests either:

- primary adrenal pathology or
- secondary adrenal insufficiency (eg ACTH deficiency or exogenous steroid therapy) with consequent atrophy of the zonae fasciculata and reticularis.

Paired basal serum cortisol and plasma ACTH levels may help to distinguish between these two possibilities (eg low cortisol with elevated ACTH in primary adrenal failure; low cortisol with inappropriately low/normal ACTH in secondary hypoadrenalism). Alternatively, a long ('depot') Synacthen test can be performed to confirm the persistent lack of responsiveness in primary adrenal failure, which contrasts with a delayed but detectable rise in cortisol in secondary adrenal insufficiency.

Hazard

When a normal result may not be normal

A normal post-Synacthen peak cortisol response in the SST does not exclude partial pituitary ACTH deficiency (decreased pituitary reserve) in patients whose basal ACTH production is sufficient to prevent adrenal atrophy, but in whom the ACTH response to stress (eg insulin-induced hypoglycaemia) is attenuated.

Congenital adrenal hyperplasia

A peak 17-OHP level of >45 nmol/L confirms the diagnosis.

3.1.2 Corticotrophin-releasing hormone test

Principle

Unlike pituitary corticotrophs, most ectopic ACTH-secreting tumours do not express corticotropin-releasing hormone (CRH) receptors and are therefore not susceptible to stimulation by CRH. Accordingly, exogenous CRH administration can help to distinguish between pituitary-dependent Cushing's disease and ectopic ACTH secretion, either alone (see below) or in combination with inferior petrosal sinus sampling (see Section 2.1.1).

Indications

To differentiate between Cushing's disease and ectopic ACTH secretion.

Contraindications

Known allergy to CRH.

Practical details

Before investigation

The patient should be fasted from midnight and warned that facial flushing is common following injection of CRH. Occasionally, transient hypotension occurs.

The investigation

1 Insert an IV cannula at 8.30am with the patient recumbent. Take samples for measurement of serum cortisol and plasma ACTH 15 and 30 minutes later (–15 and 0 min samples, respectively).
2 Give synthetic CRH 100 μg IV at 9am.
3 Measure serum cortisol and plasma ACTH at 15, 30, 45, 60, 90 and 120 minutes.

After investigation – interpretation

Most patients with Cushing's disease exhibit a normal or exaggerated increment in plasma ACTH and serum cortisol, contrasting with the lack of response from ectopic ACTH-secreting tumours. Thresholds for defining a normal response depend on whether human or ovine CRH is used.

Hazard

Up to 15% of pituitary adenomas may fail to respond to CRH.

3.1.3 Thyrotropin-releasing hormone test

Principle

Administration of thyrotropin-releasing hormone (TRH) in normal subjects promotes release of pituitary thyroid-stimulating hormone (TSH). This response is blunted in hyperthyroidism and exaggerated in primary hypothyroidism. An abnormal response may also be seen in hypothalamic–pituitary disorders. This test is rarely used now because of the availability of high precision TSH assays.

Indications

- borderline cases of thyrotoxicosis (eg normal free thyroxine (FT4) and free triiodothyronine (FT3) with suppressed TSH)
- in the investigation of hypothalamic–pituitary disorders (eg as part of a combined pituitary triple test with insulin-induced hypoglycaemia and a gonadotrophin-releasing hormone (GnRH) test)
- to distinguish a TSH-secreting pituitary adenoma (thyrotropinoma) from the genetic disorder resistance to thyroid hormone (RTH).

Contraindications

Known allergy to TRH.

Practical details

Before investigation

Non-fasting unless combined with an insulin tolerance test (see below). The patient should be warned that flushing and a desire to micturate are commonly experienced transient side effects.

The investigation

1 Insert IV cannula at 8.45am (with the patient recumbent). Take blood for basal FT4 and TSH levels immediately prior to TRH administration (0 min).
2 Give 200 μg of TRH IV at 9am.
3 Take samples for TSH measurement at 20 and 60 minutes.

After investigation – interpretation

- In normal controls TSH rises by at least 2 mU/L, with a 20-minute value that is higher than the 60-minute value.
- In hyperthyroidism, the basal TSH level is suppressed and fails to respond to TRH.
- Hypothyroidism due to hypothalamic–pituitary disorders may be associated with a subnormal or delayed TSH response.
- TSHomas (pituitary tumours that secrete TSH) show minimal response to TRH, while the TSH response in RTH is maintained/robust.

Complications

Acute pituitary tumour haemorrhage/infarction has been reported following administration of TRH, especially if undertaken as part of a combined pituitary triple test.

3.1.4 Gonadotrophin-releasing hormone test

Principle

Administration of gonadotrophin-releasing hormone (GnRH) in normal subjects leads to a prompt increase in serum luteinising hormone (LH), with a slower and lesser increment in serum follicle-stimulating hormone (FSH). This test is principally used to assess LH and FSH secretory reserves and does not *per se* diagnose gonadotrophin deficiency.

Indications

- as a part of a combined triple test in suspected hypopituitarism
- in the investigation of delayed puberty.

Contraindications

Known allergy to GnRH.

Practical details

Before investigation

Non-fasting unless combined with insulin tolerance test.

The investigation

1 Insert IV cannula at 8.45am. Take samples for basal serum LH and FSH immediately prior to GnRH administration (0 min).
2 Give 100 µg of GnRH IV at 9am.
3 Obtain further samples for measurement of serum LH and FSH at 20 and 60 minutes.

After investigation – interpretation

- In normal subjects, peak levels of LH are similar in both sexes (10–50 IU/L). Peak levels of FSH are generally lower (1–25 IU/L in females and 1–10 IU/L in males).
- In hypothalamic–pituitary disorders the GnRH response may be subnormal (especially in pituitary disease), normal or enhanced (particularly with hypothalamic dysfunction).

3.1.5 Insulin tolerance test

Principle

Insulin-induced hypoglycaemia is a powerful stimulus to ACTH/cortisol and growth hormone (GH) secretion.

Indications

The 'gold standard' test for the assessment of cortisol and GH reserves in patients with known or suspected hypothalamic–pituitary dysfunction.

Contraindications

Hazard

Contraindications to an insulin tolerance test

- ischaemic heart disease, arrhythmias and/or an abnormal resting ECG
- epilepsy
- 9am cortisol <100 nmol/L.

Practical details

Before the investigation

- Check the resting ECG and ensure that 9am serum cortisol is >100 nmol/L. Serum free thyroxine (FT4) should also be normal.

Hazard

Be aware of adrenal insufficiency

If there is any question of adrenal insufficiency, there is a risk of precipitating a hypoadrenal crisis. If in doubt, use an alternative stimulation test, eg Synacthen test (to assess cortisol reserve), glucagon test (to assess GH and/or cortisol reserve).

- Ensure point-of-care blood glucose measurement is available.
- Draw up 25 mL of 50% dextrose and 100 mg of hydrocortisone ready for intravenous use.
- Nil by mouth from midnight.
- Obtain the patient's consent, explaining the test and the symptoms of hypoglycaemia that they may experience (eg hunger, sweating, tachycardia, tremor). Reassure the patient that you will be present throughout.
- Label the blood bottles.
- Weigh the patient and calculate the dose of soluble insulin required: 0.15 units/kg (0.3 units/kg in those who are likely to be insulin resistant, eg Cushing's syndrome, acromegaly, marked obesity).

The investigation

1 Insert an IV cannula at 8.30am.
2 Take basal blood samples (for glucose, cortisol, ACTH and GH) at 9am.
3 Give the calculated dose of soluble insulin as an IV bolus.
4 Take further blood samples at 20, 30, 45, 60, 90 and 120 minutes.
5 Check bedside blood glucose at each time point.
6 The blood glucose must fall to less than 2.2 mmol/L to provide an adequate stress.
7 By 45 minutes you should expect the patient to experience symptoms of hypoglycaemia. If this does not occur and the blood sugar has not fallen below 2.2 mmol/L, you may need to administer another bolus of insulin and continue sampling for longer.
8 Throughout the test you should record the patient's pulse and BP and note the presence or absence of symptoms of hypoglycaemia.
9 Remember to reassure the patient as the test can be an unpleasant experience.
10 If the patient becomes overwhelmingly hypoglycaemic during the test (especially if there is impending or actual loss of consciousness or a

seizure) administer 50–100 mL of 20% glucose IV and continue sampling, as the hypoglycaemic stimulus will have been sufficient! Consider giving hydrocortisone 100 mg IV if the patient does not recover in response to the glucose.

After the investigation

- Give oral glucose (eg Lucozade) and lunch, and observe for 2 hours.
- Advise the patient to avoid exercise after the test (including cycling home!).

Interpretation

Look for:

- A peak cortisol concentration of 500 nmol/L is generally accepted as a normal response, with an increment of at least 170 nmol/L from the basal level also expected.
- A rise in serum GH to >9 µg/L denotes a normal response; values <3 µg/L indicate severe GH deficiency.

Complications

Provided the test is carried out according to these guidelines, it is associated with few serious adverse events.

3.1.6 Pentagastrin stimulation test

Principle

Although calcitonin is a useful marker for medullary thyroid carcinoma (MTC), levels may be normal in the early stages of tumour development or if C-cell hyperplasia (a premalignant stage) is present. Provocation with pentagastrin provides a sensitive method for detecting these early cases by inducing calcitonin release from the C cells, with a correlation between the peak following the stimulus and C-cell mass.

Indications

To screen for medullary thyroid carcinoma in patients with known multiple endocrine neoplasia type 2 (MEN-2) / familial MTC or to identify at risk relatives. The latter has, however, been largely superseded by the introduction of genetic testing (see Section 2.7.1).

Contraindications

Hypocalcaemia.

Practical details

Before investigation

- Check that both basal calcium and calcitonin levels are normal.
- Restrict to a light diet with avoidance of alcohol for 12 hours prior to the test.
- Following pentagastrin, patients should be warned that they may experience several unpleasant side effects including flushing, nausea, chest tightness and abdominal cramps.

The investigation

1. With the patient supine, establish intravenous access. Take blood for measurement of basal plasma calcitonin.
2. Give 0.5 µg/kg pentagastrin IV over 10–15 seconds.
3. Repeat samples for calcitonin estimation at 2, 5 and 10 minutes.

Key point

Measuring serum calcitonin

Blood should be transported immediately on ice to the laboratory for processing.

After investigation

Interpretation

An increment of twofold to threefold or greater following stimulation is usually taken as a positive result.

Important information for patients

It is of paramount importance that relatives understand the implications of this investigation as a screening test for MTC and MEN-2.

3.1.7 Oral glucose tolerance test

Principle

Originally used to confirm/exclude the diagnosis of diabetes mellitus (DM) in individuals with equivocal fasting / random blood glucose levels.

Indications

There is controversy over the role of the oral glucose tolerance test (OGTT) in routine practice (see Section 2.6), although it is still used in pregnancy to diagnose impaired glucose tolerance and gestational DM.

Contraindications

None.

Practical details

Before investigation

Fast from midnight.

The investigation

1. Take a basal venous plasma glucose sample.
2. Give 75 g of oral glucose.
3. Take a further venous plasma glucose sample at 2 hours.

After investigation – interpretation

Values corresponding to a normal response, impaired glucose tolerance and frank DM are shown in Table 76.

Table 76 The OGTT in the diagnosis of DM		
Diagnosis	**Fasting glucose**	**2-hour glucose**
Normal	<6.1 mmol/L	<7.8 mmol/L
Impaired glucose tolerance	<7.0 mmol/L	≥7.8 but <11.1 mmol/L
Diabetes	≥7.0 mmol/L	≥11.1 mmol/L

3.2 Suppression tests

3.2.1 Overnight dexamethasone suppression test

Principle

Unlike normal subjects, patients with Cushing's syndrome fail to fully suppress endogenous cortisol secretion following administration of dexamethasone.

Indications

Establishment of diagnosis of Cushing's syndrome.

Contraindications

Although not an absolute contraindication, care should be taken in those with active peptic ulcer disease.

Practical details

Before investigation

No specific preparation is required.

The investigation

1 **Day 0**. 11pm.

Give dexamethasone 1 mg orally.

2 **Day 1**. 9am.

Take blood for serum cortisol (ie 10 hours after dose).

After investigation

Interpretation

In normal subjects, the serum cortisol suppresses fully to undetectable levels (<50 nmol/L) following dexamethasone, which does not cross-react in the cortisol assay.

Complications

Although the procedure itself has few complications, numerous circumstances can complicate interpretation of the results, with an apparent failure to fully suppress serum cortisol, including:

- lack of compliance with dexamethasone
- pseudo-Cushing's syndrome (see Section 2.1.1)
- hepatic enzyme-inducing drugs (eg rifampicin, phenytoin may facilitate rapid metabolism of dexamethasone to levels such that there is failure to fully suppress a normal hypothalamic–pituitary–adrenal axis)
- cyclical Cushing's syndrome (see Section 2.1.1) with normal dexamethasone suppression in the quiescent phase
- a significant number of normal subjects fail to show full suppression in the overnight test. It is likely that many of these individuals are endogenous fast-metabolisers.

3.2.2 Low-dose dexamethasone suppression test

Principle

Unlike normal subjects, patients with Cushing's syndrome fail to fully suppress endogenous cortisol secretion following administration of dexamethasone.

Indications

Establishment of diagnosis of Cushing's syndrome.

Contraindications

- severe intercurrent illness or infection
- although not absolute contraindications, care should be taken in those with diabetes mellitus or active peptic ulcer disease.

Practical details

Before investigation

No specific preparation is required.

The investigation

1 **Day 0**. 9am.

Take blood for serum cortisol. A basal ACTH, if not already checked, can be measured on this sample.

2 After venesection, give dexamethasone 0.5 mg orally every 6 hours (ie at 9am, 3pm, 9pm and 3am) for 48 hours.

3 **Day 2**. 9am.

Take blood for serum cortisol (ie 6 hours after last dose).

After investigation

Interpretation

In normal subjects, the basal serum cortisol lies within the reference range (200–650 nmol/L), but suppresses fully to undetectable levels (<50 nmol/L) following 48 hours of dexamethasone, which does not cross-react in the cortisol assay.

Complications

Although the procedure itself has few complications, numerous circumstances can complicate interpretation of the results, with an apparent failure to fully suppress serum cortisol including:

- lack of compliance with dexamethasone (erroneous timing and/or missed doses)
- pseudo-Cushing's syndrome (see Section 2.1.1)
- hepatic enzyme-inducing drugs (eg rifampicin, phenytoin may facilitate rapid metabolism of dexamethasone

to levels such that there is failure to fully suppress a normal hypothalamic–pituitary–adrenal axis)

- cyclical Cushing's syndrome (see Section 2.1.1) with normal dexamethasone suppression in the quiescent phase.

Important information for patients

If the test is being performed as an outpatient, it is important to provide the patient with clear instructions as to the timing of doses, and to check for any missed doses.

3.2.3 High-dose dexamethasone suppression test

Principle

Unlike other causes of Cushing's syndrome, pituitary adenomas retain some sensitivity to glucocorticoid feedback such that ACTH release and consequently cortisol levels are reduced in response to high doses of exogenous steroid, eg dexamethasone, which does not cross-react in the cortisol assay.

Indications

To distinguish Cushing's disease from other causes of Cushing's syndrome.

Contraindications

As for the low-dose dexamethasone suppression test, but in addition care should be exercised in patients with psychiatric manifestations of Cushing's syndrome, which may significantly worsen following higher doses of dexamethasone.

Practical details

Before investigation

This test should only be undertaken in individuals in whom the diagnosis of Cushing's syndrome has been confirmed. Ideally it should be performed as an inpatient.

The investigation

1. **Day 0**. 9am.

   Take blood for serum cortisol.
2. After venesection, give dexamethasone 2.0 mg orally every 6 hours (ie at 9am, 3pm, 9pm and 3am) for 48 hours.
3. **Day 2**. 9am.

   Take blood for serum cortisol (ie 6 hours after last dose).

Note that some centres also routinely check serum cortisol after 24 hours.

After investigation

Interpretation

Serum cortisol at completion of the test suppresses to $\leq$50% of the basal value in the majority of cases of Cushing's disease but not with other causes of Cushing's syndrome.

Complications

As with the low-dose test, complications are mainly restricted to the interpretation of results. Just as no single test can reliably confirm or refute the diagnosis of Cushing's syndrome, determination of the aetiology should not be based simply upon the result of one investigation. This is important with the high-dose dexamethasone suppression test, since approximately 10% of pituitary adenomas fail to suppress, while a smaller number of ectopic ACTH-secreting tumours do so.

3.2.4 Oral glucose tolerance test in acromegaly

Principle

Growth hormone (GH) secretion is pulsatile. As the hormone is rapidly cleared from the circulation, basal GH concentrations are undetectable most of the time. For these reasons, a single random blood sample is not a reliable assessment of GH secretion and dynamic tests are preferred. Normally, glucose suppresses GH secretion. In acromegaly, however, GH levels are paradoxically increased or not suppressed by glucose.

Indications

Patients with suspected acromegaly.

Contraindications

None.

Practical details

Before the investigation

Fast from midnight.

The investigation

1. Site an intravenous cannula.
2. Take a basal blood sample for measurement of glucose and GH.
3. Give 75 g of oral glucose.
4. Take further blood samples for glucose and GH at 30, 60, 90 and 120 minutes.

After investigation – interpretation

Suppression of GH to <0.4 μg/L excludes the diagnosis of acromegaly. The glucose results may also show impaired glucose tolerance or diabetes mellitus, which can complicate acromegaly. Other conditions may give rise to non-suppressibility of GH after an oral glucose load, but these are essentially catabolic conditions associated with high GH and low insulin-like growth factor (IGF)-1 levels and are unlikely to cause confusion in the clinical context.

3.3 Other investigations

3.3.1 Thyroid function tests

Principle

There are several ways to assess the hypothalamic–pituitary–thyroid axis biochemically. Historically, many laboratories routinely measured thyroid-stimulating hormone (TSH), only going on to perform further thyroid function tests (TFTs) if they were specifically requested or indicated on the basis of an abnormal TSH result. However, most laboratories now offer combined screening (TSH and free thyroxine (FT4)). Determination of FT4 and, when indicated, free triiodothyronine (FT3) levels avoids many of the problems that are associated with interpreting the results of total hormone measurements.

Indications

TFTs are frequently requested, as hyperthyroidism and hypothyroidism are common diseases that may be difficult to diagnose clinically and are relatively easy to treat successfully.

Complications

There are a number of common pitfalls in the interpretation of TFTs.

Non-thyroidal illness or 'sick euthyroid syndrome'

In non-thyroidal illness, concentrations of FT3, FT4 and TSH can all 'sag' at various times. In particular, hospitalised patients tend to have lower T3 and higher reverse T3 (rT3) levels than healthy volunteers, due to reduced activity of the enzyme responsible for peripheral conversion of T4 to T3 and rT3 to T2 (3,5-diiodo-L-thyronine).

Key point

Do not test unless clinically indicated

It is best not to test the thyroid function of ill patients unless there is clinical evidence of thyroid disease or concern that hyperthyroidism or hypothyroidism may be contributing to the patient's problems.

During thyrotoxicosis treatment

Key point

Assessment of thyroid function during treatment of thyrotoxicosis

Focus on the FT4 levels shortly after beginning treatment for thyrotoxicosis, as the TSH may remain suppressed for weeks or months.

Pituitary disease

In clinically hypothyroid patients with a low FT4 whose TSH is not elevated, consider the possibility of pituitary disease causing secondary hypothyroidism. Check remaining anterior pituitary function (hypopituitarism, see Section 2.1.8), and remember that if there is evidence of cortisol deficiency, this must be corrected before thyroid replacement is instituted.

Key point

Assessment of thyroid function in pituitary disease

In hypopituitary patients on T4 replacement, remember to titrate the dose of T4 against the FT4 concentration: in this context it is safest to ignore the TSH.

Early pregnancy

In the first trimester of pregnancy, human chorionic gonadotrophin (hCG) secretion may result in elevated concentrations of FT4 and FT3, and suppression of TSH (hCG shares a common alpha-subunit with TSH and the gonadotrophins). This is more marked in patients with hyperemesis gravidarum.

Drugs

Various drugs can interfere with thyroid function through one or more mechanisms:

- High doses of salicylates, furosemide or phenytoin may compete with hormone binding to thyroxine-binding globulin, resulting in increased free (but not total) hormone levels.
- Amiodarone, glucocorticoids, high-dose propranolol and oral cholecystographic agents inhibit peripheral conversion of T4 to T3.
- Dopamine, L-dopa and glucocorticoids may inhibit TSH secretion.
- Heparin increases FT4 ± FT3 levels due to an *in vitro* assay artefact.

3.3.2 Water deprivation test

Principle

In the presence of diabetes insipidus (DI), water deprivation leads to intravascular depletion with an increase in plasma osmolality, and urine osmolality remains inappropriately low due to a continued diuresis.

In hypothalamic (cranial) DI (ie deficiency of antidiuretic hormone (ADH)), administration of synthetic ADH (desmopressin (DDAVP)) corrects the defect to allow concentration of urine, whereas the urine remains dilute in nephrogenic DI (ie resistance to the action of ADH).

Indications

Diagnosis of DI and distinction from primary polydipsia.

Contraindications

- suspected or confirmed thyroid and/or adrenal insufficiency. Ensure adequate hormone replacement prior to test
- hypovolaemia.

Practical details

Before the investigation

Although fluid restriction is not necessary prior to the test, ask the patient to avoid excessive intake. It may also be informative to document fluid intake for the 12 hours before the test. Allow a light breakfast but no tea or coffee. Continue normal steroid replacement if the patient is receiving this.

The investigation

1. At 8am, weigh the patient (with an empty bladder) and calculate 97% of this basal level.
2. Under direct supervision, deprive the patient of all fluid and food for 8 hours. Do not allow him/her to smoke.
3. Measure and record all urine volumes on an hourly basis.
4. Measure plasma and urine osmolalities at 0, 2, 4, 6 and 8 hours.
5. Weigh the patient at 2, 4, 6, 7 and 8 hours.
6. At the conclusion of the test, give desmopressin 2 μg IM and continue collecting urine samples and measuring urine osmolalities for a further 4 hours. Allow the patient to drink and eat freely during this period.

> **Hazard**
>
> **When to stop the test**
>
> If at any point during the test there is a greater than 3% drop in weight compared with the basal level, check plasma osmolality urgently. If this has risen to >295 mosmol/kg, give desmopressin 2 μg IM and allow the patient to drink. Otherwise consider continuing the test under close supervision. Abandon if the patient loses ≥5% of body weight.

After investigation – interpretation

- In normal subjects, plasma osmolality increases but remains below 295 mosmol/kg; urine osmolality rises as urine volume falls.
- With hypothalamic DI, urine osmolality fails to rise and a relative diuresis continues despite the increasing plasma osmolality. Following desmopressin, the urine concentrates normally.
- Nephrogenic DI is similar to hypothalamic DI, except that there is a failure of urine concentration in response to desmopressin.
- With primary polydipsia, excessive fluid intake prior to the test may result in an apparent continued diuresis despite fluid restriction. Plasma osmolality remains below 295 mosmol/kg.

4 Self-assessment

4.1 Self-assessment questions

MRCP(UK) Part 1 examination questions

Question 1

Clinical scenario

A 54-year-old woman presented with left loin pain and was found on computerised tomography (CT) scanning to have several left-sided renal calculi. A biochemical screen revealed serum calcium 2.80 mmol/L (normal range 2.20–2.60).

Question

What is the most likely diagnosis?

Answer

A carcinoma with skeletal metastases
B myeloma
C primary hyperparathyroidism
D sarcoidosis
E secondary hyperparathyroidism

Question 2

Clinical scenario

A 72-year-old man with a past medical history including ischaemic heart disease, hypertension, type 2 diabetes mellitus and bipolar disorder presented with non-specific malaise. There were no notable features on physical examination. Blood tests were unremarkable, excepting for serum calcium 2.72 mmol/L (normal range 2.20–2.60).

Question

Which medication could be responsible for the hypercalcaemia?

Answer

A atorvastatin
B furosemide
C lithium
D metformin
E ramipril

Question 3

Clinical scenario

A 59-year-old man with atrial fibrillation due to ischaemic cardiomyopathy and a history of peptic ulcer disease presented with bilateral gynaecomastia.

Question

Which medication is most likely to have caused gynaecomastia?

Answer

A amiloride
B digoxin
C furosemide
D omeprazole
E ranitidine

Question 4

Clinical scenario

A 38-year-old woman presented with hypoglycaemia and after extensive investigation was found to have an insulinoma. Concern was raised that she might have an underlying genetic predisposition to malignancy because of her relatively young age at presentation.

Question

Which condition is associated with insulinomas?

Answer

A multiple endocrine neoplasia type 1
B multiple endocrine neoplasia type 2
C neurofibromatosis type 1
D neurofibromatosis type 2
E von Hippel–Lindau syndrome

Question 5

Clinical scenario

A 24-year-old woman presented with a 12 kg weight gain over 6–9 months. She had no other medical symptoms, but had recently been made redundant from her job as an office cleaner and was taking much less exercise than she had done previously. She weighed 94 kg, with a body mass index (BMI) of 37.4 kg/m^2 (normal range 18–25). A diagnosis of simple obesity was made, and she was offered advice on diet, exercise and lifestyle, but she pressed for a medication to help weight loss and said that she was aware of a drug called liraglutide.

Question

What is the mechanism of action of liraglutide?

Answer

A glucagon-like peptide-1 analogue
B leptin analogue
C monoamine reuptake inhibitor
D pancreatic lipase inhibitor
E serotonin receptor agonist

Question 6

Clinical scenario

A 50-year-old man with no significant past medical history presented with watery diarrhoea and weight loss of 5 kg over 3 months. He also complained of facial flushing on drinking alcohol. Examination was unremarkable.

Question
What is the most likely diagnosis?

Answer
A chronic pancreatitis
B diabetic autonomic neuropathy
C neuroendocrine tumour
D systemic mastocytosis
E thyrotoxicosis

Question 7

Clinical scenario
A 42-year-old woman presented with a 6-month history of tiredness, lethargy and weight loss (5 kg), and a month of nausea and vomiting. She looked chronically unwell, with blood pressure (BP) 94/66 mmHg, but thorough physical examination revealed no other abnormalities. Blood tests taken in primary care were normal, with the exception of a slightly elevated serum thyroid-stimulating hormone (TSH) with normal serum free thyroxine (FT4).

Question
What is the most likely diagnosis?

Answer
A Addison's disease
B carcinoid syndrome
C Graves' disease
D hypothyroidism
E lymphoma

Question 8

Clinical scenario
A 48-year-old woman presented with fatigue and malaise. On examination she had a moon-like facies and plethora. Urinalysis revealed glycosuria, and a random capillary blood glucose measurement was 12 mmol/L. A diagnosis of probable Cushing's syndrome was made.

Question
Which feature would most suggest an underlying diagnosis of adrenal carcinoma?

Answer
A abdominal striae
B acne
C hypertension
D proximal myopathy
E virilisation

Question 9

Clinical scenario
A 38-year-old woman presented with 4 weeks of galactorrhoea. She had a complex past medical history including diabetes mellitus complicated by autonomic neuropathy, leading to recurrent vomiting and postural hypotension.

Question
Which drug is most likely to cause galactorrhoea?

Answer
A erythromycin
B fludrocortisone
C metformin
D metoclopramide
E midodrine

Question 10

Clinical scenario
A 48-year-old woman presented with headaches of a type that she had never had before, and which had got progressively worse over 4 weeks. She thought that her vision was 'not right', but was unable to describe the problem in more detail. Magnetic resonance imaging (MRI) revealed appearances suggestive of a craniopharyngioma.

Question
What visual field defect would be most characteristic of an early stage presentation of a craniopharyngioma?

Answer
A bitemporal hemianopia
B hemianopia
C hemianopic visual inattention
D inferior quadrantanopia
E superior quadrantanopia

Question 11

Clinical scenario
A 50-year-old man presented with a history of watery diarrhoea and facial flushing. After extensive investigation, a diagnosis of carcinoid syndrome secondary to a neuroendocrine tumour with hepatic metastases was made.

Question
What drug is most likely to relieve his symptoms?

Answer
A bortezomib
B cyproheptadine
C interferon-alpha
D nicotinic acid
E octreotide

Question 12

Clinical scenario
A 38-year-old woman presented with non-specific symptoms of tiredness and fatigue.

Question
Which feature would most strongly support a diagnosis of primary adrenal insufficiency?

Answer
A hirsutism
B hyperglycaemia
C hypotension
D pigmentation
E vitiligo

Question 13

Clinical scenario
A 28-year-old woman presented with general malaise and menorrhagia. She was pale, but there were no other abnormalities on physical examination.

Question
What condition is most likely to explain her symptoms?

Answer
A adrenal insufficiency
B Cushing's syndrome
C hypopituitarism
D hypothyroidism
E prolactinoma

Question 14

Clinical scenario

A 42-year-old woman presented with weight loss and shakiness of her hands. A clinical diagnosis of thyrotoxicosis was made.

Question

Which sign would indicate that the diagnosis was likely to be Graves' disease?

Answer

A exophthalmos
B lid lag
C lid retraction
D neck pain
E pre-existing goitre

Question 15

Clinical scenario

A 28-year-old woman presented with breathlessness, palpitations and weight loss. Physical examination revealed a smooth goitre. Investigation confirmed the diagnosis of thyrotoxicosis due to Graves' disease. She was started on treatment with carbimazole.

Question

What is the commonest side effect of carbimazole?

Answer

A acute interstitial nephritis
B agranulocytosis
C raised serum alanine aminotransferase (ALT)
D rash
E thrombocytopaenia

Question 16

Clinical scenario

A 48-year-old man with no significant past medical history presented with a non-ST elevation myocardial infarct. His cardiovascular risk factors were assessed, and he was found to have a high level of serum total cholesterol and a high level of serum low-density lipoprotein (LDL). He was started on atorvastatin.

Question

What is the main effect of statins on lipid metabolism?

Answer

A inhibition of *de novo* cholesterol synthesis
B inhibition of the conversion of VLDL (very low density lipoprotein) to LDL
C stimulation of cholesterol degradation
D stimulation of conversion of cholesterol to fatty acids
E stimulation of the reverse cholesterol transport pathway

Question 17

Clinical scenario

A 46-year-old man with no significant past medical history or family medical history was found to have glycosuria at a routine medical examination. Direct enquiry revealed features suggestive of hypogonadism, and on physical examination he appeared tanned and to have diminished body hair.

Question

What is the most likely underlying diagnosis?

Answer

A Addison's disease
B Cushing's disease
C diabetes mellitus
D hereditary haemochromatosis
E hypopituitarism

Question 18

Clinical scenario

A 36-year-old man with a history of diabetes mellitus and stage V chronic kidney disease, for which he had received a simultaneous pancreas and kidney transplant, attended a routine transplant follow-up clinic. He complained of muscular cramps. Biochemical screening revealed corrected serum calcium 1.98 mmol/L (normal range 2.20–2.60).

Question

Which medication is most likely to be responsible?

Answer

A bendroflumethiazide
B co-trimoxazole
C omeprazole
D prednisolone
E tacrolimus

Question 19

Clinical scenario

A 45-year-old woman with a long-standing history of schizoaffective disorder was found on routine investigation to be hyponatraemic. Physical examination was unremarkable.

Investigations:

serum sodium	122 mmol/L (normal range 137–144)
serum potassium	4.5 mmol/L (3.5–4.9)
serum urea	2.2 mmol/L (2.5–7.0)
serum creatinine	55 μmol/L (60–110)
plasma osmolality	262 mosmol/kg (278–300)
plasma thyroid-stimulating hormone	1.8 mU/L (0.4–5.0)
serum cortisol 9am	510 nmol/L (200–600)
urine osmolality	420 mosmol/kg (100–1,000)
urine sodium	65 mmol/L

Question

Which drug is most likely to cause this biochemical picture?

Answer

A chlorpromazine
B lithium carbonate
C olanzapine
D sodium valproate
E venlafaxine

Question 20

Clinical scenario

A 19-year-old man presented with erectile dysfunction. His past medical history was unremarkable, he was on no regular medication, and he denied excessive alcohol consumption. On examination he appeared anxious and embarrassed when asked to undress. He had bilateral gynaecomastia and only sparse pubic hair. Testicular volumes were 5 mL bilaterally, with no identifiable masses.

Investigations:

plasma luteinising hormone	45 U/L (normal range 1.0–10.0)
plasma follicle-stimulating hormone	56 U/L (1.0–7.0)
serum testosterone	3.1 nmol/L (9.0–35.0)
plasma prolactin	555 mU/L (normal threshold <360)
plasma FT4	14.5 pmol/L (10.0–22.0)
plasma thyroid-stimulating hormone	1.5 mU/L (0.4–5.0)

Question

What is the most likely cause for his hypogonadism?

Answer

A haemochromatosis
B Kallmann's syndrome
C Klinefelter's syndrome
D non-functioning pituitary adenoma
E prolactinoma

Question 21

Clinical scenario

A 41-year-old woman was referred to the endocrine clinic with suspected hypoglycaemic episodes. She had previously been fit and well, but had recently gained weight. Her daughter had well-controlled type 1 diabetes mellitus. On examination she was overweight (BMI 28.0 kg/m^2 (normal range 18–25)) and BP 120/80 mmHg lying and 110/75 mmHg standing.

She was admitted to hospital for a prolonged fast and became symptomatic at 18 hours, at which time investigations revealed:

serum sodium	137 mmol/L (normal range 137–144)
serum potassium	4.8 mmol/L (3.5–4.9)
serum creatinine	70 μmol/L (60–110)
serum albumin	40 g/L (37–49)
serum total bilirubin	10 μmol/L (1–22)
serum alanine aminotransferase	25 U/L (5–35)
serum alkaline phosphatase	100 U/L (45–105)
plasma glucose	1.9 mmol/L (3.0–6.0)
plasma insulin	65 pmol/L (normal threshold <21)

Question

Which investigation is most likely to help distinguish between the possible causes of her symptoms?

Answer

A haemoglobin A_{1c}
B plasma C-peptide
C plasma pancreatic polypeptide
D plasma sulfonylurea screen
E Synacthen test

Question 22

Clinical scenario

A 31-year-old woman presented with recurrent vaginal candidiasis. Her past medical history included hypothyroidism, for which she was on long-term thyroxine replacement. On examination she was mildly overweight (BMI 28 kg/m^2 (normal range 18–25)) and her blood pressure was 140/85 mmHg.

Investigations:

fasting plasma glucose	12.2 mmol/L (normal range 3.0–6.0)
haemoglobin A_{1c}	84 mmol/mol (20–42)

Question

Which would favour a diagnosis of type 2 rather than type 1 diabetes mellitus?

Answer

A autoimmune aetiology of hypothyroidism
B detection of islet cell autoantibodies
C elevated low-density lipoprotein (LDL) cholesterol level
D normal urinary albumin:creatinine ratio
E presence of dot and blot haemorrhages on fundoscopy

Question 23

Clinical scenario

A 26-year-old man was brought to the emergency department with a 12-hour history of nausea, vomiting and drowsiness. On examination he had a reduced Glasgow Coma Scale (GCS) score of 9/15 (E3, V2, M4). He was apyrexial, with pulse 120 beats per minute (regular) and BP 95/55 mmHg. Heart sounds were normal and his chest was clear to auscultation. There were no focal neurological signs.

Question

Which investigation should take immediate priority?

Answer

A arterial blood gas
B blood cultures
C capillary blood glucose
D serum cortisol
E urine toxicology screen

Question 24

Clinical scenario

A 48-year-old man was reviewed in the endocrine clinic with the results of an oral glucose tolerance test (OGTT), which had been carried out to investigate possible acromegaly. Growth hormone levels during the OGTT suppressed appropriately and his insulin-like growth factor-1 level was within the age- and gender-matched reference range. He had a strong family history of type 2 diabetes and at his follow-up visit asked whether there was any indication that he was developing diabetes.

Investigations:

OGTT	
0-minute plasma glucose	5.1 mmol/L
120-minute plasma glucose	7.4 mmol/L

Question

What are these results most consistent with?

Answer

A diabetes mellitus
B impaired fasting glycaemia
C impaired glucose tolerance
D normal glucose tolerance
E pre-diabetes

MRCP(UK) Part 2 examination questions

Question 25

Clinical scenario

A 72-year-old woman was referred to the endocrine clinic by her general practitioner (GP) after she was discovered to have abnormal thyroid function tests while under investigation for tiredness. She reported no other symptoms of thyroid dysfunction, but had been admitted to hospital 4 months earlier with a diagnosis of congestive cardiac failure and atrial fibrillation. She had no family history of thyroid disease. Her medication included digoxin 125 μg/day, furosemide 80 mg/day and warfarin 3 mg/day. Her pulse was 80/min (atrial fibrillation) and BP 135/85 mmHg. There was a small goitre, no cervical lymphadenopathy and no evidence of dysthyroid eye disease.

Investigations:

plasma FT4	17.5 pmol/L (normal range 10.0–22.0)
plasma free triiodothyronine (FT3)	6.2 pmol/L (3.0–7.0)
plasma thyroid-stimulating hormone	<0.1 mU/L (0.4–5.0)
serum anti-thyroid peroxidase antibodies	35 IU/mL (normal threshold <50)

Question

What is the most likely cause for her abnormal thyroid function tests?

Answer

A Graves' disease
B Hashimoto's thyroiditis
C non-thyroidal illness (sick euthyroid syndrome)
D subacute thyroiditis
E toxic multinodular goitre

Question 26

Clinical scenario

A 28-year-old man who was entirely fit and well apart from occasional indigestion had a blood test taken as part of a routine 'well man' screening programme. This revealed serum creatinine 88 μmol/L (normal range 60–110) and calcium 2.68 mmol/L (normal range 2.20–2.60), which triggered further investigations, including serum parathyroid hormone (PTH) 6 pmol/L (normal range 0.9–5.4) and a urinary calcium:creatinine clearance ratio of less than 0.01 (normal threshold >0.01).

Question

What is the most likely diagnosis?

Answer

A familial hypocalciuric hypercalcaemia
B milk-alkali syndrome
C primary hyperparathyroidism
D sarcoidosis
E secondary hyperparathyroidism

Question 27

Clinical scenario

A 48-year-old nurse was found unconscious in her room and brought to the emergency department by ambulance. A capillary blood glucose reading was 1.1 mmol/L, and she responded rapidly to an intravenous bolus of 20% dextrose. A blood sample drawn at the time of hypoglycaemia showed high levels of insulin and C-peptide.

Question

Which condition is most likely to explain her presentation?

Answer

A acute liver failure
B chronic liver disease
C insulin overdose
D metformin overdose
E sulphonylurea overdose

Question 28

Clinical scenario

A 33-year-old hairdresser with long-standing irregular periods presented with gradually worsening hirsutism and weight gain.

Question

What medication is most likely to be helpful?

Answer

A azathioprine
B danazol
C Dianette (co-cyprindiol)
D Neoral (ciclosporin)
E spironolactone

Question 29

Clinical scenario

A 15-year-old girl is referred to the endocrinology outpatient clinic because she has not yet started her menstrual periods. She is generally healthy, with no known medical problems, and physical examination is unremarkable, excepting for the fact that she is short (below the tenth centile in height). Her parents were both slightly taller than average, and both went through puberty themselves at the normal times. Measurement of luteinising hormone (LH), follicle-stimulating hormone (FSH) and oestrogen levels indicated that she had hypergonadotropic hypogonadism.

Question
What is the most likely diagnosis?

Answer
A coeliac disease
B constitutional delay
C hypothyroidism
D secondary gonadal failure
E Turner's syndrome

Question 30

Clinical scenario
A 42-year-old man presented with pain in his wrists and hands due to carpal tunnel syndrome. On examination, he had several features suggestive of acromegaly.

Question
Which would be the most appropriate next investigation?

Answer
A CT scan pituitary fossa
B formal visual field testing
C MRI pituitary fossa
D serum growth hormone (GH) level
E serum insulin-like growth factor (IGF)-1 level

Question 31

Clinical scenario
A 55-year-old man attended the cardiology outpatient clinic for review following a myocardial infarction that he had suffered 3 months previously. He was overweight (BMI 34 kg/m^2 (normal range 18–25)) and hypertensive (BP 160/96 mmHg). A lipid profile revealed a total cholesterol of 4.5 mmol/L (normal threshold <5.2), high-density lipoprotein cholesterol (HDL-C) 0.8 mmol/L (normal threshold >1.55), low-density lipoprotein cholesterol (LDL-C) 3.0 mmol/L (normal threshold <3.36) and triglycerides (TG) 2.5 mmol/L (normal range 0.45–1.69).

Question
What is the core requirement for diagnosis of the metabolic syndrome?

Answer
A central obesity
B hyperglycaemia
C hypertension
D hypertriglyceridaemia
E reduced HDL-C

Question 32

Clinical scenario
A 21-year-old woman presented with fatigue. There were no abnormal physical signs. A standard panel of blood tests were normal, excepting for serum potassium 2.4 mmol/L (normal range 3.5–4.9).

Question
Which finding would support the diagnosis of concealed vomiting?

Answer
A high serum sodium concentration
B low serum bicarbonate concentration
C low serum sodium concentration
D low urinary chloride concentration
E low urinary potassium concentration

Question 33

Clinical scenario
A 48-year-old woman presented with fatigue and weight gain of 5 kg over 6 months. On examination she had a moon-like facies and truncal obesity. Urinalysis revealed glycosuria, and a random capillary blood glucose measurement was 11 mmol/L. A diagnosis of probable Cushing's syndrome was made.

Question
Which test would be most appropriate to confirm the diagnosis of Cushing's syndrome?

Answer
A late-night salivary cortisol
B morning (9am) plasma cortisol
C MRI adrenal glands
D MRI pituitary
E plasma adrenocorticotropic hormone (ACTH)

Question 34

Clinical scenario
A 52-year-old woman's dentist noted that her bite had altered and her jaw had become more prominent. She was otherwise fit and well, with no significant past medical history and she was taking no medications. A diagnosis of acromegaly was made following an oral glucose tolerance test.

Question
What is likely to be the most appropriate first-line treatment?

Answer
A bromocriptine
B octreotide
C pegvisomant
D radiotherapy
E transsphenoidal adenomectomy

Question 35

Clinical scenario
A 58-year-old man presented with headache and visual disturbance. On examination he was found to have a bitemporal hemianopia. Investigations confirmed the presence of a prolactinoma and he was started on treatment with cabergoline.

Question
What side effect should the patient be warned about?

Answer
A diarrhoea
B hallucinations
C hypertension
D impulse control disorder
E insomnia

Question 36

Clinical scenario

A 28-year-old man developed sudden onset of severe retro-orbital headache and visual disturbance. He was photophobic, and examination revealed features of a right third nerve palsy. His GCS score was 15/15, temperature 37.7°C, pulse 96 beats per minute regular and BP 136/86 mmHg. A presumptive diagnosis of subarachnoid haemorrhage was made and he underwent an urgent brain CT scan, which revealed pituitary haemorrhage.

Question

What is the most important treatment to start immediately?

Answer

A 10% dextrose (intravenous)
B desmopressin (intranasal)
C hydrocortisone (intravenous)
D labetalol (intravenous)
E nimodipine (oral)

Question 37

Clinical scenario

A 58-year-old man presented with fatigue and loss of libido. On examination he appeared to have features suggesting hypogonadism, and he underwent testing of anterior pituitary function.

Question

What is the most appropriate investigation for possible growth hormone deficiency?

Answer

A 9am and midnight serum growth hormone (GH)
B glucose tolerance test
C insulin tolerance test
D serum insulin-like growth factor (IGF)-1
E short Synacthen® test

Question 38

Clinical scenario

A 48-year-old woman presented with paroxysmal headaches, sweating, palpitations, anxiety and hypertension. A diagnosis of phaeochromocytoma was made.

Question

In preparation for surgery, which drug should be started first?

Answer

A doxazosin
B labetalol
C phenoxybenzamine
D phentolamine
E propranolol

Question 39

Clinical scenario

A 28-year-old woman who was 9 weeks pregnant presented with palpitations and tremor. A diagnosis of thyrotoxicosis was made.

Question

What is the most appropriate treatment?

Answer

A carbimazole
B propylthiouracil
C radioiodine
D sodium iodide
E subtotal thyroidectomy

Question 40

Clinical scenario

A 78-year-old woman presented with a fragility fracture. She was started on calcium/vitamin D supplementation and weekly alendronic acid. However, she was unable to tolerate the alendronic acid due to reflux oesophagitis and it had to be discontinued.

Question

What would be the most appropriate agent to try next to treat her osteoporosis?

Answer

A calcitonin
B denosumab
C hormone replacement therapy
D testosterone
E zoledronic acid

Question 41

Clinical scenario

An 81-year-old woman with diabetes mellitus, hypertension and chronic obstructive pulmonary disease attended an outpatient clinic for routine review. She had been taking weekly alendronate for 5 years as treatment for osteoporosis, and her daughter (attending the clinic with her) asked whether this should be continued.

Question

What is the main safety concern with long-term bisphosphonate use?

Answer

A atypical femoral fracture
B breast cancer
C endometrial cancer
D stroke
E thromboembolic disease

Question 42

Clinical scenario

A 38-year-old woman with coeliac disease presented with gradual onset of generalised muscle aches and pains. Her exercise capacity was reduced, and she had particular difficulty when trying to climb stairs.

Question

What is the most likely diagnosis?

Answer

A Cushing's disease
B iron deficiency anaemia
C osteomalacia
D osteoporosis
E polymyalgia rheumatica

Question 43

Clinical scenario

A 76-year-old man, attending a routine consultation for management of his severe chronic obstructive pulmonary disease, complained of pain in his right shin, which appeared to be deformed. A plain radiograph of his leg showed localised enlargement of the tibia with cortical thickening and localised areas of both sclerosis and osteolysis.

Question

What would be the most appropriate next step in management of his painful shin?

Answer

A bisphosphonate
B bone biopsy
C calcitonin
D denosumab
E MRI

Question 44

Clinical scenario

A 44-year-old man presented with erectile dysfunction. He had been fit and well until the age of 39 years when he had been diagnosed with type 2 diabetes mellitus at an insurance medical. He was a non-smoker who consumed no alcohol. On examination he was of normal height but overweight (BMI 28.5 kg/m^2 (normal range 18–25)), with central adiposity. He appeared hypogonadal and had bilateral gynaecomastia. Examination of the external genitalia revealed bilateral testicular volumes of 10–15 mL. Visual fields were full to confrontation.

Investigations:

serum sodium	139 mmol/L (normal range 137–144)
serum potassium	4.0 mmol/L (3.5–4.9)
serum creatinine	80 μmol/L (60–110)
serum albumin	42 g/L (37–49)
serum total bilirubin	20 μmol/L (1–22)
serum alanine aminotransferase	150 U/L (5–35)
serum alkaline phosphatase	165 U/L (45–105)
haemoglobin A_{1c}	58 mmol/mol (20–42)
plasma luteinising hormone	22 U/L (1.0–10.0)
plasma follicle-stimulating hormone	31 U/L (1.0–7.0)
serum testosterone	3.1 nmol/L (9.0–35.0)

Question

Which investigation is most likely to help elucidate the cause for his erectile dysfunction?

Answer

A autonomic function testing
B karyotype analysis
C plasma prolactin
D serum oestradiol
E serum transferrin saturation

Question 45

Clinical scenario

A 65-year-old woman with type 2 diabetes mellitus and long-standing hypertension was referred to the diabetic clinic by her GP who was concerned about her declining renal function. Her medication included gliclazide 80 mg bd, metformin 500 mg tds, aspirin 75 mg/day, ramipril 10 mg/day, bendroflumethiazide 2.5 mg/day and atorvastatin 20 mg/day. She was a non-smoker. On examination she was obese (BMI 34 kg/m^2; normal range 18–25), with blood pressure 130/70 mmHg and mild peripheral oedema. Fundoscopy revealed dot and blot haemorrhages, microaneurysms and hard exudates.

Investigations:

serum sodium	142 mmol/L (normal range 137–144)
serum potassium	4.5 mmol/L (3.5–4.9)
serum urea	15 mmol/L (2.5–7.0)
serum creatinine	185 μmol/L (60–110)
estimated glomerular filtration rate (eGFR)	24 mL/min/1.73 m^2 (normal threshold >60)
serum cholesterol	4.2 mmol/L (<5.2)
serum HDL-C	0.9 mmol/L (>1.55)
haemoglobin A_{1c}	44 mmol/mol (20–42)
24-hour urinary total protein	1.8 g (<0.2)

Question

Which management step is most appropriate at this visit?

Answer

A add ezetimibe
B change bendroflumethiazide to furosemide
C start fenofibrate
D stop metformin
E stop ramipril

Question 46

Clinical scenario

A 28-year-old woman with gestational diabetes mellitus had required insulin therapy in the form of a basal bolus regimen from 28 weeks gestation. She was commenced on a sliding scale of intravenous insulin infusion during labour and the delivery proceeded uneventfully.

Question

With regard to treatment, what should she be advised to do following delivery?

Answer

A restart her basal bolus subcutaneous insulin regimen
B start gliclazide
C start metformin
D start rosiglitazone
E stop all treatment

Question 47

Clinical scenario

A 54-year-old man with type 2 diabetes mellitus was admitted to hospital with an infected second toe on the right foot. Despite 3 weeks of high-dose oral antibiotics from his GP the toe had shown no sign of improvement. On examination he was pyrexial (temperature 37.7°C) but not systemically unwell. The toe was swollen, with a small deep ulcer at the tip, with spreading cellulitis over the adjacent foot.

Question

Which investigation would it be most appropriate to organise immediately?

Answer

A bone scan
B CT of foot
C MRI of foot
D white cell scan
E X-ray of foot

Question 48

Clinical scenario

A 32-year-old man with long-standing type 1 diabetes mellitus presented with a 3-month history of tiredness and lethargy. He also reported increasingly frequent hypoglycaemic episodes, despite having reduced his total daily insulin dose on three separate occasions during the previous 2 weeks. On examination he was slim (BMI 21.05 kg/m^2 (normal range 18–25)), with pulse 68/min and BP 100/65 mmHg.

Investigations:

serum sodium	135 mmol/L (normal range 137–144)
serum potassium	5.2 mmol/L (3.5–4.9)
serum urea	7.8 mmol/L (2.5–7.0)
serum creatinine	98 µmol/L (60–110)
haemoglobin A_{1c}	42 mmol/mol (20–42)

Question

Which investigation is most likely to identify the cause for his symptoms?

Answer

A anti-tissue transglutaminase antibodies
B plasma thyroid-stimulating hormone
C serum corrected calcium
D serum vitamin B_{12}
E short tetracosactide (Synacthen®) test

Question 49

Clinical scenario

A 56-year-old woman was referred to the endocrinology clinic for further investigation of weight loss and palpitations. She had no past medical history of note, was on no regular medications and gave no family history of thyroid disease. On examination her pulse was 110 beats per minute (regular) and she had a fine resting tremor. She had a small goitre, with no discrete palpable nodules and no cervical lymphadenopathy. Her eyes were normal.

Investigations:

plasma FT4	55.5 pmol/L (normal range 10.0–22.0)
plasma FT3	15.5 pmol/L (3.0–7.0)
plasma thyroid-stimulating hormone	<0.1 mU/L (0.4–5.0)
serum anti-TSH receptor antibodies	0.4 IU/L (0–1)

Question

Which investigation would be most helpful in diagnosis?

Answer

A CT scan of neck and upper thorax
B fine needle aspiration biopsy
C sestamibi scan
D technetium uptake scan
E ultrasound neck

Question 50

Clinical scenario

A 29-year-old woman complained of excessive weight gain, despite repeated attempts to diet, following the birth of her second child 2 years earlier. Her only regular medication was the combined oral contraceptive pill. Her BMI was 42 kg/m^2 (normal range 18–25). She had mild facial hirsutism, but the remainder of the physical examination was unremarkable.

Investigations:

fasting plasma glucose	5.1 mmol/L (normal range 3.0–6.0)
plasma FT4	11.5 pmol/L (10.0–22)
plasma thyroid-stimulating hormone	1.2 mU/L (0.4–5.0)
late night salivary cortisol	3.4 nmol/L (<4.3)
24-hour urinary free cortisol	collection 1 135 nmol/24hr (<145)
	collection 2 123 nmol/24hr (<145)

Question

What is the most likely cause for her weight gain?

Answer

A Cushing's disease
B Cushing's syndrome
C exogenous oestrogen therapy
D simple obesity
E subclinical hypothyroidism

4.2 Self-assessment answers

Answer to Question 1

C: primary hyperparathyroidism

The differential diagnosis of hypercalcaemia is broad, but the presence of renal calculi usually implies that it is long-standing and therefore unlikely to be secondary to malignancy. There are no other features to suggest sarcoidosis, hence primary hyperparathyroidism is the most likely cause.

Answer to Question 2

C: lithium

Drugs that can cause hypercalcaemia include lithium (possibly by altering calcium sensing by the parathyroids and enhancing the effects of parathyroid hormone (PTH)), thiazide diuretics (by reducing urinary calcium excretion and potentiating the effects of PTH), vitamin D (either oral or topical, for example for psoriasis), milk, alkali and antacids.

Answer to Question 3

B: digoxin

Drugs that cause gynaecomastia, usually by inhibiting androgen synthesis or action, include antiandrogens, gonadotrophin-releasing hormone (GnRH) analogues, digoxin, spironolactone, ketoconazole, metronidazole, cimetidine and anabolic steroids.

Answer to Question 4

A: multiple endocrine neoplasia type 1

Multiple endocrine neoplasia type 1 (MEN-1), caused by loss of function mutations in the *MENIN* tumour suppressor gene, is associated with parathyroid hyperplasia, pancreatic tumours and pituitary tumours. Multiple endocrine neoplasia type 2 (MEN-2), caused by activating mutations in the *RET* oncogene, is associated (type 2a, now denoted as MEN-2) with medullary thyroid carcinoma (MTC), phaeochromocytoma and parathyroid hyperplasia, and (type 2b, now denoted as MEN-3) with mucosal neuromas, MTC, marfanoid habitus and phaeochromocytoma.

Answer to Question 5

A: glucagon-like peptide-1 analogue

Liraglutide is a derivative of human incretin glucagon-like peptide-1 (GLP-1) that is used as a long-acting GLP-1 receptor agonist, binding to the same receptors as does the endogenous GLP-1 to stimulate insulin secretion. It is given as a once-daily injection that can be used in the treatment of type 2 diabetes or obesity. Orlistat, commonly used in the treatment of obesity, is a pancreatic lipase inhibitor.

Answer to Question 6

C: neuroendocrine tumour

Neuroendocrine tumours (NETs) may be gastrointestinal or pancreatic in origin, and can be non-functioning or secrete a diverse array of peptides (eg 5-hydroxytryptamine (5-HT), gastrin, insulin etc). They may be slow growing, remaining asymptomatic until metastases develop, usually in the liver. Historically, the term carcinoid syndrome has been used to describe the clinical disorder characterised by flushing (which may be spontaneous or precipitated by food, alcohol or stress) and recurrent watery diarrhoea due to 5-HT release into the systemic circulation (either from hepatic metastases or a bronchial primary tumour, both of which 'escape' hepatic metabolism). Other, less common features include abdominal pain, wheeze, right-sided heart disease and pellagra (dermatitis, diarrhoea and dementia due to niacin deficiency).

Answer to Question 7

A: Addison's disease

Many of the symptoms of Addison's disease are non-specific, often leading to considerable delay in its diagnosis. Tiredness, weakness, anorexia, weight loss and gastrointestinal disturbances are commonly reported, and menstrual disturbance can be a feature. Has the patient noticed a desire to eat salt? Salt craving is not uncommon in this condition.

Answer to Question 8

E: virilisation

The presence of virilisation suggests exposure to significant excess adrenal androgens. Although hirsutism and other androgenic features (eg hair loss, acne) can occur in adrenocorticotropic hormone (ACTH)-dependent forms of Cushing's disease, virilisation should raise concerns of an adrenocortical carcinoma.

Answer to Question 9

D: metoclopramide

Dopamine antagonists such as phenothiazine and metoclopramide can cause hyperprolactinaemia, manifesting as galactorrhoea.

Answer to Question 10

D: inferior quadrantanopia

The classical visual field abnormality in a patient with a pituitary macroadenoma causing optic chiasmal compression is a bitemporal hemianopia. However, it is important to remember that pressure on the optic chiasm from below initially results in a superior quadrantanopia (either unilateral or bilateral), before progressing to a complete bitemporal field defect. By contrast, a mass arising in the suprasellar region and primarily compressing the chiasm from above (eg a craniopharyngioma) is likely in the early stages to be associated with an inferior quadrantanopia.

Answer to Question 11

E: octreotide

Octreotide and longer-acting somatostatin analogues frequently relieve symptoms of flushing and diarrhoea in the carcinoid syndrome, with more recent evidence suggesting they possess anti-proliferative properties that may inhibit tumour growth. They are administered by injection. Side effects may include steatorrhoea (which can be treated with CREON), nausea/vomiting (often transient) and gallstones.

Answer to Question 12

D: pigmentation

Common findings in primary adrenal insufficiency include: (1) pigmentation, which may be generalised or affect palmar creases, scars or buccal mucosa; (2) postural hypotension (but this is less specific than pigmentation);

and (3) loss of axillary and pubic hair in women (due to lack of adrenal sex steroids). Vitiligo may be associated with autoimmune primary adrenal insufficiency.

Answer to Question 13

D: hypothyroidism

Hypothyroidism can present with menorrhagia. Symptoms of hypopituitarism include chronic lethargy, reduced libido and oligomenorrhoea or amenorrhoea.

Answer to Question 14

A: exophthalmos

The eye signs of 'lid lag' and 'lid retraction' are commonly found in thyrotoxicosis of any cause. Proptosis/ exophthalmos, ophthalmoplegia, chemosis and periorbital oedema are specific to Graves' disease.

Answer to Question 15

D: rash

Some patients are unable to tolerate carbimazole, with rashes the most commonly reported adverse event (up to 5%). In a smaller number of cases (~0.5%), life-threatening agranulocytosis and/or thrombocytopaenia occur and require immediate cessation of therapy. All patients placed on antithyroid drugs should be warned of this potentially serious side effect, and given written instructions advising them to immediately discontinue treatment and attend their general practitioner (GP) or emergency department for a full blood count should they develop a sore throat, mouth ulceration or fever.

Answer to Question 16

A: inhibition of *de novo* cholesterol synthesis

The important rate-limiting step of the hepatic *de novo* cholesterol synthesis pathway is mediated by enzyme 3-hydroxy 3-methoxyglutaryl coenzyme A (HMG-CoA). Statins work by inhibiting this enzyme.

Answer to Question 17

D: hereditary haemochromatosis

Hereditary haemochromatosis is the most commonly known inherited disease among Caucasians of northern-European descent, with a homozygote prevalence of between 0.1 and 0.5% and an overall gene frequency of 3–10%. The classical triad of diabetes mellitus, cirrhosis and skin hyperpigmentation (bronzed diabetes) occurs relatively late. Hypogonadism may be primary, secondary or mixed in origin. Increasingly patients are identified prior to clinical presentation with evidence of iron overload on routine biochemistry or when screening is performed because a relative has the condition.

Answer to Question 18

C: omeprazole

Epidemiological studies have shown that proton-pump inhibitors (PPI) are associated with hypomagnesaemia. The mechanism is via inhibition of channels in intestinal epithelial cells that are responsible for absorption of magnesium. Magnesium depletion can cause hypocalcaemia by producing PTH resistance or by decreasing PTH secretion. There are many case reports of severe hypomagnesaemia and hypocalcaemia resolving with withdrawal of PPI medication, in some of which recurrent hypomagnesaemia and hypocalcaemia was shown to recur on rechallenge.

Answer to Question 19

E: venlafaxine

In the presence of normal renal, adrenal and thyroid function, and in a patient who is clinically euvolaemic, this biochemical profile is consistent with a diagnosis of the syndrome of inappropriate antidiuretic hormone secretion (SIADH). Venlafaxine is a well-recognised cause of this disorder.

Answer to Question 20

C: Klinefelter's syndrome

This man presents with the classical features of Klinefelter's syndrome (karyotype 47,XXY). Due to the abnormal gonadal development, testosterone levels are low, with consequent elevation of gonadotrophins. Patients are usually azoospermic and infertile.

Answer to Question 21

B: plasma C-peptide

The plasma insulin level is inappropriate for the plasma glucose concentration and is consistent with insulin-mediated hypoglycaemia. The history of weight gain suggests the possibility of insulinoma, but other causes of this biochemical picture must be excluded before embarking on a search for a pancreatic lesion. Exogenous insulin administration and sulphonylurea use may both lead to hypoglycaemia with inappropriate hyperinsulinaemia. Measurement of plasma C-peptide levels helps to distinguish exogenous insulin administration from other causes because endogenous proinsulin secretion, from which both insulin and C-peptide are derived, is suppressed if hypoglycaemia is driven by exogenous insulin. In contrast, sulphonylureas stimulate endogenous insulin and C-peptide secretion from pancreatic beta cells and measurement of plasma or urine sulphonylurea levels when the patient is hypoglycaemic may be necessary to confirm/refute clinical suspicions. In this case the patient's daughter has type 1 diabetes mellitus, hence she may have access to insulin, making it particularly important to exclude factitious insulin administration. It is also important to note that not all insulin preparations are detected by all laboratory platforms – if in doubt, check with your local clinical biochemistry team.

Answer to Question 22

E: presence of dot and blot haemorrhages on fundoscopy

Subjects with type 2 diabetes mellitus may exhibit microvascular and macrovascular complications at presentation, reflecting the fact that their diabetes has often been present for some time before being diagnosed. This is not typically the case in type 1 diabetes. Autoimmune hypothyroidism is most commonly associated with type 1 rather than type 2 diabetes, and islet cell antibodies are typical of the former.

Answer to Question 23

C: capillary blood glucose

In any patient with a reduced conscious level the first investigation should be a bedside capillary blood glucose measurement to exclude hypoglycaemia. The other listed investigations are all potentially important, and depending on the initial assessment of the patient it is likely that they would also be requested at an early stage.

If adrenal insufficiency (Addison's disease) is suspected (pigmentation, hypotension, low serum sodium and elevated serum potassium), then blood should be drawn and sent to the laboratory for cortisol and ACTH measurement, and parenteral corticosteroids administered immediately (eg hydrocortisone 50–100 mg as a stat dose) and continued thereafter until adrenal insufficiency has been excluded.

Answer to Question 24

D: normal glucose tolerance

The oral glucose tolerance test (OGTT) shows that this man has normal glucose tolerance with both the 0-minute and 120-minute values clearly falling within the normal range.

See Table 77 for an interpretation of venous plasma glucose levels.

Table 77 Interpretation of venous plasma glucose levels

Diagnosis	Fasting glucose	2-hour glucose
Normal	<6.1 mmol/L	<7.8 mmol/L
Impaired fasting glycaemia	≥6.1 but <7.0 mmol/L	<7.8 mmol/L
Impaired glucose tolerance	<7.0 mmol/L	≥7.8 but <11.1 mmol/L
Diabetes	≥7.0 mmol/L	≥11.1 mmol/L

Answer to Question 25

E: toxic multinodular goitre

This is a typical presentation of toxic multinodular goitre, which is the commonest cause of hyperthyroidism in older people, in whom classical clinical symptoms and signs of thyrotoxicosis are often absent. The diagnosis may be picked up incidentally on investigation of tiredness or as part of screening in patients with atrial fibrillation or congestive cardiac failure. In this instance, the patient has so-called 'subclinical hyperthyroidism' (normal free thyroid hormone levels, with fully suppressed thyroid-stimulating hormone (TSH)), although in reality her tiredness may be attributable to the thyroid dysfunction, which can also predispose to atrial fibrillation.

Answer to Question 26

A: familial hypocalciuric hypercalcaemia

Familial hypocalciuric hypercalcaemia is an autosomal dominant condition due to heterozygous inactivating mutation of the calcium sensing receptor (CaSR). It usually causes asymptomatic hypercalcaemia in association with an inappropriately low urinary calcium excretion and an inappropriately normal serum PTH. It is important to make the diagnosis, which can be confirmed by genetic analysis of the CaSR, to avoid unnecessary and ineffective parathyroidectomy. All the other conditions listed would cause hypercalciuria, with the urinary calcium: creatinine clearance ratio likely to be >0.02.

Answer to Question 27

E: sulphonylurea overdose

Exogenous insulin administration causes hypoglycaemia with hyperinsulinaemia, but C-peptide levels are low because endogenous insulin secretion is suppressed. By contrast, the surreptitious use of sulphonylureas (which enhance endogenous insulin secretion) gives rise to a biochemical profile similar to that seen with insulinoma: diagnosis is made by assay of plasma or urinary sulphonylurea levels.

Answer to Question 28

C: Dianette (co-cyprindiol)

The patient described has experienced a gradual onset of hirsutism with several features suggestive of polycystic ovary syndrome (PCOS) and no worrying features to indicate malignancy. Having established that initial blood tests (luteinising hormone (LH), follicle-stimulating hormone (FSH), testosterone, dehydroepiandrosterone sulphate (DHEAS), sex hormone-binding globulin (SHBG), 17alpha-hydroxyprogesterone) fit with the clinical diagnosis, a standard management plan would include diet and exercise with/without Dianette (co-cyprindiol – which has antiandrogenic actions). Maximal effects would not be seen until 9–12 months because of the long duration of the hair-growth cycle. Danazol and Neoral (ciclosporin) can cause hirsutism.

Answer to Question 29

E: Turner's syndrome

Determination of gonadotrophin (LH and FSH) and sex steroid (oestrogen or testosterone) levels together with assessment of bone age are first-line tests to establish the diagnosis of pubertal delay. Low gonadotrophins and a relatively delayed bone age are more likely to be associated with normal (but delayed) pubertal development, while low gonadotrophins and a more advanced bone age are suggestive pathology that requires further investigation. Turner's syndrome is a cause of primary gonadal failure (hence leading to high gonadotrophin levels) and may not be clinically apparent, hence all girls with delayed puberty and growth should have a karyotype analysis (45,XO)

Answer to Question 30

E: serum insulin-like growth factor (IGF)-1 level

An oral glucose tolerance test remains the 'gold standard' investigation for confirming/excluding acromegaly, with the benefit also of establishing whether or not it has been complicated by the development of diabetes, but measurement of serum IGF-1 level is the most appropriate of the investigation options given here. Single/random measurements of growth hormone (GH) are not recommended because of the pulsatile nature of GH secretion. If the diagnosis of acromegaly is confirmed, then MRI scanning of the pituitary fossa and formal visual field testing would be required.

Answer to Question 31

A: central obesity

Central obesity is the only core requirement for diagnosis of the metabolic syndrome:

- waist circumference ≥ ethnicity specific cut-offs (eg ≥94 cm for Europid men and ≥80 cm for Europid women).

This core requirement should be combined with two or more of the following:

- hyperglycaemia – fasting plasma glucose ≥5.6 mmol/L or previously diagnosed type 2 diabetes mellitus
- hypertriglyceridaemia – triglycerides (TG) >1.7 mmol/L or treated for this lipid abnormality
- reduced HDL-C <1.03 mmol/L (males) or <1.29 mmol/L (females) or treated for this lipid abnormality
- hypertension – BP ≥130/85 mmHg or treated for hypertension.

Answer to Question 32

D: low urinary chloride concentration

Vomit contains a large amount of protons and chloride ions (HCl). The renal response to the subsequent deficit is to retain protons and generate bicarbonate (hence serum bicarbonate concentration is high), and to retain chloride (hence urinary chloride concentration is very low). Because the renal priority is to retain protons to maintain acid–base homeostasis, potassium ions are lost in the urine, and this is the reason for hypokalaemia, not loss of potassium in the vomit.

Answer to Question 33

A: late-night salivary cortisol

Late-night salivary cortisol measurement offers an excellent reflection of the plasma-free cortisol concentration and, due to the simple non-invasive collection procedure, can be conveniently performed at home. Loss of diurnal variation in plasma cortisol can be assessed by sampling at 9am and midnight, but a single 9am measurement is of low sensitivity/specificity. The other tests would be relevant to diagnosing the cause of Cushing's syndrome, but not to determining if Cushing's syndrome was present. Other commonly used screening tests for confirming/excluding Cushing's syndrome include 24-hour urinary free cortisol (UFC – checked on three occasions) and either overnight or low-dose dexamethasone suppression testing.

Answer to Question 34

E: transsphenoidal adenomectomy

The first-line treatment for acromegaly is usually surgery. In experienced hands, transsphenoidal adenomectomy offers a surgical cure rate of approximately 80–90% for microadenomas, but drops to about 50% for macroadenomas. Medical treatments are generally used as an adjunct to surgical treatment, as a 'holding exercise' in patients who have had radiotherapy, or as first-line treatment in patients who are unfit for surgery.

Answer to Question 35

D: impulse control disorder

Hypersexuality, impulse control disorders and gambling have been linked with dopamine agonist therapy, and all patients (and where possible their relatives) should be advised to report any concerns immediately as treatment discontinuation may be necessary. In addition, patients should be advised that mood changes can occur, and that nausea, postural hypotension and daytime drowsiness/somnolence may complicate the early treatment period, but generally improve with continued usage. Some patients develop constipation.

Answer to Question 36

C: hydrocortisone (intravenous)

This presentation is of pituitary apoplexy. Anterior pituitary dysfunction must be assumed, intravenous access established (taking bloods for urea and electrolytes, glucose and cortisol) and intravenous hydrocortisone (100 mg) given immediately, prior to establishing on regular replacement.

Answer to Question 37

C: insulin tolerance test

The 'gold standard' investigation for possible growth hormone (GH) deficiency is the insulin tolerance test (ITT). Random GH measurements and serum insulin-like growth factor (IGF)-1 are not reliable means of diagnosing GH deficiency. The glucagon stimulation test and the arginine stimulation test provide alternative provocative tests especially in cases where the ITT is contraindicated.

Answer to Question 38

C: phenoxybenzamine

In the UK, the non-competitive alpha-adrenoceptor antagonist phenoxybenzamine remains the initial treatment of choice, with escalating dose titration. The alpha1-antagonist doxazosin provides an alternative for those intolerant of phenoxybenzamine. Beta-blockers must not be given to patients with suspected or proven phaeochromocytoma until alpha-blockade has been established, since there is a significant risk of precipitating a life-threatening hypertensive crisis due to unopposed alpha-adrenoceptor activity.

Answer to Question 39

B: propylthiouracil

Propylthiouracil (PTU) remains the drug of choice in the first trimester of pregnancy, when carbimazole is generally avoided due to the risk of inducing the congenital malformation aplasia cutis; from the second trimester onwards, carbimazole is preferred, especially given concerns regarding the risk of serious (even potentially fatal) hepatic dysfunction or vasculitis with PTU. The lowest possible dose of antithyroid drug should be used at all times, and the so-called 'block and replace' regimen must not be used. Radioiodine (131I) therapy is contraindicated in pregnancy (as are radioisotope scans), hence treatment options are limited to antithyroid drugs or, in some cases, surgery during the second trimester.

Answer to Question 40

E: zoledronic acid

Oral bisphosphonates such as alendronic acid are not well tolerated by all patients, even when they adhere to the guidance of taking it on an empty stomach, 30 minutes before food, and while sitting in an upright position. In this context, zoledronic acid (which is given by injection on an annual basis – typically for three doses) is a reasonable alternative. Denosumab is a monoclonal antibody targeting RANK ligand to inhibit osteoclast formation, function and survival. It is given by subcutaneous injection every 6 months and could also be considered here. Calcitonin is no longer available for use in osteoporosis (risk of cancer). Hormone replacement therapy (HRT) is no longer used because of risks of breast cancer, thromboembolic and cardiovascular disease, excepting in younger women with early/premature menopause. Androgen therapy is not indicated for treating osteoporosis in women.

Answer to Question 41

A: atypical femoral fracture

Bisphosphonates have a good safety record, but there have been reports of potentially serious side effects in some contexts. Osteonecrosis of the jaw is mainly seen in those with poor dentition receiving intravenous therapy. More commonly, atypical femoral fractures (eg subtrochanteric or femoral shaft) may complicate continuous long-term treatment. Accordingly, current guidelines recommend that oral therapy should be used for up to 5 years, and intravenous therapy for up to 3 years, in the first instance. The decision to continue treatment beyond this should be taken by a metabolic bone expert after careful review of the individual case.

Answer to Question 42

C: osteomalacia

The presentation of osteomalacia is often vague and insidious with a gradual onset of generalised muscle aches and pains. A history of immigration, long-term anticonvulsant use, gastric surgery, coeliac disease or other malabsorption should prompt consideration of the diagnosis. Proximal myopathy may occur and manifest as difficulty rising out of a chair or in climbing stairs.

Answer to Question 43

A: bisphosphonate

The presentation is typical of Paget's disease. Bisphosphonates are the mainstay of treatment for symptomatic Paget's disease, and produce a prolonged, marked reduction of bone resorption by inhibiting osteoclast activity, with intravenous zoledronic acid demonstrating the greatest efficacy. Administration is followed by decreased uptake on bone scanning, reduction in alkaline phosphatase, stabilisation of hearing loss and improvement in other neurological dysfunction. As a potent inhibitor of osteoclastic RANK ligand, denosumab would appear to be an attractive alternative in patients intolerant of bisphosphonates, but there is limited clinical experience of its use for this indication.

Answer to Question 44

E: serum transferrin saturation

This man has type 2 diabetes mellitus, primary hypogonadism and deranged liver function tests – a combination that raises the possibility of haemochromatosis. Genetic testing for the common mutations in the *HFE* gene is readily available, but initial screening with measurement of serum transferrin saturation will identify most cases.

Although central obesity per se may be associated with hepatic steatosis and borderline low/normal testosterone levels, the gonadotrophins are usually within the normal range, reflecting the fact that these subjects typically have normal free testosterone levels. However, measurements of total testosterone may be borderline low due to a reduction in circulating sex hormone-binding globulin (SHBG) levels.

Answer to Question 45

D: stop metformin

Metformin should not be used in patients with significant renal impairment (ie estimated glomerular filtration rate (eGFR) <30 mL/min) due to the risk of associated lactic acidosis. It is also contraindicated in moderate to severe cardiac failure or hepatic impairment.

Angiotensin converting enzyme inhibitors and angiotensin receptor blockers are renoprotective and reduce cardiovascular risk in type 2 diabetes and should be continued unless there is a high index of suspicion that renal artery stenosis is a significant contributor to the patient's renal impairment.

Fibrates must be used with caution in renal impairment as the risk of a myositis-like syndrome is increased, especially if combined with a statin.

Answer to Question 46

E: stop all treatment

Gestational diabetes mellitus (GDM) is a transient phenomenon in many patients. Dietary measures are tried in the first instance, but if blood glucose levels remain above target then insulin therapy is the mainstay of treatment during the remainder of the pregnancy. Many patients with GDM are able to discontinue all therapy following delivery of the placenta. However, women with a history of GDM are at higher risk of developing type 2 diabetes mellitus in later life and should therefore be encouraged to follow a healthy diet and lifestyle. Repeating the OGTT at 6–8 weeks after delivery can help to identify those at higher risk.

Answer to Question 47

E: X-ray of foot

It is quite likely that this man has underlying osteomyelitis and that the tiny ulcer over the tip of his right second toe extends to the bone. There are several imaging studies that would help in identifying osteomyelitis, but the most readily available and appropriate in the first instance is a plain X-ray. Although plain films may not show bony changes in the early stages of osteomyelitis, there is often some evidence of soft tissue reaction. This man has had symptoms and signs for a sufficient duration of time (>2 weeks) for X-ray changes of osteomyelitis to be evident (haziness and loss of density of the affected bone, periosteal thickening and/or elevation and focal osteopenia, or the typical lytic changes). However, if plain X-rays are negative and there is sufficient clinical concern of an underlying infection, then further imaging is required – typically an MRI or a bone scan, but CT may also be useful.

Answer to Question 48

E: short tetracosactide (Synacthen®) test

Type 1 diabetes mellitus may be associated with other autoimmune disorders, including Addison's disease, Graves' disease, Hashimoto's thyroiditis, primary gonadal failure, coeliac disease, pernicious anaemia, vitiligo, alopecia and primary hypoparathyroidism (as part of the type 2 or, less commonly, type 1 polyglandular endocrinopathy syndromes).

Tiredness and lethargy are common presenting features of several of these conditions, but the history of recurrent hypoglycaemic episodes despite adjustments to his insulin regimen, low body mass index (BMI), hypotension and abnormal electrolytes (with low serum sodium and elevated serum potassium and urea) make Addison's disease most likely in this case.

Answer to Question 49

D: technetium uptake scan

A technetium uptake scan would help in differentiating between the possible causes of thyrotoxicosis: Graves' disease – diffuse increased uptake; toxic multinodular goitre – patchy increased uptake; toxic adenoma – discrete hot nodule; thyroiditis – absent or reduced uptake.

In this case there is no relevant family history, eye signs or other features to allow a clinical diagnosis of Graves' disease to be made.

The patient is older than is classical for a new presentation of Graves' disease (although this remains a possibility), but the absence of TSH receptor antibodies in the patient's serum makes the diagnosis unlikely.

Answer to Question 50

D: simple obesity

The finding of a normal midnight cortisol level and normal urinary cortisol excretion makes the diagnosis of Cushing's syndrome unlikely. Cushing's disease refers exclusively to cases of Cushing's syndrome arising as a consequence of a corticotroph pituitary adenoma.

Weight gain occurs in some patients on the combined oral contraceptive pill, but this is usually modest and unlikely to explain the gross obesity in this case. Serious consideration should be given to recommending an alternative from of contraception in this patient given her significantly elevated BMI.

Although the free thyroxine (FT4) level is in the lower part of the reference range, the plasma thyroid-stimulating hormone level, which is the most sensitive indicator of primary thyroid dysfunction, is unequivocally normal.

Index

Note: page numbers in *italics* refer to figures, those in **bold** refer to tables.

D

E

I

K

L

M

N

O

P

T

U

V

W

Z